C000147821

Trademark Acknowledge

Wrox has endeavored to provide trademark information about all the companies and products mentioned in this book by the appropriate use of capitals. However, Wrox cannot guarantee the accuracy of this information.

Credits

Author
Ivor Horton

Technical Editor
Julian Dobson

Series Editor
Luke Dempsey

Technical Reviewer
Nick Challoner

Managing Editor
John Franklin

Production Manager
Gina Mance

Book Layout
Eddie Fisher
Greg Powell
Lee Kelly

Proof Reader
Pam Brand

Cover Design
Third Wave

For more information on Third Wave, contact Ross Alderson on 44-21 236 6616

Cover photograph supplied by The Image Bank

About the Author

Ivor Horton has been in the computer industry for 30 years. He has applied and taught most programming languages in a wide variety of contexts. He has design and implementation experience of a wide variety of systems involving mainframes, on-line control systems and PCs. He has extensive knowledge of engineering and scientific applications and systems, particulary in the context of Computer Aided Design and Computer Aided Manufacturing.

Summary of Contents

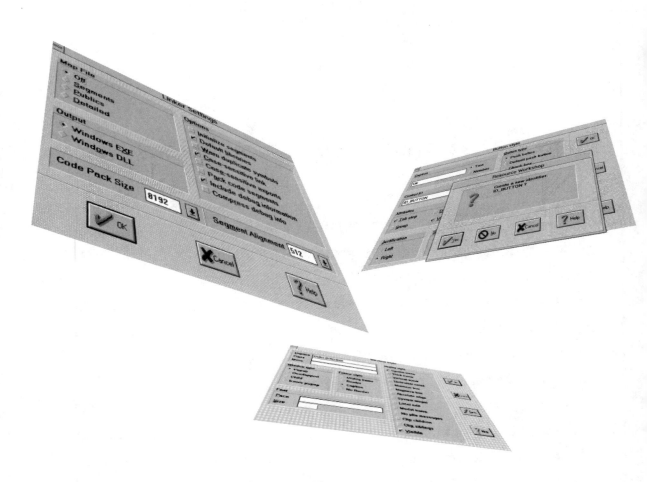

Why Windows Programming using Turbo C++ ?
Why the Beginner's Guide?

As the author of this guide says, 'Windows programming is easy', and in this latest Beginner's Guide he goes on to prove this with lots of simple but powerful Windows applications. This Guide uses Wrox's well-established process of teaching by example, with lots of Try It Out sections aimed at taking the reader through each example quickly and painlessly. The language basis of Windows programming is fully covered. C++ is the successor to one of the most popular programming languages, C. C++ has become the *de facto* language for the professional developer. C++ allows you to create your own data types, which makes it ideally suited for programming Microsoft Windows. You will quickly master the ObjectWindows library, as well as all the main features of Windows applications including menus, scroll bars, dialog boxes and so on. All you need is a willingness to learn and enjoy Windows programming from the bottom up.

What is Wrox Press?

Wrox Press is a computer book publisher which promotes a brand new concept - clear, jargon-free programming and database titles that fulfill your real demands. We publish for everyone, from the novice through to the experienced programmer. To ensure our books meet your needs, we carry out continuous research on all our titles. Through our dialog with you we can craft the book you really need.

We welcome suggestions and take all of them to heart - your input is paramount in creating the next great Wrox title. Use the reply card inside this book or mail us at:

feedback@wrox.demon.co.uk
or
Compuserve 100063, 2152

Wrox Press Ltd.
2710 W. Touhy
Chicago
IL 60645
USA

Tel: **0101 312 465 3559**
Fax: **0101 312 465 4063**

Why this book makes learning Windows Programming easy...

All source code supplied on disk

Code highlighted for easy understanding

```
                                     // Close the file
                                     // Reset file handle

    _lclose(aFile);
    aFile = 0;
  }
}
```

The only significant difference with this message response function is that, if there is a file name stored in `FileName[]`, this is used as the default name in the input field in the dialog. If there is no previous file name, the name `TEMP.DRW` is used as the default. The remainder of the code for the function is the same as that for the save operation.

Clear easy to follow text

Try it Out!

Try It Out - The Complete Program

The only other changes required to create a complete example is to add an `#include` statement for `FILEDIAL.H` to our program and add an `#include` statement for `FILEDIAL.DLG` to the resource project file.

This example is complete on the disk in the files `EX13-03.CPP`, `DRWDLG3.CPP`, `DRWDLG3.H` and `DRWG5.RC` as the resource project file.

If you run the example you can get a window which looks this.

Lots of easy to follow examples

THE ARTIST'S FRIEND

File   Shape   Color   Text   Help

File Save As

OK
Cancel

Filename: samp.drw
Directory: d:\winword\bgtcppw\bookex
Directories:

[..]
[-a-]
[-b-]
[-c-]
[-d-]
[-e-]
[-f-]
[-g-]
[-j-]
[-k-]

Oblique view of a pipe

Screenshots throughout

The Beginner's Guide to Windows Programming using Turbo C++ Visual Edition

Ivor Horton

Wrox Press Ltd.®

The Beginner's Guide to
Windows Programming using Turbo C++ Visual Edition

© 1995 Ivor Horton

Published by Wrox Press Ltd. Unit 16, 20 James Road, Birmingham, B11 2BA UK
Library of Congress Catalog Number: 94-78398
Printed in the U.S.A
ISBN 1-874416-53-2

Contents

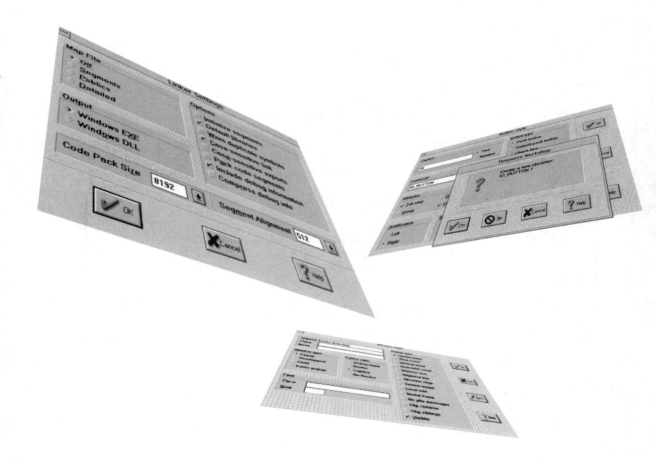

Introduction

Why the Beginner's Guide?

If you have picked up and opened this book, then you are almost certainly interested in learning to program using Borland's Turbo C++ for Windows and, like most things in life, you want it to be painless. There are plenty of computer books out there that claim to teach you C++ easily, or Windows programming easily, so why choose our book? Firstly, we do intend to do both these things. Secondly, we have designed this book with a very clear aim. We understand that it's not just descriptions of the syntax of a language, or the functions in a library that people need. They need practical guidance. C++ is C++, and this book won't change that. What we can change is the *way* we teach you C++ and Windows programming.

Our first assumption is that people don't learn for the sake of learning. Most people want to learn to program so they can achieve something with their programs - just learning C++ or Windows programming isn't an aim in itself. For this reason, wherever possible, each feature of C++, and each technique for Windows programming uses a practical, complete example of a program to show how it is used. This will help you see how things work in context, rather than simply giving you a definition of the mechanics of their operation. The method teaches you about designing programs for real. It also shows you how the language works - not just the language constructs. The examples are not trivial - indeed, some will involve quite a lot of work, the largest running to hundreds of lines of code. The reward is that their effectiveness in teaching you how C++ and the ObjectWindows library is applied in practice is much greater.

The book is based on the principle that you learn best by doing. If we promised to teach you French just by teaching you the grammar, you might find it dubious if we claimed you would be fluent by the end of the book. The only way you can become fluent is if you use what you learn in a real life way. That is why we make extensive use of complete working examples throughout the book, together with clear and thorough explanations.

How to Use This Book

Because we believe in the hands-on approach, you will write complete programs from the beginning. Every chapter has several programs to put the theory into practice, and these examples are key to making best use of the book. We would advise you to type in as many as possible. You won't always find it easy or get it right, but the very act of typing programs in is a tremendous aid to remembering the language elements. When you do get a program to work for the first time, particularly when you are trying to solve your own problems, the sense of excitement and satisfaction will make it all worthwhile. Recognizing that you may not want to type them all in - after all, after the first 100 it can get a bit tedious - they are all on the disk accompanying the book.

Each chapter covers a lot of ground. Don't expect to be able to digest it all in a few hours. Take your time and experiment with your own ideas. Try modifying the programs and see what you can do - that's when it gets really interesting. Don't be afraid of trying anything out. If you don't understand how something works, just type in a few variations and see what happens. Making mistakes (in most contexts) is usually very educational, unless you are something like a highwire walker. A good approach is to read a chapter through, and once you have a good idea of its scope, go back to the beginning and work through all the examples. For some topics you will almost certainly need to go through the material a couple of times before it really sticks.

You may find some of the programs quite hard at first. Don't worry if everything isn't all completely clear immediately. There are bound to be bits that you find difficult to understand at first, because the examples often apply what you have learnt to quite complicated problems, so persevere. Neither C++ nor Windows programming techniques are difficult, but there are quite a lot of different things to remember, and a practical context usually requires a little more insight. You will be surprised at how things you think are difficult initially become easy after you have used them a couple of times.

The largest program you will develop in the book is several hundred lines of code, but because you will be developing it one step at a time, you should find it quite straightforward. Borland Turbo C++ for Windows really does make Windows programming easy, so after you have practiced a bit with some picket fences, you should soon be leaping tall buildings at a single bound.

Who is This Book For?

All you need to use this book is an elementary knowledge of what programming is about. As long as you have at least some experience of writing simple programs in some programming language (such as BASIC, for example), then this book is for you. No prior knowledge of either C++ or Windows programming is assumed. This book will first teach you programming in C++, using the features of Turbo C++ for Windows to avoid the specifics of Windows programming at the outset. Once you are confident with C++ you will move quickly and easily to the real meat of programming for Windows. By the end of the book you will have a thorough grounding in C++, and provided you have used, understood and exercised all the examples, you should have little trouble in writing Windows programs for yourself.

What You Need To Use This Book

The only personal attributes you need to tackle programming in C++ for Windows is a basic knowledge of high school math, and sufficient enthusiasm to get through a 600+ page book. You will also need a computer with Turbo C++ for Windows installed on it, so you can run the examples.

Conventions Used

To enable you to find your way around this book easily, we have used various different styles to highlight different references.

Program Code

All programs in the book are highlighted with a gray background so you can find them easily.

```
// Calculating the how many rolls of wallpaper are required for a room
#include <iostream.h>
int main()
{
   double height = 0.0, width = 0.0, length = 0.0; // Room dimensions
   double perimeter = 0.0;                         // Room perimeter
```

When we use extracts from this code we also shade it so you can spot it quickly.

When we have shown general examples of code or the output from a program we have put it in this style:

```
The is how general code and output will look.
```

When code features in the middle of sentences, we write it in **this_style**.

When for the sake of brevity we haven't printed some lines of code we'll use three periods

...

to indicate a missing fragment.

In some instances, we repeat parts of the code in an example in various places. This is deliberate, so that you can see the program develop. We have shaded lines which are new additions to the program, and left the lines that are repeated unshaded. This will enable you to see immediately where new stuff has been added:

```
This is repeated code.
This is new code.
This is repeated code.
This is new code.
This is new code.
```

Command Definitions

When we refer to the syntax of the C++ language, we use this convention to highlight the abstract concept:

```
this  is  a  concept + not  necessarily  literal
```

4

Important Bits, Interesting Bits

Bits that you really must read are in this style.

Things that are interesting but not essential are in this style.

▶ Important words are in **this style**. These are significant words that we are meeting for the first time. Subsequently they will appear as normal text.

▶ File names are in **THIS_STYLE**. All file names appear like this in the text, even when they are conventionally written in lower case inside a program.

▶ Keys that you press are in *this style*, such as *Enter* or *Ctrl*.

▶ Things that appear in a Windows screen appear in this style.

Installing the Disk

To access the source code on the accompanying disk, simply place the floppy in your machine and move the contents of the disk onto your hard drive - your `c:` drive, for example. You can then open the code up easily and quickly.

There are no project files on the disk as these are dependent upon your system set-up. They are not essential, as Turbo C++ creates them for you, but if you want to create your own, please refer to Chapter 1, page 13, *Creating a Project File.*

Tell Us What You Think

One last thing. We've tried to make the book enjoyable and accurate. The programming community is what we're here to serve, so if you have any queries or suggestions or comments about this book, let us know - we will be delighted to hear from you. You can help us ensure that our future books are even better. Return the reply card at the back of the book, or contact us direct at Wrox. You can also use e-mail:

feedback@wrox.demon.co.uk
Compuserve: 100062,2152

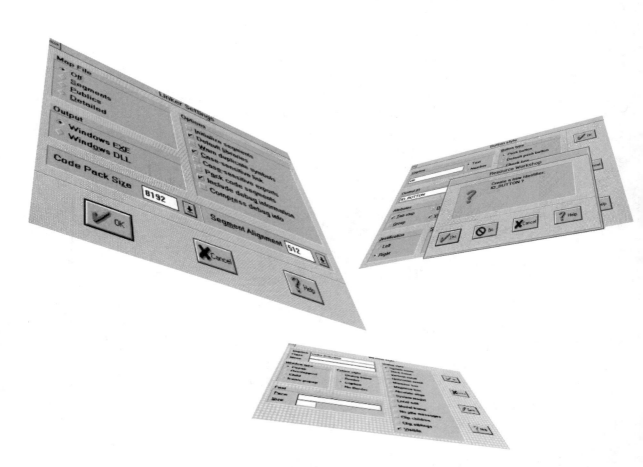

Programming with Turbo C++ for Windows

Windows programming is easy. It can seem very messy as there are always a lot of loose ends for you to tie together, but it's still easy. We have just one hurdle to bound over before we can prove that. To get to Windows programming using the ObjectWindows Library, we have to be thoroughly familiar with the capabilities of C++, particularly the object-oriented aspects of the language. In this chapter, we are going to take you quickly through operations with the Interactive Development Environment (IDE) that comes with Turbo C++ for Windows (TCW) as a basis for tackling the language. We will be concentrating on TCW throughout this book.

The IDE is very straightforward, and generally intuitive in its operation, but there is the odd subtlety. The best approach to understanding the IDE is to work through creating, compiling and executing a simple example, so as to get some insight into its capability. Being fairly fluent with the IDE makes the whole process of developing your applications very much easier. We won't deal with it exhaustively, as the product manuals contain all the fine detail, and we want to concentrate on programming. Here we will go through just enough to take you into the C++ language proper and run the examples, and the remainder we will pick up as we go along. By the end of this chapter you will have learnt:

▶ How to set up the key options in Turbo C++ for Windows

▶ How to create and edit a program in the Edit window

▶ How to compile, link and execute your first C++ program

So power up your information processor, stoke up Windows, invoke the mighty Turbo C++ for Windows, and we can begin.

The Interactive Development Environment

If the application fired up successfully, you will be looking at a fairly blank window with a menu, as illustrated below.

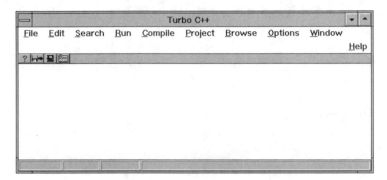

IDE Facilities

The menu items in the above screen are your doorway to all of the facilities provided by the IDE. You can create, compile, execute, and debug your programs entirely within this set of options. Below the main menu is the SpeedBar, containing four buttons. These are a short-cut to menu commands which you can click on with your mouse. Reading from the left, the four shown correspond to these menu options:

- Help
- Open a file
- Exit Turbo C++ for Windows
- Make

This last option compiles your source code and creates an executable module.

> *There are a number of other buttons which will appear once you start working with a program, and you can configure the SpeedBar by clicking on **Options** on the main menu, followed by **Environment** and **Desktop**.*

You can execute C++ programs written for DOS as well as Windows from here. While we are looking into the capabilities provided by the C++ language, all our examples will be DOS programs. Even though we will be running under Windows, you actually don't need to worry about this at all. DOS mode programs are recognized automatically by Turbo C++ for Windows (let's start using the abbreviation TCW for good now, before any more trees bite the dust!), and a facility called EasyWin is invoked. This provides a sort of envelope to allow your DOS programs to run under Windows without any effort on your part whatsoever.

Hot-keys

There are a number of hot-keys for operations within the IDE. Because I use a wide range of different systems I have trouble remembering them, but you may well have a better memory! The two you can't possibly avoid remembering are *Alt-F9* for compiling a program, and *Ctrl-F9* to compile, link and execute a program (you'll probably know that compiling is converting source code into machine code and that linking is bringing in any library functions required and joining all the bits together to make a single executable module). In the main menu the underlined character may be used in combination with the *Alt* key to select the particular menu item, *Alt-F* for File, for instance. You can also select any menu item by clicking it with the mouse. In the pull-down menus produced by selecting a main menu option, you can either click a selection, or just enter the underlined letter in the menu item from the keyboard.

IDE Options

The first menu selection you need to take a look at is the Options item. You need to set various options to make sure your program can compile and run properly. Click on this selection with the mouse (or use *Alt-O* if you are a keyboard fan) and you will get a pulldown menu.

Choosing a Hot-keys Set

Click on Environment and then on the Preferences... menu option. This will present you with the screen shown on the next page.

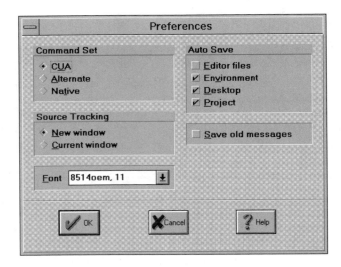

You can now choose which set of hot-keys you want to use. You have a choice of the Borland set which is there for people who have a lot of previous experience of Borland language products, or CUA (which is Common User Access). The Borland arrangement is usually the default, indicated by the Native box being checked.

CUA is a good choice if you use a variety of other packages, since this is a standard set of hot-keys supported by a lot of current Windows software, as well as packages in other environments.

> *In most word processing products, for example, you will find Ctrl-Ins will be the key for copying blocked text, and Shift-Ins the corresponding paste operation, as it is here. The cut operation for blocked text is Shift-Del. As we shall see when we get to editing a program, you can block text in the Edit windows by dragging the cursor over the text you want to block, while holding down the left mouse button. Click on the CUA box if you want to work with this arrangement.*

While you have the Preferences... dialog open, you can also make sure that the Project and Desktop boxes are ticked. These cause the current project file (which we will look into very shortly), and the current desktop, to be saved when you exit from TCW. You can also check the Editor files box to cause the contents of the editor window to be saved automatically, if you wish. I generally leave this unchecked and save my program code explicitly. This avoids accidentally overwriting good code when you may have just been fooling around with different variations on a theme, and then forget that it will be automatically saved with the current source file name when you exit.

Defining Directories

It is very important you set up the directories where include and library files are to be found. If these are not set properly, your programs won't compile and link without errors. Selecting Options from the menu bar and then choosing Directories... leads you to the Directories dialog shown below:

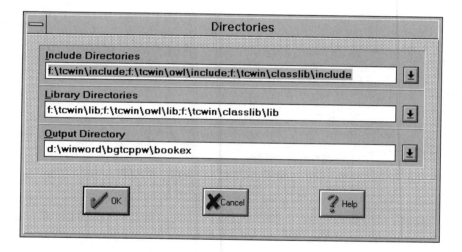

There are three sorts of directories you need to set. The first is for the include files, and the illustration shows what they are for a default installation (aside from the drive specification, your installation drive may be different - **c:** or **D:** perhaps). There are three directories specified here, separated by semicolons. These are the basic include directory, the ObjectWindows library include directory, and the include directory for class libraries. Don't worry about what these are for the moment. Just set them up now and all the examples in the book will be covered.

The next group of directories is for libraries which contain various routines supplied with the system which will be linked into your program when necessary. There are three of these with the same associations as the include directories.

The last entry specifies the directory where you want your object files to be stored. Don't copy what's here since this is specific to my system. I am storing my source files and object files in the same directory. If you haven't set up a directory, click the OK button and leave TCW for a moment - you can just minimize the window if you like. Now go to the Windows File Manager and create a directory. Once you have defined where you want your object files to go, maximize the TCW window, and pick Options and Directories... once again. You can now enter your directory in the third line and click on OK.

Setting Code Generation Options

There is one last option you must set if your programs are to compile and run correctly. There are a number of others which we won't discuss here, but we will get to some of them later in the book. For now, pick Options from the menu bar, and then Compiler. You will see another pull down menu from which you should pick the first choice, Code generation..., and you will see the dialog box shown below.

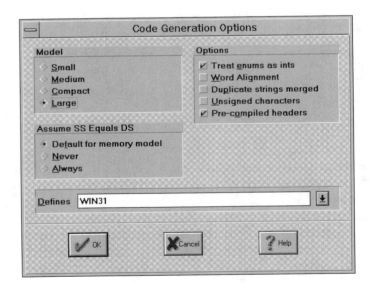

You could check the Large option from the Model options if you wish since we will need this later. This tells the compiler to use the large memory model. The other Model options provide for various ways of addressing code and data segments within your program, which can be more economical on memory usage. This can create some complications if your programs are of any size (and Windows programs often are), or if you use a lot of memory for storing data. The large memory model ensures that we sidestep these complexities at the expense of some memory.

What you *must* complete is the entry in the <u>D</u>efines box. If you don't set this properly, your code won't compile correctly. If you are running with Windows 3.1 enter WIN31 as shown in the illustration. You may need to click in the box to get the cursor there before you enter the text.

If for some strange reason you are running with Windows 3.0, enter WIN30 *instead.*

Using the Editor

Now all the essential defaults have been set, you are ready to use the IDE. The edit window is opened when you start a new program file or fetch an existing file from disk. Both of these are accomplished through the <u>F</u>ile menu option, with <u>N</u>ew in the pull-down corresponding to start a new program, and <u>O</u>pen... to fetch an existing program. Although our first program, and indeed all the programs in the book, are on the disk, you should key this in to get the feel of the IDE if you haven't used it before, so pick <u>F</u>ile then <u>N</u>ew and enter the text shown in the Window below.

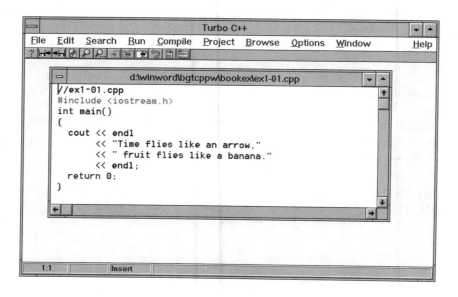

The Edit window shown has a long file name at the top, whereas yours will undoubtedly be headed **NONAME00.CPP**. This is just a default file name generated by TCW. You can assign a suitable name to your source program when you save it. Note the extension **.CPP**: this indicates to the compiler that it is a C++ source code file. Straight C programs, which can also be compiled by TCW, have the extension **.C**.

Creating Your First Program

Enter the ten lines of text just as they are shown in the illustration above. We will deal with all the language specifics in Chapter 2 onwards, but for the sake of completeness, lets look briefly now at what each line does.

```
//ex1-01.cpp
```

This is just a comment line, which in this case indicates the name of the source file on disk. Anything following two successive slashes **//** is treated as a comment and ignored by the compiler. If you intend to keep this program in a file with a different name, by all means change this.

```
#include <iostream.h>
```

This include statement brings the include file **IOSTREAM.H** into your program. This contains definitions relating to the standard library routines for input/output in C++. There are lots of different include files provided with the system, as we shall see in later chapters. You will also be creating your own include files later on. Include files are also called header files because they usually appear at the beginning or 'head' of a program (hence the extension **.H**).

```
int main()
```

This defines the start of the function called **main()**, which consists of the statements enclosed between the curly brace on the following line to the corresponding curly brace on the last line. The first word on the line, **int**, indicates the type of value which can be returned by the function **main()**. We shall see more about the meaning of this later.

Every C++ program written for DOS starts execution with the function **main()** *so every DOS program will contain this function. As we shall see, Windows programs are a little different.*

The pair of curly braces define the extent of the function **main()**, and they enclose five lines, the first four lines of which are in fact one executable statement:

```
cout << endl
     << "Time flies like an arrow, "
     << "fruit flies like a banana."
     << endl;
```

Statements can be spread over several lines in C++ if it is convenient to write them this way. There are some specific rules about this which we shall see in Chapter 2, but generally if it looks readable it is OK. The end of the statement is marked by the semicolon.

This particular statement outputs information to the screen. The word **cout** is a special name referring to the screen as an output device, and the operator **<<** is the operator for output in C++ The first thing it outputs is **endl**, which is a special symbol representing the newline character, which causes the cursor on the screen to move to a new line (**endl** for **end line**). The next output is the text string on the second line which is followed by the text string on the third line. Both these text strings will appear on the same line on the screen, the second immediately following the first. Finally, we output another **endl** to move the cursor to the next line.

A common mistake when you start with C++ is to forget the semicolon at the end of a statement. A further common mistake is to include a semicolon at the end of the function header, where there shouldn't be one.

The last line within the braces is:

```
return 0;
```

This simply ends the program by returning control back to the operating system. The zero after the word return is the value handed over to the operating system when the program ends.

Change the Colors of the Code

When you have keyed everything in, note the appearance of the code in the edit window. Some words are a different color. This is a result of the syntax highlighting facilities of TCW. If they are *not* different colors then you need to check that syntax highlighting is switched on by selecting Options, Environment, Editor... from the menu, and verify that the Syntax Highlighting option is checked (assuming you have a color monitor, of course). You can change the highlight color for various components of the C++ language by selecting Options, Environment, Highlight... from the menu. This will display the dialog shown below.

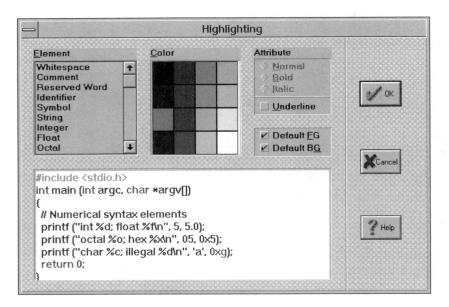

You can check the colors assigned to any of the elements listed in the Element list on the left by clicking on the name. The foreground and background colors will be indicated by FG and BG respectively in the Color box if they have been assigned. If you want to change the foreground color for, say, reserved words (these are specific words used in C++ which you must not use for your own purposes - **void** is a reserved word, for example), click on Reserved Word in the Element box, then click on the foreground color you want to be assigned to this, using the left mouse button. If you want to change the background color, simply click on a color using the right mouse button. Easy isn't it? These color cues are a good indicator of where you have misspelled a keyword or made some other mistake. For example, if it isn't in the keyword color, then it isn't a keyword.

Using the Compiler

The compiler converts your C++ source code into machine code. It checks for errors in the structure of your program - things like verifying that for every left curly brace there is a matching right curly brace - and it checks the syntax, verifying that the statements have the correct form. If there are no errors it will generate an object file with the extension **.OBJ** which will contain the machine instructions corresponding to your source code. This isn't yet executable, since it will need library routines added to do things like input and output, and we will do this in the step after compilation.

Compiling Your First Program

To compile the program you can select Compile from the main menu and then Compile from the pull-down menu, or you can just key *Alt-F9*. Either way, you should get the screen shown below.

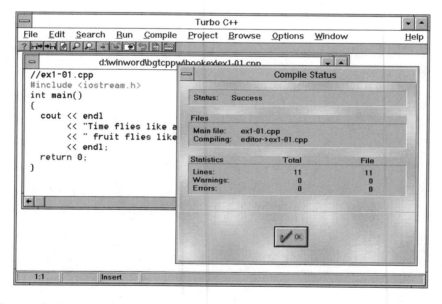

If you didn't get the same screen as this, particularly with the Warnings and Errors counts as zero, the most likely possibility is that you have typed something incorrectly. Everything should be the same as in the original illustration (for instance, upper-case letters in place of lower case can cause a problem). If you are 110% sure that your code is correct, then the next most likely problem lies with the options you set at the beginning, so you need to go back and check those again.

When you do make mistakes (and, of course, everyone *does*), the compiler will produce error messages. However, these error messages aren't always specific to the problem, and one small slip can sometimes generate an avalanche of error messages, so be prepared to delve a bit sometimes to find what is wrong. A simple small scale illustration of the kind of thing you can get will be produced if you leave out the semicolon from after the **endl** in the second to last line. You will get two error messages, only one of which refers to the fact that your problem is the absence of a semicolon.

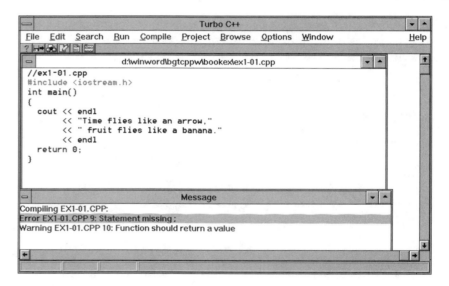

If you now have a program that compiles without error you can save it on disk (although you already have a copy available on the disk accompanying this book). If you want to save the program, click on File, Save as..., and key in the name you want to use for the source file in the pop up window. Don't forget that it should have a **.CPP** extension. You could call it **THOUGHTS.CPP**.

Executing Programs in the IDE

Running a program from within the IDE is almost as simple as compiling. However, we do need to generate an extra file to accompany our source file called a **project file**. This file will provide a definition of where all of the pieces necessary to make up a complete program can be found. In our example, we only have one source file which we have to specify (aside from the include file), **EX1-01.CPP**, or whatever you may have called it, but as we shall see, a C++ program will typically consist of several files.

Creating a Project File

We can create a project file for our example by selecting Project/Open Project from the menu bar. The window shown below will then appear.

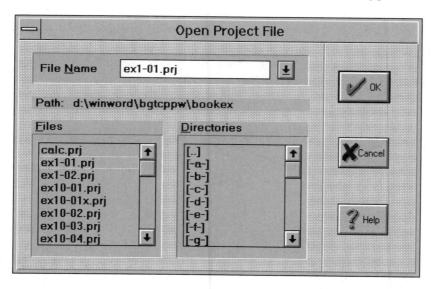

In your case, the File Name box will probably be empty and the path indicated will certainly be different. You may need to change the directory specified by the path to where you want to store your project file. You can use the same directory as the source file. You can change to a different drive by double clicking on a drive letter in the Directories box. To go to any directory shown in the box, just double click on it. To back up one directory level in the path, double click on the [..] entry. Once you have managed to get the path to indicate the directory you want to use, click in the File Name box and key in the name of your project file. It must have the extension .PRJ. You can now click on OK. TCW will create the file if it doesn't already exist (or fetch it into the current desktop if it does), and take you back to the main window where you will see an extra project window at the bottom of your screen. If you click on Project in the main menu once again, you will see the screen shown below.

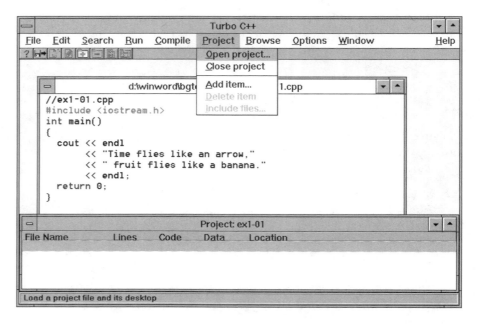

Our project file is empty at the moment (as is evident from the project window). When files have been specified, they will be shown one to a line in the project window. Since we now have an open project file, the Add item... option in the pull-down menu is available to allow file references to be added to our project file. The SpeedBar also has extra buttons, and the fifth one from the left with the plus sign is equivalent to Add item..., so we can either click on the menu or on the SpeedBar to add an item to our project. In the Add To Project List dialog box, we need to set the path to the directory containing our source file, if it's not already  indicated. If you want the directory where you will store your project files to be preset, you can use Program Manager under Windows to edit the TCW icon to specify the directory that will be used as a default. Once the correct directory is set, the name of our source file will appear in the Files box. We can select the file name by clicking on it, and it will then appear in the File Name box. If we then click on the Add button, the file name will be added to the project file and will appear in that window, as shown below.

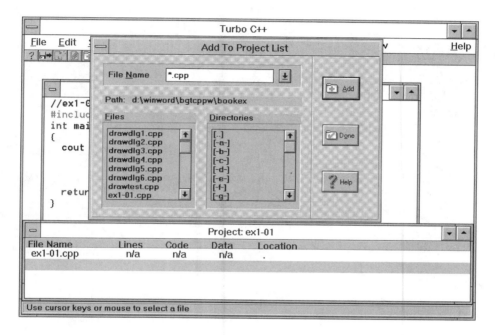

Since we have no further files to add, we can click on the Done button to close the dialog.

The line corresponding to our program file **EX1-01.CPP** is empty apart from the file name. This is because we should have created the project file before we compiled the program. In the previous compilation, TCW simply used a default project file, and in a more realistic program consisting of two or more files, TCW would be unable to deduce what these were without a project file. So let's compile our program once again using *Alt-F9*. TCW automatically compiles the code defined by the current project file. We should get no errors as before, but now more detail is filled in on the line in our project file. We can also see which include files were added to our program by clicking on the file name line in the project window and pressing the space bar.

In spite of the fact that we only have one **#include** statement in our program for **IOSTREAM.H**, we have several files included. This is because one include file can also include other include files, and in this case the additional files stem from **IOSTREAM.H**. This is because the definitions necessary for the input and output facilities of C++ are quite complex, and they are structured in several header files.

Running Your First Program

To run the program, you can either use the Run menu option or press *Ctrl-F9*. This will actually compile all the source code if necessary, link all the required library routines in to the program, and then execute it under EasyWin. You should end up with the screen shown below.

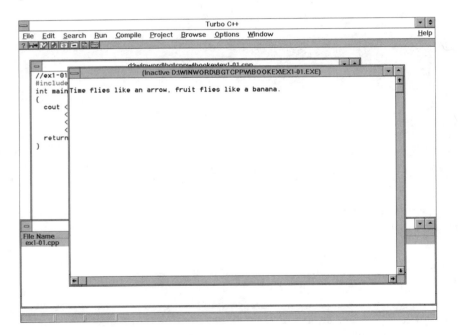

As you see, the output from the program appears in a separate window. To close the program output window, double click on the system menu box on the top left of the window. There we have it - we have compiled, linked and executed our first program.

Understanding Windows Programs

Since we are going to be spending quite a bit of time learning the elements of programming in C++ before we do any Windows programming proper, it would be as well to have an idea of how a Windows program works. This should give you a perspective on where we are heading ultimately, which you can keep in mind as you build expertise in C++.

Being Driven by Events

A distinguishing feature of a Windows program from the majority of DOS programs is that, most of the time, the sequence of events is not predetermined. If you think about what we have been doing with the IDE editor, at any point we could pick one of a number of menu items, key some text, click on a point in the existing text in the window to move the cursor, and a number of other possibilities. What happens after that will depend on what we do next, and for each of the possible things we might do, the program must have a piece of code that deals with that particular action or event. Indeed, programs of this kind are called **event driven** programs.

What Else is Happening?

Another important aspect to a Windows program is that a basic assumption must be made that there are other application programs being executed at the same time. An inevitable consequence of this is that your Windows program never talks directly to the user. The user talks to Windows, and if Windows thinks the communications is for your program, it sends a suitable message to your program - this being a supply of certain data and the execution of a particular piece of your program. Therefore, a large part of your program can turn out to be a number of pieces of code designed to process particular Windows messages.

Since there are other programs around, each of which is competing for the resources of your PC, your program doesn't get to communicate directly with any of the computer hardware. Your program talks to Windows and Windows deals with the hardware. Therefore, your typical Windows program will have the following structure:

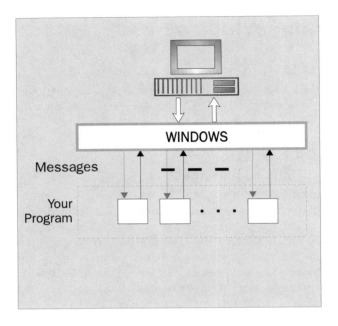

It's not quite as disjointed as the illustration might appear. One unifying element is shared data, which is accessed by the various bits of your program that process individual messages from Windows, and, of course, Windows itself. Nonetheless, we shall see when we get to write a Windows application that many of the bits of code making up a program can be written relatively independently of the rest. This has a definite plus side. The structure of a Windows programs is positive encouragement for you to develop and test your program *incrementally*. You can implement the code necessary for one kind of event, a menu selection say, and when that is working add the next menu option. Naturally, you still need to have worked out an overall design for your program at the outset. If you don't know where you are going, you won't know when you get there!

This discussion has been just to give you the flavor of Windows programming. We shall obviously get down to the specifics once we have looked at C++.

Summary

In this chapter we have looked at the basics of setting up TCW, and using the IDE to compile link and execute a program. If you are not one for studying the manuals that came with the product, you should be able to pick up anything else you need on the IDE as you go along. Don't forget the TCW Help facility under the IDE. It's a mine of information which you will find is extremely useful - especially when writing Windows programs.

The next few chapters are going to give you the grounding in C++ which is essential for effective use of the ObjectWindows Library. We will cover C++ fairly comprehensively, especially the object-oriented aspects of the language. The only bit we will really skimp on is input from the keyboard and output to the display, since we need to talk to Windows to do this, and the standard stream facilities of C++ don't apply. However, we will do enough to be able to exercise C++ in a practical fashion. The real fun is in getting your programs working.

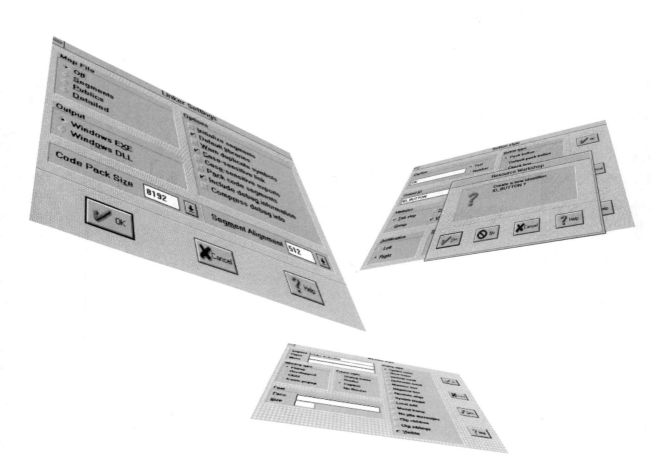

Data, Variables and Calculations

In this chapter we will get down to the essentials of programming in C++. By the end of this chapter you will be able to write a simple C++ program of the traditional form: input - process - output.

As we will explore these aspects of the language using working examples, you will have an opportunity to get some additional practice with the IDE. All of the examples are on disk, but it would be a good idea to key at least some of the examples in yourself. This will help you to recognize the effects of the typical mistakes that inevitably creep in, and show you how the compiler reacts to them.

In this chapter you will learn about:

- C++ program structure
- Variables in C++
- Defining variables and constants
- Basic input from the keyboard and output to the screen
- Performing arithmetic calculations
- Variable scope

The Structure of a C++ Program

A program in C++ consists of one or more functions. We saw examples consisting of simply the function **main()** in Chapter 1, where **main** is the name of the function. Every C++ program in the DOS environment will contain the function **main()** and all C++ programs of any size will consist of several functions. A function is simply a self-contained block of code with a unique name which is invoked by using the name of the function. A typical DOS program might be structured as shown in the figure below.

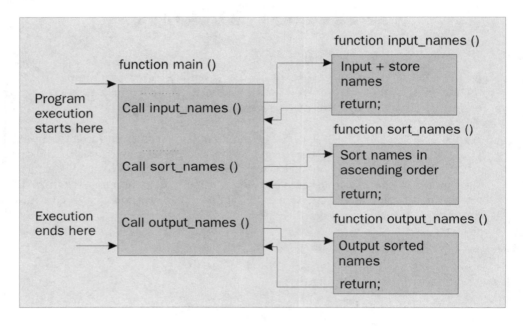

The above figure illustrates that execution of the program starts at the beginning of the function **main()**. From **main()**, execution transfers to a function **input_names()** which returns execution to the position immediately following the point where it was called in **main()**. The function **sort_names()** is then called from **main()** and after it returns to **main()**, the final function **output_names()** is called. Eventually, once output has been completed, execution returns once again to **main()** and the program ends. Of course, different programs under DOS may have radically different functional structures, but they will all start execution at the beginning of **main()**.

We will see more on creating and using functions in Chapter 6.

Try It Out - A Simple Program

Let's look at a simple example to understand the elements of a program a little better:

```
// EX2-01.CPP
// A Simple Example of a Program
#include <iostream.h>
int main()
{
    int apples, oranges;       // Declare two integer variables
    int fruit;                 // ..then another one

    apples = 5; oranges = 6;   // Set initial values
    fruit = apples + oranges;  // Get the total fruit

    cout << endl;              // Start output on a new line
    cout << "Oranges are not the only fruit... " << endl
         << "- and we have " << fruit << " fruits in all.";

    return 0;                  // Exit the program
}
```

Note that the above example is intended to illustrate a range of possibilities, rather than to be a model of good programming style.

If you compile and run this program you should get the following output:

```
Oranges are not the only fruit...
- and we have 11 fruits in all.
```

Program Comments

The first two lines in the program are comments. Comments are not part of the program - they are there to help the human reader, and all comments are ignored by the compiler. Two successive slashes on a line (that are not part of a text string as we shall see) indicate that the rest of the line is a comment. You can see several lines of the program contain comments as well as program statements. You can also use an alternative form of comment bounded by /* and */. For example the first line of the program could have been written:

```
/* EX2-01.CPP   */
```

The comment using // only covers the portion of a line following the two successive slashes, whereas the /*....*/ form can span several lines. We could write for example:

```
/*
    EX2-01.CPP
    A Simple Program Example
*/
```

and all four lines are comments. If you want to highlight some particular comment lines you can always embellish them with a frame of some description:

```
/*****************************
 *   EX2-01.CPP              *
 *   A Simple Program Example *
 *****************************/
```

As a rule, you should always comment your programs comprehensively. The comments should be sufficient for another programmer to understand the purpose of any particular piece of code, and to understand how it works. You should also comment the purpose of variables that you use where they are less than obvious (which is a lot of the time).

The #include Directive - Header Files

Following the comments we have the **#include** directive

```
#include <iostream.h>
```

which makes the compiler introduce the contents of the file **iostream.h** into the program before compilation. This file is called a header file, because it is usually brought in at the beginning of a program file, and it contains program code necessary for you to be able to use input and output statements in C++. There are many different header files provided by TCW in the include directories we defined in Chapter 1, providing a wide range of capability, and we shall be seeing more of them as we progress through the language facilities.

An **#include** statement is one of several preprocessor directives. These are commands executed by the compiler that generally act on your source code in some way before it is compiled. They all start with the character **#**. We will be introducing other preprocessor directives as we need them.

The Function main()

The function **main()** in our example consists of the function header defining it as **main()**, plus everything from the first opening curly brace to the corresponding closing curly brace. The curly braces enclose the executable statements in the function, which are referred to collectively as the **body** of the function. This is illustrated in the figure below.

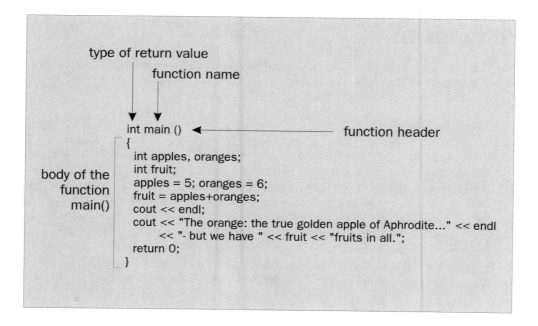

As we shall see, all functions consist of a header (defining the function name amongst other things), followed by the function body.

Program Statements

The program statements making up the function body of **main()** are each terminated with a semicolon. The program statement is the basic unit in defining what a program does. The action of a function is always expressed by a number of statements each ending with a semicolon. Statements are executed in the sequence in which they are written, unless a statement specifically causes the natural sequence to be altered. In Chapter 3 we will look at statements which alter the sequence of execution.

There are a number of different kinds of statements in C++, and we shall accumulate knowledge on these as we progress through the book.

Whitespace

Whitespace is the term used to describe blanks, tabs, newline characters and comments. Whitespace separates one part of a statement from another to prevent any confusion. Therefore, in the statement

```
int number = 0;
```

there must be at least one whitespace character - usually a space between **int** and **number** - for the compiler to be able to distinguish them. No whitespace characters are necessary between **number** and **=**, or between **=** and **0**, although you are free to include some if you wish. Apart from its use as a separator between elements in a statement that might otherwise be confused, the compiler ignores whitespace (except of course in a string of characters between quotes). You can therefore include as much whitespace as you like to make your program more readable, as we did when we spread our output statement in the last example over several lines.

Statement Blocks

We can enclose several statements between a pair of curly braces, in which case they become a **block**, or a **compound statement**. The body of a function is a block. Such a compound statement can be thought of as a single statement (as we shall see when we look at the decision making possibilities in C++ in Chapter 3). In fact, wherever you can put a single statement in

C++, you could equally well put a block between braces. As a consequence, a block can be placed inside another block. In fact, blocks can be nested, one within another, to any depth.

A statement block also has important effects on variables, but we will defer discussion of this until later in this chapter when we discuss something called variable scope.

Defining Variables

Now we are beyond our first program, we are going to want to manipulate some meaningful information and get some answers. An essential element in this process is having a piece of memory that we can call our own, that we can refer to using a meaningful name, and where we can store an item of data. Each individual piece of memory so specified is called a **variable**. Each variable will store a particular kind of data that is fixed when we introduce the variable in our program. One variable might store whole numbers (that is, integers) in which case it couldn't be used to store numbers with fractional values. The value each variable contains at any point is determined by the instructions in our program, and of course its value will usually change many times as the calculation progresses.

Let's look first at the rules for naming a variable when we introduce it into a program.

Naming Variables

The name we give to a variable is called an **identifier**, or more conveniently a **variable name**, and it can be defined very flexibly. It is a string of one or more letters and digits beginning with a letter, and where the underscore counts as a letter. Examples of good variable names are:

- `Price`
- `discount`
- `pShape`
- `Value_`
- `COUNT`

A variable name can't include any other characters and mustn't start with a digit so `8_Ball`, `2big`, *and* `6_pack` *are not legal. Neither is* `Hash!` *or* `Mary-Ann`. *This last example is a common mistake.* `Mary_Ann` *would be quite acceptable though. Of course,* `Mary Ann` *would not be because blanks are not allowed in variable names. Note that the variable names* `democrat` *and* `Democrat` *are quite different, as upper and lower case letters are differentiated.*

In TCW, up to 32 characters are permitted for identifiers. In fact, there are quite a few things that have names in C++ apart from variables, as we shall see, and they can all have names of up to 32 characters with the same definition rules as a variable name.

Since an underscore counts as a letter you can use variables such as `_This` and `_That` which start with an underscore. However, this is best avoided, as there are standard system variables which have this form, and your examples could conceivably clash with them and create a deal of mayhem.

Keywords in C++

There are reserved words in C++, also called **keywords**, which have special significance within the language. You met the keyword `int` in Chapter 1 and you will collect many more as you progress through the book. You must ensure that the names you choose for entities such as variables in your program, are not the same as any of the keywords in C++. A complete list of keywords used in TCW appears in Appendix B.

Declaring Variables

A variable declaration is a program statement which specifies the name of a variable, and what sort of data it can store. For example, the statement

```
int value;
```

declares a variable with the name **value** that can store integers. The type of data that can be stored in the variable value is specified by the keyword `int`. Because `int` is a keyword you can't use `int` as a name for one of your variables.

Note that a declaration always ends with a semicolon.

A single declaration can specify the names of several variables. For example, to declare the three integer variables **value**, **count**, and **number** we can write

```
int value, count, number;
```

Each of the variable names following the keyword **int** are separated by commas.

A variable declaration can appear virtually anywhere in a program but all variables must be declared before you can use them.

Initial Values for Variables

When you declare a variable, you can also assign an initial value to it. You just need to write an equals sign followed by the initializing value after the variable name in the declaration. We can write the statement

```
int value = 0, count = 10, number = 5;
```

to give each of the variables in the declaration an initial value. In this case **value** will have the value **0**, **count** will have the value **10**, and **number** will have the value **5**.

There is another way of writing the initial value for a variable in C++ called **functional notation**. Instead of an equals sign and the value, you can simply write the value in parentheses following the variable name. So we could rewrite the previous declaration as

```
int value(0), count(10), number(5);
```

If you don't supply an initial value for a variable, then it will usually contain whatever garbage was left in the memory location it occupies by the previous program you ran (there is an exception to this as we shall see later). You should always initialize your variables when you declare them (wherever possible). It makes it easier to work out what is happening when things go wrong if your variables start out with known values.

Data Types in C++

The sort of information a variable can hold is called its **data type**. All data and variables in your program have to be of some defined type. C++ provides you with a range of standard data types, specified by particular keywords. As part of the object-oriented aspects of the language, you can also create your own data type, as we shall see later. For the moment, let's take a look at elementary numerical data types.

Integer Variables

Integer variables are variables that can only have values that are whole numbers. The number of players in a football team is an integer, at least at the beginning of the game. We have already seen integer variables declared using the keyword **int**. These are variables which occupy 2 bytes in memory and can therefore have values from -32,768 to +32,767.

> *The upper and lower limits for the values of a variable of type* int, *correspond to the maximum and minimum signed binary numbers which can be represented by 16 bits. The upper limit is 2^{16}-1, and the lower limit is -2^{16}.*

In TCW, the keyword **short** is equivalent to **int**, so instead of the declarations above, you could write

```
short value(0), count(10), number(5);
```

The keyword **short** is equivalent to **short int** so you can also write

```
short int value(0), count(10), number(5);
```

> *Note that with other C++ compilers* short *and* short int *may not be the same as* int, *so if you expect your programs to be compiled in other environments, do not assume that* short *and* int *are equivalent.*

The range of values supported by variables of type **int** is rather limited for many purposes (not enough for the mileage record of the average astronaut, for instance). C++ provides another integer type, **long**, which can also be written as **long int**, to accommodate this situation. In this case we can write the statement

```
long BigNumber = 1000000L, LargeValue = 0L;
```

where we declare the variables **BigNumber** and **LargeValue** with initial values **1000000** and **0** respectively. The letter **L** appended to the end of the constant values specify that they are **long** constants. You can also use the small letter **l** for the same purpose, but it has the disadvantage that it is easily confused with the numeral 1. Integer variables declared as **long** occupy 4 bytes and can have values from -2,147,483,648 to 2,147,483,647. This is sufficient for everybody's mileage expenses.

> *Note that we don't include the commas when writing large integer values in a program.*

The char Data Type

The **char** data type serves a dual purpose. It specifies a one byte integer variable or a variable storing a single **ASCII** character, which is the American Standard Code for Information Interchange, and the ASCII character set appears in Appendix A. We can declare a **char** variable with this statement:

```
char letter = 'A';
```

This declares the variable **letter** and initializes it with the value **'A'**. Note that we specify a constant which is a single character between single quotes, not double quotes (which we have used for defining a string of characters to be displayed). Because the character **'A'** is represented as the decimal value 65 (have a look at Appendix A if you don't believe me), we could have written this

```
char letter = 65;       // Equivalent to A
```

to produce the same result as the previous statement.

We can also use hexadecimal constants to initialize **char** variables (and other integer types). A hexadecimal constant is written using the standard representation for hexadecimal digits, 0 to 9, and A to F (or a to f) for digits with values 10 to 15. It is also preceded by the 0x (or 0X) to distinguish it from a decimal value. Thus we could rewrite the last statement as follows:

```
char letter = 0x41;     // Equivalent to A
```

to get exactly the same result.

Integer Type Modifiers

Variables of the integral types **char**, **int** or **short**, and **long** which we have just discussed, contain signed values by default, that is, they can store both positive and negative values. This is because the type modifier **signed** is assumed for these types by default. So wherever we wrote **char**, **int**, or **long**, we could have written **signed char**, **signed int**, or **signed long** respectively. If you are sure that you don't need to store negative values in a variable, the astronauts mileage record again for instance, you can specify a variable as **unsigned**:

```
unsigned long mileage = 0UL;
```

In this case the minimum value that can be stored is zero, and the maximum increases to 4,294,967,295. You can apply the **unsigned** modifier to **int** as well, in which case such variables may assume values from 0 to 65,535. Note how a **U** (or **u**) is appended to **unsigned** constant values. In the above example we also have **L** appended to indicate that the value is also **long**. You can use either upper or lower case for **U** and **L** and the sequence is unimportant, but it is a good idea to adopt a consistent way of specifying such constants.

> *Of course, both* signed *and* unsigned *are keywords, so you can't use them as variable names.*

The TCW compiler also provides you with an option to change the default for **char** declarations to **unsigned**, although this isn't commonly used, so unless you have a good reason to do it, it's best to leave it as the default.

Floating Point Variables

Values which are not integral are stored as **floating point** numbers. A floating point number can be expressed as just a decimal value such as 112.5, or with an exponent such as 1.125E2 where the decimal part is multiplied by the power of 10 specified after the E (for Exponent). Our example is therefore 1.125×10^2, which is 112.5.

> **Note that a floating point constant must contain a decimal point or an exponent or both. If you write neither, then you have an integer.**

You can specify a floating point variable using the keyword **double**, as in this statement:

```
double in_to_mm = 25.4;
```

A **double** variable occupies 8 bytes of memory and stores values accurate to 15 decimal digits. The range of values stored is much wider than that indicated by the 15 digits accuracy, being from 1.7×10^{-308} to 1.7×10^{308}, positive and negative.

If you don't need 15 digits precision, and you don't need the massive range of values provided by **double** variables, you can opt to use the keyword **float** to declare floating point variables occupying 4 bytes. For example, the statement

```
float Pi = 3.14159f;
```

defines a variable **Pi** with the initial value 3.14159. The **f** at the end of the constant specifies it to be a **float** type. Without the **f** the constant would have been double. Variables declared as **float** are of 7 decimal digits precision and can have values from 3.4×10^{-38} to 3.4×10^{38}, positive and negative.

Financial Data

C++ also provides a type **long double** which provides floating point values with more precision than **double**, which is intended for financial calculations. To declare and initialize a **long double** variable, a typical statement would be this:

```
long double Payola = 1.2345678987654321E17L;
```

The fact that the initializing constant is **long** is indicated by the suffix **L**. Variables of this type provide 19 digits precision and support numbers in the range 3.4×10^{-4932} to 1.1×10^{4932}.

> *TCW also provides the type bcd which is also intended for financial calculations to minimize round-off errors which plague those who need to account for every cent. This data type may not be supported by other C++ compilers. You need to include the header file BCD.H if you want to use it. You will find more details in the TCW Programmer's Guide.*

Variables with Specific Sets of Values

You will sometimes be faced with the need for variables that have a limited set of possible values - the days of the week for example, or months of the year. There is a specific facility in C++ to handle this situation, and it is called an **enumeration**. Let's take one of the examples we have just mentioned, of a variable that can assume values corresponding to days of the week. We can define this as follows:

```
enum Week (Mon, Tues, Wed, Thurs, Fri, Sat, Sun) This_week;
```

This declares an enumeration type called **Week**, and the variable **This_week** that is an instance of **Week** that can only assume the values in parentheses. If you try to assign to **This_week** anything other than the set of values specified it will cause an error. The symbolic names listed between the parentheses are known as **enumeration constants**. In fact, the names of the days will be defined as having a fixed integer values. The first name in the list, **Mon**, will have the value 0, **Tues** will be 1, and so on. If you prefer the implicit numbering to start at a different value, you can just write:

```
enum Week (Mon = 1, Tues, Wed, Thurs, Fri, Sat, Sun) This_week;
```

and they will be equivalent to 1 through 7. Having defined the form of an enumeration, you can define another variable thus:

```
enum Week Next_week;
```

This defines a variable **Next_week** as an enumeration that can assume the values previously specified.

You can also assign specific values if you wish. We could define this enumeration for example:

```
enum Punctuation (Comma=',', Exclamation='!', Question='?' )things;
```

Here we have defined the possible values for the variable **things** as the numerical equivalents of the appropriate symbols. If you look in the ASCII table in Appendix A you will see they are in decimal 44, 33, and 63 respectively. As you can see, the values assigned don't have to be in ascending order. If you don't specify all the values explicitly, they continue to be assigned incrementing by 1 from the last specified value, as in our second **Week** example. You could also use this to define the idea of logical variables as:

```
enum Boolean (False, True) B1, B2, B3;
```

This defines three variables having the possible values **False** or **True**. Note that here the sequence of values results in **True** and **False** being assigned the values of 1 and 0 respectively, consistent with the usual interpretation of **True** and **False**.

If you don't intend to define any other enumeration variables of the same type, you can omit the type, in which case you have an anonymous enumeration. For example, we could write

```
enum (False, True) B1, B2, B3;
```

which would define **B1**, **B2**, and **B3** as each having the values **True** or **False**.

Defining Your Own Data Types

The **typedef** keyword enables you to define your own data type specifier. Using **typedef** you could redefine the standard **long int** type as the type name **BigOnes** with the declaration:

```
typedef long int BigOnes;          // Defining BigOnes as a type name
```

This defines **BigOnes** as an alternative type specifier for **long int**, so you could declare a variable **mynum** as **long int** with the declaration:

```
BigOnes mynum = 0;                 // Define a long int variable
```

There is no difference between this declaration, and that using the built in type name. You could equally well use

```
long int mynum = 0;                // Define a long int variable
```

for exactly the same result. In fact, if you define your own type name such as **BigOnes**, you can use both type specifiers within the same program for declaring different variables that will end up as having the same type.

Since **typedef** only defines a synonym for an existing type, it may appear to be a bit superficial. We will see later that it can fulfil a very useful role in enabling us to simplify more complex declarations than we have met so far.

Basic Input/Output Operations

We will only look at enough of C++ input and output here to get us through learning about C++. It's not that it's difficult - quite the opposite - but for Windows programming we won't need it at all. (If you want more details, you will find it in the reference material with TCW.)

C++ input/output revolves around the notion of a data stream, where we can insert data into an output stream or extract data from an input stream. We have already seen that the standard output stream to the screen is referred to as **cout**. The input stream from the keyboard is referred to as **cin**.

Input from the Keyboard

We obtain input from the keyboard through the stream **cin**, and using the extractor operator for a stream **>>**. To read two values from the keyboard into integer variables **num1** and **num2**, you can write this:

```
cin >> num1 >> num2;
```

Any leading whitespace is skipped and the first integer value is read into **num1**. This is because the input statement executes from left to right. Whitespace following **num1** is ignored, and a second integer value is read into **num2**. Of course, errors can arise if you key in the wrong data, but we will assume that you always get it right!

Floating point values are read from the keyboard in exactly the same way as integers, and of course we can mix the two. For example, in the statements:

```
int num1 = 0, num2 = 0;
double factor = 0.0;
cin >> num1 >> factor >> num2;
```

the last line will read an integer into **num1**, then a floating point value into **factor**, and finally an integer into **num2**.

Try It Out - Output to the Display

Writing information to the display operates in a complementary fashion to input. The stream is called **cout**, and we use the inserting operator **<<**. We have already used this operator to output a text string between quotes. We can demonstrate the process of outputting the value of a variable with a simple program:

```
// EX2-02.CPP
// Exercising output
#include <iostream.h>
int main()
{
   int num1 = 1234, num2 = 5678;
   cout << endl;                          //Start on a new line
   cout << num1 << num2;
   return 0;                              //Exit program
}
```

How It Works

The first statement in the body of **main()** declares and initializes two integer variables, **num1** and **num2**. This is followed by two output statements, the first of which moves the screen cursor position to a new line. Because output statements execute from left to right, the second output statement displays the value of **num1** followed by the value of **num2**.

If you compile and execute this you will get the output

```
12345678
```

This is correct, but not exactly helpful. We really need the two output values separated by at least one space. The default for stream output is to just output the digits in the output value, which doesn't provide for spacing different values out nicely so that they can be differentiated. As it is, we can't tell where the first number begins and the second one ends.

Try It Out - Manipulators

We can fix this quite easily though, using what is called a **manipulator**. A manipulator modifies the way in which data output to (or input from) a stream is handled. Manipulators are defined in the header file **iomanip.h** so we need to add an **#include** statement for it. The manipulator we will use is **setw(n)** which will output a following value left justified in a field **n** spaces wide, so **setw(6)** requests the output in a field with a width of 6 spaces. We can change our program to the following:

```
// EX2-03.CPP
// Exercising output
#include <iostream.h>
#include <iomanip.h>
int main()
{
    int num1 = 1234, num2 = 5678;
    cout << endl;                                  //Start on a new line
    cout << setw(6) << num1 << setw(6) << num2;
    return 0;                                      //Exit program
}
```

How It Works

The only changes from the last example are the addition of the **#include** statement for **iomanip.h**, and the insertion of the **setw()** manipulator in the output stream preceding each value, to output the values in a field 6 characters wide. Now we get nice neat output where we can actually separate the two values:

```
1234   5679
```

Note how the **setw()** manipulator only works for the single output value immediately following it. We have to insert it into the stream immediately preceding each value we want to output within a given field width. If we put only one **setw()**, it would apply to the first value to be output after it was inserted. Any following value would be output in the default manner. You could try this out by deleting the second **setw(6)** and its insertion operator in our example.

Escape Sequences

When we write a character string between quotes, we can include special characters called **escape sequences**. They are called escape sequences because they allow characters to be included in a string that otherwise could not be represented. An escape sequence starts with a backslash character, \. For example, a tab character is written as \t, so these two output statements

```
cout << endl << "This is output.";
cout << endl << "\tThis is output after a tab.";
```

will produce these lines:

```
This is output.
        This is output after a tab.
```

In fact, instead of using `endl` we could include the escape sequence for the newline character, \n, in each string, so we could rewrite the statements above as follows:

```
cout << "\nThis is output.";
cout << "\n\tThis is output after a tab.";
```

Here are some escape sequences which may be particularly useful:

Escape Sequence	What It Does
\a	Sounds a beep
\n	Newline
\'	Single quote
\\	Backslash
\b	Backspace
\t	Tab
\"	Double quote

Obviously, if you want to be able to include a backslash or a double quote as a character to be output in a string between quotes, you must use the escape sequences to represent them. Otherwise, the backslash would be interpreted as another escape sequence, and a double quote would indicate the end of the character string.

You can also use characters specified by escape sequences in the initialization of **char** variables. For example:

```
char Tab = '\t';        // Initialize with tab character
```

That gives us enough of a toehold in input/output. We will collect a few more bits as we go along.

Calculating in C++

This is where we actually start doing something with the data we enter. We are beginning the 'process' part of a C++ program. Almost all of the computational aspects of C++ are fairly intuitive, so we should slide through this like a hot knife through butter.

The Assignment Statement

A typical assignment statement would look like this:

```
whole = part1 + part2 +part3;
```

The assignment statement enables you to calculate the value of an expression which appears on the right hand side, in this case the sum of **part1**, **part2**, and **part3**, and store the result in the variable specified on the left hand side, in this case **whole**. In this statement, the **whole** is only the sum of its parts, and no more.

Note that the statement ends with a semicolon.

You can also write repeated assignments such as the following

```
A = B = 1;
```

where this is equivalent to assigning the value 1 to **B**, then assigning the value of **B** to **A**.

Understanding Lvalues

An **lvalue** is something that refers to an address in memory, and is so-called because it can appear on the left of an equals sign in an assignment. Most variables are lvalues since they specify a place in memory. However, as we shall see, there are variables which are not lvalues and so cannot appear on the left of an assignment because their values have been defined as constant. The variables **A** and **B** appearing in the preceding paragraph are lvalues, whereas the expression **A+B** would not be, since its result does not determine an address in memory where a value might be stored.

Lvalues will pop up at various times throughout the book, sometimes where you least expect it, so keep the idea in mind.

Arithmetic Operations

The basic arithmetic operators we have at our disposal are addition, subtraction, multiplication, and division, represented by the symbols **+**, **-**, ***** and **/** respectively. These operate generally as you would expect with the exception of division, which has a slight aberration when working with integer variables or constants as we'll see. You can write statements such as the following:

```
NetPay = Hours*Rate - Deductions;
```

Here the product of **Hours** and **Rate** will be calculated, and then **Deductions** subtracted from the value produced. The multiply and divide operators are executed before addition and subtraction. We will discuss the order of execution more fully later in this chapter. The overall result of the expression will be stored in the variable **NetPay**.

The minus sign used in the last statement applies to two operands - it subtracts one from another. This is called a binary operation because two values are involved. The minus sign can also be used with one operand to change the sign of its value, in which case it is called a unary minus. You could write this:

```
int A = 0; B = -5;
A = -B;                         // Changes the sign of the operand
```

Here **A** will be assigned the value +5 because the unary minus changes the sign of the value of the operand **B**.

Note that an assignment is not the equivalent of the equation you saw in high school algebra. It specifies an action to be carried out rather than a statement of fact. The statement:

```
A = A + 1;
```

means add 1 to the current value stored in **A** and then store the result back in **A**. As a normal algebraic statement it wouldn't make sense.

Try It Out - Exercising Basic Arithmetic

We can exercise basic arithmetic in C++ by calculating how many standard rolls of wallpaper are needed to paper a room. This is done with the following example:

```cpp
// EX2-04.CPP
// Calculating how many rolls of wallpaper are required for a room
#include <iostream.h>
int main()
{
   double height = 0.0, width = 0.0, length = 0.0; // Room dimensions
   double perimeter = 0.0;                          // Room perimeter

   const double ROLLWIDTH =21.0;           // Standard roll width
   const double ROLLLENGTH = 12.*33.;      // Standard roll length(33ft.)

   int Strips_per_Roll = 0;                // Number of strips in a roll
   int Strips_Reqd = 0;                    // Number of strips needed
   int Nrolls = 0;                         // Total number of rolls

   cout << endl                            // Start a new line
        << "Enter the height of the room in inches: ";
   cin >> height;

   cout  << endl                           // Start a new line
        << "Now enter the length and width in inches: ";
   cin >> length >> width;

   Strips_per_Roll = ROLLLENGTH/height;    // Get number of strips in a roll
   perimeter = 2.0*(length + width);       // Calculate room perimeter
   Strips_Reqd = perimeter/ROLLWIDTH;      // Get total strips required
   Nrolls = Strips_Reqd/Strips_per_Roll;   // Calculate number of rolls
```

```
    cout << endl
        << "For your room you need " << Nrolls << " rolls of wallpaper."
        << endl;

    return 0;
}
```

How It Works

One thing needs to be clear at the outset. No responsibility is assumed for you running out of wallpaper as a result of using this program! All errors in the estimate of the number of rolls required are due to the way C++ works, as we shall see, and due to the wastage that inevitably occurs when you hang your own wallpaper - usually 50%+!

We can work through the statements in this example in sequence, picking out the interesting, novel, or even exciting features. The statements down to the start of the body of **main()** are familiar territory by now, so we will take those for granted.

A couple of general points are worth noting about the layout of the program. Firstly, the statements in the body of **main()** are indented to make the extent of the body visually clearer, and secondly, various groups of statements are separated by a blank line to indicate that they are functional groups. Indenting statements is a fundamental technique in laying out program in C++. You will see that this is applied universally to visually cue various logical blocks in a program.

The const Modifier

We have a block of declarations for the variables used in the program right at the beginning of the body of **main()**. These statements are also fairly familiar, but there are two which contain some new features:

```
    const double ROLLWIDTH =21.0;          // Standard roll width
    const double ROLLLENGTH = 12.*33.;      // Standard roll length(33ft.)
```

They both start out with a new keyword **const**. This is a type modifier which indicates that the variables are not just of type **double**, but are also constants. Because we effectively tell the compiler that these are constants, the compiler will check for any statements which attempt to change the values of these variables, and if it finds any it will generate an error message. This is relatively easy since a variable declared as **const** is not an lvalue, and therefore can't legally be placed on the left of an assignment operation.

You could check this out by adding, anywhere after the declaration of **ROLLWIDTH**, a statement such as

```
ROLLWIDTH = 0;
```

and you will find the program no longer compiles.

Note that the variable names declared as **const** are written here with capital letters. It is a common convention in C++ to write identifiers that represent constants in capitals to distinguish them from other variable which are, well, more variable. It can be very useful defining constants by means of **const** variable types, particularly when you use the same constant several times in a program. For one thing, if you need to change it, you will be able to change its definition at the beginning and all uses of it will automatically be changed. We will see this technique used quite often.

Constant Expressions

The **const** variable **ROLLLENGTH** is also initialized with an arithmetic expression **(12.*33.)**. Being able to use a constant expression as an initializer saves having to work out the value yourself, and can also be more meaningful, as 33 feet times 12 inches is much clearer than simply writing 396. The compiler will generally evaluate constant expressions accurately, whereas if you do it yourself, depending on the complexity of the expression and your ability to number crunch, there is a finite probability it may be wrong.

You can use any expression that can be calculated as a constant at compile time, including **const** objects you have already defined. So for instance if it was useful in the program to do so, we could declare the area of a standard roll of wallpaper as:

```
const double ROLLAREA = ROLLWIDTH*ROLLLENGTH;
```

This statement obviously would need to be placed after the declarations for the two **const** variables used in the initialization of **ROLLAREA**.

Program Input

The next four statement in the program handle input:

```
cout << endl                              // Start a new line
     << "Enter the height of the room in inches: ";
cin >> height;

cout  << endl                             // Start a new line
     << "Now enter the length and width in inches: ";
cin >> length >> width;
```

Here we have used **cout** to prompt for the input required, and then read the input from the keyboard using **cin**. We first obtain the room **height**, and then read the **length** and **width** successively. In a practical program we would need to check for errors, and possibly make sure that the values read are sensible, but we don't have enough knowledge to do that yet!

Calculating the Result

We have four statements involved in calculating the number of standard rolls of wallpaper required for the size of room given:

```
Strips_per_Roll = ROLLLENGTH/height;    // Get number of strips in a roll
perimeter = 2.0*(length + width);       // Calculate room perimeter
Strips_Reqd = perimeter/ROLLWIDTH;      // Get total strips required
Nrolls = Strips_Reqd/Strips_per_Roll;   // Calculate number of rolls
```

The first statement calculates the number of strips of paper with a length corresponding to the height of the room we can get from a standard roll, by dividing one into the other. So if the room is 8 feet high we divide 96 into 396, which would produce the floating point result 4.125. There is a subtlety here however. The variable where we stored the result, **Strips_per_Roll**, was declared as **int**, so it can only store integer values. Consequently any floating point value to be stored as an integer is rounded down to the nearest integer, 4 in our case, and this value is stored. This is actually the result you want here since, although it may fit under a window or over a door, fractions of a strip are best ignored when estimating.

Note how we calculate the perimeter of the room in the next statement. In order to multiply the sum of the **length** and the **width** by two, we enclose the expression summing the two variables between parentheses. This ensures that the addition is performed first, and the result of that is multiplied by 2.0 to give us the correct value for the perimeter. We can use parentheses to make sure a calculation is carried out in the order we require, since expressions in parentheses are always evaluated first and, where there are nested parentheses, the expressions within the parentheses are evaluated in sequence from the innermost to the outermost.

The third statement, calculating how many strips of paper are required to cover the room, uses the same effect we observed in the first statement, where the result is rounded down to the nearest integer because it is to be stored in the integer variable, `Strips_Reqd`. This is not what we need in practice. It would be best to round up for estimating, but we don't have enough knowledge of C++ yet to do this. After you have read the next chapter you can come back and fix it!

The last arithmetic statement calculates the number of rolls required, by dividing the number of strips required (integer), by the number of strips in a roll (also integer). Because we are dividing one integer by another the result has to be integer, and any remainder is ignored. This would still be the case if the variable `Nrolls` were floating point. The resulting integer value would be converted to floating point form, before it was stored in `Nrolls`. The result we obtain is essentially the same as if we produced a floating point result and rounded down to the nearest integer. This again is not what we want, so you will need to fix this too, if you want to use this.

Displaying the Result

The result of the calculation is displayed by the following statement:

```
cout << endl
     << "For your room you need " << Nrolls << " rolls of wallpaper."
     << endl;
```

This is a single output statement spread over three lines. It first outputs a newline character, then the text string `"For your room you need "`. This is followed by the value of the variable `Nrolls`, and finally the text string `" rolls of wallpaper."`. Output statements are very easy in C++ as you can see.

Finally the program ends when this statement

```
return 0;
```

is executed. The value zero here is a return value which in this case will be returned to the operating system. We will see more about return values in Chapter 6.

Calculating a Remainder

We have seen in the last example that dividing one integer value by another produces an integer result that ignores any remainder, so that 11 divided by 4 gives the result 2. Since the remainder after division can be of great interest, particularly when you are dividing cookies amongst children for example, C++ provides a special operator **%** for this. So we can write the statements:

```
int Residue = 0, Cookies = 19, Children = 5;
Residue = Cookies%Children;
```

and the variable **Residue** will end up with the value 4, the number left after dividing 19 by 5. To calculate how many they received each you just need to use division, as in the statement

```
Each = Cookies/Children;
```

Modifying a Variable

It's often necessary to modify the existing value of a variable, such as incrementing it, or doubling it. We could increment a variable **count** using the statement

```
count = count + 5;
```

This simply adds 5 to the current value stored in **count**, and stores the result back in **count**, so if **count** started out at 10 it would end up as 15. You have an alternative shorthand way of writing the same thing in C++:

```
count += 5;
```

This says, take the value in **count**, add 5 to it and store the result back in **count**.

We can use other operators with this notation as well. For example,

```
count *=5;
```

has the effect of multiplying the current value of **count** by 5, and storing the result back in **count**. In general, we can write statements of the form

```
rhs op= lhs;
```

where **op** is any of the following operators

```
+        -        *        /        %
<<       >>       &        ^        |
```

The first five of these we have already met, and the remainder, which are shift and logical operators, we will see later in this chapter.

The general form of the statement is equivalent to this:

```
rhs = rhs op ( lhs );
```

This means that we can write statements such as

```
A /= B + C;
```

which will be identical in effect to

```
A = A/(B + C);
```

The Increment and Decrement Operators

We will now take a brief look at some unusual arithmetic operators called the increment and decrement operators, as we will find them to be quite an asset once we get further into applying C++ in earnest. These are unary operators used to increment or decrement a variable. For example, assuming the variables are of type **int**, the following three statements all have exactly the same effect:

```
count = count + 1;      count += 1;      ++count;
```

They each increment the variable **count** by 1. The last form using the increment operator is clearly the most concise. The action of this operator in an expression is to increment the value of the variable, then use the incremented value in the expression. For example, if **count** has the value 5, then the statement:

```
total = ++count + 6;
```

results in the variable **total** being assigned the value 12.

So far, we have written the operator in front of the variable to which it applies. This is call the **prefix** form. It can also be written after the variable to which it applies, the **postfix** form, where the effect is slightly different. The incrementing of the variable to which it applies occurs after its value is used in context. For example, if we rewrite the previous example as:

```
total = count++ + 6;
```

with the same initial value for **count**, **total** is assigned the value 11, since the initial value of **count** is used to evaluate the expression, then the increment by 1 is applied. The statement above is equivalent to the two statements:

```
total = count + 6;
++count;
```

Generally, it isn't a good idea to use the increment operator in the way that we have here. It would be clearer to write:

```
total = 6 + count++;
```

Where we have an expression such as **a++ + b**, or **a+++b**, it becomes less obvious what is meant, or what the compiler will do. They are actually the same, but in the second case you might really have meant **a + ++b** which is different. It evaluates to one more than the other two expressions.

Exactly the same rules as we have discussed in relation to the increment operator, apply to the decrement operator, **--**. For example, if **count** has the initial value 5, then the statement:

```
total = --count + 6;
```

results in **total** having the value 10 assigned, whereas:

```
total = 6 + count-- ;
```

sets the value of **total** to 11. Both operators are usually applied to integers, particularly in the context of loops as we shall see in Chapter 3, but we shall also see in later chapters that they can be applied to other data types in C++ as well.

Try It Out - The Comma Operator

The comma operator allows you to specify several expressions where one might normally occur. This is best understood through an example of its use.

```cpp
// EX2-05.CPP
// Exercising the comma operator
#include <iostream.h>
int main()
{
   long num1 = 0, num2 = 0, num3 = 0, num4 = 0;

   num4 = ( num1 = 10, num2 = 20, num3 = 30 );
   cout << endl
           << "The value of a series of expressions "
           << "is the value of the right most: "
           << num4;

   return 0;
}
```

How It Works

You will get three compiler warnings from this example as a consequence of not using the values of **num1**, **num2**, and **num3**. This is because having variables you don't use usually doesn't make sense, and can indicate some kind of error, but since this is purely for demonstration purposes you can ignore them. If you compile and run this program you will get this output:

```
The value of a series of expressions is the value of the right most: 30
```

which is fairly self explanatory. The variable **num4** receives the value of the last of the series of three assignments, the value of an assignment being the value assigned to the left hand side. The parentheses in the assignment for **num4** are essential. You could try executing this without them to see the effect. Without the parentheses the first expression in the series separated by commas will become

num4 = **num1** = 10

so **num4** will have the value 10.

The expressions separated by the comma operator do not have to be assignments, of course. We could equally well write the following:

```
long num1 = 1, num2 = 10, num3 = 100, num4 = 0;
num4 = ++num1, ++num2, ++num3;
```

The effect of this assignment would be to increment the variables `num1`, `num2`, and `num3` by 1, and to set `num4` to the value of the last expression which will be 101.

We will come across the comma operator quite a few times in subsequent chapters.

The Sequence of Calculation

So far we haven't talked about how the sequence of calculations involved in evaluating an expression is arrived at. It generally corresponds to what you will have learnt at school when dealing with basic arithmetic operators, but there are many other operators in C++. To understand what happens with these we need to look at the mechanism used in C++ to determine this sequence. It is referred to as operator precedence.

Operator Precedence

Operator precedence orders the operators in a priority sequence. Operators with the highest precedence are always executed before operators of a lower precedence. The precedence of the operators in C++ is shown in the following table.

Operators	Associativity
() [] -> :: .	Left to right
! ~ +(unary) -(unary) ++ &(unary) *(unary) (typecast) sizeof	Right to left
new delete	
.*(unary) ->*	Left to right
* / %	Left to right
+ -	Left to right
<< >>	Left to right
< <= > >=	Left to right

Operators	Associativity
== !=	Left to right
&	Left to right
^	Left to right
|	Left to right
&&	Left to right
||	Left to right
?:(conditional operator)	Right to left
= *= /= %= += -= &= ^= |= <<= >>=	Right to left
,	Left to right

There are a lot of operators you haven't seen yet, but you will know them all by the end of the book. They all appear in the precedence table here rather than spread around, so you can always refer back here if you are uncertain in the future.

Operators with the highest precedence appear at the top of the table. Operators in the same row are all of equal precedence. If there are no parentheses in an expression, then operators of equal precedence are executed in a sequence determined by their associativity. Thus, if the associativity is 'left to right', then the left-most operator in an expression is executed first, progressing through the expression to the right-most.

Note that where an operator has a unary (working with one operand) and a binary (working with two operands) form, the unary form is always of a higher precedence and is therefore executed first.

You can always override the precedence of operators by using parentheses. Since there are so many operators in C++ it is hard to be sure what takes precedence over what. It is a good idea to insert parentheses to make sure. A further plus is that parentheses often make the code much easier to read.

Variable Types and Casting

Calculations in C++ can only be carried out between values of the same type. When you write an expression involving variables or constants of different types, for each operation to be performed the compiler has to convert the type of one of the operands to match that of the other. This conversion process is called **casting**. For example, if you want to add a double value to an integer, the integer value is first converted to **double**, and then the addition is carried out. Of course, the variable which contains the value to be cast is not itself changed. The compiler will store the converted value in a temporary memory location which will be discarded when the calculation is finished.

There are rules that govern which operand is selected to be converted in any operation. Any expression to be calculated breaks down into a series of operations between two operands. For example, the expression `2*3-4+5` amounts to the series `2*3` resulting in `6`, `6-4` resulting in `2`, and finally `2+5` resulting in `7`. Thus, the rules for casting operands where necessary only need to be defined in terms of decisions about pairs of operands. So, for any pair of operands, the following rules are checked in the sequence they are written until one applies, then that rule is used.

Rules for Casting Operands

1   If either operand is **long double** the value of the other is cast to **long double**

2   If either operand is **double** the value of the other is cast to **double**

3   If either operand is **float** the value of the other is cast to **float**

4   If either operand is **long** the value of the other is cast to **long**

5   If either operand is **int** then the value of the other is cast to **int**

We could try these rules on a hypothetical expression to see how they work. Let's suppose we have a sequence of variable declarations as follows:

```
double value = 5.0;
int count = 3;
float many = 2;
char num = 4;
```

Let's also suppose we have the following rather arbitrary arithmetic statement:

```
value = (value - count)*(count + num)/many + num/many;
```

We can now work out which casts the compiler will apply. The first operation is to calculate **(value - count)**. Rule 1 doesn't apply but Rule 2 does, so the value of **count** is converted to **double** and the **double** result 15.0 is calculated. Next **(count - num)** must be evaluated, and here the first rule in sequence which applies is Rule 5, so **num** is converted from **char** to **int** and the result 12 produced as type **int**. The next calculation is the product of the first two results, a **double** 15.0 and an **int** 12. Rule 2 applies here and the 12 is converted to 12.0 as **double**, and the **double** result 180.0 is produced. This result now has to be divided by **many**, so Rule 2 applies again and the value of **many** is converted to **double** before generating the **double** result 90.0. The expression **num/many** is calculated next, and here Rule 3 applies to produce the **float** value 2.0f after converting the value of **num** from **char** to **float**. Lastly, the **double** value 90.0 is added to the **float** value 2.0f for which Rule 2 applies, so after converting the 2.0f to 2.0 as **double**, the final result of 92.0 is stored in **value**.

In spite of the last paragraph reading a bit like *The Auctioneer's Song*, I hope you get the general idea.

Casts in Assignment Statements

As we saw in example **EX2-04.CPP** earlier in this chapter, you can cause an implicit cast by writing an expression of the right-hand side of an assignment that is of a different type to the variable on the left-hand side. This can cause values to be changed and information to be lost. For instance, if you assign a **float** or **double** value to an **int** or a **long** variable, at least the fractional part of the **float** or **double** will be lost and just the integer part will be stored, assuming that does not exceed the range of values available for the integer type concerned.

For example, after executing the following code fragment:

```
int number;
float decimal = 2.5f;
number = decimal;
```

the value of **number** will be 2. Note the **f** at the end of the constant 2.5. This indicates to the compiler that this constant is single precision floating point. Without the **f**, the default would have been **double**. Any constant containing a decimal point is floating point and if you don't want it to be double precision you need to append the `f`. A capital `F` would do as well. We can also define `long` integer constants by appending an `l`, or better still an `L` to avoid confusion, to the integer value. Thus `99` is a two byte integer and `99L` is a four byte integer.

Explicit Casts

Sometimes the default cast rules can be inconvenient. Suppose you have an expression

```
result = x+i/j;
```

where `x` is double and `i` and `j` are integers. Because of the way integer division works, you won't get an exact result here unless `i` is a multiple of `j`. You can use an explicit type cast to convert a value from one type to another. We can rewrite the last statement as

```
result = x + (double)i/j;
```

As may be obvious to you, the value of `i` and `j` are converted to type `double` before the division occurs, so we now get an exact result produced.

The way the cast is written above is called cast notation. You can also use functional notation which would look like this:

```
result = x + double(i)/j;
```

This works exactly the same as the previous version. As `i` is cast to double, `j` is cast to double according to the rules for mixed expressions we saw earlier.

You can write an explicit cast for any standard type, but you should be conscious of the possibility of losing information. If you cast a `float` or `double` value to `long`, for example, you will lose the fractional part of the value converted, so if the value started out as less than 1.0 the result will be 0. If you cast `double` to `float` you will lose accuracy because a `float` variable has only 7 digits precision whereas `double` variables maintain 19. Even casting between integer types provides potential for losing data depending on the values involved. For example, the value of an integer of type `long` can exceed the maximum you can store in a variable of type `int`, so casting from a `long` value to an `int` may lose information.

The Bitwise Operators

The bitwise operators treat their operands as a series of individual bits rather than a numerical value. They only work with integer variables or constants as operands, so only data types **short**, **int**, **long**, and **char** can be used. They are useful in programming hardware devices where the status of a device is often represented as a series of individual flags, and you will meet them when we look at input output in detail, where single bits are used to control various options in the way data is handled.

There are six bitwise operators:

Operator	Meaning
&	Bitwise AND
|	Bitwise OR
^	Bitwise exclusive OR
~	Bitwise NOT
>>	Shift right
<<	Shift left

Let's take a look at how each of them works.

The Bitwise AND

The bitwise AND, **&**, is a binary operator that combines corresponding bits in its operands. If both corresponding bits are 1, then the result is a 1 bit, and if either or both operand bits are 0, then the result is a 0 bit. We can represent this in a table:

Bitwise AND	0	1
0	0	0
1	0	1

For each row and column combination the result of **&** combining the two is at the entry corresponding to the intersection of the row and column.

Let's see how this works on an example.

```
char Letter1 = 'A', Letter2 = 'Z', Result = 0;
Result = Letter1 & Letter2;
```

We need to look at the bit patterns to see what happens. The letters `'A'` and `'Z'` correspond to hexadecimal values 41h and 5Ah respectively (see Appendix A) for ASCII codes. So we can write the operation as:

```
Letter1    0100 0001
Letter2    0101 1010
```
ANDed produce:
```
Result     0100 0000
```

You can confirm this by looking at how corresponding bits combine with `&` in the truth table. After the assignment `Result` will have the value 40h which corresponds to the character `'@'`.

Because the `&` produces zero if either bit is zero, we can use this operator to make sure unwanted bits are zero in a variable. We achieve this by creating what is called a 'mask' which is combined with the original variable using `&`. We create the mask by putting a 1 where we want to keep bits, and 0 where we want to set a bit to zero. The result will be 0s where the mask bit is 0, and the same value as the original bit in the variable where the mask is 1. Suppose we have a **char** variable **Letter** where, for the purposes of illustration, we want to eliminate the high order 4 bits, but keep the low order 4 bits. This is easily done by setting up a mask as **0Fh** and combining it with the letter using `&` thus:

```
Letter = Letter & 0x0F;
```

or, more concisely,

```
Letter &= 0x0F;
```

If **Letter** started out as 41h, it would end up as 01h as a result of either of these statements. Similarly, you can use a mask of 0xF0 to keep the 4 high order bits, and zero the 4 low order bits. Therefore, this statement:

```
Letter &= 0xF0;
```

will result in the value of **Letter** being changed from 41h to 40h.

The Bitwise OR

The bitwise OR, |, sometimes called the inclusive OR, combines corresponding bits such that the result is a 1 bit if either operand bit is a 1, and 0 if both operand bits are 0. The truth table for the bitwise OR is:

Bitwise OR	0	1
0	0	1
1	1	1

We can exercise this with the same variables we used with AND:

```
char Letter1 = 'A', Letter2 = 'Z', Result = 0;
Result = Letter1 | Letter2;
```

We can show how the result is generated by representing the operation as:

Letter1	0100 0001
Letter2	0101 1010

ORed produce:

Result	0101 1011

This is quite a different result from the & operation. Again you can verify by using the truth table for | on corresponding bits of Letter1 and Letter2. The variable Result ends up with the value 5Bh which corresponds to the character '['.

The OR can be used to turn bits on. If we want to be sure that the fifth bit in a char variable flag is on, but want to leave the other bits as whatever they are, we could use the statement:

```
flag |= 0x08h;
```

The value ORed with flag is 0000 1000 in binary, which forces the fifth bit to be 1, and leaves the others as they were. A constant combined with a variable using a bitwise logical operator in this way is usually referred to as a **mask**.

The Bitwise Exclusive OR

The exclusive OR, ^, is so called because it operates similar to the inclusive OR but produces 0 when both operand bits are 1. Its truth table is therefore as follows:

Bitwise EOR	0	1
0	0	1
1	1	0

Using the same variable values as we used with the OR, we can look at the result of the following statement:

```
Result = Letter1 ^ Letter2;
```

This operation can be represented as:

```
                    Letter1    0100 0001
                    Letter2    0101 1010
EORed produce:
                    Result     0001 1011
```

The variable `Result` is set to 1Bh or 27 in decimal notation.

The ^ operator has a rather surprising property. Suppose we have two `char` variables, `First` with the value `'A'`, and `Last` with the value `'Z'`, corresponding to binary values 0100 0001 and 0101 1010. If we write the statements:

```
First ^= Last;      // Result First is 0001 1011
Last ^= First;      // Result Last is 0100 0001
First ^= Last;      // Result First is 0101 1010
```

then the result of these is that `First` and `Last` have exchanged values without using any intermediate memory location. This works with any integer values.

The Bitwise NOT

The bitwise NOT, ~, takes a single operand for which it inverts the bits: 1 becomes 0, and 0 becomes 1. Thus when we execute the statement

```
Result = ~Letter1;
```

if **Letter1** is 0100 0001, the variable **Result** will have the value 1011 1110, which is BEh or 190 as a decimal value.

The Bitwise Shift Operators

These operators shift the value of an integer variable a specified number of bits to the left or right. Bits that go off either end of the variable are lost. The right operand determines how many positions the bit shifts. Let's take a **char** variable **Number** with the decimal value 14. The statement

```
Number <<= 2;
```

results in the value of **Number** which to start with is 0000 1110 in binary, being shifted two positions left. This results in **Number** ending up as the value 0011 1000. This is equivalent to decimal 56, which is four times the original value. As long as bits are not lost, shifting left n bits is equivalent to multiplying the value by 2, n times. In other words, it is equivalent to multiplying by 2^n. Similarly, shifting right n bits is equivalent to dividing by 2^n. But beware, if we initialize **Number** with the value 16385, and execute the statement:

```
Number <<= 2;
```

the variable **Number** will have the value 4, which might not be what you anticipated. This is because the high order bits have fallen off the end and are lost.

The right shift operation is, in the main, similar. For example, if the variable **Number** has the value 24, and we execute the statement:

```
Number >>= 2;
```

it will result in **Number** having the value 6, effectively dividing by 4.

The right shift operates in a special way with **signed** integers types that are negative (that is, the sign bit, which is the leftmost bit, is 1). In this case, the sign bit is propagated to the right. So if **Number** of type **char** has the value -104 in decimal, which is 1001 1000 in binary, and we shift it right 2 bits with the operation:

```
Number >>= 2;          // Result 1110 0110
```

then the decimal value of the result is -26 as the sign bit is repeated. With operations on **unsigned** integer types, of course, the sign bit is not repeated and zeros appear.

> *These shift operations can be faster than the regular multiply or divide on some computers, but you should only use them in this way if you are sure you are not going to lose bits you can ill afford to be without.*

Variable Scope

All variables have a finite lifetime. They come into existence from the point you declare them, and then at some point, at the latest when your program terminates, they disappear. The lifetime of a variable is called its **scope**.

Try It Out - Automatic Variables

All of the variables we have declared so far have been declared within a block, that is, within the extent of a pair of curly braces. These are called **automatic** variables, and are said to have **local scope** or **block scope**. They are born when they are declared and they cease to exist at the end of the block containing the declaration. There are other kinds of variables (as we shall see later in this chapter when we come to discuss **static** variables), and **dynamic** variables. We can demonstrate the effect of scope on automatic variables with the following example:

```
// EX2-06.CPP
// Demonstrating variable scope.
#include <iostream.h>
int main()
{                                          // Function scope starts here
   int count1 = 10;
```

Try it Out!

```
    int count3 = 50;
    cout << endl
        << "Value of outer count1 = " << count1;

    {                                // New scope starts here...
        int count1 = 20;            //This hides the outer count1
        int count2 = 30;
        cout << endl
            << "Value of inner count1 = " << count1;
        count1 += 3;                // This affects the inner count1
        count3 += count2;
    }                               // ...and ends here.

    cout << endl
        << "Value of outer count1 = " << count1
        << endl
        << "Value of outer count3 = " << count3;

    // cout << endl << count2;  // uncomment to get an error
    return 0;
}                                   // Function scope ends here
```

How It Works

The output from this example will be

```
Value of outer count1 = 10
Value of inner count1 = 20
Value of outer count1 = 10
Value of outer count3 = 80
```

The first two statements declare and define two integer variables count1 and count3 with initial values of 10 and 50 respectively. Both these variables exist from this point, to the closing brace at the end of the program. Following the variable definitions the value of count1 is output to produce the first of the lines shown above.

There is then a second curly brace which starts a new scope. Two variables count1 and count2 are then defined with values 20 and 30 respectively. This count1 is different from the first count1, but the first is masked by the second because they have the same name.

Note this is not a good approach to programming in general. The output statement shows by the value in the second line that we are using the count1 in the inner scope - that is, inside the innermost braces. If it were the outer count1, it would have the value 10. The variable count1 is incremented and the increment applies to the variable in the inner scope since the outer one is still hidden. However, **count3** which was defined in the outer scope is incremented without any problem showing that the variables that were defined at the beginning of the outer scope are accessible in the inner scope. Note that they could be defined after the second of the inner pair of braces and still be within the outer scope, in which case they would not exist at this point.

After the brace ending the inner scope, **count2** and the inner **count1** cease to exist. The variables **count1** and **count3** are still there in the outer scope and the values displayed show that **count3** was indeed incremented in the inner scope. If you uncomment the line

```
// cout << endl << count2;   // uncomment to get an error
```

the program will no longer compile correctly because it attempts to output a nonexistent variable. You will get the error message

Undefined symbol 'count2'

since **count2** is out of scope at this point. The scopes of the variables in this example are shown in the figure below.

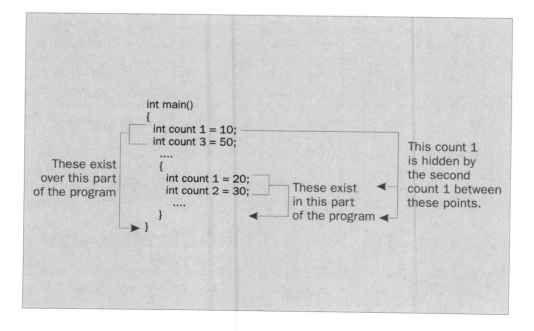

Positioning Variable Declarations

You have great flexibility in where you place the declarations for your variables. The most important aspect to consider is what scope they should have. Beyond that, you should generally place them close to where they are to be first used in a program. You should write your programs with a view to making them as easy as possible for another programmer to understand, and declaring a variable at its first point of use can be helpful in achieving that. It is also possible to place declarations for variables outside of all the functions that make up a program. Let's look into that.

Global Variables

Variables declared outside of all blocks and classes (you might not know what these are yet but we will come to them later) are called **globals** and have **file scope**. This means that they are accessible throughout all the functions in the file following the point at which they are declared. If you declare them at the very beginning, they will be accessible throughout the file.

Since global variables are declared outside of all the blocks in a program, they continue to exist as long as the program is running. This might raise the question in your mind 'why not make all variables global and avoid all this messing about with local variables that disappear?'. This sounds very attractive at first, but, like the Sirens of mythology, there are serious disadvantages which completely outweigh any advantages you might gain. Real programs are generally composed of a large number of statements, a significant number of functions, and a great many variables. Declaring all variables at the global scope greatly magnifies the possibility of accidental erroneous modification of a variable, as well as making the job of naming them sensibly quite intractable. By keeping variables local to a function or a block they have almost complete protection from external effects, and the whole development process becomes much easier to manage.

Try It Out - The Scope Resolution Operator

Note that global variables can still be hidden by a local variable with the same name. In this case it is possible to access them using the scope resolution operator, `::`. We can demonstrate how this works with a revised version of the last example:

```
// EX2-07.CPP
// Demonstrating the global scope resolution operator
#include <iostream.h>

int count1 = 100;                        // Global version of count1

int main()
{
    int count1 = 10;                     // Function scope starts here
    int count3 = 50;
    cout << endl
        << "Value of outer count1 = " << count1;

    cout << endl
        << "Value of global count1 = "<< ::count1;

    {                                    // New scope starts here...
        int count1 = 20;       //This hides the outer count1
        int count2 = 30;

        cout << endl
            << "Value of inner count1 = " << count1;

        cout << endl
            << "Value of global count1 = "<< ::count1;

        count1 += 3;                     // This affects the inner count1
        count3 += count2;
    }                                    // ...and ends here.

    cout << endl
        << "Value of outer count1 = " << count1
        << endl
        << "Value of outer count3 = " <<count3;

    // cout << endl << count2;  //remove first // to get an error
    return 0;
}                                        // Function scope ends here
```

How It Works

If you compile and run this example you will get the following output:

```
Value of outer count1 = 10
Value of global count1 = 100
Value of inner count1 = 20
Value of global count1 = 100
Value of outer count1 = 10
Value of outer count3 = 80
```

You can see from the listing the changes we have made to the previous example. We will just discuss the effects of those. The declaration of **count1** prior to the definition of the function **main()** is global, so it is available in principle through the function **main()**. This global variable is initialized with the value of 100. However, we have two other variables called **count1** which also defined in **main()**, so throughout the program the global **count1** is hidden by the local **count1** variables. In fact, in the inner block it is hidden behind two variables called **count1**, the inner **count1** and the outer **count1**. The first additional output statement:

```
cout << endl
     << "Value of global count1 = "<< ::count1;
```

uses the scope resolution operator to make it clear to the compiler that we want to reference the global variable **count1**. You can see that this works from the value displayed by this statement. The global scope resolution operator also does its stuff within the inner block, as you can see from the output generated by the statement we have added there. A global is always reached by the long arm of the scope resolution operator.

We shall see a lot more of this operator when we get to object-oriented programming.

Static Variables

It is conceivable that you might want to have a variable that is defined and accessible locally, but which also continues to exist after exiting the block in which it is declared. This will become more apparent when we come to deal specifically with functions. The **static** specifier provides this. In fact, a **static** variable will continue to exist for the life of a program. To declare a **static** variable **count** you would write:

```
static int count;
```

Static variables are always initialized for you if you don't provide an initializer yourself. The variable **count** declared here will be initialized with 0.

Summary

In this chapter we have covered the basics of computation in C++. We have learnt about all of the elementary types of data provided for in the language, and all the operators that manipulate these types directly. The essentials of what we have discussed up to now are as follows:

▶ A DOS program in C++ consists of at least one function called `main()`.

▶ The executable part of a function is made up of statements contained between curly braces.

▶ A statement in C++ is terminated by a semicolon.

▶ Named objects in C++, such as variables or functions, can have names that consist of a sequence of letters and digits, the first of which is a letter, and where an underscore is considered to be a letter. Upper and lower case letters are distinguished.

▶ All the objects such as variables that you name in your program must not have a name that coincides with any of reserved words in C++. The full set of reserved words in TCW appear in Appendix B.

▶ All constants and variables in C++ are of a given type. The basic types are **char**, **int**, **long**, **float**, and **double**.

▶ The name and type of a variable is defined in a declaration statement ending with a semicolon. Variables may also be given initial values in a declaration.

▶ You can protect the value of a variable of a basic type by using the modifier **const**. This will prevent direct modification of the variable within the program.

▶ By default, a variable is automatic, which means that it only exists from the point at which it is declared to the end of the scope in which it is defined, indicated by the next closing brace after its declaration.

▶ A variable may be declared as `static`, in which case it continues to exist for the life of the program. It can only be accessed within the scope in which it was defined.

▶ Variables can be declared outside of all blocks within a program, in which case they have global scope. Variables with global scope are accessible throughout a program, except where a local variable exists

▶ with the same name as the global variable. Of course, they can still be reached with the scope resolution operator.

▶ An lvalue is an object that can appear on the left hand side of an assignment. Non-**const** variables are examples of lvalues.

▶ You can mix different types of variables and constants in an expression, but they will be automatically converted to a common type where necessary. Conversion of the type of the right hand side of an assignment to that of the left hand side will also be made where necessary. This can cause loss of information when the left hand side type can't contain the same information as the right hand side: **double** converted to **int**, or **long** converted to **int**, for example.

▶ The keyword **typedef** allows you to define synonyms for other types.

Although we have discussed all the basic types, don't be misled into thinking that's all there is. There are more complex types based on the basic set as we shall see, and eventually you will be creating original types of your own.

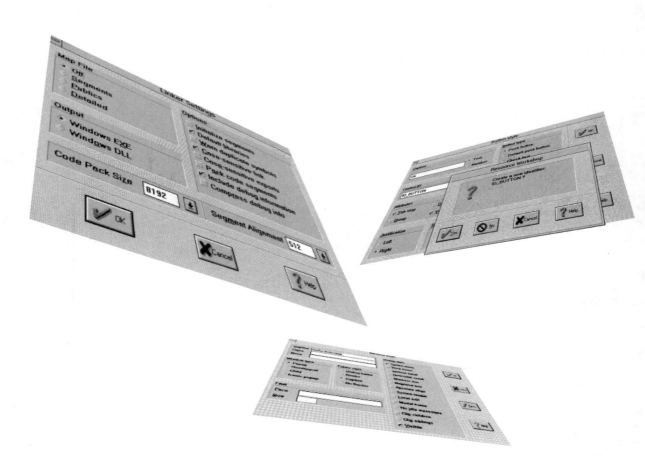

Decisions and Loops

This chapter introduces to us the capability of making decisions and of repeating a set of actions until a specific condition is met. This will enable you to handle variable amounts of input as well as make validity checks on the data you read in. You will also be able to write programs that can adapt their actions depending on the input data, and to deal with problems where logic is fundamental to the solution. By the end of this chapter you will have learnt:

▶ How to compare data value and alter the sequence of program execution based on the result

▶ What logical operators and expressions are and how to apply them

▶ How to deal with multiple choice situations

▶ How to write and use loops in your programs

We will start with one of the most powerful programming tools, the ability to compare variables with other variables and constants and based on the outcome, choose to execute one set of statements or another.

Comparing Values

Unless we want to forever work on the basis of tossing a coin in order to make a decision we need a mechanism for comparing things. This involves some new operators which are called **relational operators**. Since we are dealing one way or another with numbers (as character information is ultimately represented by numeric codes), comparing numerical values is basic to practically all decision making. We have six fundamental operators for comparing two values:

Symbol	What it means	Symbol	What it means
<	Less than	<=	Less than or equal to
>	Greater than	>=	Greater than or equal to
==	Equal to	!=	Not equal to

The 'equal to' comparison operator has two successive equal signs. You will almost certainly mistakenly use one equals sign on occasions, which will cause considerable confusion until you spot the problem!

Each of these operators compare two values and result in a value of 1, representing **True**, if the comparison is true, or the value 0, representing **False**, if the comparison is not true. We can see how this works by having a look at a few simple examples of comparisons. Suppose we have integer variables i and j with the values 10 and -5 respectively. Then the expressions

$i > j$ $i\ != \ j$ $j > -8$ $i <= \ j+15$

are all **True**.

Let's further assume we have the following variables defined:

```
char First = 'A', Last = 'Z';
```

We can now write some examples of comparing values. Take a look at these:

```
First==65     First<Last    'E'<=First    First!=Last
```

All four of these involve comparing ASCII code values. The first expression is true since **First** was initialized with 'A' which is the equivalent of decimal 65. The second expression checks whether the value of **First**, which is 'A', is less than the value of **Last**, which is 'Z'. If you check the ASCII codes for these characters in Appendix A you will see that the capital letters are represented by an ascending sequence of numerical values from 65 to 90, 'A' representing 65 and 90 representing 'Z', so this comparison will result in 1 since it is true. The third expression is false and so returns 0, since 'E' is greater than the value of **First**. The last expression is true since 'A' is definitely not equal to 'Z'.

Look at the following straight numerical comparisons:

```
int i = -10, j = 20;
double x = 1.5, y = -0.25E-10
```

```
-1<y j <( 10 - i )          2.0*x >=( 3 + y )
```

As you can see, we can use expressions resulting in a numerical value as operands in comparisons. If you check with the precedence table we saw in Chapter 2, you will see that none of the parentheses are strictly necessary, but I feel the parentheses help to make the expressions clearer. The first comparison is true and so produces 1. The variable **y** has a very small negative value, -0.000000000025, and so is greater than -1. The second comparison results in 0 since it is false. The expression **10-i** has the value 20 which is the same as **j**. The third expression is true since the expression **3+y** is slightly less than 3.

We can use the relational operators to compare any types of values, so all we need now is a practical way of using the results of a comparison to modify the behaviour of a program, so let's look into that immediately.

The if Statement

The basic **if** statement allows you to execute a single statement, or a block of statements enclosed within curly braces if a given condition is **True**. This is illustrated graphically in the figure on the following page.

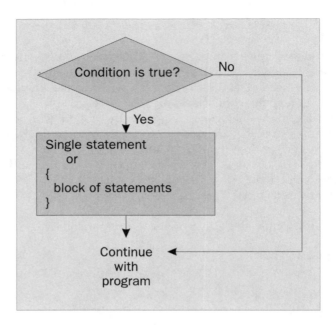

A simple example of an **if** statement is as follows:

```
if( Letter == 'A' )
    cout << "The first capital, alphabetically speaking.";
```

The condition to be tested appears in parentheses immediately following the keyword, **if**. Note the position of the semicolon here. It goes after the statement following the **if**. There shouldn't be a semicolon after the condition in parentheses. You can also see how the statement following the **if** is indented to indicate it is only executed as a result of the **if** condition being **True**. The relational operators return 1 as representing **True**, but actually any positive integer value will be interpreted as **True** in an **if** statement.

The output statement will only be executed if the variable **Letter** has the value **'A'**. We could extend this example to change the value of **Letter** if it contains the value **'A'**:

```
if( Letter == 'A' )
{
    cout << "The first capital, alphabetically speaking.";
    Letter = 'a';
}
```

Here we execute the statements in the block only if the condition is **True**. Without the braces, only the first statement would be the subject of the **if**, and the statement assigning the value **'a'** to **Letter** would always be executed. Note that there is only a semicolon after each of the statements in the block, not after the closing brace at the end of the block. There can be as many statements as you like within the block. Now as a result of **Letter** having the value **'A'**, we change its value to **'a'** after outputting the same message as before. Neither of these will be executed if the condition is **False**.

Try It Out - Using ifs

The statement that is to be executed if the condition in an **if** is **True**, can also be an **if**. This is called a **nested if**. We can demonstrate this with a working example:

```
// EX3-01.CPP
// A nested if demonstration
#include <iostream.h>
int main()
{
    char Letter = 0;                        // Store input in here

    cout << endl
         << "Enter a letter: ";
    cin >> Letter;

    if( Letter >= 'A' )                     // Test for 'A' or larger
       if( Letter <= 'Z' )                  // Test for 'Z' or smaller
          cout << endl
               << "You entered a capital letter.";

    if( Letter >= 'a' )                     // Test for 'a' or larger
       if( Letter <= 'z' )                  // Test for 'z' or smaller
          cout << endl
               << "You entered a small letter.";
    return 0;
}
```

How It Works

This is a very straightforward program starting out with the usual comment lines and the **#include** statement for the header file supporting input/output. The first action in the body of **main()** is to prompt for a letter to be entered. This is stored in the **char** variable **Letter**.

The `if` that follows the input checks whether the character entered is `'A'` or larger. If it is, the nested `if` is executed which checks for the input being `'Z'` or less. If it is `'Z'` or less, then the message is displayed. The next `if` checks whether the character entered is a small letter by essentially the same mechanism as the first `if`.

You can see that the relationship between the nested `if`s and the output statement is cued by the indentation applied to each. This helps make the logic of the program easier to follow.

A typical output from this example is

```
Enter a letter: H
You entered a capital letter.
```

This program is rather poorly constructed. It has the disadvantage that the test for lower case is carried out even when upper case has already been discovered. It is also completely silent if you enter a character that is not alphabetic. It's the best we can do with the tools we have accumulated so far, but we will be able to improve on this very soon.

You could easily arrange to change upper case to lower case by adding just one extra statement to the `if`, checking for upper case:

```
if( Letter >= 'A' )                      // Test for 'A' or larger
    if( Letter <= 'Z' )                  // Test for 'Z' or smaller
    {
        cout << endl
             << "You entered a capital letter.";
        Letter += 'a' - 'A';             // Convert to lower case
    }
```

This involves adding the curly brackets plus one additional statement. This statement for converting from upper to lower case works because the ASCII codes for `'A'` to `'Z'` and `'a'` to `'z'` are two groups of consecutive numerical codes, so that the expression `'a'-'A'` represents the value to be added to an upper case letter in order to get the equivalent lower case letter.

You could equally well use the equivalent ASCII values for the letters here, but using the letters means this would work on computers where the characters were not ASCII.

The Extended if Statement

The `if` statement we have been using so far executes a statement if the condition specified is `True`. Program execution then continues with the next statement in sequence. We also have a version of the `if` which allows one statement to be executed if the condition is `True`, and another to be executed if the condition is `False`. Execution then continues with the next statement in sequence. Of course, a block can always replace a single statement as we saw in Chapter 2.

Try It Out - Extending the if

An example of using an extended `if` would be as follows:

```
// EX3-02.CPP
// Using the extended if
#include <iostream.h>
int main()
{
   long number = 0;                  // Store input here
   cout << endl
        << "Enter a number less than 2 billion: ";
   cin >> number;

   if( number%2L )                   // Test remainder after division by 2
      cout << endl                   // Here if remainder 1
           << "Your number is odd.";
   else
      cout << endl                   // Here if remainder 0
           << "Your number is even.";
   return 0;
}
```

A typical example of output from this program is:

```
Enter a number less than 2 billion: 12345
Your number is odd.
```

How It Works

After reading the input value into `number`, the value is tested by taking the remainder after division by 2 and using that as the condition for the `if`. If the remainder is 1(`True`), then the statement immediately following the `if` is executed. If the remainder is 0 (`False`), then the statement following the `else` keyword is executed. After either outcome, the `return` statement is executed to end the program.

Note that the `else` keyword is written without a semicolon, similar to the `if` part of the statement. Again, indentation is used as a visible indicator of the relationship between various statements. You can clearly see which statement is executed for a `True` result, and which for a `False` result. You should always indent the statements in your programs to show their logical structure.

The `if-else` combination is providing a choice between two options. The general logic of the `if-else` is shown in the illustration below.

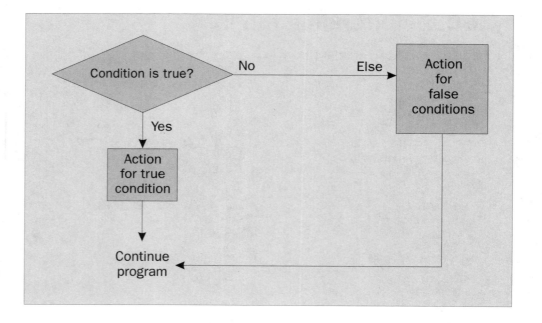

Nested if-else Statements

You can nest `if` statements within `if` statements as we have seen. You can also nest `if-else` statements within `if`s, `if`s within `if-else` statements, and `if-else` statements within `if-else` statements. This provides us with considerable room for confusion so let's look at these with a few examples. Taking the first case first, an example of an `if-else` nested within an `if` might be:

```
    if( coffee == 'y' )
       if( donuts == 'y' )
          cout << "We have coffee and donuts.";
       else
          cout << "We have coffee at least...";
```

The test for **donuts** is executed if the result of the test for **coffee** is **True**, so the messages reflect the correct situation in each case. It is easy to get this confused, however. If we write much the same thing with incorrect indentation we can be trapped into the wrong conclusion:

```
if( coffee == 'y' )
     if( donuts == 'y' )
        cout << "We have coffee and donuts.";
 else                                    // This else is indented incorrectly
    cout << "We have no coffee...";      // Wrong!
```

This mistake is easy to see here, but with more complicated **if** structures we need to keep in mind the rule about which **if** owns which **else**.

> An **else** always belongs to the nearest preceding **if** that is not already spoken for by another **else**.

Whenever things look a bit complicated, you can apply this rule to sort things out. When you are writing your own programs, you can always use braces to make the situation clearer. It isn't really necessary in such a simple case, but we could write the last example as follows:

```
    if( coffee == 'y' )
    {
       if( donuts == 'y' )
          cout << "We have coffee and donuts.";
       else
          cout << "We have coffee at least...";
    }
```

Now it's absolutely clear.

Now that we know the rules, understanding the case of the **if** within the **if-else** becomes easy:

```
    if( coffee == 'y' )
    {
       if( donuts == 'y' )
```

```
        cout << "We have coffee and donuts.";
   }
   else
      if( tea == 'y' )
         cout << "We have tea at least...";
```

Here the braces are essential. If we leave them out then the **else** would belong to the **if** which is looking out for **donuts**. In this kind of situation it is easy to forget to include them and create an error which may be hard to find. A program with this kind of error will compile fine, and even produce the right results some of the time.

The last case can get very messy, even with just one level of nesting. Let's flog the coffee and donuts analysis to death by using it again:

```
if( coffee == 'y' )
   if( donuts == 'y' )
      cout << "We have coffee and donuts.";
   else
      cout << "What only coffee, no donuts?";
else
   if( tea == 'y' )
      cout << "We have tea at least...";
   else
      cout << "No tea or coffee, but maybe donuts...";
```

This starts to look a bit muddled. No braces are necessary as the rule will verify this is correct, but it would look a bit clearer if they were there:

```
if( coffee == 'y' )
{
   if( donuts == 'y' )
      cout << "We have coffee and donuts.";
   else
      cout << "What only coffee, no donuts?";
}
else
{
   if( tea == 'y' )
      cout << "We have tea at least...";
   else
      cout << "No tea or coffee, but maybe donuts...";
}
```

There are much better ways of dealing with this kind of logic in a program. If you put enough nested **if**s together you can almost guarantee a mistake somewhere. The next paragraph will help to simplify things.

Logical Operators and Expressions

Where we have two or more related conditions, using **if**s can be a bit cumbersome as we have just seen. We have tried our iffy talents on looking for coffee and donuts, but in practice you may want to check much more complex conditions. You could be searching a personnel file for someone who is over 21 but under 35, is female with a college degree, and who is unmarried and speaks Hindi or Urdu. Defining a test for this could involve the mother of all **if**s.

Logical operators provide a neat and simple solution. We can combine a series of comparisons using logical operators into a single expression, so we end up needing just one **if**, virtually regardless of the complexity of the set of conditions.

We have just three logical operators:

Operator	Meaning
&&	logical AND
||	logical OR
!	logical negation(NOT)

Let's first consider for each of these, what they are used for in general terms, and then look at an example.

Logical AND

You would use the first operator, **&&**, where you have two conditions and you want both to be **True** for a true result. This is the case when testing for upper case. The value being tested must be both greater than or equal to 'A', AND less than or equal to 'Z'. If either or both conditions are not true, then the value is not a capital letter. If we take the example we used previously, of a value stored in a **char** variable **Letter**, we could write the test, in which we used two **if**s, as a single **if**:

```
if( (Letter >='A') && (Letter<='Z') )
    cout << "This is a capital letter.";
```

The parentheses inside the `if` expression ensures there is no doubt that the comparison operations are executed first, and makes the statement clearer. Here, the output statement will be executed only if both of the conditions combined by the operator `&&` are `True`. The effect of logical operators is often shown using what is called a 'truth' table, which shows for various possible combinations of operands what the result is. The truth table for `&&` is as follows:

&&	0	1
0	0	0
1	0	1

The row headings of the left, and the column headings at the top, represent the value of the logical expressions to be combined by the operator `&&`. Thus to determine the result of combining a `True` condition (1) with a `False` condition (0), select the row with 1 at the left, and the column with 0 at the top, and look at the intersection of the row and column for the result (0). This is exactly the same as the `&` operation we have already seen, which applied to logical values which were typically the result of comparisons.

Logical OR

The OR operator, `||`, applies when you have two conditions and you want a `True` result if either or both of them are true. For example, you might be considered creditworthy for a loan from the bank if your income was at least $100,000 a year, or you had $1,000,000 in cash. This could be tested using the following `if`:

```
if( (Income >= 100000.00) || ( Capital >= 1000000.00) )
    cout << "How much would you like to borrow, Sir, (grovel, grovel)?";
```

The ingratiating response emerges when either or both of the conditions are `True`. A better response might be '*Why* do you want to borrow?'. We can also construct a truth table for the `||` operator:

			0	1
0	0	1
1	1	1

As you can see you only get a `False` result if both conditions are `False`.

Logical NOT

The third logical operator, **!**, takes one operand with a logical value, **True** or **False**, and inverts its value. So if the value of **Test** is **True** then **!Test** becomes **False**, and if it is **False** then **!Test** becomes **True**. To take the example of a simple expression, if **x** has the value 10, then the expression

```
!( x>5 )
```

is **False**, since **x** **>5** is **True**.

Try It Out - Combining Logical Operators

You can combine conditional expressions and logical operators to any degree you feel comfortable with. For example, we could construct a test for whether a variable contained a letter just using a single **if**. Let's write it as a working example:

```
// EX3-03.CPP
// Testing for a letter using logical operators
#include <iostream.h>
int main()
{
 char Letter = 0;                              // Store input in here

    cout << endl
         << "Enter a character: ";
    cin >> Letter;

    if( ((Letter>='A')&&(Letter<='Z')) ||
        ((Letter>='a')&&(Letter<='z')) )  // Test for alphabetic
       cout << endl
            << "You entered a letter.";
    else
       cout << endl
            << " You didn't enter a letter.";
    return 0;
}
```

How It Works

This example starts out in the same way a **EX3-01.CPP** by reading a character after a prompt for input. The interesting part of the program is in the **if** statement condition. This consists of two logical expressions combined with the **||** (OR) operator, so that if either is true the condition returns **True**, and the following message:

```
You entered a letter.
```

is displayed. If both logical expressions are **False** then the **else** statement is executed which displays this message

```
You didn't enter a letter.
```

Each of the logical expressions combines a pair of comparisons with the operator **&&** (AND), so both comparisons must be **True** if the logical expression is to be true. The first logical expression is **True** if the input is a capital letter, and the second is **True** if the input is a small letter.

The Conditional Operator

The conditional operator is sometimes called the ternary operator because it involves three operands. It is best understood by looking at an example. Suppose we have two variables, **a** and **b**, and we want to assign the maximum of **a** and **b** to a third variable **c**. We can do this with the statement:

```
c = a>b ? a : b;          // Set c to the maximum of a and b
```

The conditional operator has a logical expression as its first argument, in this case **a>b**. If this expression has the value 1(**True**), the second operand - **a** in this case - is returned as a value. If it is **False** the third operand - **b** in this case - is returned as a value. Thus the result of the conditional expression is **a** if **a** is greater than **b**, and **b** otherwise. This value is stored in **c**. This use of the conditional operator is equivalent to the following **if** statement:

```
if( a> b )
   c = a;
else
   c = b;
```

The conditional operator can be written generally as:

```
condition   ?   expression1   :   expression2
```

If the condition evaluates as **True** that the result is the value of *expression1*, and if it evaluates to **False** then the result is the value of *expression2*.

Try It Out - Conditional Operator as an lvalue

A curious property of the conditional operator is that it can produce an lvalue in which you can store a result, so it can appear on the left hand side of an assignment statement. We can demonstrate this with a small working example.

```
// EX3-04.CPP
// The conditional operator producing an lvalue
#include <iostream.h>
int main()
{
    int num1 = 0, num2 = 0;               // Input stored here
    cout << endl
         << "Enter two different integers: ";
    cin >> num1 >> num2;

    num1< num2 ? num1 : num2 += 10;    // Increment the smaller number by 10

    cout << endl
         << "num1 is now " << num1 << endl
         << "num2 is now " << num2;
    return 0;
}
```

This is typical output from this program

```
Enter two different integers: 23 94
num1 is now 33
num2 is now 94
```

How It Works

After you enter two integer values the interesting action occurs in the rather odd looking statement which includes the conditional operator. The conditional operator works out what variable has the lowest value stored, then this is used as the variable on the left of the **+=** operation. We could equally well have set it to zero or to the result of some completely different expression. The conditional operator generates a perfectly good address in these instances.

Not all results of the conditional operator produce an lvalue. If the result is a constant, for example, it won't be an lvalue. Clearly an expression such as

```
num1>num2  ?  1  :  2
```

will produce a numeric result which is not an lvalue.

Equally, the expression

```
num1>num2  ?   ++num1  :   --num2
```

is a perfectly good conditional expression but it doesn't produce an lvalue, so it can't appear on the left of an assignment statement.

It is even possible to have the conditional operator on both sides of an assignment operation. For example:

```
num1<num2 ? num1 : num2 = num1 > num2 ? num1-1 : num2 -1;
```

The effect of the left conditional operator is to select the lower of **num1** and **num2** as the destination for the result of the right conditional operator, which has the value of one less than the larger of **num1** and **num2**. The net effect is to set the smaller of **num1** and **num2** to one less than the larger of the two, so we end up with two consecutive numbers (assuming we are still dealing with integer variables).

Try It Out - The switch Statement

Try it Out!

The **switch** statement enables you to select from multiple choices based on a set of fixed values for a given expression.

We can examine how the **switch** statement works with the following example:

```
// EX3-05.CPP
// Using the switch statement
#include <iostream.h>
int main()
{
  int choice = 0;                          // Store selection value here

  cout << endl
       << "Your electronic recipe book is at your service." << endl
       << "You can choose from the following delicious dishes: "
       << endl
       << endl << "1 Boiled eggs"
       << endl << "2 Fried eggs"
       << endl << "3 Scrambled eggs"
       << endl << "4 Coddled eggs"
       << endl << endl << "Enter your selection number: ";
  cin >> choice;
```

```
    switch( choice )
    {
       case 1: cout << endl << "Boil some eggs.";
               break;
       case 2: cout << endl << "Fry some eggs.";
               break;
       case 3: cout << endl << "Scramble some eggs.";
               break;
       case 4: cout << endl << "Coddle some eggs.";
               break;
       default: cout << endl <<"You entered a wrong number, try raw eggs.";
    }
    return 0;
}
```

How It Works

This sort of program needs really good quality packaging to sell well. After defining your options, and reading a selection number into the variable **choice**, the **switch** statement is executed with the condition specified as simply **choice** in parentheses immediately following the keyword **switch**. The possible choices in the **switch** are enclosed between braces and are each identified by a **case label**. A case label is the keyword **case** followed by the value of choice for this option terminated by a colon. The statements to be executed for a particular case are written following the colon, and terminated by a **break** statement, as you can see. The **break** transfers execution to the statement after the **switch**. The break isn't mandatory, but if you don't include it all the statements for the cases following the one selected will be executed, which isn't usually what you want. You can demonstrate this by removing the **break** statements from this example and seeing what happens.

If the value of **choice** doesn't correspond with any of the case values specified, the statements preceded by the **default** label are executed. A **default** case isn't essential. In its absence, the **switch** is exited and the program continues with the next statement after the **switch**.

The general form of the **switch** statement is illustrated in the figure on the following page.

```
                    switch (switch_expression)
                    {
                                                          Each expression
                                                          must be constant
       If switch                                          and different.
  expression results   case constant_expression1:
          in a value
      corresponding              statements;
         to a case
constant_expression,              break;
  the class statements  case constant_expression2:
      are executed.
                                   statements;           Executing break
                                                         transfers control
                                   break;                out of the switch
                          .....                          to here.
  If switch_expression  default:
  does not correspond
    to any case value,           statements;
    default statements
      are executed.    }
```

Try It Out - Sharing a case

Each of the case constant expressions must be constant and must be unique. No two case constants must be the same, otherwise the compiler has no way of knowing which should be executed for that value. However, different cases don't need to have a unique action. Several cases can share the same action, as is shown in the following example:

```cpp
// EX3-06.CPP
// Multiple case actions
#include <iostream.h>
int main()
{
   char Letter = 0;
   cout << endl
        << "Enter a small letter: ";
   cin >> Letter;

   switch( Letter*( Letter>='a' && Letter <='z' ) )
   {
     case 'a':
     case 'e':
     case 'i':
     case 'o':
     case 'u': cout << endl << "You entered a vowel.";
               break;
```

```
      case 0: cout << endl << "It is not a small letter.";
              break;

      default: cout << endl << "You entered a consonant.";
   }
   return 0;
}
```

How It Works

In this example, we have a more complex expression in the `switch`. If the character entered is not a small letter then the expression

```
  ( Letter>='a' && Letter <='z' )
```

will result in the value 0. `Letter` is multiplied by this expression, so the `switch` expression would be set to 0 if a small letter was not entered. This will then cause the statements following the case label `case 0` to be executed.

If a small letter was entered, then the expression above will result in the value 1. Multiplying `Letter` by one results in the `switch` expression having the same value as `Letter`. For all values corresponding to vowels, the same output statement is executed. You can effect this by writing each of the case labels one after the other before the statements to be executed. If a small consonant is entered then the `default` case label statement is executed.

Unconditional Branching

The `if` statement provides you with the flexibility to choose to execute one set of statements or another, depending on a specified condition, so the statement execution sequence is varied depending on the values of the data in the program. The `goto` statement, in contrast, is a blunt instrument. It enables you to branch to a specified program statement unconditionally. The statement to be branched to must be identified by a statement label, which is an identifier defined according to the same rules as a variable name. This is followed by a colon, and placed before the statement requiring labelling. Here is an example of a labelled statement:

```
   MyLabel: x = 1;
```

This statement has the label `MyLabel`, and an unconditional branch to this statement would be written as follows:

```
   goto MyLabel;
```

Using `goto`s in your program should be avoided whenever possible. They tend to encourage very convoluted code that can be extremely difficult to follow, and if you ever get the program working it will become a nightmare to maintain.

> *As the `goto` is theoretically unnecessary - there is always an alternative approach to using `goto` - a significant cadre of programmers say you should never use the `goto`. I don't subscribe to such an extreme view. It is a legal statement after all, and there are occasions when it can be convenient. However, I do recommend that you only use it where you can see an obvious advantage over other options that are available.*

Repeating a Block of Statements

The ability to repeat a group of statements is fundamental to most applications. Without this ability, an organisation would need to modify the payroll program every time an extra employee was hired. Without it, you would need to reload Tetris every time you wanted to play another game. So let's first understand how a loop works.

What is a Loop?

A loop executes a sequence of statements until a particular condition is true (or false). We can actually write a loop with the C++ statements we have met so far. We just need an **if** and the dreaded **goto**. Look at this example:

```
// EX3-07.CPP
// Creating a loop with an if and a goto
#include <iostream.h>
int main()
{
   int i = 0, sum = 0;
   const int MAX = 10;

   i = 1;
loop:
   sum += i;               // Add current value of i to sum
   if (++i <= MAX)
      goto loop;           // Go back to loop until i = 11
```

```
     cout << endl
         << "sum = " << sum
         << endl
         << "i = " << i;
     return 0;
}
```

This example accumulates the sum of integers from 1 to 10. The first time through the sequence of statements, **i** is 1 and is added to **sum** which is zero. In the **if**, **i** is incremented to 2 and as long as it is less than or equal to **MAX** the unconditional branch to **loop** occurs and the value of **i**, now 2, is added to **sum**. This continues with **i** being incremented and added to **sum** each time, until finally **i** is incremented to 11 in the **if**, and the branch back will not be executed. If you run this example you will get this output:

```
sum = 55
i = 11
```

This shows quite clearly how the loop works. However, it uses a **goto**, and introduces a label into our program, both of which are things we should be avoiding if possible. We can achieve the same thing, and more, with the next statement, which is specifically for writing a loop.

Try It Out - Using the for Loop

We can rewrite the last code fragment as a working example using what is known as a **for** loop:

```
// EX3-08.CPP
// Summing integers with a for loop
#include <iostream.h>
int main()
{
   int i = 0, sum = 0;
   const int MAX = 10;

   for ( i = 1 ; i <= MAX ; i++ )    // Loop specification
      sum += i;                      // Loop statement

   cout << endl
          << "sum = " << sum
          << endl
          << "i = " << i;
   return 0;
}
```

Try it Out!

How It Works

If you compile and run this you will get the following output:

```
sum = 55
i = 11
```

This reflects an exact parallel with the position we obtained in the previous example, so they seem to be the same in effect, but the code is much simpler here. The conditions determining the operation of the loop appear in parentheses after the keyword **for**. There are three expressions that appear within the parentheses:

▶ The first sets **i** to 1

▶ The second determines that the loop statement following is executed as long as **i** is less than or equal to **MAX**

▶ The third increments **i** each iteration.

Actually this loop is not the same as the version in **EX3-07.CPP**. You can demonstrate this if you set the value of **MAX** to 0 in both programs and run them again. You will find that the value of **sum** is 1 in **EX3-07.CPP** and 0 in the **for** loop version, and the value of **i** differs too. The reason for this is that the **if** version of the program always executes the loop at least once, since the condition is not checked until the end. The **for** loop does not do this, so evidently the condition is actually checked at the beginning.

The general form of the **for** loop is as follows:

```
for(initializing_expression ; test_expression ; increment expression)
      loop_statement;
```

Of course *loop_statement* can be a block between braces. The sequence of events in executing the **for** loop is shown in the figure opposite.

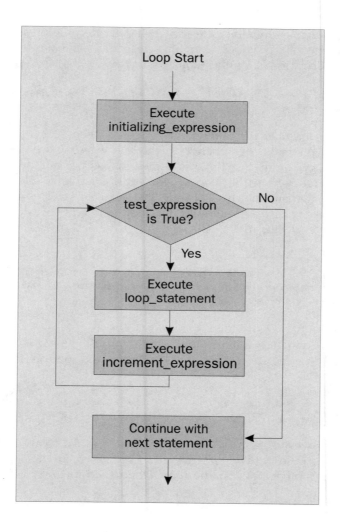

Variations on the for Loop

Usually, the expressions in a **for** loop are used as they are intended, the first for initializing one or more loop counters, the second to test if the loop should continue, and the third to increment or decrement one or more loop counters. However, you are not obliged to use these expressions in this way and quite a few variations are possible which we should look at more closely.

The initialization expression can also include a declaration for a loop variable. Using our previous example, we could have written the loop to include the declaration for the loop counter **i**:

```
for ( int i = 1 ; i <= MAX ; i++ )    // Loop specification
    sum += i;                          // Loop statement
```

Naturally, the original declaration for **i** would need to be omitted in the program. If you make this change to the last example, you will find that it runs exactly as before, but there is something odd about this. The counter **i** is now declared within the loop scope, but we are still able to refer to it in the output statement which is outside the scope of **i**. This is because a special extension has been allowed for loop counters to extend their scope to the scope enclosing the loop.

> *I recommend you don't write programs which take advantage of this, since recent changes to the draft standard for C++ suggest that this may not be supported by future C++ compilers.*

You can also omit the initialization expression altogether. If we initialize **i** appropriately in the declaration, we can write the loop as follows:

```
int i = 1;
for (; i <= MAX ; i++ )             // Loop specification
    sum += i;                        // Loop statement
```

The increment expression is also flexible as to what it can contain. For example, we could actually put the loop statement in the last example into the increment expression, so the loop would become:

```
for( i = 0 ; i <= MAX ; sum += i++ );      // The whole loop
```

We still need the semicolon after the closing parentheses to indicate the loop statement is now empty. If it is omitted then the next statement will be interpreted as the loop statement.

Try It Out - Using Multiple Counters

You can use the comma operator to include multiple counters in a **for** loop. We can show this in operation in the following program:

```
// EX3-09.CPP
// Using multiple counters to show powers of 2
#include <iostream.h>
#include <iomanip.h>
int main()
{

    long i = 0, power = 0;
    const int MAX = 10;

    for( i = 0, power = 1 ; i <= MAX ; i++, power += power )
       cout << endl
            << setw(10) << i << setw(10) << power;       // Loop statement

    return 0;
}
```

How It Works

We initialize two variables in the initialization part of the **for**, separated by the comma operator, and increment each of them in the increment part. Clearly, you can put as many expressions as you like in each position. You can even specify multiple conditions separated by commas in the test part of the **for**, but only the right-most one will affect when the loop ends.

For each increment of **i**, the value of the variable power is doubled by adding it to itself. This produces the powers of two we are looking for and so the program will produce the following output:

```
 0         1
 1         2
 2         4
 3         8
 4        16
 5        32
 6        64
 7       128
 8       256
 9       512
10      1024
```

Try it Out!

The **setw()** manipulator we saw in the previous chapter is used to align the output nicely. This requires the file **IOMANIP.H** to be included, as you have seen.

Try It Out - The Infinite for Loop

If you omit the test condition, the value is assumed to be **True** so the loop will continue indefinitely unless you provide some other means of exiting from it. In fact, you can omit all the expressions in the parentheses after **for** if you like. This may not seem to be very useful, but in fact quite the reverse is true. Have a look at the following example:

```cpp
// EX3-10.CPP
// Using an infinite for loop to compute an average
#include <iostream.h>
int main()
{
    double value = 0.0;            // Value entered stored here
    double sum = 0.0;              // Total of values accumulated here
    int i = 0;                     // Count of number of values
    char indicator = 'n';          // Continue or not?

    for( ;; )                      // Infinite loop
    {
        cout << endl
            << "Enter a value: ";
        cin >> value;              // Read a value
        ++i;                       // Increment count
        sum += value;              // Add current input to total

        cout << "Do you want to enter another value ( enter n to end )?";
        cin >> indicator;          // Read indicator
        if ( (indicator == 'n') || ( indicator == 'N') )
            break;                 // Exit from loop
    }

    cout << endl
        << "The average of  the " << i
        << " values you entered is " << sum/i << ".";
    return 0;
}
```

How It Works

This program will compute the average of an arbitrary number of values. After each value is entered you need to indicate whether you want to enter another value by entering a single character *y* or *n*. Typical output from executing this example is as follows:

```
Enter a value: 10
Do you want to enter another value ( enter n to end )? y

Enter a value: 20
Do you want to enter another value ( enter n to end )? y

Enter a value: 30
Do you want to enter another value ( enter n to end )? n

The average of the 3 values you entered is 20.
```

After declaring and initializing the variables we need, we start a **for** loop with no expressions specified, so there is no provision for ending it here. The block immediately following is the subject of the loop which is to be repeated.

The loop block performs two basic actions:

1 It reads a value

2 It checks whether you want to continue to enter values.

The first action within the block is accomplished by prompting for input and reading a value into the variable **value**. The value entered is added to **sum** and the count of the number of values, **i**, is incremented. The second action is achieved through prompting for 'y' or 'n' to be entered and storing the character in the variable **indicator**, and then testing for 'n' or 'N' in the **if**. If neither is found the loop continues, otherwise a **break** is executed. The effect of **break** is similar here to that in the **switch** statement. It exits the loop immediately by transferring to the statement following the closing brace of the loop block.

Finally, the output is presented including the count of the number of values entered, and the average, which is calculated by dividing **sum** by **i**. Of course, **i** will be promoted to **double** before the calculation, as you will remember from the casting discussion in Chapter 2.

The continue Statement

There is another statement besides **break** that is used to affect the operation of a loop: the **continue** statement. This is written simply as:

```
continue;
```

Executing **continue** within a loop starts the next loop iteration immediately, skipping over any statements remaining in the current iteration. We can demonstrate this with the following code fragment:

```
int i = 0, value = 0, product = 1;
for( i = 1 ; i <= 10 ; i++ )
{
   cin << value;

   if( value == 0 )                    // If value is zero
      continue;                        // skip to next iteration

   product *= value;
}
```

This loop reads 10 values with the intention of producing the product of the values entered. The **if** checks whether the value entered was zero, and if it was the **continue** statement skips to the next iteration. Obviously, if this occurred on the last iteration the loop would end. There are clearly other ways of achieving the same result, but **continue** provides a very useful capability, particularly with complex loops where you may need to skip to the end of the current iteration from various points in the loop.

The effect of the **break** and **continue** statements on the logic of a **for** loop is illustrated in the figure opposite.

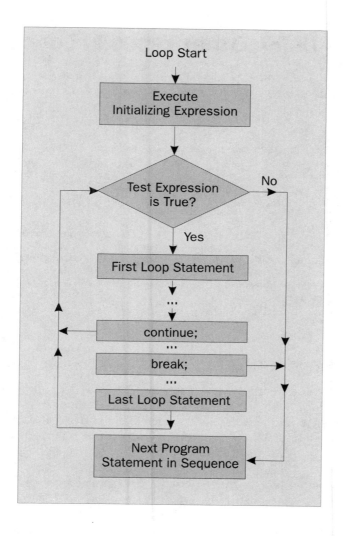

The **break** and **continue** statements can also be used with the other kinds of loop discussed in the following sections.

Try It Out - Using Other Types in Loops

We have only used integers to count loop iterations so far. You are in no way restricted as to what type of variable you use to count iterations. Look at the following example:

```
// EX3-11.CPP
// Display ASCII codes for alphabetic characters
#include <iostream.h>
#include <iomanip.h>
int main()
{
   for(char capital='A',small='a'; capital<='Z'; capital++,small++)
      cout << endl
           << "\t" << capital                   // Output capital as character
           << hex << setw(10) << int (capital) // Output capital as hex
           << dec << setw(10) << int (capital) // Output capital as decimal
           << "\t" << small                     // Output small as character
           << hex << setw(10) << int (small)    // Output small as hex
           << dec << setw(10) << int (small);   // Output small as decimal

   return 0;
}
```

How It Works

The loop in this example is controlled by the **char** variable **capital** which we declare along with the variable **small** in the initializing expression. We also increment both variables in the increment part, so that the value of **capital** varies from 'A' to 'Z', and the value of **small** correspondingly varies from 'a' to 'z'.

The loop contains just one output statement spread over seven lines, the first of which starts a new line. On each iteration after outputting a tab character, the value of **capital** is displayed three times, as a character, as a hexadecimal value, and as a decimal value. We insert the manipulator **hex** which causes succeeding data values to be displayed as hexadecimal values for the second output of **capital**, and we then insert the manipulator **dec** to cause succeeding values to be output as decimal once more. We get the **char** variable **capital** to output as a numeric value by casting it to **int**. The value of **small** is output in a similar way. As a result the program will generate the following output:

A	41	65	a	61	97
B	42	66	b	62	98
C	43	67	c	63	99
D	44	68	d	64	100

E	45	69	e	65	101
F	46	70	f	66	102
G	47	71	g	67	103
H	48	72	h	68	104
I	49	73	i	69	105
J	4a	74	j	6a	106
K	4b	75	k	6b	107
L	4c	76	l	6c	108
M	4d	77	m	6d	109
N	4e	78	n	6e	110
O	4f	79	o	6f	111
P	50	80	p	70	112
Q	51	81	q	71	113
R	52	82	r	72	114
S	53	83	s	73	115
T	54	84	t	74	116
U	55	85	u	75	117
V	56	86	v	76	118
W	57	87	w	77	119
X	58	88	x	78	120
Y	59	89	y	79	121
Z	5a	90	z	7a	122

You can also use a floating point value as a loop counter. An example of a **for** loop with this kind of counter is as follows:

```
double a = 0.3, b = 2.5;
for( double x = 0.0 ; x <= 2.0 ; x += .25 )
   cout << "\n\tx = " << x
        << "\ta*x +b = " << a*x + b;
```

This calculates the value of **a*x+b** for values of **x** from 0.0 to 2.0 in steps of 0.25.

The while Loop

A second kind of loop in C++ is the **while** loop, which is another C++ keyword. Where the **for** loop is primarily intended to count a number of iterations, the **while** loop will continue as long as a specified statement is true. The general form of the **while** loop is as follows:

```
while(   condition  )
      loop_statement;
```

where **loop_statement** will be executed repeatedly as long as the **condition** expression has the value **True**. Once the condition becomes

False, the program continues with the statement following the loop. Of course, a block of statements between braces could replace the single **loop_statement**. The logic of the **while** loop is represented in the figure shown below:

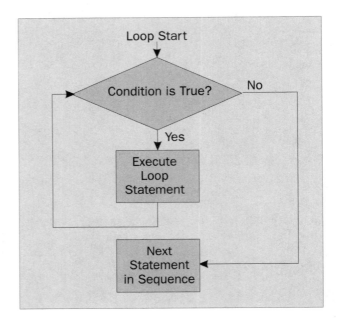

Try It Out - Using the while Loop

We could rewrite our program to compute averages to use the **while** form of loop:

```
// EX3-12.CPP
// Using a while loop to compute an average
#include <iostream.h>
int main()
{
    double value = 0.0;          // Value entered stored here
    double sum = 0.0;            // Total of values accumulated here
    int i = 0;                   // Count of number of values
    char indicator = 'y';        // Continue or not?

    while( indicator == 'y' )    // Loop as long as y is entered
    {
```

```
        cout << endl
            << "Enter a value: ";
        cin >> value;              // Read a value
        ++i;                       // Increment count
        sum += value;             // Add current input to total

        cout << "Do you want to enter another value ( enter n to end )?";
        cin >> indicator;          // Read indicator
    }

    cout << endl
        << "The average of  the " << i
        << " values you entered is " << sum/i << ".";
    return 0;
}
```

How It Works

For the same input this version of the program will produce the same output as before. The statement that has changed and the one that has been added are highlighted above. The **for** loop statement was replaced by the **while** statement, and the test for **indicator** in the **if** was deleted, as this function is performed by the **while** condition. You need to initialize **indicator** with **'y'** in place of **'n'** which appeared previously, otherwise the **while** loop will terminate immediately. As long as the condition in the **while** is **True**, the loop continues. You can put any expression resulting in **True** or **False** as the loop condition. It would be better if the loop condition were extended to allow **'Y'** to be entered to continue the loop as well as **'y'**. Modifying the **while** to this:

```
while( (indicator=='y') || (indicator=='Y') )
```

would do the trick.

You can also create an infinite **while** loop by using a condition that is always **True**. This can be written as follows:

```
while( 1 )
{
    ...
}
```

Naturally the same requirement applies here as in the case of the indefinite **for** loop, namely that there must be some way of exiting the loop within the loop block. We will see some other ways to use the **while** loop in Chapter 4.

The do-while Loop

The **do-while** loop is similar to the **while** loop in that the loop continues as long as the specified loop condition remains **True**. The main difference is that the condition is checked at the end of the **do-while** loop, not at the beginning as in the case of the **while** loop (and the **for** loop). Thus the loop statement is always executed at least once. The general form of the **do-while** loop is as follows:

```
do
{
        loop_statements;
}while(    condition    );
```

The logic of this form of loop is shown in the illustration below.

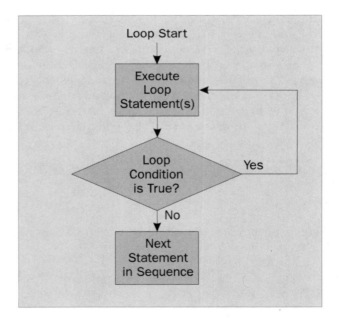

We could replace the **while** loop in the last version of the program to calculate an average with a **do-while** loop:

```
   do
{
     cout << endl
          << "Enter a value: ";
     cin >> value;                    // Read a value
     ++i;                             // Increment count
     sum += value;                    // Add current input to total

     cout << "Do you want to enter another value ( enter n to end )?";
     cin >> indicator;                // Read indicator
}while( (indicator=='y') || (indicator=='Y') );
```

There is little to choose between them except that this version doesn't depend on the initial value set in **indicator** for a correct operation. As long as you want to enter at least one value, which is not unreasonable for the calculation in question, this version of the loop is preferable.

Try It Out - Nested Loops

You can nest one loop inside another. The usual application of this will become more apparent in Chapter 4, but is usually concerned with repeating actions at different levels of classification. An example might be calculating the total marks for each student in a class, then repeating the whole thing for each class in a school. We can illustrate the effects of nesting one loop inside another by calculating a simple formula. A factorial of an integer is the product of all the integers from 1 to the integer in question. The following program will compute the factorial of integers that you enter (until you have had enough):

```
// EX3-13.CPP
// Demonstrating nested loops to compute factorials
#include <iostream.h>
int main()
{
   char indicator = 'n';
   long value = 0,
        factorial = 0;

   do
   {
      cout << endl
           << "Enter an integer value: ";
      cin >> value;
```

```
      factorial = 1;
      for( int i = 2 ; i<=value ; i++ )
         factorial *= i;

      cout << "Factorial " << value << " is " << factorial;
      cout << endl
           << "Do you want to enter another value( y or n )? ";
      cin >> indicator;
   }while( (indicator=='y') || (indicator=='Y') );

   return 0;
}
```

How It Works

If you compile and execute this example, the typical output produced will be as follows:

```
Enter an integer value: 5
Factorial 5 is 120
Do you want to enter another value( y or n)? y

Enter an integer value: 10
Factorial 10 is 3628800
Do you want to enter another value( y or n)? y

Enter an integer value: 23
Factorial 23 is 862456760
Do you want to enter another value( y or n)? n
```

Factorial values grow very fast. In fact, 23 is the last value for which this example will produce a correct value. If you run it with larger values, leading digits will be lost and you may well get negative values for the factorial. Note that the fact that you don't get an error message indicates that there is a problem. This shows the importance of being sure the values you are dealing with can be contained in the permitted range of the type of variable you are using. Errors of this kind can be very hard to find.

The outer of the two nested loops is the **do-while** loop which controls when the program ends. As long as you keep entering *y* or *Y* at the prompt, the program will continue to calculate factorial values. The factorial for the integer entered is calculated in the inner **for** loop. This is executed **value** times to multiply the variable **factorial** (with an initial value of 1) with successive integers from 2 to **value**.

Try It Out - Another Nested Loop

If you haven't dealt much with nested loops they can be a little confusing, so let's try another example. This program will generate a multiplication table of a given size.

```
// EX3-14.CPP
// Using nested loops to generate a multiplication table
#include <iostream.h>
#include <iomanip.h>
int main()
{
   const int SIZE = 12;                // Size of table
   int i = 0, j = 0;                   // Loop counters

   cout << endl                        // Output table title
        << SIZE << " by " << SIZE
        << " Multiplication Table" << endl << endl;

   cout << endl << "    |";
   for( i=1 ; i<=SIZE ; i++ )          // Loop to output
      cout << setw(3) << i << "  ";    // column headings

   cout << endl;                       // Newline for underlines
   for( i=0 ; i<=SIZE ; i++ )
      cout << "_____";                 // Underline each heading

   for( i=1 ; i<=SIZE ; i++ )                    // Outer loop for rows
   {
      cout << endl
           << setw(3) << i << " |";    // Output row label

      for( j=1 ; j<=SIZE ; j++ )                 // Inner loop to output the
         cout << setw(3) << i*j << "  ";   // rest of the row

   }                                            // End of outer loop
   return 0;
}
```

How It Works

If you compile and run this you will see the output shown in the figure on the following page. This shows the output window when execution is complete.

```
(Inactive D:\WINWORD\BGTCPP\BOOKEX\EX3-12.EXE)

12 by 12 Multiplication Table

    |  1    2    3    4    5    6    7    8    9   10   11   12
------------------------------------------------------------------
  1 |  1    2    3    4    5    6    7    8    9   10   11   12
  2 |  2    4    6    8   10   12   14   16   18   20   22   24
  3 |  3    6    9   12   15   18   21   24   27   30   33   36
  4 |  4    8   12   16   20   24   28   32   36   40   44   48
  5 |  5   10   15   20   25   30   35   40   45   50   55   60
  6 |  6   12   18   24   30   36   42   48   54   60   66   72
  7 |  7   14   21   28   35   42   49   56   63   70   77   84
  8 |  8   16   24   32   40   48   56   64   72   80   88   96
  9 |  9   18   27   36   45   54   63   72   81   90   99  108
 10 | 10   20   30   40   50   60   70   80   90  100  110  120
 11 | 11   22   33   44   55   66   77   88   99  110  121  132
 12 | 12   24   36   48   60   72   84   96  108  120  132  144
```

The table title is produced by the first output statement in the program. The next output statement, combined with the loop following it, generates the column headings. Each column will be five characters wide, so the heading value is displayed in a field width of 3 specified by the **setw(3)** manipulator, followed by two blanks. The output statement preceding the loop outputs four spaces and a vertical bar above the first column which will contain the row headings. A series of underline characters are then displayed beneath the column headings.

The nested loop generates the main table contents. The outer loop repeats once for each row so **i** is the row number. The output statement:

```
cout << endl
     << setw(3) << i << " |";        // Output row label
```

goes to a newline for the start of a row, and then outputs the row heading given by the value of **i** in a field width of 3, followed by a space and a vertical bar.

A row of values is generated by the inner loop:

```
for( j=1 ; j<=SIZE ; j++ )               // Inner loop to output the
    cout << setw(3) << i*j << "   ";      // rest of the row
```

This loop outputs values `i*j` corresponding to the product of the current row value `i`, and each of the column values in turn by varying `j` from 1 to `SIZE`. So for each iteration of the outer loop, the innerloop executes `SIZE` iterations. The values are positioned in the same way as the column headings.

When the outer loop is completed, the `return` is executed to end the program.

Summary

In this chapter we have assembled all of the essential mechanisms for making decisions in C++. We have also gone through all the facilities for repeating a group of statements. The essentials of what we have discussed are as follows:

- The basic decision making capability is based on the set of relational operators, which allow expressions to be tested and compared yielding a value `True` or `False`.

- `True` is represented by 1 and `False` is represented by 0, although any positive integer will be interpreted as `True` when a condition is tested.

- The primary decision making capability in C++ is provided by the `if` statement. Further flexibility is provided by the `switch` statement and the conditional operator.

- There are three basic methods provided for repeating a group of statements: the `for` loop, the `while` loop, and the `do-while` loop. The `for` loop allows the loop to repeat a given number of times, the `while` loop allows a loop to continue as long as a specified condition is `True`, and the `do-while` executes the loop at least once and allows continuation of the loop as long as a specified condition is `True`.

- Any kind of loop may be nested within any other kind of loop.

- The keyword `continue` allows you to skip the remainder of the current iteration in a loop, and go straight to the next iteration.

- The keyword `break` provides an immediate exit from a loop. It also provides an exit from a switch at the end of a group of `case` statements.

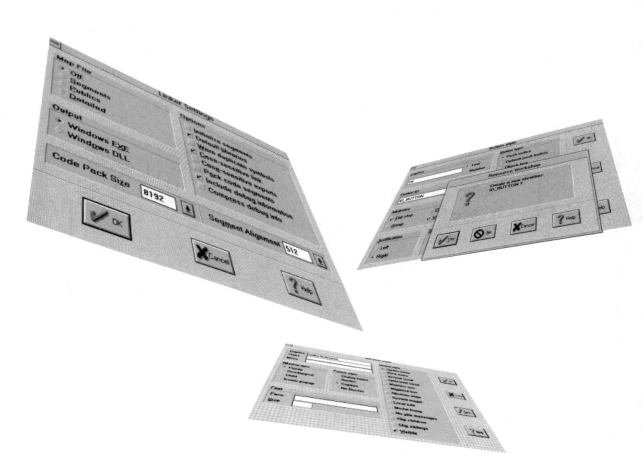

4

Arrays, Pointers and References

So far we have covered all the basic data types of consequence, and we have accumulated a basic knowledge of how to perform calculations and make decisions in a program. This chapter is about broadening the application of the basic programming techniques from single data elements to whole collections of data items. In this chapter you will learn:

- What an array is and how it is used

- How to declare and initialize arrays of different types

- How to declare and use multi-dimensional arrays

- What a pointer is and how it can be used

- How to declare and initialize pointers of different types

- The relationship between arrays and pointers

- What a reference is, how it is declared, and some initial ideas on its uses

- How to create and allocate memory for variables dynamically

Handling Multiple Data Values of the Same Type

We already know how to declare and initialize variables of various types which each hold a single item of information, a single character in a **char** variable, a single integer in a variable of type **int** or of type **long**, and so on. The most obvious extension to these functions, which will enable you to handle applications of a broader scope, is to be able to reference several data elements with a single variable name. It wouldn't be very practical to try to deal with names defined by a string of characters, for instance, by using a separate variable for each character. Equally, to write a payroll program using a separately named variable for each individual's pay, tax liability, and so on, would be an uphill task to say the least. What you would really want to do is reference an employee by some kind of generic name - **EmployeeName** to take an imaginative example - and to have other generic names for the kinds of data related to each employee, such as **Pay**, **Tax**, and so on. Of course, there would also need to be some means of picking out a particular employee from the whole bunch, together with the data associated with him or her.

Arrays

The basis for the solution to all of these problems is provided by the **array** in C++. An array is simply a number of memory locations, each of which can store an item of data of the same type, **int** or **double** say, which are all referenced through a common variable name. Each of the items connected with the payroll could be an array. Individual items in an array are specified by an index value, which is simply an integer representing the sequence number of the elements in the array, the first having the sequence number 0, the second 1, and so on. For our payroll, we could arrange that for an employee corresponding to a given index value in an array **EmployeeName**, the arrays **Pay** and **Tax** would store the associated data in the positions with the same index value.

The basic structure of an array is illustrated in the figure opposite:

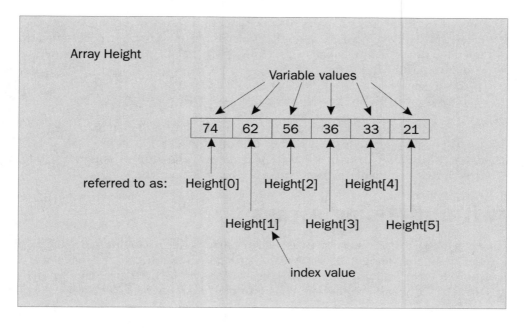

This shows an array, **Height**, with six elements each storing a different value. These might be the heights of members of a family, for instance. As there are six elements, the index values run from 0 through to 5. To refer to a particular element you write the array name followed by the index value of the particular element between square brackets, the third element being referred to as **Height[2]** for example.

Declaring Arrays

You declare an array in essentially the same way as you declared the variables we have seen up to now, the only difference is that the array dimension, which is specified between square brackets, follows the array name. For example, we could declare the integer array **Height** shown in the previous figure, with the following declaration statement:

```
int Height[6];
```

Since each **int** value occupies two bytes, the whole array requires 12 bytes. Arrays can be of any dimension, subject to the constraints imposed by the amount of memory in your personal computer.

119

You can declare arrays to be of any type, and you can declare multiple arrays of a given type in a single statement. For example, to declare arrays intended to store the capacity and power output of a series of engines, you could write the following:

```
double cu_in[10], bhp[10];
```

This would enable you to store the cubic capacity and power output of up to 10 engines, referenced by index values from 0 to 9. In practice, it is better to declare them in separate statements. This allows you to include a descriptive comment for each to say what they are for.

Try It Out - Using Arrays

As a basis for an exercise in exercising arrays, let's imagine we have kept a record of the amount of gas we have bought for the car, and have recorded the odometer reading on each occasion. We can write a program to analyze this data to see how the gas consumption looks on each occasion we bought gas:

```cpp
// EX4-01.CPP
// Calculating gas mileage
#include <iostream.h>
#include <iomanip.h>

int main()
{
    const int MAX = 20;              // Maximum number of values
    double gas[ MAX ];               // Gas quantity in gallons
    long miles[ MAX ];               // Odometer readings
    int count = 0;                   // Loop counter
    char indicator = 'n';            // Input indicator

    for( count=0 ; count < MAX ; count++ )
    {
        cout << endl
             << "Enter gas quantity: ";
        cin >> gas[count];                       // Read gas quantity
        cout << "Enter odometer reading: ";
        cin >> miles[count];                     // Read odometer value

        cout << "Do you want to enter another( y or n )? ";
        cin >> indicator;
        if( indicator =='n' || indicator == 'N')
            break;                               // Exit loop if N or n entered
    }
```

```
    if( count < 1)                          // First was index 0 so index
    {                                       // on exit should be at least 1
        cout << endl
            << "Sorry - at least two readings are necessary.";
        return 0;
    }

// Output results from 2nd entry to last entry
    for( int i=1 ; i <= count ; i++ )
    cout << endl
        << setw(2) << i << "."                  // Output sequence number
        << "Gas purchased = " << gas[ i] << " gallons" // Output gas
        << " resulted in "                      // Output miles per gallon
        << (miles[i] - miles[i-1])/gas[i] << " miles per gallon.";

    return 0;
}
```

How It Works

Since we need to take the difference between two odometer readings to calculate the miles covered for the gas used, only the odometer reading from the first pair of input values is used - the gas bought is ignored. Typical output produced by this example is shown in the figure below:

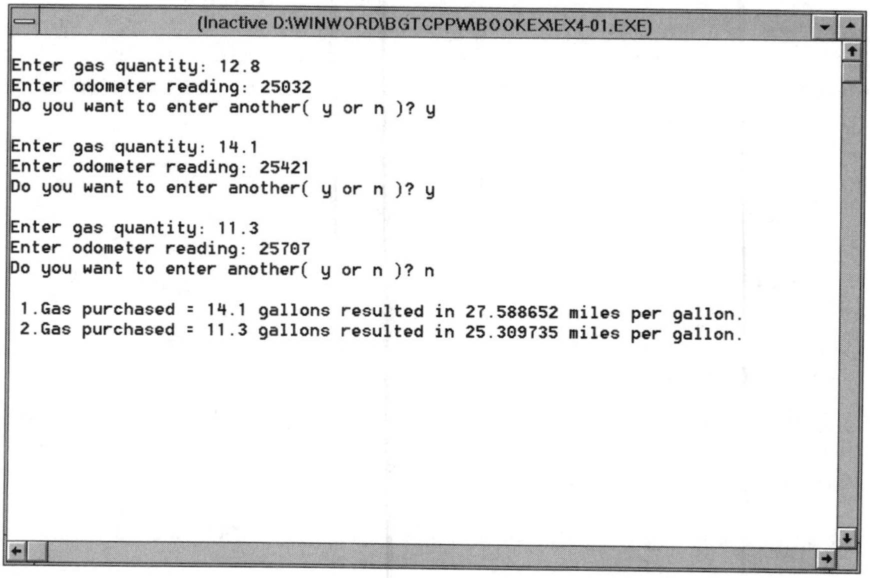

```
─                (Inactive D:\WINWORD\BGTCPPWBOOKEX\EX4-01.EXE)          ▼ ▲
                                                                            ↑
Enter gas quantity: 12.8
Enter odometer reading: 25032
Do you want to enter another( y or n )? y

Enter gas quantity: 14.1
Enter odometer reading: 25421
Do you want to enter another( y or n )? y

Enter gas quantity: 11.3
Enter odometer reading: 25707
Do you want to enter another( y or n )? n

 1.Gas purchased = 14.1 gallons resulted in 27.588652 miles per gallon.
 2.Gas purchased = 11.3 gallons resulted in 25.309735 miles per gallon.
                                                                            ↓
←                                                                         →
```

The dimensions of the two arrays **gas** and **miles**, used to store the input data, is determined by the value of the constant variable **MAX**. By changing the value of **MAX**, you can change the program to accommodate a different maximum numbers of input values. This is a commonly used technique to make a program flexible in the amount of information it can handle. Of course, all the program code must be written to take account of the array dimensions, or of any other parameters being specified by **const** variables. However, this presents little difficulty in practice, so there is no reason not to adopt this approach generally.

Inputting the Data

The data values are read in the first **for** loop. Since the loop variable **count** can run from 0 to **MAX-1**, the limit on the maximum number of values that can be stored, **MAX**, is automatically taken care of. There is a prompt for each input value required, and the value is read into the appropriate array element. The element used to store a particular value is determined by the variable **count**, which is the loop control variable. The array element is specified in the **cin** statement by using **count** as an index. Since **count** varies from 0 to **MAX-1**, successive values of each array are used according to the current value of **count**.

After each value is entered, there is a prompt for confirmation that another value is to be entered. The character entered is read into the variable **indicator**, and then tested in the **if** statement. If the character *n* or *N* was entered, the loop is terminated by executing **break**. The loop will end in any event once **MAX** pairs of input values have been read.

Once the input loop ends (one way or another), the value of **count** contains the index value of the last element entered in each array. This is checked in order to verify that at least two pairs of values were entered. If this wasn't the case, the program ends with a suitable message, since two odometer values are necessary to calculate a mileage value.

Producing the Results

The output is generated in the second **for** loop. The control variable **i** runs from 1 to **count**, allowing mileage to be calculated as the difference between the current element **miles[i]**, and the previous element **miles[i-1]**. Note that an index value can be any expression that evaluates to an integer that represents a legal index for the array in question.

The output is generated by a single **cout** statement for all values entered, except for the first. A line number is also generated for each line of output using the loop control variable **i**. The miles per gallon is calculated directly in the output statement. You can use array elements in exactly the same way as any other variables in an expression.

Initializing Arrays

To initialize an array, the initializing values are enclosed within braces in the declaration, and are placed following an equals sign after the array name. An example of a declaration and initialization of an array would be this:

```
int cu_in[5] = { 200, 250, 300, 350, 400 };
```

The values in the initializing list correspond to successive index values of the array, so in this case **cu_in[0]** will have the value 200, **cu_in[1]** the value 250, **cu_in[2]** the value 300, and so on.

You mustn't specify more initializing values than there are elements in the list, but you can include less. If there *are* less, then the values are assigned to successive elements, starting with the first element which has the index 0. The array elements without initializing values will be initialized with zero. This is not the same as supplying no initializing list. Without an initializing list the array elements will contain junk values. Also, if you include an initializing list there must be at least one initializing value in it, otherwise the compiler will generate an error message. We can illustrate this with the following, rather limited, example:

Try It Out - Initializing an Array

```
// EX4-02.CPP
// Demonstrating array initialization
#include <iostream.h>
#include <iomanip.h>

int main()
{
   int value1[5] = { 1, 2, 3 };
   int value2[5];

   cout << endl;
   for( int i=0 ; i<5 ; i++)
      cout << setw(10) << value1[i];
```

Try it Out!

```
    cout << endl;
    for( i=0 ; i<5 ; i++)
        cout << setw(10) << value2[i];

    return 0;
}
```

In this example we declare two arrays, the first of which, **value1**, is initialized in part, and the second of which, **value2**, is not initialized at all. The program generates two lines of output, which on my computer look like this:

1	2	3	0	0
6864	7104	29679	8192	0

The second line (corresponding to values of **value2[0]** to **value2[4]**) may well be different on your computer.

How It Works

The first three values of the array **value1** are the initializing values, and the last two are default 0. In the case of **value2**, all the values are spurious, being whatever values were left there by the program which last used these memory locations.

A convenient way to initialize a whole array to zero is simply to specify a single initializing value as 0. For example, the statement:

```
long data[100] = {0};    // Initialize all elements to zero
```

declares the array **data**, with all elements initialized with 0.

You can also omit the dimension of an array of numeric type, providing you supply initializing values. The number of elements in the array will be determined by the number of initializing values. For example, the array declaration:

```
int value[] = { 2, 3, 4 };
```

defines an array with three elements which will have the values 2, 3, and 4.

Character Arrays and String Handling

An array of type **char** is called a character array, and it is generally used to store a character string. A character string is a sequence of characters with a special character appended to indicate the end of the string. The string terminating character is defined by the escape sequence **'\0'**, and is sometimes referred to as a **null** character, being a byte with all bits as zero. The representation of a string in memory is shown in the figure below:

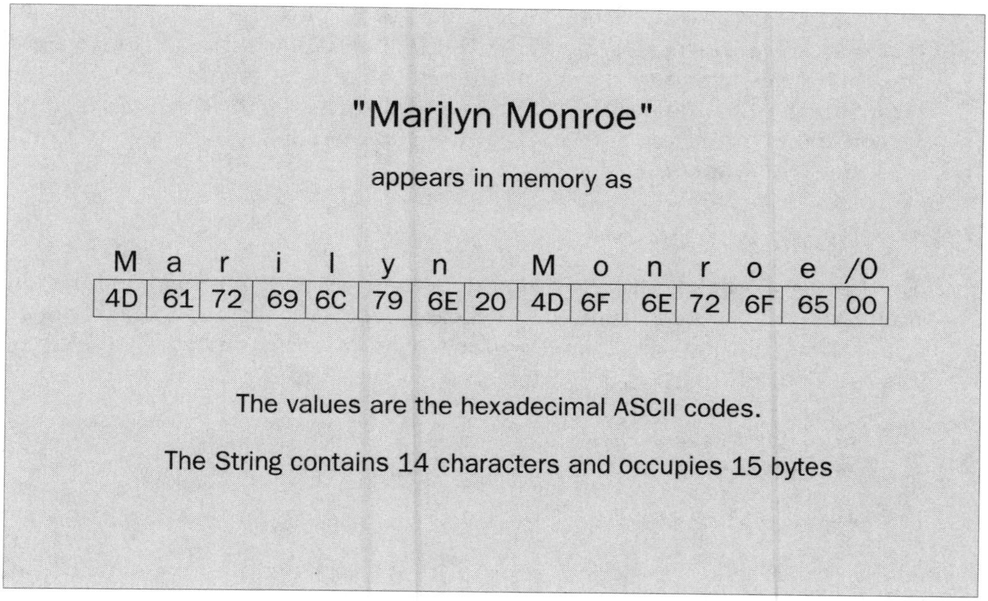

"Marilyn Monroe"

appears in memory as

M	a	r	i	l	y	n		M	o	n	r	o	e	/0
4D	61	72	69	6C	79	6E	20	4D	6F	6E	72	6F	65	00

The values are the hexadecimal ASCII codes.

The String contains 14 characters and occupies 15 bytes

Each character in the string occupies one byte, so together with the null character, a string requires a number of bytes that is one greater than the number of characters contained in the string.

We can declare a character array and initialize it with a string constant between quotation marks. For example:

```
char movie_star[15] = "Marilyn Monroe";
```

Note that the terminating `'\0'` will be supplied automatically by the compiler. If you include one explicitly in the string constant then you will end up with two of them.

You can let the compiler work out the length of an initialized array for you. Have a look at the following declaration:

```
char president[] = "Ulysses Grant";
```

Because the dimension is unspecified, the compiler will allocate space for enough elements to hold the initializing string plus the terminating null, in this case, 14 elements for the array **president**. Of course, if you want to use this array later for storing a different string, its length (including the terminating null) must not exceed 14 bytes. In general, it is your responsibility to ensure the array is large enough for any string you might subsequently want to store.

String Input

The header file **IOSTREAM.H** contains definitions of a number of functions for reading characters from the keyboard. The one that we shall look at here is the function **getline()**, which reads a string into a character array. This is typically used with statements such as this:

```
const int MAX = 80;
char name[MAX];
...
cin.getline( name, MAX, '\n' );
```

These statements first declare a **char** array name with **MAX** elements, and then read characters from **cin** using the function **getline()**. The source of the data is written as shown, with a period separating it from the function name. The significance of various parts of the input statement is shown opposite.

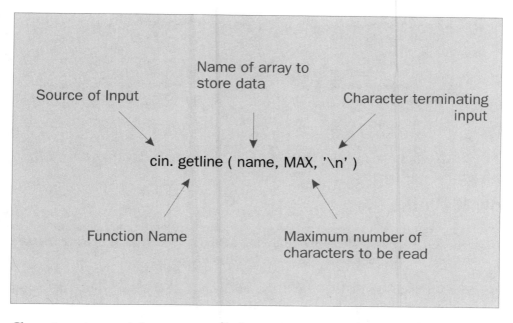

Characters are read from **cin** until the **'\n'** (endline) character is read, or when **MAX-1** characters have been read, whichever occurs first. The **'\n'** character is generated when you press the *Return* key on your keyboard, and thus is usually the most convenient character to end input, but you can specify something else if you wish. The **'\n'** isn't stored in the input array **name**, but a **'\0'** is added at the end of input string in the array.

We will learn more about this form of syntax when we discuss classes later on. Meanwhile, we can take it for granted, and use it in an example.

Try It Out - Programming With Strings

We now have enough knowledge to write a simple program to read a string, and then count how many characters it contains.

```
// EX4-03.CPP
// Counting string characters
#include <iostream.h>

int main()
{
   const int MAX = 80;                  // Maximum array dimension
```

```
    char buffer[MAX];                  // Input buffer
    int count = 0;                     // Character count

    cin.getline( buffer, MAX, '\n' );  // Read a string until \n

    while( buffer[count] != '\0' )     // Increment count as long as
        count++;                       // the current character is not null

    cout << endl
        << "The string \"" << buffer
        << "\" has " << count << " characters.";
    return 0;
}
```

How It Works

This program declares a character array **buffer**, and reads a character string from the keyboard. Reading from the keyboard ends when the *Return* key is pressed, or **MAX-1** characters have been read.

A **while** loop is used to count the number of characters read. The loop continues as long as the current character referenced to **buffer[count]** is not **'\0'**. This sort of checking on the current character (while stepping through an array) is a common technique in C++. The only action in the loop is to increment **count** for each non-null character.

Finally, the string and the character count is displayed with a single output statement. Note how we need to use the escape character **'\"'** in order to output a quote. The typical output from this program is illustrated below.

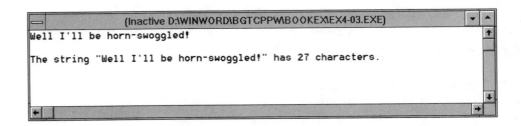

Multi-Dimensional Arrays

The arrays we have defined so far with one index are referred to as one-dimensional arrays. An array can also have more than one index value. Suppose we have a field in which we are growing bean plants in rows of ten, and the field contains 12 such rows, (so 120 plants in all). We could perhaps declare an array to record the weight of beans produced by each plant, using the following statement:

```
double beans[12][10];
```

This declares the two dimensional array **beans**, the first index being the row number, and the second index the number within the row. To refer to any particular element requires two indices. For example, we could set the value of the element reflecting the fifth plant in the third row with the following statement:

```
beans[2][4] = 10.7;
```

Remembering that the index values start from zero, the row index value is **2**, and the index for the fifth plant within the row is **4**.

Being successful bean farmers, we might have several identical fields planted with beans in the same pattern. Assuming we have eight fields, we could use a three-dimensional array declared thus:

```
double beans[8][12][10];
```

This will record production for all of the plants in each of the fields, the leftmost index referencing a particular field. If we ever get to bean farming on an international scale, we will be able to use a four dimensional array, with the extra dimension designating the country. This sort of quantity of beans, however, may start to affect the ozone layer.

Arrays are stored in memory such that the right-most index value varies most rapidly. You can visualize the array **data[3][4]** as 3 one dimensional arrays of 4 elements each. The arrangement of this array is illustrated on the following page.

```
int data[3][4];

       data[0][0]        ...
       data[0][1]        ...
       data[0][2]        ...
       data[0][3]        ...
       data[1][0]        ...
       data[1][1]        ...
       data[1][2]        ...
       data[1][3]        ...
       data[2][0]        ...
       data[2][1]        ...
       data[2][2]        ...
       data[2][3]        ...
```

Initializing Multi-Dimensional Arrays

To initialize a multi-dimensional array you use an extension of the method used for a one-dimensional array. For example, you can initialize a two dimensional array, **data**, with the following declaration:

```
long data[2][4] = {
                    { 1,   2 ,  3 ,  5 },
                    { 7,  11 , 13 , 17 }
                  };
```

Thus, the initializing values for each row of the array are contained within their own pair of braces. Since there are 4 elements in each row, there are 4 initializing values in each group, and since there are two rows there are two groups between braces, each group of initializing values being separated from the next by a comma. There is also a comma between rows.

You can omit initializing values in any row, in which case the remaining array elements in the row will be zero. For example, with the declaration

```
long data[2][4] = {
                    { 1,   2 , 3      },
                    { 7, 11          }
                  };
```

the initializing values have been spaced out to show where values have been omitted. The elements **data[0][3]**, **data[1][2]**, and **data[1][3]** have no initializing values and will therefore be zero.

If you wanted to initialize the whole array with zeros you could simply write:

```
long data[2][4] = {0};
```

If you are initializing arrays with even more dimensions, then remember that there are typically as many nested braces for initializing values as there are dimensions in the array.

Try It Out - Storing Multiple Strings

We can use a single two dimensional array to store several strings. We can see how this works with an example.

```
// EX4-04.CPP
// Storing strings in an array.
#include <iostream.h>
int main()
{
   char stars[6][80] = { "Robert Redford",
                         "Hopalong Cassidy",
                         "Clint Eastwood",
                         "Slim Pickens",
                         "Boris Karloff",
                         "Oliver Hardy"
                       };
   int dice = 0;

   cout << endl
        << " Pick a lucky star!"
        << " Enter a number between 1 and 6: ";
   cin >> dice;
```

Try it Out!

```
    if( dice >= 1 && dice <= 6 )                    // Check input validity
       cout << endl                                 // Output star name
             << "Your lucky star is " << stars[dice-1];
    else
       cout << endl                                 // Invalid input
             << "Sorry, you haven't got a lucky star.";

    return 0;
}
```

How It Works

Apart from its inherent entertainment value, the main point of interest in this example is the declaration of the array **stars**. It is a two dimensional **char** array, which can hold up to six strings, each of which can be up to 80 characters including the terminating null character. The terminating null for each string is automatically added by the compiler. The initializing strings for the array are enclosed between braces and separated by commas.

> *One disadvantage of using arrays in this way is the memory that is almost invariably left unused. All of our strings are less than 80 characters, and the surplus elements in each row of the array are wasted.*

You can also let the compiler work out how many strings you have by omitting the first array dimension, and declare it as follows:

```
    char stars[][80] = { "Robert Redford",
                         "Hopalong Cassidy",
                         "Clint Eastwood",
                         "Slim Pickens",
                         "Boris Karloff",
                         "Oliver Hardy"
                       };
```

This will cause the compiler to define the first dimension to accommodate the number of initializing strings you have specified. Since we have six, the result is exactly the same, but it avoids the possibility of an error.

> *Note the semicolon at the end of the declaration. It is easy to forget it when there are initializing values for an array.*

Where we need to reference a string for output in the statement

```
cout << endl                              // Output star name
     << "Your lucky star is " << stars[dice-1];
```

we only need to specify the first index value. A single index value selects a particular 80 element sub-array, and the output operation will display the contents up to the terminating null character. The index as specified as **dice-1** as the **dice** values are from 1 to 6, whereas the index values clearly need to be from 0 to 5.

Indirect Data Access

The variables we have dealt with so far provide you with the ability to name a memory location in which you can store data of a particular type. The contents of a variable are either entered from an external source, such as the keyboard, or calculated from other values that are entered. There is another kind of variable in C++ which does not store data that you normally enter or calculate, but it greatly extends the power and flexibility of your programs. This kind of variable is called a **pointer**.

What is a Pointer?

Each memory location that you use to store a data value has an address. The address provides the means for your PC hardware to reference a particular data item. A pointer is a variable that stores an address of another variable of a particular type. A pointer has a variable name just like any other variable, and it also has a type which designates what kind of variables its contents refer to.

Declaring Pointers

The declaration for a pointer is similar to that of an ordinary variable except that the pointer name has an asterisk in front of it to indicate that it is a variable which is a pointer. For example, to declare a pointer **pnumber** of type **long**, you could use the following statement:

```
long* pnumber;
```

133

This declaration has been written with the asterisk close to the type name. You can also write it as

```
long *pnumber;
```

if you wish - the compiler won't mind at all. However, the type of the variable **pnumber** is 'pointer to **long**' and placing the asterisk close to the type name is often adopted to indicate this.

You can mix declarations of ordinary variables and pointers in the same statement. For example:

```
long *pnumber, number = 99;
```

This declares the pointer **pnumber** of type **long** as before, and also declares the variable **number**, also of type **long**. On balance, it is probably better to declare pointers separately from other variables, otherwise the statement can appear misleading as to the type of the variables declared, particularly if you place the * adjacent to the type name. The following statements certainly look clearer

```
long number = 99;      // Declaration and initialization of long variable
long* pnumber;         // Declaration of variable of type pointer to long
```

You are free to add comments for them individually - it makes for a program that is easier to read.

It is a common convention in C++ to use variable names beginning with **p** to denote pointers. This makes it easier to see which variables in a program are pointers, which in turn can make a program easier to follow.

Let's take an example to see how this works, without worrying about what it is for. We will come on to how this is used very shortly. Suppose we have the **long** integer variable **number**, as we declared it above containing the value 99. We also have the pointer, **pnumber**, of type **long**, which we could use to store the address of our variable **number**. But how can we obtain the address of a variable?

The Address Operator

What we need is the address operator, **&**. This is a unary operator which obtains the address of a variable. It is also called the reference operator for reasons we will discuss later in this chapter. To set up the pointer we have just discussed, we could write this assignment statement:

```
pnumber = &number;          // Store address of number in pnumber
```

The result of this operation is illustrated below.

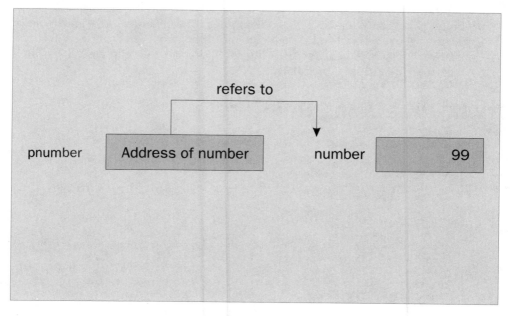

You can use the operator **&** to obtain the address of any variable, but you need a pointer of the same type to store it. If you want to store the address of a **double** variable for example, the pointer must have been declared as type pointer to **double**.

Using Pointers

Taking the address of a variable and storing it in a pointer is all very well, but the really interesting aspect is in how you can use it. Fundamental to using a pointer is accessing the data value in the variable to which a pointer points. This is done using the indirection operator, *****.

The Indirection Operator

The indirection operator, *, is used with a pointer to access the contents of the variable pointed to. The name 'indirection operator' stems from the fact that the data is accessed indirectly. It is also called the de-reference operator, and the process of accessing the data in the variable pointed to by a pointer is termed 'de-referencing' the pointer.

One aspect of this operator that can seem confusing is the fact that we now have several different uses for the same symbol, *. It is the multiply operator, the indirection operator, and it is used in the declaration of a pointer. The compiler is able to distinguish the meaning in each instance you use * by its context. When you multiply two variables, A*B for instance, there is no meaningful interpretation of this expression for anything other than a multiply operation.

Try It Out - Using Pointers

We can try out various aspects of pointer operations with an example.

```
//EX4-05.CPP
// Exercising pointers
#include <iostream.h>

int main()
{
   long* pnumber;                        // Pointer declaration
   long num1 = 55, num2 = 99;

   pnumber = &num1;                      // Store address in pointer
   *pnumber += 11;                       // Increment num1 by 11
   cout << endl
        << "num1 = " << num1
        <<"    &num1 = " << hex << pnumber;

   pnumber = &num2;                      // Change pointer to address of num2
   num1 = *pnumber*10;                   // 10 times num2

   cout << endl
        << "num1 = " << num1
        << "  pnumber = " << pnumber
        << "    *pnumber = " << *pnumber;
   return 0;
}
```

How It Works

There is no input to this example. All operations are with the initializing values. After storing the address of **num1** in the pointer **pnumber**, the value of **num1** is incremented indirectly through the pointer in this statement:

```
*pnumber += 11;                          // Increment num1 by 11
```

The indirection operator determines that we are adding 11 to the contents of the variable pointed to, **num1**. If we forget the *****, we would be attempting to add 11 to the address stored in the pointer.

The values of **num1**, and the address of **num1** stored in **pnumber**, are displayed. The output operation will automatically generate the address output in hexadecimal notation.

You can obtain the value of ordinary integer variables as hexadecimal output by using the manipulator **hex**. You send it to the output stream in the same way as we have applied **endl**, and all following output will be in hexadecimal notation. If you want the following output to be decimal, you need to use the manipulator **dec** in the next output statement in order to switch the output back to decimal mode again.

After the first line of output, the contents of **pnumber** are set to the address of **num2**. The variable **num1**, referenced directly, is then changed to the value of 10 times **num2**:

```
num1 = *pnumber*10;                      // 10 times num2
```

This is calculated by accessing the contents of **num2** indirectly through the pointer. The second line of output shows the results of these calculations. On my computer, the example generates the following output:

```
num1 = 66      &num1 = 0x1b04
num1 = 990     pnumber = 0x1b00      *pnumber = 99
```

The address values on your computer may well be different, since they reflect where the program is loaded in memory, and this depends on how your operating system is configured. The **0x** prefixing the address values indicate that they are hexadecimal numbers. Note that the addresses for **num1**, and **pnumber** when it contains **&num2**, differ by four bytes. This shows that **num1** and **num2** occupy adjacent memory locations, as a **long** variable requires 4 bytes. The output demonstrates that everything is working as we expect.

Initializing Pointers

Using pointers that are not initialized is extremely hazardous. You can overwrite anywhere in memory by this means, and the consequential damage just depends on how unlucky you are, so it is always a good idea to initialize your pointers. To initialize a pointer to the address of a variable that already has been defined is very easy. To initialize the pointer **pnum** with the address of the variable **number** you just use the operator **&** with the variable name, so you might have the following statements to do this:

```
int number = 0;            // Initialized integer variable
int* pnum = &number;       // Initialized pointer
```

When initializing a pointer with another variable, clearly the variable must already have been declared prior to the pointer declaration.

Of course, you may not want to initialize a pointer with the address of a specific variable when you declare it. In this case, you can initialize it with the pointer equivalent of zero. TCW provides the mnemonic **NULL** for this, so you can declare and initialize using the following statement:

```
int* pnum = NULL;          // Pointer not pointing to anything
```

This ensures that the pointer does not contain a valid address, and provides the pointer with a value that you can check in an **if** statement, such as:

```
if( pnum == NULL )
   cout << endl << "pnum is null.";
```

You can also initialize a pointer with 0, which will also ensure that it is assigned a value that doesn't point to anything. In spite of it being arguably somewhat less legible, if you expect to run your code with other compilers it is preferable to use 0 as an initializing value for a pointer you want to be null.

> This is also more consistent with the current 'good practice' in C++, the argument being that if you have an object with a name in C++, it should have a type, but *NULL* does not have a type.

To use 0 as the initializing value for a pointer you would simply write

```
int* pnum = 0;             // Pointer not pointing to anything
```

To check whether a pointer contains a valid address you could use the statement

```
if( pnum == NULL )    // or pnum == 0
    cout << endl << "pnum is null.";
```

or you could equally well use the statement

```
if( !pnum )
    cout << endl << "pnum is null.";
```

which does exactly the same as the previous example.

A pointer of type **char** has the interesting property that it can be initialized with a string constant. For example, we can declare and initialize such a pointer with the statement:

```
char* proverb = "A miss is as good as a mile.";
```

This looks very similar to initializing a char array but it is slightly different. This will create the string constant (actually a constant array of type **char**) with the character string appearing between the quotes, and terminated with **/0**, and store the address of the constant in the pointer **proverb**. This is shown graphically below.

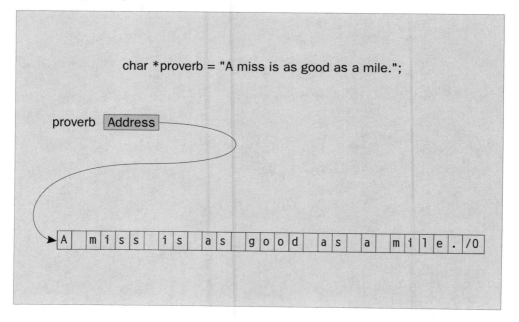

Try It Out - Lucky Stars With Pointers

We could rewrite our lucky stars example using pointers instead of an array to see how that would work:

```cpp
// EX4-06.CPP
// Initializing pointers with strings
#include <iostream.h>
int main()
{
   char *pstr1 = "Robert Redford",
        *pstr2 = "Hopalong Cassidy",
        *pstr3 = "Clint Eastwood",
        *pstr4 = "Slim Pickens",
        *pstr5 = "Boris Karloff",
        *pstr6 = "Oliver Hardy",
        *pstr  = "Your lucky star is ";

   int dice = 0;

   cout << endl
        << " Pick a lucky star!"
        << " Enter a number between 1 and 6: ";
   cin >> dice;

   cout << endl;
   switch(dice)
   {
      case 1: cout << pstr << pstr1;
              break;

      case 2: cout << pstr << pstr2;
              break;

      case 3: cout << pstr << pstr3;
              break;

      case 4: cout << pstr << pstr4;
              break;

      case 5: cout << pstr << pstr5;
              break;

      case 6: cout << pstr << pstr6;
              break;

      default: cout << "Sorry, you haven't got a lucky star.";
   }

   return 0;
}
```

How It Works

The array in **EX4-04.CPP** has been replaced by the six pointers, **pstr1** to **pstr6**, each initialized with a name. We also have declared an additional pointer, **pstr**, initialized with the phrase we want to use at the start of a normal output line. Because we have discrete pointers, it is easier to use a **switch** statement to select the appropriate output message than an **if**, as we had in the original version. Incorrect values entered are all taken care of by the **default** option of the **switch**.

Outputting the string pointed to by a pointer couldn't be easier. As you can see, you simply write the pointer name. It may cross your mind at this point that in **EX4-05.CPP** we wrote a pointer name in the output statement and the address it contained was displayed. Why is it different here? The answer lies in the way the output operation views a pointer of type pointer to **char**. It treats a pointer of this type as a string (which is an array of **char**) and so outputs the string itself, rather that its address.

Using pointers has eliminated the waste of memory that occurred with the array version of this. The program seems a little long winded now. There must be a better way. And indeed there is - using an array of pointers.

Try It Out - Arrays of Pointers

We can declare an array of pointers in the same way as we declare a normal array. Let's go straight to rewriting the previous example using a pointer array.

```
// EX4-07.CPP
// Initializing pointers with strings
#include <iostream.h>
int main()
{
   char *pstr[] =  { "Robert Redford",      // Initializing a pointer array
                     "Hopalong Cassidy",
                     "Clint Eastwood",
                     "Slim Pickens",
                     "Boris Karloff",
                     "Oliver Hardy"
                   };
   char *pstrt = "Your lucky star is ";

   int dice = 0;

   cout << endl
```

```
        << " Pick a lucky star!"
        << " Enter a number between 1 and 6: ";
  cin >> dice;

  cout << endl;
  if( dice >= 1 && dice <= 6 )                   // Check input validity
     cout << pstrt << pstr[dice-1];              // Output star name

  else
     cout << "Sorry, you haven't got a lucky star."; // Invalid input

  return 0;
}
```

How It Works

In this case, we are nearly getting the best of all possible worlds. We have a one dimensional array of **char** pointers declared such that the compiler works out what the dimension should be from the number of initializing strings. The memory usage that results from this is illustrated below.

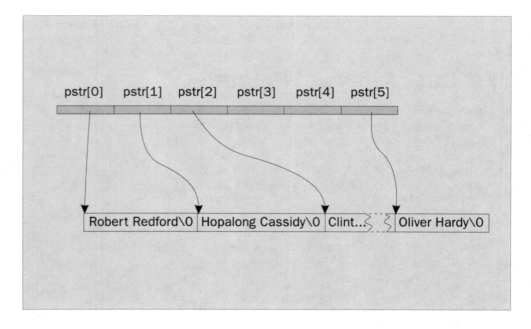

We select the string that we want to output by means of a very simple `if` statement similar to that of the original version of the example. We either display a star selection, or a suitable message in the case of an invalid value being entered.

One weakness of the way the program has been written is that the code assumes there are six options, even though the compiler is allocating the space for the pointer array from the number of initializing strings we supply. So if we add a string to the list, we have to alter other parts of the program to take account of this. It would be nice to be able to add strings and have the program automatically adapt to however many strings there are.

The sizeof Operator

A new operator will help us here. The `sizeof` operator produces an integer constant that gives the size of how much memory is occupied by its operand in bytes. For example, with the variable `dice` from the previous example, this expression

```
sizeof dice
```

will result in the value 2 since `dice` was declared as `int`.

When the operator is applied to an array name by itself, it produces the number of bytes occupied by the whole array, whereas when it is applied to a single element with the appropriate index value or values, it results in the number of bytes occupied by that element. Thus in the last example, we can obtain the number of elements in the `pstr` array with the expression

```
sizeof pstr/sizeof pstr[0]
```

The `sizeof` operator can also be applied to a type name rather than a variable, in which case the number of bytes occupied by a variable of that type is the result. The type name should be enclosed between parentheses. For example, after executing the statement

```
long_size = sizeof(long);
```

the variable `long_size` will have the value 4.

Try It Out - Using the sizeof Operator

We can use this to amend the last example so that it automatically adapts to an arbitrary number of string values from which to select:

```
// EX4-08.CPP
// Flexible array management using sizeof
#include <iostream.h>
int main()
{
   char *pstr[] =                               // Initializing a pointer array
                  { "Robert Redford",
                    "Hopalong Cassidy",
                    "Clint Eastwood",
                    "Slim Pickens",
                    "Boris Karloff",
                    "Oliver Hardy"
                  };
   char *pstrt = "Your lucky star is ";
   int count = sizeof pstr/sizeof pstr[0]; // Number of array elements

   int dice = 0;

   cout << endl
        << " Pick a lucky star!"
        << " Enter a number between 1 and " << count << ": ";
   cin >> dice;

   cout << endl;
   if( dice >= 1 && dice <= count )            // Check input validity
      cout << pstrt << pstr[dice-1];           // Output star name

   else
      cout << "Sorry, you haven't got a lucky star."; // Invalid input

   return 0;
}
```

How It Works

As you can see, the changes required in the example are very simple. We just calculate the number of elements in the pointer array **pstr** and store the result in **count**. Then, wherever the total number of elements in the array was referenced as 6, we just use the variable **count**. You could now just add a few more names to the list of lucky stars and everything affected in the program will be adjusted automatically.

Constant Pointers and Pointers to Constants

The array `pstr` in the last example is clearly not intended to be modified in the program - nor are the strings being pointed to. Neither is the variable `count`. It would be a good idea to ensure that these didn't get modified in error in the program. We could protect the variable `count` from accidental modification very easily by writing this:

```
const int count = sizeof pstr/sizeof ptr[0];
```

However, the array of pointers bears some closer examination. As the program stands, a statement such as this:

```
*pstr[0] = 'X';
```

is perfectly legal and results in Mr. Redford being re-christened Xobert. If we rewrite the declaration of the array as follows:

```
const char* pstr[] = { "Robert Redford",   // Array of pointers to constants
                       "Hopalong Cassidy",
                       "Clint Eastwood",
                       "Slim Pickens",
                       "Boris Karloff",
                       "Oliver Hardy"
                     };
```

then we are declaring the objects pointed to by elements of the pointer array as constant, and therefore the compiler will inhibit any direct attempt to change these, so the last assignment statement would be flagged as an error. However, we could still legally write this statement:

```
pstr[0] = pstr[1];
```

so those lucky individuals due to be awarded Mr. Redford would get Mr. Cassidy instead, since both pointers now point to the same name. We should therefore inhibit this kind of change as well, since some people may reckon that good old Hoppy may not have the same sex appeal as Robert. We can do this with the following statement:

```
const char* const pstr[] = { "Robert Redford",// Array of constant pointers
                             "Hopalong Cassidy", // to constants
                             "Clint Eastwood",
```

```
        "Slim Pickens",
        "Boris Karloff",
        "Oliver Hardy"
   };
```

To summarize, we can distinguish three situations relating to `const`, pointers, and the objects to which they point:

1   A pointer to a constant object

```
const char* pstring = "Some text";
```

Here the object pointed to cannot be modified but we can set the pointer to point to something else.

2   A constant pointer to an object

```
char* const pstring =  "Some text";
```

Here, the address stored in the pointer can't be changed, but the object pointed to can be.

3   A constant pointer to a constant object

```
const char* const pstring = "Some text";
```

Here, both the pointer and the object pointed to have been defined as constant and therefore neither can be changed.

Of course, all this applies to pointers of any type. Type **char** *is used here purely for illustration purposes.*

Pointers and Arrays

Array names can behave like pointers in certain circumstances. In most circumstances, if you use the name of a one-dimensional array by itself, it is automatically converted to a pointer to the first element of the array. The exceptions are if the array name is the operand of the address operator, **&**, or of the operator **sizeof**. If we have these declarations:

```
double* pdata;
double data[10];
```

then we can write this assignment:

```
pdata = data;        // Initialize pointer with the array address
```

This is assigning the address of the array **data** to the pointer **pdata**. Using the array name by itself refers to the address of the array. If we use the array name **data** with an index value, it defines the contents of the element corresponding to that index value. So, if we want to store the address of that element in the pointer, we have to use the address operator:

```
pdata = &data[1];
```

and the pointer **pdata** will contain the address of the second element of the array.

Pointer Arithmetic

You can perform arithmetic operations with pointers. You are limited to addition and subtraction in terms of arithmetic, but you can also perform comparisons using pointers to produce a logical result. Arithmetic with a pointer implicitly assumes that the pointer points to an array, and the arithmetic operation is on the address contained in the pointer. For the pointer **pdata** for example, we could assign the address of the third element of the array **data** to a pointer with this statement:

```
pdata = &data[2];
```

In this case, the expression **pdata+1** would refer to the fourth element, the array data, or in other words the address of **data[3]**. We could make the pointer point to this element by writing this statement:

```
pdata += 1;          // Increment pdata to the next element
```

The address contained in **pdata** has been incremented by the number of bytes occupied by one element of the array **data** by this statement. In general, the expression **pdata+n**, where **n** can be any expression resulting in an integer, will add **n*sizeof(double)** to the address contained in the pointer **pdata**, since it was declared to be of type pointer to **double**. This is illustrated below.

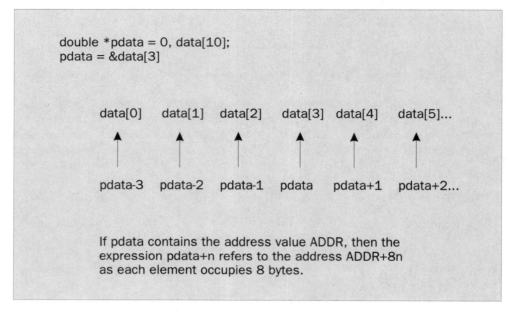

```
double *pdata = 0, data[10];
pdata = &data[3]
```

data[0]   data[1]   data[2]   data[3]   data[4]   data[5]...

pdata-3   pdata-2   pdata-1   pdata   pdata+1   pdata+2...

If pdata contains the address value ADDR, then the
expression pdata+n refers to the address ADDR+8n
as each element occupies 8 bytes.

In other words, incrementing or decrementing a pointer works in terms of the type of the object pointed to. Incrementing a pointer to **long** by 1 increments the address by 4, and incrementing a pointer to **int** by one will increment the address by 2. The more common notation for incrementing a pointing is using the increment operator. For example, this:

```
pdata++;              // Increment pdata to the next element
```

is equivalent to (and more usual than) the **+=** form. However, the **+=** form was simply used to make it clear that while the increment value is actually specified as 1, the effect is usually an increment greater than 1, except in the case of a pointer to **char**.

The address resulting from an arithmetic operation on a pointer can be a value from the address of first element of the array to which it points, to the address which is one beyond the last element. Outside of these limits the behavior of the pointer is undefined.

You can, of course, de-reference a pointer on which you have performed arithmetic, (there wouldn't be much point to it otherwise). For example, assuming **pdata** is still pointing to **data[3]**, this statement:

```
*(pdata+1) = *(pdata+3);
```

is equivalent to this statement:

```
data[4] = data[6];
```

The parentheses are necessary when you want to de-reference a pointer after incrementing the address it contains, as the precedence of the indirection operator is higher than that of the arithmetic operators, **+** or **-**. If you write the expression ***pdata+1**, instead of ***(pdata+1)**, this would add one to the value stored at the address contained in **pdata**, which is equivalent to executing **data[3] +1**. Since this is not an lvalue, its use in the assignment statement above would cause the compiler to generate an error message.

We can use an array name as though it were a pointer for addressing elements of an array. If we have the same one dimensional array as before, declared as

```
long data[10];
```

then we can refer to the element **data[3]**, for example, as ***(data+3)** using pointer notation. This kind of notation can be applied generally so that corresponding to the elements **data[0]**, **data[1]**, **data[2]**, **...** we can write ***data**, ***(data+1)**, ***(data+2)**, and so on.

Try It Out - Array Names as Pointers

We could exercise this aspect of array addressing with a program to calculate prime numbers (a prime number is a number divisible only by itself and 1).

```
// EX4-09.CPP
// Calculating primes
#include <iostream.h>
#include <iomanip.h>
int main()
{
   const int MAX = 100;            // Number of primes required
```

Try it Out!

```
  long primes[MAX] = { 2,3,5 };   // First three primes defined
  long trial = 5;                 // Candidate prime
  int count = 3;                  // Count of primes found
  int found = 0;                  // Indicates when a prime is found

  do
  {
    trial += 2;                        // Next value for checking
    found = 0;                         // Set found indicator
    for ( int i = 0; i < count; i++ )  // Try division by existing primes
    {
      found = ( trial % *(primes+i))==0;// Result is 1 for exact division
      if( found )                       // If division is exact
        break;                          // it's not a prime
    }
    if (found == 0 )                   // We got one...
      *(primes+count++) = trial;       // ...so save it in primes array
  }while (count < MAX );

  // Output primes 5 to a line
  for( int i = 0 ; i < MAX ; i++)
  {
    if( i%5 == 0 )                     // New line on 1st, and every 5th line
      cout << endl;
    cout << setw(10) << *(primes+i);
  }
  return 0;
}
```

How It Works

We have the usual **#include** statements for **IOSTREAM.H** for input and output, and for **IOMANIP.H** since we will be using a stream manipulator to set the field width for output.

This program will work for **MAX** primes automatically. The **primes** array which stores the results has the first three primes already defined to start the process off. All the work is done in the **do-while** loop which continues until **MAX** primes have been found. The algorithm is very simple, and is based on the fact that if a number is not a prime, it must be divisible by one of the primes found so far, all of which are less than the number in question, since all numbers are either prime, or a product of primes. (In fact, only division by primes less than the square root of the number in question needs to be checked, so this example isn't as efficient as it might be.)

This statement:

```
found = ( trial % *(primes+i)) == 0;   // Result is 1 for exact division
```

sets the variable found to be 1 if there is no remainder from dividing the value in **trial** by the current prime ***(primes+i)** (equivalent to **primes[i]**), and 0 otherwise. The **if** causes the loop to be terminated if **found** has the value 1, since the candidate in **trial** can't be a prime in that case.

After the loop ends (for whatever reason), it is necessary to decide whether or not the value in **trial** was prime. This is indicated by the value in the indicator variable **found**. If **trial** *does* contain a prime, this statement:

```
*(primes+count++) = trial;     // ...so save it in primes array
```

stores the value in **primes[count]** and then increments **count** through the postfix increment operator.

Once **MAX** number of primes have been found, they are output with a field width of 10 characters, 5 to a line, as a result of this statement:

```
cout << endl;
```

being executed when **i** has the values 0, 5, 10, and so on.

If you compile and execute this example you should get the output shown below.

(Inactive D:\WINWORD\BGTCPPW\BOOKEX\EX4-09.EXE)				
2	3	5	7	11
13	17	19	23	29
31	37	41	43	47
53	59	61	67	71
73	79	83	89	97
101	103	107	109	113
127	131	137	139	149
151	157	163	167	173
179	181	191	193	197
199	211	223	227	229
233	239	241	251	257
263	269	271	277	281
283	293	307	311	313
317	331	337	347	349
353	359	367	373	379
383	389	397	401	409
419	421	431	433	439
443	449	457	461	463
467	479	487	491	499
503	509	521	523	541

Try It Out - Counting Characters Revisited

To see how handling strings works in pointer notation we could produce a version of the program we looked at earlier for counting the characters in a string.

```
// EX4-10.CPP
// Counting string characters using a pointer
#include <iostream.h>

int main()
{
    const int MAX = 80;                   // Maximum array dimension
    char buffer[MAX];                     // Input buffer
    char* pbuffer=buffer;                 // Pointer to array buffer

    cin.getline( buffer, MAX, '\n' );     // Read a string until \n

    while( *pbuffer )                     // Continue until \0
        pbuffer++;

    cout << endl
        << "The string \"" << buffer
        << "\" has " << pbuffer-buffer << " characters.";
    return 0;
}
```

How It Works

Here the program operates using the pointer **pbuffer** rather than the array name **buffer**. We don't need the **count** variable since the pointer is incremented in the loop until **\0** is found. The count of the number of characters in the string entered is the difference between the address stored in the pointer and the address of the beginning of the array denoted by **buffer**.

We could also have incremented the pointer in the loop by writing the loop like this:

```
while( *pbuffer++ );                     // Continue until \0
```

Now the loop contains no statements, only the test condition. This would work adequately, except for the fact that the pointer would be incremented after **/0** was encountered so the address would be one more than in the example. We would therefore need to express the count of the number of characters in the string as **pbuffer-buffer-1**.

Note that we can't use the array name in the same way that we have used the pointer. The expression **buffer++** is strictly illegal since you can't modify an array name - it is not a pointer.

Pointer Notation with Multi-Dimensional Arrays

You need to keep clear in your mind what is happening when you use pointer notation with multi-dimensional arrays. By way of illustration we can use an array **beans**, declared as follows:

```
double beans[3][4];
```

and the pointer **pbeans** declared as follows:

```
double* pbeans=&beans[0][0];
```

Note that we could also have declared and initialized the pointer as follows:

```
double* pbeans=beans[0];
```

but we could not initialize it with just **beans**, because although **beans** will refer to an address, that address will contain the address of **beans[0]**, that is, it is an address of an address, or in other words, effectively a pointer to a pointer. A legal initialization using just the array name would be this:

```
double* pbeans=*beans;
```

so that **beans** is de-referenced to an address.

You can reference each element of the array in three ways:

1 Using the array name with two index values

2 Using the array name in pointer notation

3 Using a separate pointer.

Therefore the following are equivalent:

```
beans[i][j]
```
```
*(*(beans+i)+j)
```
```
*(pbeans+4*i+j)
```

153

If you really want to be obscure, and it is not recommended that you do so, the following are also legal references to the same element of the array:

▶ `*(beans[i]+j)`

▶ `(*(beans+i))[j]`

▶ `(pbeans+4)[j]`

where we have mixed array and pointer notation.

There is yet another aspect to the use of pointers which is really the most important of all - the ability to create variables dynamically. We will look into that next.

Dynamic Memory Allocation

Working with a fixed set of variables in a program can be very restrictive. The need often arises within an application to adjust the amount of space available for storing different types of variables at execution time, depending on the input data for the program. Obviously, since any dynamically allocated variables can't have been defined at compile time, they can't be named in your source program. When they are created, they are identified by their address in memory and a pointer is used to contain such an address. With the power of pointers and the dynamic memory management tools in TCW, you can write your programs to have this kind of flexibility, quickly and easily.

The Free Store, Alias the Heap

In most instances, there is unused memory in your computer when your program is executed. This unused memory is usually called the **free store** in C++, or sometimes the **heap**. You can allocate space within the free store for a new variable of a given type, using a special operator in C++ which returns the address of the space allocated. This is the operator **new**, which is complemented by the operator **delete** which deallocates memory previously allocated by **new**.

You can allocate space in the free store for some variables in one part of a program, and then release the allocated space and return it to the free store once you have finished with the variables concerned. This makes it available for re-use by other dynamically allocated variables, later in the same program. This enables you to use memory very efficiently, and in many cases results in programs that can handle much larger problems involving considerably more data than otherwise might be possible.

The Operators new and delete

Suppose we need space for a **double** variable. We can define a pointer to type **double** and then request that the memory be allocated using the operator **new** with the following statements:

```
double* pvalue=0;     // Pointer initialized with null
pvalue = new double; // Request memory for a double variable
```

This is a good moment to recall that **all pointers should be initialized**. Using memory dynamically typically involves a number of pointers floating around, so it is important that they should not contain spurious values. You should try to arrange that if a pointer doesn't contain a legal address value, then it is set to null.

The **new** operator in the second line of code above should return the address of the memory in the free store allocated to a **double** variable, and this address will be stored in the pointer **pvalue**. We can then use this pointer to reference the variable using the indirection operator as we have seen. For example:

```
*pvalue = 9999.0;
```

However, using a dynamic variable as shown here is very risky. The memory may not have been allocated, because the free store has been used up; or it could be that the free store is fragmented by previous usage such that there is not a sufficient number of contiguous bytes to accommodate the variable for which you want to obtain space. In this case, the operator **new** will return a null pointer value, so we should always test for a valid address being returned and stored in our pointer before using it. We could have done this by writing the following:

```
if( !(pvalue = new double) )
{
   cout << endl
        << "Out of memory.";
   exit(1);
}
```

Here we have called for the space to be allocated, and the address stored in the pointer, **pvalue**, all within the **if** statement. If a null pointer value was returned, the **if** expression will be **True**, so the message will be displayed and the **exit()** function called to end the program. The function **exit()** is used when you want to terminate a program abnormally. The value between the parentheses is an integer (**int**) value that can be used to indicate the circumstances under which the program was terminated. If you use the **exit()** function, you need to include the header file **STDLIB.H** into your program.

You can also initialize a variable created by **new**. Taking our example of the **double** variable which was allocated by **new** and the address stored in **pvalue**, we could have set the value to 999.0 as it was created with this statement:

```
pvalue = new double( 999.0 );   // Allocate a double and initialize it
```

When you no longer have a need for a variable that has been dynamically allocated, you can free up the memory it occupies in the free store with the **delete** operator:

```
delete pvalue;                  // Release memory pointed to by pvalue
```

This ensures that the memory can be used subsequently by another variable. If you don't use **delete**, and subsequently store a different address value in the pointer **pvalue**, then it will be impossible to free up the memory or to use the variable it contains, since access to the address will have been lost.

Allocating Memory Dynamically for Arrays

Allocating memory for an array dynamically is very straightforward. If we wanted to allocate an array of type **char**, assuming **pstr** is a pointer to **char** we could write this:

```
pstr = new char[20];     // Allocate a string of twenty characters
```

156

This allocates space for a **char** array of 20 characters and stores its address in **pstr**.

To remove the array we have just created in the free store, we must use the **delete** operator. The statement would look like this:

```
delete[] pstr;          // Delete array pointed to by pstr
```

Note the use of square brackets to indicate that what we are deleting is an array. When removing arrays from the free store, you should always include the square brackets or the results will be unpredictable. Note also that you do not specify any dimensions here, simply [].

Try It Out - Using Free Store

We can see how this works in practice by rewriting our program to calculate an arbitrary number of primes, but use memory in the free store to store them.

```
// EX4-11.CPP
// Calculating primes using dynamic memory allocation
#include <iostream.h>
#include <iomanip.h>
#include <stdlib.h>                    // For the exit function

int main()
{
   long* pprime=0;                     // Pointer to prime array
   long trial = 5;                     // Candidate prime
   int count = 3;                      // Count of primes found
   int found = 0;                      // Indicates when a prime is found
   int max = 0;                        // Number of primes required

   cout << endl
        << "Enter the number of primes you would like: ";
   cin >> max;                         // Number of primes required

   if( !(pprime=new long[max]) )
   {
      cout << endl
           << "Memory allocation failed.";
      exit(1);                         // Terminate program
   }

   *pprime = 2;                        // Insert three
   *(pprime+1) = 3;                    // seed primes
```

157

```
   *(pprime+2) = 5;

   do
   {
      trial += 2;                          // Next value for checking
      found = 0;                           // Set found indicator
      for ( int i = 0; i < count; i++ ) // Try division by existing primes
      {
         found=( trial % *(pprime+i)) == 0;    // Result is 1 for exact
division
         if( found )                       // If division is exact
            break;                         // it's not a prime
      }
      if (found == 0 )                     // We got one...
         *(pprime+count++) = trial;        // ...so save it in primes array
   }while (count < max );

   // Output primes 5 to a line
   for( int i = 0 ; i < max ; i++)
   {
      if( i%5 == 0 )                       // New line on 1st, and every 5th line
         cout << endl;
      cout << setw(10) << *(pprime+i);
   }
   delete [] pprime;                       // Free up memory
   return 0;
}
```

How It Works

Apart for the prompt for the number of primes required, the output from this example is the same as the previous version (assuming the same number of primes is being generated) so we won't reproduce it again here.

In fact, the program is very similar. We have an extra **#include** statement for **STDLIB.H** because we are using the function **exit()** if we run out of memory. After receiving the number of primes required in the **int** variable **max**, we allocate an array of that size in the free store using the operator **new**. We specify the size of the array required by putting the variable **max** between the square brackets following the array type specification. The pointer value returned by **new** and stored in the pointer **pprime** is validated in the **if**. If it turns out to be null, a message is displayed and the program is exited.

Assuming the memory allocation is successful, the first three array elements are set to the values of the first three primes.

Note that we can't specify initial values for elements of an array allocated dynamically, so we have to use explicit assignment statements if we want to set initial values elements of the array.

The calculation of the prime numbers is exactly as before. The only change is that the name of the pointer we have here, **pprime**, is substituted for the array name **primes**, used in the previous version. Equally, the output process is the same. Acquiring space dynamically is really not a problem to deal with at all. Once it has been allocated, it doesn't in any way affect how the computation is written.

Once we have finished with the array, we remove it from the free store using the **delete** operator, not forgetting to include the square brackets to indicate it is an array we are deleting.

Dynamic Allocation of Multi-Dimensional Arrays

Allocating memory in the free store for a multi-dimensional array involves using the operator **new** in only a slightly more complicated form than that for a one dimensional array. Assuming we have already declared the pointer **pbeans** appropriately, to obtain the space for our array **beans[3][4]** we used earlier in this chapter, we could write this:

```
pbeans = new double [3][4];         // Allocate memory for a 3x4 array
```

Allocating space for a three dimensional array simply requires the extra dimension specified with **new** as in this example:

```
pBigArray = new double [5][10][10]; // Allocate memory for a 5x10x10 array
```

However many dimensions there are in the array that has been created, to destroy it and release the memory back to the free store you write the following:

```
delete [] pBigArray;                 // Release memory for array
```

You use just one pair of square brackets regardless of the dimensionality of the array with which you are dealing.

We have already seen that we can use a variable as the specification of the dimension of a one dimensional array to be allocated by **new**. This extends to two or more dimensions only in that the leftmost dimension may be specified by a variable. All the other dimensions must be constants. So we could write this:

```
pBigArray = new double[max][10][10];
```

However, specifying a variable for any other dimension will cause an error message to be generated by the compiler.

Using References

A **reference** is similar to a pointer in many respects (which is why it is introduced here). Its real significance will only become apparent when we get to discuss its use with functions, and particularly in the context of object-oriented programming. So don't be misled by its simplicity and what might seem to be a trivial concept. As you will see later, it provides some extraordinarily powerful facilities, and in some contexts will enable you to achieve results that would be impossible without using references.

What is a Reference?

A reference is an alias for another variable. It has a name that can be used in place of the original variable name. Since it is an alias, and not a pointer, the variable for which it is an alias has to be specified when the reference is declared, and unlike a pointer, a reference can't be altered to represent another variable.

Declaring and Initializing References

If we have a variable declared as follows:

```
long number = 0;
```

then we can declare a reference for this variable using the following declaration statement:

```
long& rnumber=number;      // Declare a reference to variable number
```

The ampersand following the type **long**, and preceding the name **rnumber**, indicates that a reference is being declared, and the variable name it represents, **number**, is specified as the initializing value following the equals sign. Therefore, **rnumber** is of type **reference to long**. The reference can now be used in place of the original variable name. For example, this statement:

```
rnumber += 10;
```

has the effect of incrementing the variable **number** by 10.

Let's contrast the reference **rnumber** with the pointer **pnumber**, declared in this statement

```
long pnumber = &number;   // Increment number through a reference
```

This initializes the pointer with the address of the variable **number**, which then allows the variable number to be incremented with a statement such as:

```
*pnumber += 10;            // Increment number through a pointer
```

You should see a significant distinction between using a pointer and using a reference. The pointer needs to be de-referenced, and whatever address it contains is used to access the variable to participate in the expression. With a reference there is no need for de-referencing. In some ways, a reference is like a pointer that has already been de-referenced, although it can't be changed to reference another variable. The reference is the complete equivalent of the variable for which it is a reference. A reference may seem like just an alternative notation for a given variable, and here it certainly appears to behave like that. However, we shall see when we come to discuss functions in C++ that this is not quite true, and it can provide some very impressive extra capabilities.

Summary

You are now familiar with all of the basic types of values in C++, how to create and use arrays of those types, and how to create and use pointers. You have also been introduced to the idea of a reference. However, we have not exhausted all of these topics. We will come back to arrays, pointers and references again later in the book. The important points that we have discussed in this chapter are:

▶ An array allows you to manage a number of variables of the same type using a single name. Each dimension of an array is defined between square brackets following the array name in the declaration of the array.

▶ Each dimension of an array is indexed starting from zero. Thus the fifth element of a one dimensional array will have the index value 4.

▶ Arrays can be initialized by placing the initializing values between braces in the declaration.

▶ A pointer is a variable that contains the address of another variable. A pointer is declared as a 'pointer to type', and may only be assigned addresses of variables of the given type.

▶ A pointer can point to a constant object. Such a pointer can be reassigned to another object. A pointer may also be defined as **const**, in which case it can't be reassigned.

▶ A reference is an alias for another variable, and can be used wherever the variable it references can be used. A reference must be initialized in its declaration.

▶ A reference can't be reassigned to another variable.

▶ The operator **sizeof** returns the number of bytes occupied by the object specified as its argument. Its argument may be a variable, or a type name between parentheses.

▶ The operator **new** allocates memory dynamically in the free store. When memory is allocated it returns a pointer to the beginning of the memory area. Memory allocated by **new** can only be freed using the **delete** operator with the address originally returned by **new** as an argument.

The pointer mechanism is sometimes a bit confusing because it can operate at different levels within the same program. Sometimes it is operating as an address, and at other times it can be operating with the value stored at an address. It is very important that you feel at ease with the way pointers are used, so if you find they are in anyway unclear, try them out with a few examples of your own until you feel confident about applying them.

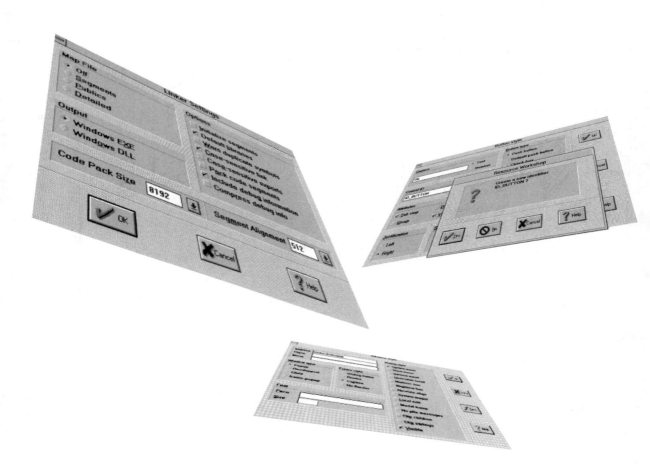

5

Introducing Structure Into Your Programs

Up to now we have not really been able to structure our program code in a modular fashion since we have only been able to construct a program as a single function, **main()**, but we *have* been using library functions of various kinds. Whenever you write a C++ program you should have a modular structure in mind from the outset, and a good understanding of how to implement functions is essential to object-oriented programming in C++ as we shall see. In this chapter you will learn:

▶ How to declare and write your own C++ functions

▶ What function arguments are and how they are defined and used

▶ How arrays can be passed to and from a function

▶ What pass-by-value means

▶ How to pass pointers to functions

▶ How to use references as function arguments and what pass-by-reference means

▶ How the **const** modifier affects function arguments

▶ How to return values from a function

▶ What recursion is and how it can be used

There is quite a lot to delve into on structuring your C++ programs, so we won't try to swallow the whole thing in one gulp. This chapter is complemented by the following chapter, More About Program Structure, where we will dig deeper into the topic, once we have chewed over and digested all the crunchy bits listed above.

Understanding Functions

A function is a self-contained block of code with a specific purpose. A function has a name that both identifies it and is used to call it for execution in a program. The name of a function is not necessarily unique in C++, as we shall see later in this chapter, but functions which perform different actions generally should have a unique name. The name of a function is governed by the same rules as that for a variable name. A function name is therefore a sequence of letters and digits, the first of which is a letter, and where an underscore counts as a letter. A function can be executed as many times as necessary from different points in a program.

Structure of a Function

As we have seen when writing the function **main()**, a function consists of a function header which identifies the function, followed by the body of the function between curly braces which contains the executable code for the function. Let's look at an example. We could write a function to raise a value to a given power, that is compute x^n:

```
double power( double x, int n )          // Function header
{                                         // Function body starts here...
   double result = 1.0;                   // Result stored here
   for( int i = 1 ; i<=n ; i++ )
      result *=x;
   return result;
}                                         // ...and ends here
```

The Function Header

Let's first examine the function header in this example. This is the first line of the function:

```
double power( double x, int n )     // Function header
```

It consists of three parts: the type of the **return value** which is **double** in this case, the name of the function, **power**, and then the parameters of the function enclosed between parentheses.

The return value is returned to the calling function when the function is executed, so when the function is called it will have a value of type **double** in the expression in which it appears.

Our function has two parameters which are **x**, the value to be raised to a given power, which is of type **double**, and the value of the power **n** which is of type **int**. The computation the function performs is written using these parameter variables together with another variable, **result**, declared in the body of the function.

Note that no semicolon is required at the end of the function header.

The General Form of a Function Header

The general form of a function header can be written as follows:

```
return_type      FunctionName(  parameter_list  )
```

The *return_type* can be any legal type. If the function does not return a value, the return type is specified by the keyword **void**. It is also used to indicate the absence of parameters, so a function that has no parameters and does not return a value would have this header:

```
void  MyFunction(  void  )
```

A function with a return type specified as void should not be used in an expression in the calling program. Because it doesn't return any value it can't sensibly be part of an expression, so using it in this way will cause the compiler to generate an error message.

The Function Body

The computation is performed by the statements in the function body following the function header. The first of these declares a variable **result** which is also initialized with the value 1.0. (It is initialized to this particular value because any number raised to the power 0 is 1.0.) The variable **result** is local to the function, as are all variables within the function body. This means the variable **result** ceases to exist after the function has completed execution.

The calculation is performed in the **for** loop. A loop control variable **i** is also declared in the **for** loop which will assume successive values from 1 to **n**. The variable **result** is multiplied by **x** once for each loop iteration, so this occurs **n** times to generate the required value. If **n** is 0 then the statement in the loop will not be executed at all because the loop continuation condition will immediately fail, and **result** will be left as 1.0.

As we have said, the names of all the variables declared within the body of a function, as well as the parameter names, are all local to the function. There is nothing to prevent you from using the same names for variables in other functions for quite different purposes. Indeed, it is just as well this is so, as it would be extremely difficult to ensure variables names were always unique within a program containing a large number of functions, particularly if they were not all written by the same person.

The return Statement

The **return** statement returns the value of **result** to the point where the function was called. What might immediately strike you is that we just said **result** ceases to exist on completing execution of the function - so how is it returned? The answer is that a copy is made of the value being returned, and this copy is available to the return point in the program.

The general form of the return statement is as follows:

```
return expression;
```

where **expression** must evaluate to a value of the type specified in the function header for the return value. The expression can be any expression as long as you end up with a value of the required type. It can include function calls - even a call of the same function in which it appears, as we shall see later in this chapter.

If the type of return value has been specified as **void**, then there must be no expression appearing in the **return** statement. It must be written simply as:

```
return;
```

Using a Function

Before you can use a function in a program you must declare the function using a statement called a **function prototype**.

Function Prototypes

A prototype for a function provides the basic information the compiler needs to implement the use of a function. It specifies the parameters to be passed to the function, the function name, and the type of the return value, so it contains essentially the same information as appears in the function header, with the addition of a semicolon. The prototypes for the functions used in a program must appear before the statements calling them, and are usually placed at the beginning of a program. The header files (that is, the files with the extension **.H** which appear between **<** and **>** in an **include** statement) we have been including for standard library functions include the prototypes of the functions provided by the library.

For our example **power()**, we could write the prototype as follows:

```
double power( double value, int index );
```

Don't forget that a semicolon is required at the end of a function prototype. Without it, you will get error messages from the compiler.

Note that we have specified different names for the parameters to the function in this instance, just to indicate that it is possible. Most often, the same names are used in the prototype and in the function header in the definition of the function, but this doesn't *have* to be so. The parameter names in the function prototype can be selected to aid understanding of the significance of the parameters.

You can also omit the names altogether in the prototype if you like, and just write the following:

```
double power( double, int );
```

This is enough for the compiler to do its job. However, it is better practice to use some meaningful name in a prototype as it aids readability, and in some cases it can make all the difference between opacity and lucidity. If you have a function with two parameters of the same type (suppose our index was also of type **double** in the function **power()** for example), the use of suitable names can indicate which parameter appears first and which second.

Try it Out!

Try It Out - Using a Function

We can see how all this goes together in an example exercising our **power()** function.

```
// EX5-01.CPP
// Declaring, defining, and using a function
#include <iostream.h>

double power( double x, int n );    // Function prototype

int main(void)
{
   int index = 3;                // Raise to this power
   double x = 3.0;               // Different x from that in function power
   double y = 0.0;

   y = power( 5.0, 3 );          // Passing constants as arguments
   cout << endl
        << "5.0 cubed = " << y;

   cout << endl
        << "3.0 cubed = "
        << power( 3.0, index ); // Outputting return value

   x = power( x, power( 2.0, 2.0 ) );  // Using a function as an argument
   cout << endl                  // with auto conversion of 2nd parameter
        << "x = " << x;

   return 0;
}

// Function to compute integral powers of a double value
// First argument is value, second argument is power index
double power( double x, int n )
```

```
{
    double result = 1.0;         // Result stored here
    for( int i = 1 ; i<=n ; i++ )
    result *=x;
    return result;
}                                // ...and ends here
```

This shows some of the ways in which we can use the function `power()` with variety in the way arguments are specified. If you run this example you will get the following output:

```
5.0 cubed = 125
3.0 cubed = 27
x = 81
```

How It Works

After the usual `#include` statement for input/output we have the prototype for the function `power()`. Try deleting this and recompiling the program. Without the prototype the compiler can't process the calls of the function in `main()`. In the function `main()` where the parameter list would usually appear, we have used the new keyword, **void**, that we introduced earlier in this chapter. This indicates that no parameters are to be supplied. In previous examples, we left the parentheses enclosing the parameter list empty, and this is interpreted in C++ as indicating that there are no parameters, but it is better to specify the fact by using the keyword **void**. As we saw, the keyword **void** can also be used as the return type for a function to indicate that no value is returned. If you specify the return type of a function as **void** then you must not place a value in any **return** statement within the function, otherwise you will get an error message from the compiler.

You will have gathered from some of our previous examples that using a function is very simple. To use the function `power()` to calculate 5.0^3 and store the result in a variable **y** in our example, we have written this:

```
y = power( 5.0, 3 );
```

The values **5.0** and **3** here are called **arguments**. They happen to be constants, but any expression can be used as an argument, as long as a value of the correct type is ultimately produced. The arguments substitute for the parameters **x** and **n** which were used in the definition of the function. The computation is performed using these values and a copy of the result, 125, will be returned to the calling function, **main()**, and will be stored in **y**. You can think of the function as having this value in the statement or expression in which it appears. We then output the value of **y** to the screen:

```
cout << endl
        << "5.0 cubed = " << y;
```

The next call of the function is used within the output statement:

```
    cout << endl
        << "3.0 cubed = "
        << power( 3.0, index ); // Outputting return value
```

so the value returned is transferred directly to the output mechanism. Since we have not stored the returned value anywhere, it is otherwise unavailable to us. The first argument in the call of the function here is a constant and the second is a variable.

The function **power()** is next used in this statement:

```
    x = power( x, power( 2.0, 2.0 ) );   // Using a function as an argument
```

and here the function will be called twice. The first call of the function will be the right-most in the expression, appearing as an argument to the second call. Although the arguments are both specified as **2.0**, the function will actually be called with the first argument as **2.0** and the second argument as **2**. The compiler will convert the **double** value specified for the second argument to **int** because it knows from the function prototype that the type of the second parameter has been specified as such. The **double** result 4.0 will be returned, and after converting this to **int**, the compiler will insert this value as the second argument in the next call of the function, with **x** as the first argument. Since **x** has the value 3.0, the value of 3.0^4 will be computed and the result, 81, stored in **x**. This sequence of events is illustrated opposite.

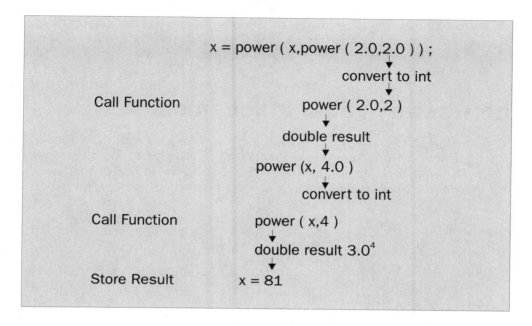

Passing Arguments to a Function

It is very important to understand how arguments are passed to a function in C++, as it will affect how you write functions and how they will ultimately operate. There are also a number of pitfalls to be avoided, so we will look at the mechanism for this quite closely.

The arguments specified when a function is called should usually correspond in type and sequence to the parameters appearing in the definition of the function. As we have seen in the last example, if the type of an argument specified in a function call doesn't correspond with the type of parameter in the function definition, it will be converted to the required type where possible. If this turns out not to be possible, you will get an error message from the compiler.

One mechanism used generally in C++ to pass parameters to functions applies when the parameters are specified as ordinary variables which are not references. This is called the **pass-by-value** method of transferring data to a function.

The Pass-by-value Mechanism

With this mechanism, the values of the variables or constants you specify as arguments are not passed to a function at all. Copies of the arguments are created and these copies are used as the values to be transferred. We can show this diagrammatically using the example of our function `power()`:

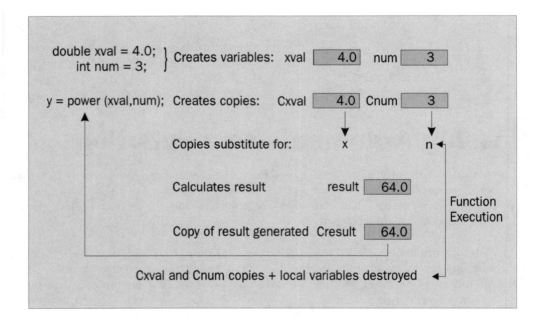

We have used pseudo-names for the copies generated in the illustration, and these are purely to help your understanding of the diagram. They do not exist in reality in this form.

Try It Out - Passing-by-value

One consequence of the pass-by-value mechanism is that a function can't directly modify the arguments passed. We can demonstrate this by deliberately trying to do so in an example.

```
// EX5-02.CPP
// A futile attempt to modify caller arguments
#include <iostream.h>

int incr10( int num );                    // Function prototype

int main( void )
{
   int num = 3;

   cout << endl
        << "incr10( num ) = " << incr10( num )
        << endl
        << "num = " << num;
   return 0;
}

// Function to increment a variable by 10
int incr10( int num )            // Using the same name might help...
{
   num += 10;                    // Increment the caller argument - hopefully
   return num;                   // Return the incremented value
}
```

How It Works

Of course this program is doomed to failure. If you run it you will get this output:

```
incr10( num ) = 13
num = 3
```

thus confirming that the original value of **num** remains untouched. The incrementing occurred on the copy of **num** which was generated, and was eventually discarded on exiting from the function.

Clearly the pass-by-value mechanism provides a high degree of protection from having caller arguments mauled by a rogue function, but it is conceivable that we might actually want to arrange to modify caller arguments. Of course, there is a way to do this. Didn't you just know that pointers would turn out to be incredibly useful?

Pointers as Arguments to a Function

When you use a pointer as an argument, the pass-by-value mechanism still operates as before. However, a pointer is an address of another variable, and if you take a copy of this address, the copy still points to the same variable. This is how specifying a pointer as a parameter enables your function to get at a caller argument.

Try It Out - Pass-by-pointer

We can change the last example to use a pointer to demonstrate the effect:

```
// EX5-03.CPP
// A successful attempt to modify caller arguments
#include <iostream.h>

int incr10( int* num );              // Function prototype

int main( void )
{
    int num = 3;
    int* pnum = &num;                // Pointer to num

    cout << endl
         << "Address passed = " << pnum;

    cout << endl
         << "incr10( pnum ) = " << incr10( pnum );

    cout << endl
         << "num = " << num;

    return 0;
}

// Function to increment a variable by 10
int incr10( int* num )               // Function with pointer argument
```

```
{
    cout << endl
        << "Address received = " << num;

    *num += 10;                 // Increment the caller argument - confidently
    return *num;                // Return the incremented value
}
```

How It Works

In this example, the principle alterations from the previous version relate to passing a pointer **pnum** in place of the original variable **num**. The prototype for the function now has the parameter type specified as a pointer to **int**, and the **main()** function has the pointer **pnum** declared and initialized with the address of **num**. The function **main()** and the function **incr10()** output the address sent and the address received respectively, to verify that the same address is indeed being used in both places.

If you run this program, you will get output similar to this:

```
Address passed = 0x782f1c5a
Address received = 0x782f1c5a
incr10( pnum ) = 13
num = 13
```

> *The address values produced by your computer may be different from those shown above, but the two values should be identical.*

The output shows that this time the variable **num** has been incremented, and has a value that is now identical to that returned by the function.

In the rewritten version of the function **incr10()**, both the statement incrementing the value passed to the function, and the **return** statement, now need to dereference the pointer in order to use the value stored.

Passing Arrays to a Function

You can also pass an array to a function, but in this case the array is not copied, even though a pass-by-value method of passing arguments still applies. The array name is converted to a pointer, and a copy of the pointer to the beginning of the array is passed to the function. This is quite advantageous, as copying large arrays could be very time consuming.

Try It Out - Passing Arrays

We can illustrate the ins and outs of this by writing a function to compute the average of a number of values that are passed to a function in an array.

```cpp
// EX5-04.CPP
// Passing an array to a function
#include <iostream.h>
double average( double array[], int count );        //Function prototype

int main(void)
{
   double values[] =
              { 1.0, 2.0, 3.0, 4.0, 5.0, 6.0, 7.0, 8.0, 9.0, 10.0 };

   cout << endl
        << "Average = "
        << average( values, sizeof values/sizeof values[0] );

   return 0;
}

// Function to compute an average
double average( double array[], int count )
{
   double sum = 0.0;                     // Accumulate total in here
   for( int i = 0 ; i<count ; i++ )
     sum += array[i];                    // Sum array elements

   return sum/count;                     // Return average
}
```

How It Works

The function **average()** is designed to work with an array of any length. As you can see from the prototype, it accepts two arguments, the array and a count of the number of elements. The array parameter appears without a dimension specified, since we want it to work with arrays of arbitrary length.

The function is called in **main()** in this statement:

```cpp
   cout << endl
        << "Average = "
        << average( values, sizeof values/sizeof values[0] );
```

with the first argument as the array name, **values**, and the second argument as an expression which evaluates to the number of elements in the array.

> You will recall this expression using the operator *sizeof* from when we looked at arrays in Chapter 4.

Within the body of the function the computation is expressed in the way you would expect. There is no significant difference between this and the way we would write the same computation if we implemented it directly in `main()`.

If you run the example it will produce the following output

```
Average = 5.5
```

confirming that everything works as we anticipated.

Try It Out - Using Pointer Notation When Passing Arrays

However, we haven't exhausted all the possibilities here. As we determined at the outset, the array name is passed as a pointer, in fact as a copy of a pointer, so within the function we need not necessarily deal with the data as an array at all. We could modify the function in the example to work with pointer notation throughout, in spite of the fact we are using an array.

```cpp
// EX5-05.CPP
// Handling an array in a function as a pointer
#include <iostream.h>
double average( double* array, int count );        //Function prototype

int main(void)
{
   double values[] =
            { 1.0, 2.0, 3.0, 4.0, 5.0, 6.0, 7.0, 8.0, 9.0, 10.0 };

   cout << endl
           << "Average = "
           << average( values, sizeof values/sizeof values[0] );

   return 0;
}
```

```
// Function to compute an average
double average( double* array, int count )
{
    double sum = 0.0;                    // Accumulate total in here
    for( int i = 0 ; i<count ; i++ )
        sum += *array++;                 // Sum array elements

    return sum/count;                    // Return average
}
```

How It Works

It needed very few changes to work with the array as a pointer, as you can see. The prototype and the function header have been changed, although neither change is absolutely necessary. If you change both back to the original version with the first parameter specified as a **double** array, and leave the function body written in terms of a pointer, it will work just as well. The most interesting aspect of this version is the **for** loop statement:

```
sum += *array++;                 // Sum array elements
```

where we apparently break the rule about not being able to modify an address specified as an array name. Here, we are incrementing the address stored in **array**. In fact, we're not breaking the rule. Remember that the pass-by-value mechanism makes a copy of the original array address and passes that, so here we are modifying the copy, and the original array address will be quite unaffected. As a result, whenever we pass a one dimensional array to a function, we are free to treat the value passed as a pointer in every sense, and change the address in any way that we wish.

Naturally, this version produces exactly the same output as the original.

Passing Multi-Dimensional Arrays to a Function

Passing a multi-dimensional array to a function is quite straightforward. To pass a two dimensional array, for instance the array declared as follows:

```
double beans[2][4];
```

you could write the prototype of a hypothetical function **yield()** like this:

```
double yield( double beans[2][4] );
```

You may be wondering how the compiler can know that this is defining an array of the dimensions shown as an argument, and not a single array element. The answer is simple. You can't write a single array element as a parameter, only as an argument. For a parameter accepting a single element of an array as an argument, the parameter would have just a variable name. The array context doesn't apply.

You can also omit the first dimension value when defining a multidimensional array as a parameter. Of course, the function will need some way of knowing the extent of the first dimension. For example you could write this:

```
double yield( double beans[][4], int index );
```

where the second parameter would provide the necessary information about the first dimension. Here, the function can operate with a two dimensional array with any value for the first dimension, but with the second dimension fixed at 4.

Try It Out - Passing Multi-dimensional Arrays

We could define such a function in an example:

```
// EX5-06.CPP
// Passing a two dimensional array to a function
#include <iostream.h>

double yield( double array[][4], int n )

int main(void)
{
   double beans[3][4] =
               {   { 1.0,  2.0,  3.0,  4.0 },
                   { 5.0,  6.0,  7.0,  8.0 },
                   { 9.0, 10.0, 11.0, 12.0 }  };

   cout << endl
        << "Yield = " << yield( beans, sizeof beans/sizeof beans[0] );
   return 0;
}
```

Try it Out!

181

```
// Function to compute total yield
double yield( double beans[][4], int count )
{
    double sum = 0.0;
    for( int i=0 ; i<count ; i++)          // Loop through number of rows
        for( int j=0 ; j<4 ; j++)          // Loop through elements in a row
            sum += beans[i][j];
    return sum;
}
```

How It Works

Here, we have used different names for the parameters in the function
header from that in the prototype just to remind you that this is possible,
but in this case it doesn't really improve the program at all. The first
parameter is defined as an array of an arbitrary number of rows, each row
having four elements. We actually call the function using the array **beans**
with 3 rows. The second argument is specified by dividing the total length
of the array in bytes by the length of the first row. This will evaluate to the
number of rows in the array.

The computation in the function is simply a nested **for** loop with the inner
loop summing elements of a single row, and the outer loop repeating this
for each row. For what it's worth, the program will display this result:

```
Yield = 78
```

Using a pointer in a function as an alternative to a multi-dimensional array
as an argument doesn't really apply particularly well. When the array is
passed, it passes an address value which points to an array of four
elements (a row). This doesn't lend itself to an easy pointer operation within
the function. We would need to modify the statement in the nested **for**
loop to the following:

```
sum += *(*(beans+i)+j);
```

so the computation is probably clearer in array notation.

References as Arguments to a Function

Specifying a parameter to a function as a reference changes the method of passing data for that parameter. The method used is not pass-by-value where an argument is copied before being passed, but pass-by-reference, where the parameter acts as an alias for the argument passed. This eliminates any copying and allows the function to access the caller argument directly. It also means that the dereferencing which is required when passing and using a pointer to a value is also unnecessary.

Try It Out - Pass-by-reference

Let's go back to a revised version of a very simple example, **EX5-03.CPP**, to see how it would work using reference parameters.

```
// EX5-07.CPP
// Using a reference to modify caller arguments
#include <iostream.h>

int incr10( int& num );              // Function prototype

int main( void )
{
    int num = 3;
    int value = 6;

    cout << endl
        << "incr10( num ) = " << incr10( num );

    cout << endl
        << "num = " << num;

    cout << endl
        << "incr10( value ) = " << incr10( value );

    cout << endl
        << "value = " << value;


    return 0;
}
```

```
// Function to increment a variable by 10
int incr10( int& num )          // Function with reference argument
{
    cout << endl
        << "Value received = " << num;

    num += 10;                  // Increment the caller argument - confidently
    return num;                 // Return the incremented value
}
```

How It Works

You should find the way this works quite remarkable. This is the same as **EX5-03.CPP** except that the function uses a reference as a parameter. The prototype has been changed to reflect this. When the function is called, the argument is specified just as though it was a pass-by-value operation, so it is no different from the earlier version in its usage. The argument value isn't passed to the function. Here, the function parameter is **initialized** with the address of the argument, so whenever the parameter **num** is used in the function, it accesses the caller argument directly.

Just to confirm there is nothing fishy about the use of the identifier **num** in **main()** as well as in the function, the function is called a second time with the variable **value** as the argument. At first sight, this may give you the impression that this contradicts what we said was a basic property of a reference - that once declared and initialized, it couldn't be reassigned to another variable. The reason that it is not contradictory is that a reference as a function parameter is created and initialized when the function is called, and destroyed when the function ends, so we get a completely new reference each time the function is called.

Within the function, the value received from the calling program is displayed on the screen. Although the statement is essentially the same as that used to output the address stored in a pointer, because **num** is now a reference we obtain the data value rather than the address.

> *This demonstrates clearly the difference between a reference and a pointer. A reference is an alias for another variable, and therefore can be used as an alternative way of referring to it. It is equivalent to using the original variable name.*

The output from this example is as follows:

```
Value passed = 3
incr10( num ) = 13
num = 13
Value passed = 6
incr10( value ) = 16
value = 16
```

This clearly demonstrates that the function `incr10()` is directly modifying the variable passed as a caller argument.

You will find you can even use a numeric value such as 20 as an argument to `incr10()`, and it will still run without a problem. However, there will be a warning from the compiler in this case, which indicates that a copy of the constant will be created and placed as an argument to the function rather than the original. This is to protect the constant from modification. This copy is often referred to as a **temporary**. Similarly, if you try to pass a `const` variable to the function, the compiler will make a copy of the variable before calling the function, so the variable will not be updated. You can demonstrate this by simply changing the declaration of `num` in the last example to the following:

```
const int num = 3;
```

and by running the example again.

This security is all very well, but if the function did not modify the value, we would not want the compiler to create all these spurious copies every time we pass a reference argument that was a constant. Surely there ought to be some way to accommodate this? As Ollie would have said, there most certainly is Stanley!

Use of the const Modifier

We can use the `const` modifier with a parameter to a function to tell the compiler that we don't intend to modify it in any way. This will avoid the creation of temporaries when passing `const` variables or other constants to the function.

Try It Out - Passing a const

We can modify the previous program to show how the **const** modifier changes the situation with regards to temporary variables.

```cpp
// EX5-08.CPP
// Using a reference to modify caller arguments
#include <iostream.h>

int incr10( const int& num );                    // Function prototype

int main( void )
{
    const int num = 3;        // Declared const to test for temporary creation
    int value = 6;

    cout << endl
        << "incr10( num ) = " << incr10( num );

    cout << endl
            << "num = " << num;

    cout << endl
        << "incr10( value ) = " << incr10( value );

    cout << endl
            << "value = " << value;


    return 0;
}

// Function to increment a variable by 10
int incr10( const int& num )        // Function with const reference argument
{
    cout << endl
            << "Value received = " << num;

//    num += 10;        // this statement would now be illegal
    return num+10;                      // Return the incremented value
}
```

How It Works

The variable **num** in **main()** has been declared as **const** to show that now the parameter to the function **incr10()** is declared as **const**, we no longer get a compiler message when passing a **const** object.

It has also been necessary to comment out the statement which increments **num** in the function **incr10()**. If you uncomment this line, you will find the program will no longer compile, as the compiler won't allow **num** to appear on the left-hand side of an assignment. When you specified **num** as **const**, you promised not to modify it, so the compiler checks that you kept your word.

Everything works as before except that the variables in **main()** are no longer changed in the function, so the program produces the following output:

```
Value passed = 3
incr10( num ) = 13
num = 3
Value passed = 6
incr10( value ) = 16
value = 6
```

Now, using reference arguments we have the best of both worlds. On one hand, we can write a function that can access caller arguments directly and avoid the copying implicit in the pass-by-value mechanism. On the other hand, where we do not intend to modify an argument, by using a **const** modifier with a reference, we can get all the protection we need against accidental modification.

The compiler will also create a temporary variable when a conversion is necessary to match a reference type parameter. This is necessary to accommodate the result of the conversion. The reference will then access the converted value directly. Obviously, there is no way to avoid the creation of a temporary object in this case, unless you avoid causing the conversion being initiated in the first place by only specifying an argument which matches the reference type. You should keep this potential for temporary objects being created in mind though, particularly if you are writing functions which are intended to modify the arguments provided by the calling program.

> *Obviously, if a temporary object is created, the temporary will be modified, not the original.*

References provide a remarkably powerful facility when used as function parameters. But that isn't all. We shall see a lot more about references when we get to investigating user defined types and object-oriented programming.

Returning Values from a Function

All the example of functions we have created have returned a single value. Is it possible to return anything other than a single value? Well, directly no, but the single value returned need not be a numeric value, it can also be an address, so this provides the key to returning any amount of data. You simply use a pointer. But here is where the pitfalls start, so you need to be careful.

Returning a Pointer

Returning a pointer value is very easy. A pointer value is just an address, so if you want to return the address of some variable **value**, you can just write the following:

```
return &value;          // Returning an address
```

As long as the function header and function prototype indicate the return type appropriately, we have no problem. Assuming the variable **value** is of type **double**, the prototype of a function which might contain the above **return** statement might be as follows:

```
double* treble( double data );
```

The parameter list has been defined arbitrarily here.

So let's look at a function which will return a pointer. You should know in advance that this function doesn't work. Let's assume we need a function which will return a pointer to three times its argument value. Our first attempt might look like this:

```
// Function to treble a value - mark 1
double* treble( double data )
{
   double result = 0;

   result = 3.0*data;
   return &result;
}
```

188

Try It Out - Returning a Bad Pointer

We could create a little test program to see what happens:

```
//EX5-09.CPP
#include <iostream.h>

double* treble( double );                    // Function prototype

int main(void)
{
    double num = 5.0;                        // Test value
    double* ptr=0;                           // Pointer to returned value

    ptr = treble( num );

    cout << endl
         << "Three times num = " << 3.0*num;

    cout << endl
         << "Result = " << *ptr;             // Display 3*num

    return 0;
}
```

```
// Function to treble a value - mark 1
double* treble( double data )
{
    double result = 0;

    result = 3.0*data;
    return &result;
}
```

How It Works

The function **main()** calls the function **treble()** and stores the address returned, which should point to a value which is three times the argument **num**, in the pointer **ptr**. We then display the result of computing three times **num** followed by the value at the address returned from the function.

On my computer I get this output:

```
Three times num = 15
Result = 9,068591e-160
```

Clearly, the second line doesn't reflect the correct value of 15. Where's the error? The error arises because we are returning the address of a variable which is local to the function. The variable `result` in the function `treble()` is created when the function begins execution, and is destroyed on exiting from the function. The memory previously allocated to `result` becomes available for other purposes, and here it has evidently been used for something else.

A Cast Iron Rule for Returning Addresses

So there is an absolutely cast iron rule for returning addresses:

Never return the address of a local variable from a function.

Now we have a function that doesn't work, we need to think about how we can get it to work. We could use a reference and modify the original variable, but that's not what we set out to do. One answer lies in dynamic memory allocation. With the operator `new` we can create a new variable in the free store which will continue to exist until it is eventually destroyed by `delete` or until the program ends. The function would then look like this:

```
// Function to treble a value - mark 2
double* treble( double data )
{
   double* result = new double(0.0);
   if( !result )
   {
     cout << "Memory allocation failed.";
     exit(1);
   }

   *result = 3.0*data;
   return result;
}
```

Rather than declaring `result` as of type `double`, we now declare it as `double*` and store the address returned by the operator `new` in it. We then have the necessary check that we got a valid address back, and exit the program if anything is wrong.

Since the result is a pointer, the rest of the function is changed to reflect this, and the address contained in the result is finally returned to the calling program. You could exercise this by replacing the function in the last working example with this version.

You need to remember with dynamic memory allocation within a function like this, that more memory is allocated each time the function is called. The onus is on the calling program to delete the memory when it is no longer required. It is easy to forget to do this in practice, with the result that the free store is gradually eaten up until at some point it is exhausted, and the program will fail.

Returning a Reference

You can also return a reference from a function. This is just as fraught with potential error as returning a pointer, so you need to take care with this too. Because a reference has no existence in its right (as it is always an alias for something else), you must ensure that the object referred to still exists after the function completes execution. It is very easy to forget this when you use references in a function, because they appear to be just like ordinary variables.

References as return types are of primary significance in the context of object-oriented programming where they will enable you to do things which would be impossible without them. The principle characteristic that a return value which is a reference type has, is that it is an lvalue. This means that you can use the result of a function on the left side of an assignment statement.

Try It Out - Returning a Reference

Let's look at one example which illustrates the use of reference return types and also demonstrates how a function can be used when it returns an lvalue. We will assume that we have an array containing a mixed set of values. Whenever we want to insert a new value into the array we want to replace the lowest value.

Try it Out!

```cpp
// EX5-10.CPP
// Returning a reference
#include <iostream.h>
#include <iomanip.h>

double& lowest(double A[], int len );   // Prototype of function
                                        //   returning a reference

int main(void)
{
   double array[] =
               { 3.0, 10.0, 1.5, 15.0, 2.7, 23.0,
                 4.5, 12.0, 6.8, 13.5, 2.1, 14.0 };
   int len = sizeof array/sizeof array[0]; // Initialize to number
                                           // of elements

   cout << endl;
   for(int i = 0 ; i<len ; i++ )
      cout << setw(6) << array[i];

   lowest(array, len) = 6.9;                    // Change lowest to 6.9
   lowest(array, len) = 7.9;                    // Change lowest to 7.9

   cout << endl;
   for( i = 0 ; i<len ; i++ )
      cout << setw(6) << array[i];

   return 0;
}

double& lowest( double A[], int len )
{
   int j=0;                             // Index of lowest element
   for( int i=1 ; i<len ; i++)
      if(A[j]>A[i])                     // Test for a lower value...
          j = i;                        // ...if so update j
   return A[j];                         // Return reference to lowest element
}
```

How It Works

Let's first take a look at how the function is implemented. The prototype uses **double&** as the specification of the return type for the function **lowest()**, which is therefore of type **reference to double**. A reference type of return value is written in exactly the same way as the same type in a reference declaration. The function has two parameters specified, a one dimension array of type **double**, and an **int** parameter **len**, which should specify the length of the array.

The body of the function has a straightforward **for** loop to determine the element of the array passed which contains the lowest value. The index of the lowest value is arbitrarily set to 0, and then modified within the loop if the current element **A[i]** is less than **A[j]**. Thus, on exit from the loop, **j** will contain the index value corresponding to the array element with the lowest value. The **return** statement is as follows:

```
return A[j];                          // Return reference to lowest element
```

In spite of the fact that this appears identical to the statement which would return a value, because the return type was declared as a reference, this returns a reference to **A[j]**. The address of **A[j]** is used to initialize a reference which is created by the compiler because the return type was declared as a reference.

Don't confuse returning **&A[j]** with returning a reference. If you write **&A[j]** as the return value, you are specifying the address of **A[j]** which is a pointer. You will get an error message from the compiler if you do this, having specified the return type as a reference.

The function **main()**, which exercises our function **lowest()**, is very simple. An array of type **double** is declared and initialized with 12 arbitrary values, and an **int** variable **len** is initialized to the length of the array. The initial values in the array are output for comparison purposes.

> *Note the use of the stream manipulator* **setw()** *to space the values uniformly. The use of this manipulator requires the* **#include** *statement for* **IOMANIP.H.**

The function **main()** then calls the function **lowest()** on the left side of an assignment to change the lowest value in the array. This is done twice to show it does actually work and is not an accident. The contents of the array are then output to the display again with the same field width as before, so corresponding values line up. The output you should see if you run this example is as follows:

```
3    10   1.5   15   2.7   23   4.5   12   6.8   13.5   2.1   14
3    10   6.9   15   2.7   23   4.5   12   6.8   13.5   7.9   14
```

With the first call to **lowest()**, the third element of the array, **array[2]**, contained the lowest value so the function returned a reference to it, and its value was changed to 6.9, as you can see. Similarly, on the second call, **array[10]** was changed to 7.9.

This demonstrates quite clearly that returning a reference allows the use of the function on the left side of an assignment statement. The effect is as if the variable specified in the **return** statement appeared on the left of the assignment.

Of course, you can also use it on the right side of an assignment, or in any other suitable expression, if you want to. If we had two arrays **x** and **y**, with **lenX** and **lenY** elements respectively, we could set the lowest element in the array **x** to twice the lowest element in the array **y** with this statement:

```
lowest(X, lenX) = 2.0*lowest(Y, lenY);
```

This statement would call our function **lowest()** twice, once with arguments **Y** and **lenY** in the expression on the right side of the assignment, and once with arguments **X** and **lenX** to obtain the address where the result of the right-hand expression is to be stored.

A Further Rule: Returning References

A similar rule to that applicable to returning a pointer from a function also applies to returning references:

Never return a reference to a local variable in a function.

We will leave the topic of returning a reference from a function for now, but we haven't finished with it yet. We will come back to it again in the context of user-defined types and object-oriented programming, when we shall unearth a few more magical things we can do with references.

Static Variables in a Function

There are some things you can't do with automatic variables within a function. You can't count how many times a function is called, for example, because you can't accumulate a value from one call to the next. There is more than one way to get around this if you need to. You could use a reference parameter to update a count in the calling program, for instance, but this wouldn't help if the function was called from lots of different places within a program. You could use a global variable which you increment from within the function, but globals are risky things to use as they can be referenced from anywhere in the program, which makes it very easy to change them accidentally.

For a general solution, you can declare a variable within a function as **static**. You use exactly the same form of declaration for a **static** variable that we saw in Chapter 2. For example, to declare a variable **count** as **static** you could use this statement:

```
static int count = 0;
```

This also initializes the variable to zero.

> *Initialization of a static variable within a function only occurs the first time the function is called. In fact, on the first call of a function the static variable is created and initialized. It then continues to exist for the duration of program execution, and whatever value it contains when the function is exited, is available when the function is next called.*

Try It Out - Using Static Variables in Functions

We can demonstrate this with a simple example.

```cpp
// EX5-11.CPP
// Using a static variable within a function
#include <iostream.h>
void record(void);    // Function prototype, no arguments or return value

int main(void)
{
```

Try it Out!

```
   record();

   for( int i = 0 ; i<= 3 ; i++ )
      record();

   return 0;
}

// A function that records how often it is called
void record(void)
{
   static int count = 0;
   cout << endl
        << "This is the " << ++count;
   if( (count>3) && (count<21) )                    // All this....
      cout <<"th";
   else
      switch(count%10)                              // is just to get...
      {
         case 1: cout << "st";
                 break;
         case 2: cout << "nd";
                 break;
         case 3: cout << "rd";
                 break;
         default: cout << "th";                     // the right ending for...
      }                                             // 1st, 2nd, 3rd, 4th, etc.
   cout << " time I have been called";
   return;
}
```

How It Works

Our function here serves only to record the fact that it was called. If you compile and execute it you will get this output:

```
This is the 1st time I have been called
This is the 2nd time I have been called
This is the 3rd time I have been called
This is the 4th time I have been called
This is the 5th time I have been called
```

The **static** variable **count** is initialized with 0, and is incremented in the first output statement in the function. Because the increment operation is prefix, the incremented value is displayed by the output statement, and it will be 1 on the first call, 2 on the second, and so on. Because the variable **count** is **static**, it continues to exist and retain its value from one call of the function to the next.

The remainder of the function is all concerned with working out when `"st"`, `"nd"`, `"rd"`, or `"th"` should be appended to the value of `count` that is displayed. It's surprisingly irregular. (I guess 101 should be 101st rather than 101th, shouldn't it?)

> Note the `return` statement. Because the return type of the function is `void`, to include a value would be an error. You don't actually need to put a `return` statement in this particular case. Running off the closing brace for the body of the function is equivalent to the `return` statement without a value, so the program will compile and run without error without the `return`. However, I prefer to include the `return` anyway, as at least it confirms you didn't just forget to put it in.

Recursive Function Calls

When a function contains a call to itself, it is referred to as a **recursive function**. A recursive function call can also be indirect, where a function `fun1` calls a function `fun2`, which in turn calls `fun1`.

Recursion may seem to be a recipe for an infinite loop, and if you are not careful it certainly can be. An infinite loop will lock up your machine and require *Ctrl-Alt-Del*, which is always a nuisance. A prerequisite for avoiding an infinite loop is that the function contains some means of stopping the process. Unless you have come across the technique before, the sort of things to which recursion may be applied may not be obvious. There are in physics and mathematics many things which can be thought of as involving recursion. A simple example is the factorial of an integer which for a given integer N, is the product 1x2x3...xN. This is very often the example given to show recursion in operation. However, we shall take something even simpler.

Try It Out - A Recursive Function

Earlier we produced a function to compute the integral power of a value, that is to compute x^n. This is equivalent to x multiplied by itself *n* times. We can implement this as a recursive function as an elementary illustration of recursion in action.

Try it Out!

```
// EX5-12.CPP
// A recursive version of x to the power n
#include <iostream.h>
#include <stdlib.h>                         // This for the exit() function

double power( double x, int n );        // Function prototype

int main(void)
{
    int index = 3;              // Raise to this power
    double x = 3.0;             // Different x from that in function power
    double y = 0.0;

    y = power( 5.0, 3 );                // Passing constants as arguments
    cout << endl
        << "5.0 cubed = " << y;

    cout << endl
        << "3.0 cubed = "
        << power( 3.0, index ); // Outputting return value

    x = power( x, power( 2.0, 2.0 ) );  // Using a function as an argument
    cout << endl                        // with auto conversion of 2nd parameter
        << "x = " << x;

    return 0;
}
// Recursive function to compute integral powers of a double value
// First argument is value, second argument is power index
double power( double x, int n )
{
    if(n<0)
    {
        cout << endl
            << "Negative index, program terminated.";
        exit(1);
    }
    switch(n)
    {
        case 0: return 1.0;

        case 1: return x;

        default: return x*power( x, n-1 );
    }
}
```

The function **main()** is exactly the same as the previous version so the output is also the same:

```
5.0 cubed = 125
3.0 cubed = 27
x = 81
```

We have added the **#include** statement for **STDLIB.H** because we use the **exit()** function in our revised function **power()**. Let's now look at how the function works.

How It Works

We only intend to support positive powers of **x**, so the first action is to check that the value for the power that **x** is to be raised to, **n**, is not negative. With a recursive implementation this is essential, otherwise we could get an infinite loop because of the way the rest of the function is written. The **switch** statement provides for the value 1.0 being returned if **n** is zero, and the value of **x** being returned if **n** has the value 1. In all other cases it returns the result of the expression appearing in the default option of the switch, **x*power(x, n-1)**. This causes a further call of the function **power()** with the index value reduced by 1. Because the statements for each case in the switch are **return** statements, there is no need to put a **break** statement after the statement for each case. More than that, if you do so the compiler will give you an error message since it is evident that these **break** statements can never be executed.

Clearly, within the function **power()**, if the value of **n-1** is greater than 1, a further call of the function **power()** will occur. In fact, for a given value of **n** greater than 1, the function will call itself **n-1** times. The mechanism is illustrated in the figure on the next page, assuming the value 5 for the index value.

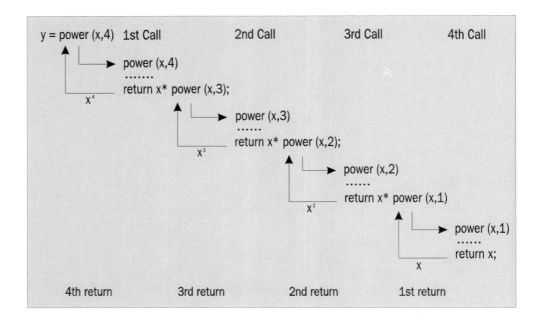

Using Recursion

Unless you have a problem which particularly lends itself to using recursive functions, or if you have no obvious alternative, it is generally better to use an alternative approach such as a loop. This will be much more efficient than using recursive function calls. Think about what happens with our last example to evaluate a simple product, `x*x*...x n` times. On each call, the compiler will generate copies of the two arguments to the function, and it also has to keep track of the location to return to when each `return` is executed. It will also be necessary to arrange to save the contents of various registers in your computer so that they can be used within the function `power()`, and of course these will need to be restored to their original state at each return from the function. With a quite modest depth of recursive call, the overhead can be considerably greater than that when using a loop.

This is not to say you should never use recursion. Where the problem suggests the use of recursive function calls as a solution, the technique can be immensely powerful, and it can greatly simplify the code. We will see an example where this is the case in the following chapter.

Summary

In this chapter you have learned about the basics of program structure. You should have a good grasp of how functions are defined, how data can be passed to a function, and how results are returned to a calling program. Functions are fundamental to programming in C++, so everything we do from here on will involve using multiple functions in a program. The key points you should keep in mind about writing your own functions are these:

▶ Functions should be compact units of code with a well-defined purpose. A typical program will consist of a large number of small functions, rather than a small number of large functions.

▶ Always provide a function prototype for each function defined in your program.

▶ Passing values to a function using a reference can avoid the copying implicit in the call-by-value transfer of arguments. Parameters which are not modified in a function should be specified as **const**.

▶ When returning a reference or a pointer from a function, ensure that the object being returned has the correct scope. Never return a pointer or a reference to an object which is local to a function.

The use of references as arguments is a very important concept, so make sure you are confident about using them. We will see a lot more about references as arguments to functions when we look into object-oriented programming.

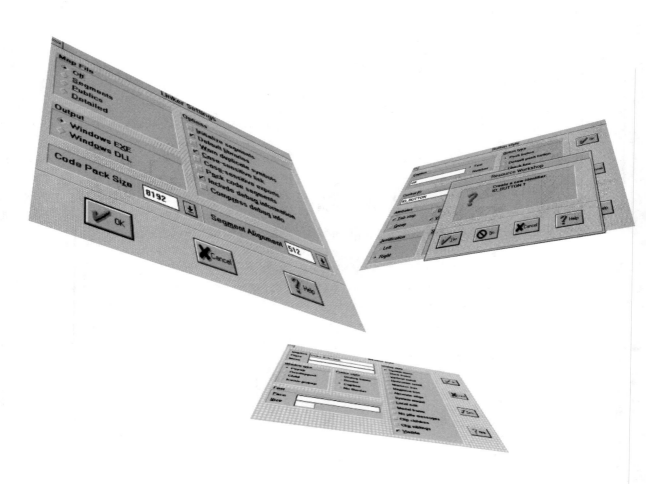

More About Program Structure

In the previous chapter you learned about the basics of defining functions, the various ways in which data can be passed to a function and results returned to a calling program.

In this chapter we will cover the various uses of functions, including:

- What is a pointer to a function
- How to define and use pointers to functions
- How to write a function to manage dynamic memory allocation errors
- How to define and use arrays of pointers to functions
- How to write multiple functions with a single name to handle different kinds of data automatically
- How to write a substantial program example using several functions

Pointers to Functions

A pointer stores an address value which up to now has been the address of another variable with the same basic type as the pointer. This has provided considerable flexibility in allowing us to use different variables at different times through a single pointer. A pointer can also point to the address of a function. This enables you to call a function through a pointer, and the specific function that will be called will be the function that was last assigned to the pointer.

A pointer to a function obviously must contain the address of the function to which it points, but more information is necessary if it is to work properly. It has to maintain information about the parameter list for the function it points to, as well as the return type. Therefore, when we declare a pointer to a function the parameter types and the return type of the functions it can point to have to be specified in addition to the name of the pointer.

Declaring Pointers to Functions

Let's declare a pointer **pfun** that can point to functions that take two arguments of type **char*** and **int**, and will return a value of type **double**. The declaration would be as follows:

```
    double (*pfun)(char*, int);          // Pointer to function declaration
```

This may look a little weird at first because of all the parentheses. The parentheses around the pointer name, **pfun**, and the asterisk are necessary since without them it would be a function declaration rather than a pointer declaration. In this case, it would look like this:

```
    double *pfun(char*, int); // Prototype for a function
                              // returning type double*
```

which is clearly not what we want at the moment.

The general form of a declaration of a pointer to a function is given here:

```
    return_type  (*pointer_name)(list_of_parameter_types);
```

The pointer can only point to functions with the specified `return_type` *and* `list_of_parameter_types` *in the declaration.*

This shows that the declaration breaks down into three components:

▶ The return type of the functions that can be pointed to

▶ The pointer name preceded by an asterisk to indicate it is a pointer

▶ The parameter types of the functions that can be pointed to

If you attempt to assign a function to a pointer that does not conform to the types in the pointer declaration, you will get an error message from the compiler.

You can initialize a pointer to a function with the name of a function within the declaration of the pointer. This is what it might look like:

```
long sum( long num1, long num2); // Function prototype
long (*pfun)(long, long) = sum;  // Pointer to function pointing to sum()
```

Here, the pointer can be set to point to any function that accepts two arguments of type `long`, and also returns a value of type `long`.

Of course, you can also initialize a pointer to a function with an assignment statement. Assuming the pointer `pfun` has been declared as above, we could set the value of the pointer with these statements:

```
long product(long, long);        // Function prototype
...
pfun = product;                  // Set pointer to function product()
```

As with pointers to variables, you must ensure that a pointer to a function is initialized before you use it to call a function. Without initialization, catastrophic failure of your program is guaranteed.

Try It Out - Pointers to Functions

To get a proper feel for these new-fangled pointers let's try one out in a program.

```cpp
// EX6-01.CPP
// Exercising pointers to functions
#include <iostream.h>

long sum(long a, long b);                // Function prototype
long product(long a, long b);            // Function prototype

int main(void)
{
   long (*pdo_it)(long, long);           // Pointer to function declaration

   pdo_it = product;
   cout << endl
        << "3*5 = " << pdo_it(3, 5);     // Call product thru a pointer

   pdo_it = sum;                         // Reassign pointer to sum()
   cout << endl
        << "3*(4+5) + 6 = "
        << pdo_it(product(3, pdo_it(4, 5)), 6); // Call thru a pointer
                                                // twice

   return 0;
}

// Function to multiply two values
long product(long a, long b)
{
   return a*b;
}

// Function to add two values
long sum(long a, long b)
{
   return a+b;
}
```

How It Works

This is hardly a useful program, but it does show very simply how a pointer to a function is declared, assigned a value, and subsequently used to call a function.

After the usual preamble, we declare a pointer to a function, **pdo_it**, which can point to either of the other two functions we have defined, **sum()** and

product(). The pointer is given the address of the function **product()** in this assignment statement:

```
pdo_it = product;
```

The name of the function is used in a parallel way to that of an array name when initializing an ordinary pointer. No parentheses or other adornments are required. The function name is automatically converted to an address which is stored in the pointer.

The function **product()** is then called indirectly through the pointer **pdo_it** in the output statement. The name of the pointer is used just as if it were a function name, and it is followed by the arguments between parentheses exactly as they would appear if the original function name were being used directly.

Just to show we can do it, the pointer is then changed to point to the function **sum()**. We then use it again in an incredibly convoluted expression to do some simple arithmetic. This shows that a pointer to a function can be used in exactly the same way as a function. The sequence of actions in the expression is shown below.

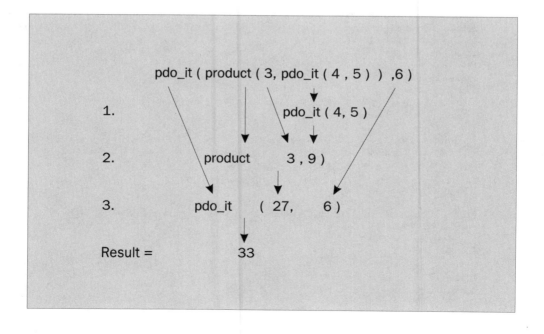

A Pointer to a Function as an Argument

Since a pointer to a function is a perfectly reasonable type, a function can also have an argument that is a pointer to a function. The function can then call the function pointed to by the argument. At different times, the function can be called with an argument that points to different functions. This allows the particular function that is to be called from inside a function to be determined in the calling program. You can pass a function explicitly as an argument in this case.

Try It Out - Passing a Function Pointer

We can look at this with an example. Suppose we need a function that will process an array of numbers by producing the sum of the squares of each of the numbers on some occasions, and the sum of the cubes on other occasions. One way of achieving this is using a pointer to a function as an argument.

```cpp
//EX6-02.CPP
// A pointer to a function as an argument
#include <iostream.h>

// Function prototypes
double squared(double);
double cubed(double);
double sumarray(double array[], int len, double (*pfun)(double));

int main(void)
{
    double array[] = { 1.5, 2.5, 3.5, 4.5, 5.5, 6.5, 7.5 };
    int len = sizeof array/sizeof array[0];

    cout << endl
        << "Sum of squares = "
        << sumarray(array,len,squared);

    cout << endl
        << "Sum of cubes = "
        << sumarray(array,len,cubed);

    return 0;
}

// Function for a square of a value
double squared( double x)
```

```
{
   return x*x;
}

// Function for a cube of a value
double cubed( double x)
{
   return x*x*x;
}

// Function to sum functions of array elements
double sumarray(double array[], int len, double (*pfun)(double))
{
   double total = 0.0;        // Accumulate total in here

   for(int i=0 ; i<len ; i++)
      total +=pfun(array[i]);

   return total;
}
```

How It Works

The first statement of interest is the prototype for the function **sumarray()**. Its third parameter is a pointer to a function which has a parameter of type **double**, and returns a value of type **double**. We call this function twice in **main()**, the first time with **squared** as the third argument, and the second time using **cubed**. In each case, the address corresponding to the function name used as an argument will be substituted for the function pointer in the function **sumarray()**, so the appropriate function will be called within the **for** loop.

There are obviously easier ways of achieving what this example does. But using a pointer to a function provides you with a lot of generality. You could pass any function you care to define to the function **sumarray()**, as long as it takes one **double** argument and returns a value of type **double**.

The example will generate this output:

```
Sum of squares = 169.75
Sum of cubes = 1015.875
```

Writing a Function to Handle Memory Allocation Errors

When we have used the operator **new**, we have had to test the value of the pointer returned for null, since **new** returns null if the memory was not allocated. This can be a bit tedious with an **if** statement after every use of **new**, and if you have a lot of dynamic memory allocation in your program it can add quite a few statements to the overall program size. There is an alternative to this which makes use of a pointer to a function.

TCW supplies a function called **set_new_handler()** which accepts a pointer to a function as an argument. The pointer argument should point to a function that you supply which handles the problem of the operator **new** not being able to allocate memory. This is how the function gets its name. The function that you write will be called if **new** fails to allocate the memory requested. Once you have called the function **set_new_handler()** with a pointer to your function as an argument, the problem of dealing with the failure of **new** to work properly is fixed for the entire program.

Try It Out - Real Use of Function Pointers

We can demonstrate this with an example:

```
// EX6-03.CPP
// Using your own error handler for new
#include <iostream.h>              // For stream I/O
#include <stdlib.h>                // For the exit() function
#include <new.h>                   // For the set_new_handler() function

void mem_error(void);    //Prototype of function to handle error from new
int main(void)
{
   double* pmem=0;                 // Pointer to memory allocated
   set_new_handler( mem_error );   // Operator new to call our function

   for( int i=0 ; i<1000 ; i++ )
   {
      pmem = new double[4096];     // Request 32K bytes
      cout << endl
           << i << "th call to new."
           <<"Allocated total of " << 32*i << "K bytes";
   }
   delete[] pmem;                  // So the compiler doesn't complain
```

```
    return 0;
}

// Function to handle out of memory conditions
void mem_error(void)
{
    cout << endl
         << "Out of memory";
    exit(1);
}
```

How It Works

If you are lucky enough to have more than 32 megabytes of memory on your computer, this program may not run out of memory. It also can cause some strange effects, because windows sometimes is not happy if you use all of the available memory, so you run this example at your own risk. On my machine, I have to restart Windows after running it.

We have three include statements for the reasons given in the comments, followed by the prototype for our function which is going to handle out of memory conditions. All the function does is display a message and call **exit()** to end the program. In **main()** we set up our function by a call to the function **set_new_handler()** with the name of our function as an argument. This will be passed as a pointer to function. We then repeatedly allocate memory in the **for** loop, 32K bytes at a time, and display a message about how many times we have invoked **new** and how much memory has been allocated. Sooner or later we should run out, and at this point we will see a message from our function handling this condition. The **delete[]** and the **return** statements will never be executed, but the compiler doesn't know that, and will generate error messages without them.

Implementing your own function to handle out of memory conditions removes the need to test for null each time you request some memory be allocated. In future examples we will assume that we will work this way, so we won't clutter up the code with tests for a null pointer return from **new**, but don't forget that you should do one or the other.

Arrays of Pointers to Functions

As with regular pointers you can declare an array of pointers to functions. You can also initialize them in the declaration. An example of declaring an array of pointers would be:

```
double sum( double, double);          // Function prototype
double product( double, double);      // Function prototype
double difference( double, double);   // Function prototype
double (*pfun[3])(double,double) =
         { sum, product, difference }; // Array of function pointers
```

Each of the elements in the array are initialized by the corresponding function address appearing in the initializing list between braces. To call the function **product()** using the second element of the pointer array, you would write:

```
pfun[1](2.5, 3.5);
```

The square brackets to select the function pointer array element appear immediately after the array name and before the arguments to the function being called. Of course, you place a function call through an element of a function pointer array in any appropriate expression that the original function might legitimately appear in, and the index value selecting the pointer can be any expression producing a valid index value.

Initializing Function Parameters

You can initialize function parameters in the declaration of a function. For example, we could write a function to display a message. Here is the definition of the function:

```
void showit(char* message)
{
   cout << endl
        << message;
   return;
}
```

We can initialize the parameter to this function by specifying the initializing value in the function prototype as follows:

```
void showit(char* = "Something is wrong."); // Initialized function
                                            // declaration
```

Here the parameter message is initialized with the string shown. But why would you want to do this? After all, the argument specified when the function is called will replace the value here. That is exactly the point. If you initialize a parameter to a function in the prototype, you can leave that argument out when you call the function.

Try It Out - Omitting Function Arguments

Leaving out the function argument when you call the function will execute it with the default value, and if you supply the argument it will replace the default value. We can use the previous function to output a variety of messages.

```
//EX6-04.CPP
// Omitting function arguments
#include <iostream.h>

void showit(char* = "Something is wrong.");

int main(void)
{
   char* mymess = "The end of the world is nigh.";

   showit();                                // Display the basic message
   showit("Something is terribly wrong!");  // Display an alternative
   showit();                                // Display the default again
   showit(mymess);                          // Display a predefined message

   return 0;
}

void showit(char* message)
{
   cout << endl
        << message;
   return;
}
```

How It Works

If you execute this example it will produce this output:

```
Something is wrong.
Something is terribly wrong!
Something is wrong.
The end of the world is nigh.
```

As you can see, we get the default message specified in the function prototype whenever the argument is left out. Otherwise, the function behaves normally.

If you have a function with several arguments, you can provide initial values for as many of them as you like. If you want to omit more than one argument to take advantage of a default value, only the right-most arguments can be omitted. For example, if you have the following function:

```
int do_it( long arg1=10, long arg2=20, long arg3=30, long arg4=40);
```

then if you want to omit one argument in a call of this function you can only omit the last one, **arg4**, if you want to omit **arg3** you must also omit **arg4**, if you omit **arg2** then **arg3** and **arg4** must be omitted, and if you want to use the default value for **arg1**, you have to omit all of the arguments in the function call.

You can conclude from this that you need to put the arguments for which you put default values in the function prototype together in sequence at the end of the parameter list, with the most likely argument to be omitted appearing last.

Function Overloading

Suppose we have a function which generates the maximum value of an array of values of type **double**:

```
// Function to generate the maximum value in an array of type double
double maxdouble(double array[], int len)
{
   double max = array[0];

   for( int i=1 ; i<len ; i++ )
      if(max<array[i])
         max = array[i];

   return max;
}
```

We now want to create a function which produces the maximum value from an array of type **long**, so we write another function very similar to the first, with this prototype:

```
long maxlong(long array[], int len);
```

We now have to be careful to choose the appropriate function name to match the particular task in hand. We may also need the same function for other types of argument. It seems a pity that we have to keep inventing new names. Ideally, we would want to use the function **max()** for whatever type, and have the appropriate version executed.

The mechanism which enables you to do this is called **function overloading**.

What is Function Overloading?

Function overloading allows you to use the same name in different functions, and have the compiler choose the correct version for the job in each instance. There has to be a clear method for the compiler to decide which function is to be called in any particular instance, and the key to this being done is the parameter list. A series of functions with the same name but differentiated by their parameter lists is a set of overloaded functions. So following on from our **max()** function example, we could have overloaded functions with the following prototypes:

```
int max(int array[], int len);        // Prototypes for
long max(long array[], int len);      // a set of overloaded
double max(double array[], int len);  // functions
```

Each of the functions must have a different parameter list. Note that a different return type does not distinguish a function adequately. You can't add the function

```
double max(long array[], int len);
```

to the above set . It would cause the compiler to complain and the program containing these would not compile. This may seem slightly unreasonable, until you remember that you can write statements such as this:

```
long numbers[] = {1,2,3,3,6,7,11,50,40};
int len = sizeof numbers/sizeof number[0];
...
max( numbers, len);
```

If the return type were permitted as a distinguishing feature, then the version of **max()** taking a **long** array as an argument and returning a **double** value would be allowed, along with the original three. In the instance of the code above, the compiler would be unable to decide whether to choose the version with a **long** return type or a **double** return type.

Try It Out - Using Overloaded Functions

We can exercise the overloading capability with the function **max()** we have already defined. We can include the three versions for **int**, **long** and **double** arrays.

Try it Out!

```
// EX6-05.CPP
// Using overloaded functions
#include <iostream.h>

int max(int array[], int len);          // Prototypes for
long max(long array[], int len);         // a set of overloaded
double max(double array[], int len);     // functions

int main(void)
{
   int small[] = { 1,24,34,22};
   long medium[] = { 23,245,123,1,234,2345};
   double large[] = { 23.0,1.4,2.456,345.5,12.0, 21.0};
   int lensmall = sizeof small/sizeof small[0];
   int lenmedium = sizeof medium/sizeof medium[0];
   int lenlarge = sizeof large/sizeof large[0];

   cout << endl << max( small, lensmall);
   cout << endl << max( medium, lenmedium);
   cout << endl << max( large, lenlarge);

   return 0;
}

// Maximum of ints
int max( int x[], int len )
{
   int max = x[0];
   for( int i=1 ; i<len ; i++ )
      if( max<x[i] )
         max = x[i];
   return max;
}

// Maximum of longs
long max( long x[], int len )
{
   long max = x[0];
   for(int i=1 ; i<len ; i++ )
      if( max<x[i] )
         max = x[i];
   return max;
}

// Maximum of doubles
double max(double x[], int len )
{
 double max = x[0];
   for(int i=1 ; i<len ; i++ )
      if( max<x[i] )
         max = x[i];
   return max;
}
```

How It Works

We have three prototypes for the three overloaded versions of the function `max()`. The appropriate version of the function `max()` is selected by the compiler in each of the three output statements based on the argument list types. The example works as expected and produces this output:

```
34
2345
345.5
```

Each function in a set of functions is sometimes said to have a unique **signature**, determined by the parameter list.

When to Overload Functions

Function overloading provides you with the means of ensuring that a function name is a descriptor for the function being performed, and is not confused by extraneous information such as the type of data being processed. This is akin to what happens with basic operations in C++. To add two numbers you use the same operator regardless of the type of the operands. Our overloaded function `max()` has the same name regardless of the type of data being processed. This helps make the code more readable and eases the use of such functions.

The intent of function overloading is clear: to enable the same operation to be performed with different operands using a single function name. So whenever you have a series of functions that do essentially the same thing, but with different types of arguments, you should overload them and use a common function name.

An Example Using Functions

We have covered a lot of ground in C++ up to now, and a lot on functions in this chapter. After wading through a varied menu of language capabilities, it's not always easy to see how they relate to one another. Now would be a good time to see how some of this goes together to produce something with more meat than a simple demonstration program.

Let's work through a more realistic example to see how a problem can be broken down into functions. The process will involve defining the problem to be solved, analyzing the problem to see how it can be implemented in C++, and finally writing the code.

Implementing a Calculator

Suppose we need a program that will act as a calculator, not one of these fancy devices with lots of buttons and gizmos, but one where we can enter a calculation from the keyboard as a single arithmetic expression, and have the answer displayed immediately. An example of the sort of thing we might enter is

$$2*3.14159*12.6*12.6/2 \ + \ 25.2*25.2$$

We won't allow parentheses in the expression, so as not to complicate things unduly, and the whole computation must be entered in a single line. We *will* allow blanks to be placed anywhere, however, to allow the user to make the input look attractive. The expression entered may contain the operators multiply, divide, add, and subtract represented by *, /, +, and - respectively, and should be evaluated with normal arithmetic rules, so that multiply and divide take precedence over add and subtract.

The program should allow as many successive calculations to be performed as required, and should terminate if an empty line is entered. It should also have helpful and friendly error messages.

Analyzing the Problem

A good place to start is with the input. The program will read in an arithmetic expression of any length on a single line, which can be any construction within the terms given. Since nothing is fixed about the elements making up the expression, we will have to read it as a string of characters, and then work out within the program how it's made up. We can decide arbitrarily that we will handle a string of up to 80 characters, so we could store it in an array declared within these statements:

```
const int MAX = 80;        // Maximum expression length including '\0'
char buffer[MAX];          // Input area for expression to be evaluated
```

To change the maximum length of the string processed by the program, we will only need to alter the initial value of **MAX**.

We need to determine the basic structure of the information in the input string, so let's look at it top-down.

The first thing to do is make sure it is as uncluttered as possible, so we will get rid of all the blanks in the input string before we start analyzing it. The function we will use to do this we can call `eatspaces()`. This can work by copying the input buffer to itself using two indexes to the buffer, `i` and `j`, corresponding to the destination element and source element in the buffer, respectively. As we progress through the elements, each time we copy a blank we don't increment `i`, so it gets overwritten by the next element. We can illustrate the logic of this in the following figure:

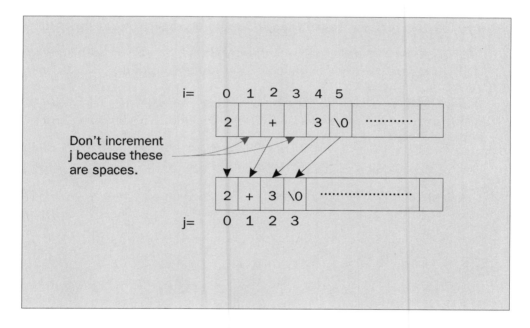

The next operation we can define evaluates the expression, so we will define the function `expr()`, which will return the value of the whole expression in the input buffer. To decide what goes on inside the function, we need to look into the structure of the input in more detail. The add and subtract operators have the lowest precedence and so are evaluated last. We can envisage the string as one or more terms connected by 'add' operators which can be either the operator + or the operator -, so we can represent the general expression as follows:

```
expression:  term  addop  term  ...  addop  term
```

where the expression will contain at least one **term**, and can have an arbitrary number of following **addop term** combinations. In fact, after each **term**, there are three legal possibilities:

1   The next character is `'\0'` so we are at the end of the string.

2   The next character is `'-'`, in which case we should subtract the next term from the value accrued for the expression up to this point.

3   The next character is `'+'`, in which case we should add the value of the next **term** to the value of the expression accrued so far.

If anything else follows a **term** then the string is not what we expect, so we will display a message and exit from the program. The function **expr()** is illustrated below.

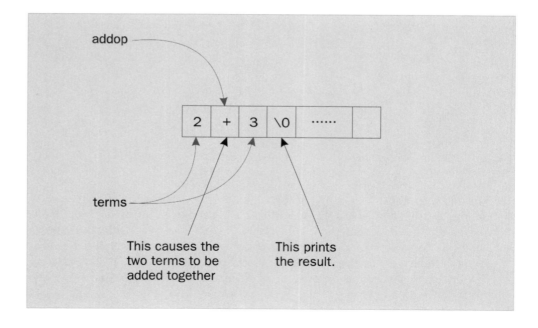

addop

2 + 3 \0 ......

terms

This causes the two terms to be added together

This prints the result.

The next thing we need to know about an input expression is the definition of a **term**. A **term** is simply a series of numbers that are connected by either the operator ***** or the operator **/**. Therefore, a **term** (in general) will look like this:

```
term:  number  multop  number  ...  multop  number
```

where by **multop** we mean either multiply or divide. What we need is a function **term()** to return the value of a **term**. This will need to progress through the string by first finding a number, and then looking for a **multop** followed by another number. If a character is found that is not a **multop**, then we will assume that it is an **addop** and return the value we have found up to that point.

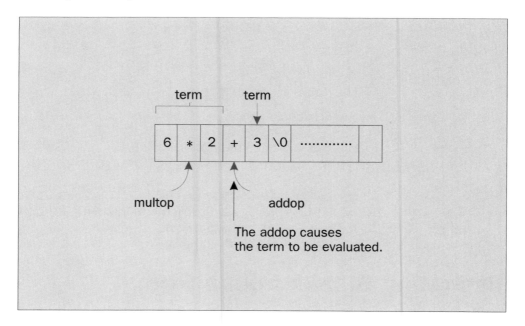

The last thing we need to understand before writing the program is what is a number. To avoid unnecessary complications, we will only allow a number to be unsigned. Therefore, a number consists of a series of digits that may be followed by a decimal point and some more digits. This is what we need to do to determine the value of a number: progress through the buffer finding digits, and if we find anything that isn't a digit we look for a decimal point. If it's not a decimal point, it's nothing to do with a number, so we return what we have got. If it is a decimal point, we look for more digits. As soon as we find anything that's not a digit, we have the complete number and we return that. We will creatively call the function to sort this out **number()**.

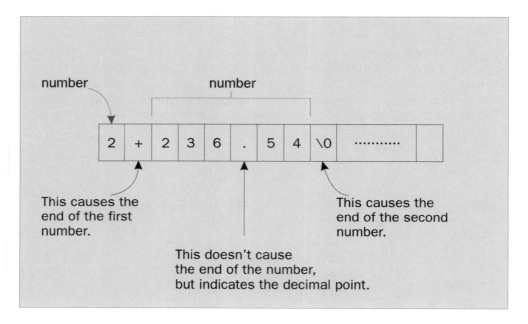

We now have enough understanding of the problem to write some code. We can work through the functions we need, then write a **main()** function to tie them all together. The first and perhaps easiest function to write is **eatspaces()**, which is going to eliminate the blanks from the input string.

Eliminating Blanks from a String

We can write the prototype for **eatspaces()** as follows:

```
void eatspaces(char *str); // Prototype of function to eliminate blanks
```

It doesn't need to return any value since the blanks can be eliminated from the string *in situ*, modifying the original string directly through the pointer provided as an argument. We can define the function as follows:

```
// Function to eliminate blanks from a string
void eatspaces(char* str)
```

```
{
   int i=0;          // 'Copy to' index to string
   int j=0;          // 'Copy from' index to string

   while( (*(str+i) = *(str+j++)) != '\0' )    // Loop while character
                                               // copied is not \0
      if(*(str+i) != ' ')                      // Increment i as long as
         i++;                                  // character is not a blank
   return;
}
```

How the Function Functions

All the action is in the **while** loop. The loop condition copies the string by moving the character at position **j** to the character at position **i**, and then increments **j** to the next character. If the character copied was **'\0'**, then we have reached the end of the string, and we are done.

The only action in the loop statement is to increment **i** to the next character if the last character copied was not a blank. If it *is* a blank, **i** will not be incremented and therefore the blank will be overwritten by the character copied on the next iteration.

That wasn't hard, was it? Next, we can try writing the function providing the result of evaluating the expression.

Evaluating an Expression

The function **expr()** needs to return the value of the expression specified in the string that is supplied as an argument, so we can write its prototype as follows:

```
double expr(char* str); // Prototype of function evaluating an expression
```

The function accepts a string as an argument and returns the result as type **double**.

We can now write the function:

```
// Function to evaluate an arithmetic expression
double expr(char* str)
{
   double value = 0;          // Store result here
```

```
int index = 0;               // Keeps track of current character position

value = term( str, index ); // Get first term

for(;;)                      // infinite loop, all exits inside
{
    switch( *(str+index++) ) // Choose action based on current character
    {
        case '\0':                       // We're at the end of the string
            return value;                // so return what we have got

        case '+':                        // + found so add in the
            value += term(str, index);   // next term
            break;

        case '-':                        // - found so subtract
            value -= term(str, index);   // the next term
            break;
        default:                         // If we reach here the string
            cout << endl                 // is junk
                << "Arrrgh!*#!! There's an error";
            exit(1);
    }
}
}
```

How the Function Functions

Considering this function is analyzing any arithmetic expression you care to throw at it, it's not a lot of code. We define a variable **index** of type **int**, which is intended to keep track of the current position in the string where we are working, and we initialize it to 0 which corresponds to the index position of the first character in the string. We also define a variable **value** of type **double** in which we will accumulate the value of the expression passed to the function in the **char** array **str**.

Since an expression must have at least one term, the first action in the function is to get the value of the first term by calling the function **term()** which we have yet to write. This actually places three requirements on the function **term()**:

1   It should accept a **char*** pointer and an **int** variable as parameters, the second being an index to the first character of the term in the string supplied.

2   It should update the index value passed to position it at the character following the last character of the term found.

3   It should return the value of the term as type `double`.

The rest of the program is an infinite `for` loop. Within the loop, the action is determined by a `switch` statement which is controlled by the current character in the string. If it is a `'+'`, we call the function `term()` to get the value of the next term in the expression and add it to the variable `value`. If it is a `'-'`, we subtract the value returned by `term()` from the variable value. If it is a `'\0'`, we are at the end of the string, so we return the current contents of the variable `value` to the calling program. If it is any other character, it shouldn't be there, so after remonstrating with the user we end the program!

If either a `'+'` or a `'-'` was found, the loop continues. Each call to `term()` will have moved the value of the variable `index` to the next character after the last term, which should be either another `'+'` or `'-'`, or the end of string character `'\0'`. Thus the function either terminates normally when `'\0'` is reached, or abnormally by calling `exit()`. We need to remember the `#include` for `STDLIB.H` to provide the prototype for the function `exit()` when we come to put the whole program together.

Getting the Value of a term

The function `term()` needs to return a `double` value, and receive two arguments, the string being analyzed and an index to the current position in the string. There are other ways of doing this, but this arrangement is quite straightforward. We can therefore write the prototype of the function `term()` as follows:

```
double term( char* str, int& index);      // Function analyzing a term
```

We have specified the second parameter as a reference. This is because we want the function to modify the value of the variable `index` in the calling program to position it at the character following the last character of the term found in the input string. We could return `index` as a value but then we would need to return the value of the term in some other way, and the arrangement we have chosen seems quite natural.

We can write the definition of the function **term()** as follows:

```
// Function to get the value of a term
double term( char* str, int& index )
{
   double value = 0;                    // Somewhere to accumulate the result

   value = number(str, index);          // Get the first number in the term

   while((*(str+index)=='*')||(*(str+index)=='/')) // Loop as long as we
   {                                                // have a good operator

      if( *(str+index)=='*')                   // If it's multiply,
         value *= number(str, ++index);        // multiply by next number

      if(*(str+index)=='/')                    // If it's divide,
         value /= number(str, ++index);        // divide by next number
   }
   return value;                        // We're finish so return what we've got
}
```

How the Function Functions

We first declare a local **double** variable value in which we will accumulate
the value of the current term. Since a term must contain at least one
number, the first action in the function is to obtain the value of the first
number by calling the function **number()**, and storing the result in the
variable **value**. We implicitly assume that the function **number()** will accept
the string and an index to the string as arguments, and will return the
value of the number found. Since the function **number()** must also update
the index to the string to the position after the number that was found, we
will again specify the second parameter as a reference when we come to
define the function.

The rest of the function is a **while** loop which continues as long as the next
character is '*' or '/'. Within the loop, if the character found at the
current position is '*', we increment the variable **index** to position it at the
beginning of the next number, call the function **number()** to get the value of
the next number, and then multiply the contents of the variable **value** by
the value returned. In a similar manner, if the current character is '/', we
increment the variable **index**, and divide the contents of **value** by the value
returned from **number()**. Since the function **number()** automatically alters
the value of the variable index to the character following the number found,
index is already set to select the next available character in the string on
the next iteration.

The loop terminates when a character other than a multiply or divide operator is found, whereupon the current value of the term accumulated in the variable **value** is returned to the calling program.

The last analytical function we require is **number()**, which needs to determine the numerical value of any number which appears in the string.

Analyzing a Number

Based on the way we have used the function **number()** within the function **term()**, we need to declare it with this prototype:

```
double number(char* str, int& index);  // Function to recognize a number
```

The specification of the second parameter as a reference will allow the function to update the argument in the calling program directly, which is what we require.

We can make use of a function provided in a standard C++ library here. The header file **CTYPE.H** provides declarations for a range of functions for testing single characters. These include these functions:

Function	Meaning
int isalpha(int c)	Returns True if the argument is alphabetic, False otherwise.
int isupper(int c)	Returns True if the argument is an upper case letter, False otherwise.
int islower(int c)	Returns True if the argument is a lower case letter, False otherwise.
int isdigit(int c)	Returns True if the argument is a digit, False otherwise.

*There are also a number of other functions provided by **CTYPE.H**, but we won't grind through all the detail. You can look them up if you are interested in TCW Help. Simply search for **CTYPE.H** and you will get a complete list, which you can then look up further if you so wish.*

We only need the last of the functions shown above in our program. Remember that **isdigit()** is testing for a character, such as the character '9' (ASCII character 57 in decimal notation) for instance, not a numeric 9, because the input is a string.

We can define the function **number()** as follows:

```
// Function to recognize a number in a string
double number(char* str, int& index)
{
   double value = 0.0;                       // Store the resulting value

   while(isdigit( *(str+index) ) )        // Loop accumulating leading digits
      value=10*value + (*(str+index++) - 48);

                                             // Not a digit when we get to here
   if(*(str+index)!='.')                    // so check for decimal point
      return value;                         // and if not, return value

   double factor = 1.0;                     // Factor for decimal places
   while(isdigit( *(str+(++index)) ) )   // Loop as long as we have digits
   {
      factor *= 0.1;                        // Decrease factor by factor of 10
      value=value + (*(str+index)-48)*factor; // Add decimal place
   }

   return value;                            // On loop exit we are done
}
```

How the Function Functions

We declare the local variable **value** as **double** which will hold the value of the number. We initialize it with 0.0 because we will add in the digit values as we go along.

As the number in the string is a series of digits as ASCII characters, the function will walk through the string accumulating the value of the number digit by digit, as we saw earlier in the logic diagram for this function. This will occur in two steps, accumulating digits before the decimal point, and then if we find a decimal point, accumulating the digits after it.

The first step is in the **while** loop that continues as long as the current character selected by the variable **index** is a digit. The value of the digit is extracted and added to the variable **value** in the loop statement:

```
value=10*value + (*(str+index++) - 48);
```

The way this is constructed might bear a little closer examination. A digit character will have an ASCII value between 48, corresponding to the digit 0, and 57 corresponding to the digit 9. Thus, if we subtract 48 from the ASCII code for a digit, we will convert it to its equivalent numeric value, which is the actual digit. We have put parentheses around the sub-expression `*(str+index++) - 48` to make it a little clearer what's going on. The contents of the variable **value** are multiplied by 10 in order to shift the value left one decimal place before adding in the digit, since we will find digits from left to right (that is, the most significant digit first). This process is illustrated below.

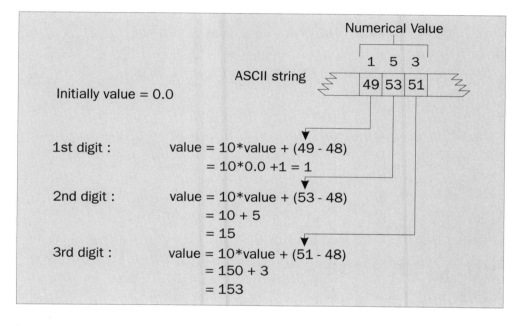

As soon as we come across something other than a digit, it is either a decimal point, or something else. If it is the latter, we have finished, so we return the current contents of the variable **value** to the calling program. If it is a decimal point, we accumulate the digits corresponding to the fractional part of the number in the second loop. In this loop we use the variable **factor**, which has the initial value 1.0, to set the decimal place for the current digit, and consequently it is multiplied by 0.1 for each digit found. Thus, the first digit after the decimal point will be multiplied by 0.1, the second by 0.01, the third by 0.001, and so on. This process is illustrated on the next page.

Initially: value = 153
        factor = 1.0

ASCII string

Numeric Value

1 5 3 . 5 8 6

| 49 | 53 | 51 | 46 | 53 | 56 | 54 |

After the decimal point:

1st digit: factor = factor*0.1
                    = 0.1
            value = value + factor*(53 - 48)
                    = 153 + 0.1*5
                    = 153.5

2nd digit: factor = factor*0.1
                    = 0.01
            value = value + factor*(56 - 48)
                    = 153.5 + 0.01*8
                    = 153.58

3rd digit: factor = factor*0.1
                    = 0.001
            value = value + factor*(54 - 48)
                    = 153.58 + 0.001*6
                    = 153.586

As soon as we find a non-digit character we are done, so after the second loop we return the value of the variable **value**.

We now have almost the whole thing. We just need a **main()** function to read the input and drive the process.

Putting the Program Together

We first ought to collect the **#include** statements together and assemble the function prototypes at the beginning of the program:

```
// EX6-06.CPP
// A program to implement a calculator

#include <iostream.h>                  // For stream input/output
#include <stdlib.h>                    // For the exit() function
#include <ctype.h>                     // For the isdigit() function

void eatspaces(char *str );            // Function to eliminate blanks
double expr(char* str);                // Function evaluating an expression
double term(char* str, int& index);    // Function analyzing a term
double number(char* str, int& index);  // Function to recognize a number

const int MAX = 80;          // Maximum expression length including '\0'
```

We have also defined a global variable **MAX** which is the maximum number of characters in the expression processed by the program including the termination null.

Now all we need to define is the function **main()** and our program is complete. It needs to read a string and exit if it is empty, otherwise call the function **expr()** to evaluate the input and display the result. This process should repeat indefinitely. That doesn't sound too difficult, so let's give it a try.

```
int main(void)
{
   char buffer[MAX];          // Input area for expression to be evaluated

   for(;;)
   {
       cin.getline(buffer, sizeof buffer);   // Read an input line
       eatspaces(buffer);                     // Remove blanks from input

       if(!buffer[0])                         // Empty line ends calculator
          return 0;

       cout << "\t= " << expr(buffer)         // Output value of expression
            << endl << endl;
   }
}
```

How the Function Functions

In **main()**, we set up the **char** array **buffer** to accept an expression up to 80 characters long (including the terminating null). The expression is read within the infinite **for** loop using the input function **getline()**, and after obtaining the input, blanks are eliminated from the string by calling the function **eatspaces()**.

The only other things the function **main()** provides for are within the loop. They are to check for an empty string which will consist of just the null character, **'\0'**, in which case the program ends, and to output the value of the string produced by the function **expr()**. The typical output from the program is shown on the next page.

```
┌─────────────────────────────────────────────────────────────┐
│ ─        (Inactive D:\WINWORD\BGTCPP\BOOKEX\EX6-06.EXE)    ▼ ▲ │
├─────────────────────────────────────────────────────────────┤
│2×3+4-0.35×6                                                 ↑ │
│       = 7.9                                                   │
│                                                               │
│2.5×3.5/1.4+7.8×.76/7                                          │
│         = 7.096857                                            │
│                                                               │
│1.0+2.5×3.4/1.175                                              │
│          = 8.234043                                           │
│                                                               │
│1/2+1/3+1/4+1/5+1/6                                            │
│         = 1.45                                                │
│                                                             ↓ │
├─────────────────────────────────────────────────────────────┤
│ ← │                                                       │ → │
└─────────────────────────────────────────────────────────────┘
```

As many calculations as you like can be entered and, when you are fed up with it, you just press *Enter* to end the program.

Extending the Program

It would be nice to be able to handle parentheses in an expression. It can't be that difficult, can it? Let's give it a try. We need to think about the relationship between something in parentheses which might appear in an expression, and the kind of expression analysis we have made so far. Let's look at an example of the kind of expression we want to handle:

$$2*(3+4)/6-(5+6)/(7+8)$$

The first thing to notice is that the expressions in parentheses always form part of a term in our original parlance. Whatever sort of computation you come up with, this is always true. In fact, if we could substitute the value of the expressions within parentheses back in the original string, we would have something that we can already deal with. This indicates a possible approach to handling parentheses. Why don't we treat an expression in parentheses as just another number, and modify the function `number()` to sort out the value of whatever appears between the parentheses?

That sounds like a good idea, but 'sorting out' the expression in parentheses requires thinking about - but not for very long as it happens. The clue is in our terminology. An **expression** appears within parentheses, a minute replica of a full-blown expression, and we already have a function **expr()** which will return the value of an expression. All we need to do is to get the function **number()** to work out what the contents of the parentheses are, and extract those from the string to be passed to the function **expr()**, so recursion really simplifies the problem. What's more, we don't need to worry about nested parentheses. Since any set of parentheses will contain what we have defined as an expression, they will be taken care of automatically. Recursion wins again.

Let's have a stab at rewriting the function **number()** to recognize an expression between parentheses.

```
// Function to recognize an expression in parentheses
// or a number in a string
double number(char* str, int& index)
{
   double value = 0.0;                     // Store the resulting value

   if(*(str+index) == '(' )                // Start of parentheses
   {
      char* psubstr = 0;                    // Pointer for sub-string
      psubstr = extract( str, ++index );    // Extract sub-string in brackets
      value = expr(psubstr);                // Get the value of the sub-string
      delete[]psubstr;                      // Clean up the free store
      return value;                         // Return sub-string value
   }

   while(isdigit( *(str+index) ) )          // Loop accumulating leading digits
      value=10*value + (*(str+index++) - 48);
                                            // Not a digit when we get to here
   if(*(str+index)!='.')                    // so check for decimal point
      return value;                         // and if not, return value

   double factor = 1.0;                     // Factor for decimal places
   while(isdigit( *(str+(++index) ) ) )     // Loop as long as we have digits
   {
      factor *= 0.1;                        // Decrease factor by factor of 10
      value=value + (*(str+index)-48)*factor; // Add decimal place
   }

   return value;                            // On loop exit we are done
}
```

How the Function Functions

Look how little has changed to support parentheses. I suppose it is a bit of a cheat, since we use a function we haven't written yet. But for one extra function you get as many levels of nested parentheses. This really is icing on the cake. All down to the magic of recursion!

The first thing the function `number()` now does is to test for a left parenthesis. If it finds one it calls another function, `extract()`, to extract the sub-string between the parentheses from the original string. The address of this new sub-string is stored in the pointer `psubstr` so we then apply the function `expr()` to the sub-string by passing this pointer as an argument. The result is stored in `value`, and after releasing the memory allocated on the free store in the function `extract()` (as we will eventually implement it), we return the value obtained for the sub-string as though it were a regular number. Of course, if there is no left parenthesis to start with, the function `number()` continues exactly as before.

We now need to write the function `extract()`. It's not difficult - it's also not trivial. The main complication derives from the fact that the expression within parentheses may also contain other sets of parentheses, so we can't just go looking for the first right parenthesis we can find. We need to watch out for more left parentheses as well, and for every one we find, ignore the corresponding right parenthesis. We can do this by maintaining a count of left parentheses as we go along, adding 1 to the count for each left parenthesis we find, and if the count is not zero, subtracting one for each right parenthesis. Of course, if the count is zero, and we find a right parenthesis, then we are at the end of the sub-string. The mechanism is illustrated in the following figure:

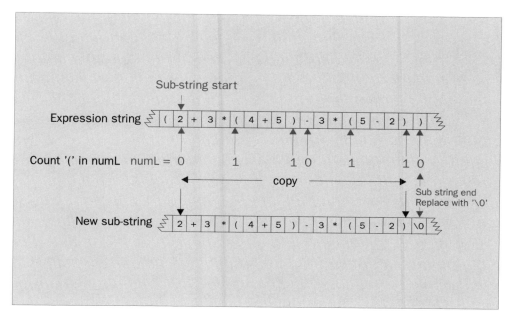

The function **extract()** will also need to allocate memory for the sub-string and return a pointer to it. Of course, the index to the current position in the original string will need to end up selecting the character following the sub-string, so the parameter for that will need to be specified as a reference. The prototype of **extract()** will therefore be as follows:

```
char* extract(char* str, int& index); // Function to extract a sub-string
```

We can now have a shot at the definition of the function.

```
// Function to extract a sub-string between parentheses
char* extract( char* str, int& index)
{
   char buffer[MAX];          // Temporary space for sub-string
   char* pstr=0;              // Pointer to new string for return
   int numL = 0;              // Count of left parentheses found
   int bufindex = index;      // Save starting value for index

   do
   {
     buffer[index-bufindex] = *(str+index) ;
     switch( buffer[index-bufindex])
     {
```

```
        case ')':
          if(numL==0)
          {
            buffer[index-bufindex] = '\0';    // Replace ')' with '\0'
            ++index;
            pstr = new char[index-bufindex];
            if(!pstr)
            {
               cout << "Memory allocation failed, program terminated.";
               exit(1);
            }
            strcpy(pstr,buffer);      // Copy sub-string to new memory
            return pstr;              // Return sub-string in new memory
          }
          else
            numL--;                   // Reduce count of '(' to be matched
          break;

        case '(':
          numL++;                     // Increase count of '(' to be matched
          break;
      }
   }while(*(str+index++) != '\0'); // Loop but don't overrun end of string

   cout << "Ran off the end of the expression, must be bad input.";
   exit(1);
   return pstr;
}
```

How the Function Functions

We declare a **char** array to hold the sub-string temporarily. We don't know how long the sub-string will be, but it can't be more than **MAX** characters. We can't return the address of **buffer** to the calling function because it is local and will be destroyed on exit from the function. We will therefore need to allocate some memory on the free store when we know how long the string is, so we declare a pointer to **char**, **psubstr**, which we will return by value when we have the sub-string safe and sound in the free store memory.

We also declare a counter **numL**, to keep track of left parentheses in the sub-string (as we discussed earlier). The initial value of **index** (when the function begins execution) is stored in the variable **bufindex**. This will be used in combination with incremented values of **index** to index the array **buffer**.

The executable part of the function is basically one big **do-while** loop. Within the loop, the sub-string is copied from **str** to **buffer** one character at each iteration, with a check for left or right parentheses each cycle. If a left parenthesis is found, **numL** in incremented, and if a right parenthesis is found and **numL** is non-zero, it is decremented. When we find a right parenthesis and **numL** is zero, we have found the end of the sub-string. The **')'** in the sub-string in **buffer** is then replaced by **'\0'**, and sufficient memory is obtained on the free store to hold the sub-string. The sub-string in **buffer** is then copied to the memory obtained through the operator **new** by using the function **strcpy()**, which is defined in the header file **STRING.H**. This function copies the string specified by the second argument, **buffer**, to the address specified by the first argument, **pstr**.

If we fall through the bottom of the loop, it means that we hit the null at the end of the expression in **str** without finding the complementary right bracket, so we display a message and terminate the program.

Running the Modified Program

After replacing the function **number()** in the old version of the program, adding the **#include** statement for **STRING.H**, and incorporating the prototype and the definition for the new function, **extract()**, we have just written, you are ready to roll with an all-singing, all-dancing calculator. If you have assembled all that without error, you will get output something like that shown below.

```
(Inactive D:\WINWORD\BGTCPPW\BOOKEX\EX6-18.EXE)
2×(3+4×(3.25-1.5/2)) - (2.3-0.7)×1.5
        = 23.6

(1/2 + 1/3)×(1/4 + 1/5)×(1/6 +1/7)
        = 0.116071

(1/2+1/3)/(1/3+1/4) + (1/3 + 1/4)/(1/5 + 1/6)
        = 3.019481

(1/(2+3) + 2/(3+4))×(3/(4+5) - 4/(5_6))

Arrrgh!×#!! There's an error
```

The error in the last output is the underline instead of the minus sign in the expression. As you can see, we get nested parentheses to any depth with a relatively simple extension of the program, all due to the amazing power of recursion. The complete version of this program appears on the disk as **EX6-07.CPP**.

Summary

You now have a reasonably comprehensive knowledge of writing and using functions. You have used a pointer to a function in a practical context for handling out of memory conditions in the free store, and you have used overloading to implement a set of functions providing the same operation with different types of parameters. We will see more of overloading functions in the following chapters.

You have also worked through the calculator example which is implemented using several functions. But remember that all the uses of functions up to now have been in the context of a traditional procedural approach to programming. When we come to look at object-oriented programming, we will still use functions extensively, but with a very different approach to program structure, and the design of a solution to a problem.

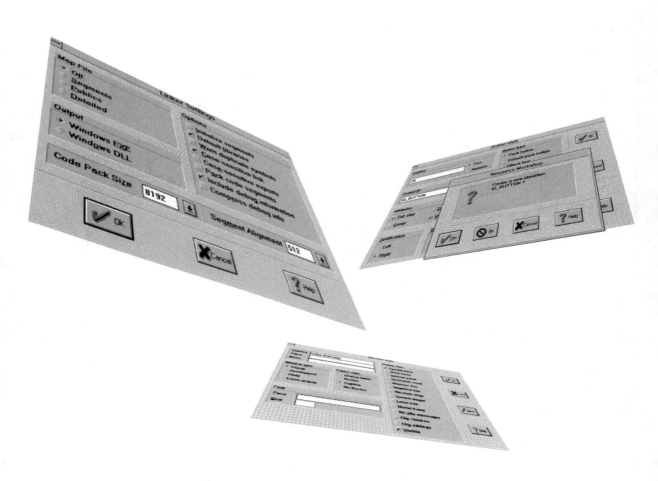

7

Creating Your Own Data Types

This chapter is about creating your own data types to suit your particular problem. It is also about creating objects, the objects of object-oriented programming. An object can seem a bit mysterious to the uninitiated, but an object is just an instance of one of your own data types, as we shall see in this chapter.

In this chapter you will learn about:

▶ Classes

▶ The basic components of a class and how a class is declared

▶ Structures

▶ The creation and usage of objects of a class

▶ Constructors and how to create them

▶ Destructors and how to create them

▶ Unions

▶ Overloaded operators and how to create them

Data Types, Objects, Classes and Instances

Before we get into the language syntax and programming aspects of classes, we should get the basic ideas and terminology straight.

So far, we have learnt that C++ lets you create variables which can be any of a range of data types, **int**, **long**, **double**. When we declare a variable of a particular type, say **long**, we are creating an instance of that type. For any given type, there are a set of operations that we can perform on them. We can add two instances of type **long**, for example. Note that we can't add instances of two different types directly. If we write an expression to add a **double** variable to a variable of type **long**, the variable of type **long** has to be converted to type **double** before the addition operation can occur. All this may seem pretty obvious, but the point of going through these obvious aspects of the built-in data types is that they are a model of how new types that you will create need to behave, as the ideas for user-defined types and basic types are the same in essence.

The variables of the basic types are very basic in the sense that, if you want to represent a physical object such as a box, you can't define a variable that adequately represents a box. You could, however, use several variables. You could define variables, **length**, **breadth** and **height**, to represent the dimensions of the box, but you still have no way to define, say, a variable **BigBox**, that was in any way representative of a box. Worse than that, if you want to be able to compare two boxes, perhaps represented by variables, **length1**, **breadth1**, and **height1**, for the first box, and **length2**, **breadth2**, and **height2**, to see which has the larger capacity, you have no direct way of doing this. Clearly, you could write a function to do this, but it would be rather cumbersome, not least because you would need six arguments for the dimensions of the boxes.

C++ allows you to create new data types to represent whatever you like. A data type for boxes is no problem. You can arrange to declare different boxes, **Box1**, **Box2**, or whatever you want to call them, using statements such as these:

```
Box Box1;
Box Box2;
```

where **Box** is the name of your data type. Any particular reference to a **Box**, **Box2** for instance, will implicitly contain all the information you have decided is necessary to represent a **Box**, such as its **length**, **breadth**, and **height** for example. Also, if you need to be able to compare boxes you can arrange that statements such as these:

```
if(Box1 > Box2 )          // Fill the larger box
   Box1.fill();
else
   Box2.fill();
```

will have the meaning you would want them to have. Don't worry about the detail of how these statements are made up. We will get to that soon enough.

We are talking about incredibly powerful medicine here. Instead of programming in terms of what are essentially computer-related data types, integer numbers, floating point numbers and so on, we are going to be programming in terms of problems-related data types. Types which might be named **Employee**, or **Cowboy**, or **Cheese**, each defined specifically for the kind of problem you are going to solve, complete with the operators that are necessary to combine instances of your new types. Program design now starts with deciding what new application-specific data types you need to solve the problem in hand, and writing the program in terms of operations on the specific kinds of things the problem is concerned with, be it **coffins** or **cowpokes**.

Instances of types that you define are referred to as **objects**, and the programming style you use based on the idea of defining your own data types is **object-oriented programming**. You will be defining your own data types using the keyword **class** in C++, so your data types are also referred to as **classes**. Declaring an object of a class is sometimes referred to as **instantiation**, because you are creating an instance of a class. The idea of an object containing the data implicit in its definition, together with the functions that operate on it, is referred to as **encapsulation**.

When we get into the detail of object-oriented programming, it may seem a little complicated in places, particularly in Chapter 9, but getting back to the basics of what this is about can often help to make things clearer, so always keep in mind what objects are really about. We can now get down to the business of understanding classes.

Understanding Classes

A class is a data type that you define. It can contain data elements which can be variables of the basic types in C++, or of other user-defined types. The data elements may be arrays or pointers or arrays of pointers, so you have a lot of flexibility in what you can include in your data type. A class can also contain functions which operate on objects of the class. So a class combines both the definition of the elementary data making up an object, and the means of manipulating objects.

The data and functions within a class are called **members**. Funnily enough, the members of a class that are data items are called **data members**, and the members that are functions are called **member functions**.

When you define a class you define a blue print for a data type. This doesn't actually define any data, it defines what the class name means. It's much the same as if you wrote a description of the basic type **double**. This wouldn't be a variable of type **double**. You would have to create that using a declaration. It is exactly the same with classes, as you will see.

Defining a Class

Let's define the class we started talking about in the beginning, a class of boxes. We can define this data type using the keyword **class** as follows:

```
class Box
{
   public:
      double length;        // Length of a box in inches
      double breadth;       // Breadth of a box in inches
      double height;        // Height of a box in inches
};
```

That's it! The name we want to give to our class appears following the keyword, and the three data members are defined between curly braces. The data members are defined for the class using the declaration statements we already know and love. The whole class definition is terminated with a semi-colon.

Access Control in a Class

There is one new keyword aside from `class` here, and that is `public`. It looks a bit like a label, but in fact it's more than that. It determines the access attributes of the members of the class that follow it. Specifying the data members as `public` here, means that these members can be used by any function. You can also specify the members as `private` or `protected`, but we'll look into the effect of these keywords in a class definition later on.

Remember that all we have defined so far is a class, which is a data type. We have not declared any objects of the class. When we talk about accessing a class member, say `height`, we are talking about accessing the data member of a particular object that needs to be declared somewhere.

Declaring Objects of a Class

We declare objects of a class with exactly the same sort of declaration that we use to declare objects of basic types. We saw this at the beginning of this chapter. We could declare object of our class `Box` with these statements:

```
Box Box1;        // Declare Box1 of type Box
Box Box2;        // Declare Box2 of type Box
```

Both of the objects `Box1` and `Box2` will have their own data members, of course. This is illustrated in the following figure:

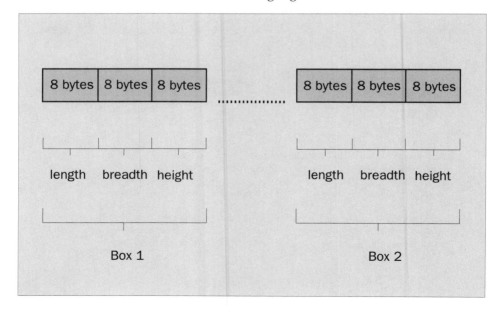

The object name **Box1** embodies the whole object (including its three data members). Of course, they are not initialized to anything. The data members of each object will simply contain junk values. So we need to look at how we can access them for the purpose of setting them to some specific values.

Accessing the Data Members of a Class

The data members of objects of a class can be referred to using the object name, followed by a period, followed by the data member name. The period is called the **direct member selection operator**. So to set the value of the data member **height** of the object **Box2** to 18.0 say, we could write this assignment statement:

```
Box2.height = 18.0;          // Setting the value of a data member
```

We can only access the data member in this way in a function because the member **height** was specified as having **public** access. We will see more about this shortly.

Try It Out - Your First Use of Classes

Let's first use our class in an example:

```
// EX7-01.CPP
#include <iostream.h>

class Box                        // Class definition at global scope
{
   public:
      double length;             // Length of a box in inches
      double breadth;            // Breadth of a box in inches
      double height;             // Height of a box in inches
};

int main(void)
{
   Box Box1;        // Declare Box1 of type Box
   Box Box2;        // Declare Box2 of type Box

   double volume = 0.0;      // Store the volume of a box here

   Box1.height = 18.0;                  // Define the values
   Box1.length = 78.0;                  // of the members of
   Box1.breadth = 24.0;                 // the object Box1
```

```
    Box2.height = Box1.height - 10;      // Define Box2
    Box2.length = Box1.length/2.0;       // members in
    Box2.breadth = 0.25*Box1.length;     // terms of Box1

// Calculate volume of Box1
    volume = Box1.height*Box1.length*Box1.breadth;

    cout << endl
        << "Volume of Box1 = " << volume;

    cout << endl
        << "Box2 has sides which total "
        << Box2.height+ Box2.length+ Box2.breadth
        << " inches.";

    cout <<endl                          // Display the size of a box in memory
        << "A Box object occupies "
        << sizeof Box1 << " bytes.";

    return 0;
}
```

How It Works

The first thing to notice is that the definition of the class appears outside of the function **main()**,and therefore it has global scope. This enables objects to be declared in any function in the program. We have declared two objects of type **Box**, **Box1** and **Box2**, within the function **main()**. Of course, as with variable of the basic types, the objects **Box1** and **Box2** are local to **main()**. Objects of type **Box** obey the same rules with respect to scope as variables declared as one of the basic types (such as the variable **volume**).

The first three assignment statements set the values of the data members of **Box1**. The data members can be used just like ordinary variables of the same type. We define the values of the data members of **Box2** in terms of the data members of **Box1** in the next three assignment statements.

We then have a statement which calculates the volume of **Box1** as the product of its three data members. This value is then output to the screen. We then output the sum of the data members of **Box2** by writing the expression for the sum of the data members directly in the output statement. The final action in the program is to output the number of bytes occupied by **Box1**, which is produced by the operator **sizeof**.

If you run this program you should get this output:

```
Volume of Box1 = 33696
Box2 has sides which total 66.5 inches.
A Box object occupies 24 bytes.
```

The last line shows that the object **Box1** occupies 24 bytes of memory, which is a result of having three, 8 byte data members. The statement which produced the last line of output could equally well have been written like this:

```
cout <<endl                     // Display the size of a box in memory
     << "A Box object occupies "
     << sizeof (Box) << " bytes.";
```

where we have used the type name, rather than a specific object name.

This example has demonstrated the mechanism for accessing the **public** data members of a class. It also shows that they can be used in exactly the same way as ordinary variables. We now should take a look at member functions of a class.

Member Functions of a Class

A member function of a class is a function that has its definition or its prototype within the class definition. A member function of a class operates on any object of the class of which it is a member, and has access to all the members of a class for that object.

Try It Out - Adding a Member Function to Box

Let's create an example (which is an extension of the **Box** class) to include a member function to see how accessing the members of the class works.

```
// EX7-02.CPP
#include <iostream.h>

class Box                       // Class definition at global scope
{
   public:
      double length;            // Length of a box in inches
      double breadth;           // Breadth of a box in inches
      double height;            // Height of a box in inches
```

```
      // Function to calculate the volume of a box
      double volume(void)
      {
          return length*breadth*height;
      }
};

int main(void)
{
   Box Box1;          // Declare Box1 of type Box
   Box Box2;          // Declare Box2 of type Box

   double volume = 0.0;      // Store the volume of a box here

   Box1.height = 18.0;                   // Define the values
   Box1.length = 78.0;                   // of the members of
   Box1.breadth = 24.0;                  // the object Box1

   Box2.height = Box1.height - 10;       // Define Box2
   Box2.length = Box1.length/2.0;        // members in
   Box2.breadth = 0.25*Box1.length;      // terms of Box1

   volume = Box1.volume();   // Calculate volume of Box1
   cout << endl
        << "Volume of Box1 = " << volume;

   cout << endl
        << "Volume of Box2 = "
        << Box2.volume();

   cout << endl                          // Display the size of a box in memory
        << "A Box object occupies "
        << sizeof Box1 << " bytes.";

   return 0;
}
```

How It Works

You can see the bit we have added to the class definition (it is shaded). It's just the definition of the function `volume()`, which is a member function of the class. It also has the access attribute **public** which the data members have. It returns the volume of a **Box** object as a value of type **double**. The expression in the **return** statement is just the product of the three data members of the class.

> *Note that there is no need to qualify the names of the data members in any way in member functions.*

249

The member function **volume()** is used in the highlighted statements in **main()**, after initializing the data members (as in the first example). You can call a member function by writing the name of the object to be processed, followed by a period, followed by the member function name. The function will automatically access the data members of the object for which it was called, so the first use of **volume()** calculates the volume of **Box1**. Using just the name of a member will always refer to the member of the object for which the member function has been called. The second use of the member function is used directly in the output statement to produce the volume of **Box2**. If you execute this example it will produce this output:

```
Volume of Box1 = 33696
Volume of Box2 = 6084
A Box object occupies 24 bytes.
```

Note that the **Box** object is still the same size. Adding a function member doesn't affect the size of the objects. Obviously, a member function has to be stored in memory somewhere, but there is only one copy, regardless of how many class objects have been declared. The use of the names of the class data members in the member function automatically refer to the data members of the specific object used to call the function, and the function can only be called by prefixing the name of an object (and the period, of course).

If you try to call a member function without specifying an object name, your program will not compile.

Positioning a Member Function Definition

A member function need not be placed inside the class definition. If you want to put it outside the class definition, you need to put the prototype for the function inside the class. If we rewrite the previous class with the function definition outside, the class definition would look like this:

```
class Box                       // Class definition at global scope
{
   public:
      double length;            // Length of a box in inches
      double breadth;           // Breadth of a box in inches
      double height;            // Height of a box in inches
      double volume(void);      // Function prototype
};
```

Now we need to write the function definition, but there has to be some way of telling the compiler that the function belongs to the class **Box**. This is done by placing the name of the class prefixing the function name, and separating the two with the **scope resolution operator**, **::**. The function definition would now look like this:

```
// Function to calculate the volume of a Box
   double Box::volume(void)
   {
      return length*breadth*height;
   }
```

If you want to run this version of the last example, it appears on the disk as **EX7-03A.CPP**. It will produce the same output as the last example. However, it isn't exactly the same program. When we specify the definition of the function within the definition of the class, the compiler will treat the function as an **inline** function, if this is possible. With an **inline** function, the compiler tries to expand the code in the body of the function in place of a call of the function, avoiding much of the overhead of calling the function. This is illustrated in the following figure:

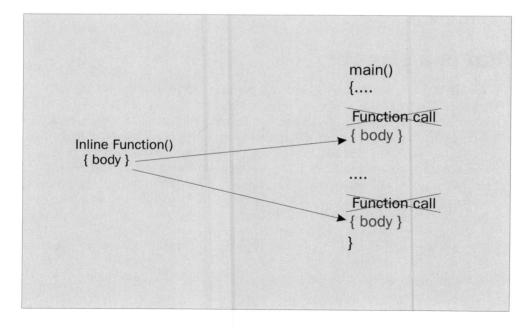

Of course, the compiler takes care of ensuring that expanding a function inline doesn't cause any problems with variable names or scope.

Inserting the code for a function inline is not always possible, but generally it works for very short simple functions, such as our function `volume()`. With the function definition outside of the class definition, the compiler treats the function as a normal function, and a call of the function will work in the usual way. However, it is also possible to tell the compiler that we would like the function to be considered as inline if possible. This is done by simply placing the keyword **inline** at the beginning of the function header. So for our function, the definition would be as follows:

```
// Function to calculate the volume of a Box
   inline double Box::volume(void)
   {
      return length*breadth*height;
   }
```

With this definition for the function, the program would be exactly the same as the original. You can apply the keyword **inline** to ordinary functions in your program that have nothing to do with classes, and get the same effect, but remember that it only works for short simple functions.

We now need to understand a little more about what happens when we declare an object of a class.

What is a struct?

We need a slight diversion here for the sake of completeness. There is another kind of entity in C++, and it is called a **struct**. A **struct** is a class whose members are **public** by default, so the use of the keyword **public** in its definition for public members is optional. It is defined by using the keyword **struct** instead of the keyword **class**. In all other respects, it is the same as a class, however the material in the next chapter on inheritance will not apply to a **struct**. Since you can do everything a **struct** can do by using a class, we won't dwell further on **struct**. We will only use classes throughout this book.

The **struct** is included in the language for historical reasons as much as anything else. You can look it up in the *TCW Programmer's Guide* if you want to know more, but there really isn't that much more to it.

Class Constructors

After we declared our **Box** objects, **Box1** and **Box2**, it was necessary to work through each of the data members laboriously for each object, in order to assign an initial value to it. This is unsatisfactory from several points of view. First of all, it would be easy to overlook initializing a data member, particularly with a class which had many more data members than the class **Box**. It's also going to be very cumbersome with more complicated classes. Initializing several objects of a complex class could involve pages of assignment statements for initializing the data members of the objects. There has to be a better way, and of course there is: the class **constructor**.

What is a Constructor?

A class constructor is a special function in a class which can be called when a new object of the class is declared. It therefore provides the opportunity to initialize objects as they are created, and to ensure that data members only contain valid values. For instance, a **Box** object with a negative dimension would not make much sense, at least not in this universe.

A class constructor has the same name as the class in which it is defined. The function **Box()** for example is a constructor for our class **Box**. It also has no return type. It is an error to specify a return type for a constructor - you must not even write it as **void**. The primary function of a class constructor is to assign initial values to the data elements of the class, and no return type is necessary or permitted.

Try It Out - Adding a Constructor to Box

Let's extend our **Box** class to incorporate a constructor.

```
// EX7-03.CPP
#include <iostream.h>

class Box                        // Class definition at global scope
{
   public:
      double length;             // Length of a box in inches
      double breadth;            // Breadth of a box in inches
      double height;             // Height of a box in inches
```

Try it Out!

```
      Box(double lv, double bv, double hv)   // Constructor definition
      {
         cout << endl << "Constructor called.";
         length = lv;                         // Set values of
         breadth = bv;
         height = hv;                         // data members
      }

   // Function to calculate the volume of a box
   double volume()
   {
      return length*breadth*height;
   }
};

int main(void)
{
   Box Box1(78.,24.0,18.0);    // Declare and initialize Box1 of type Box
   Box CigarBox(8.0,5.0,1.0); // Declare and initialize CigarBox

   double volume = 0.0;        // Store the volume of a box here

   volume = Box1.volume();  // Calculate volume of Box1
   cout << endl
        << "Volume of Box1 = " << volume;

   cout << endl
        << "Volume of CigarBox = "
        << CigarBox.volume();

   return 0;
}
```

How It Works

The constructor `Box()` has been written with three double parameters corresponding to initial values for the **length**, **breadth**, and **height** of an object. The first statement in the constructor outputs a message so we can tell when it is called. You wouldn't do this in practice, but since it is very helpful in showing when a constructor is called, we will use it regularly for the purposes of illustration. The code in the body of the constructor is very simple. It just assigns the arguments passed to the corresponding data members. We could also include checks that valid non-negative arguments are supplied here if necessary, and in practice you would want to do this, but here our primary interest is how the mechanism works.

Within **main()** we declare the object **Box1** with initializing values for the data members **length**, **breadth** and **height** in sequence. These are in parentheses following the object name. This uses the functional notation for initialization which, as we saw in Chapter 2, can also be applied to initializing ordinary variables of basic types. We also declare a second object of type **Box**, called **CigarBox** which also has initializing values.

The volume of **Box1** is calculated using the member function **volume()** as in the previous example, and it is then displayed on the screen. We also display the value of the volume of **CigarBox**. The output from the example is as follows:

```
Constructor called.
Constructor called.
Volume of Box1 = 33696
Volume of CigarBox = 40
```

The first two lines are output from the two calls of the constructor **Box()**, once for each variable declared. The constructor we have supplied in the class definition is automatically called when a **Box** object is declared, so both **Box** objects are initialized with the initializing values appearing in the declaration. These are passed to the constructor as arguments, in the sequence they are written in the declaration. As you can see, volume of **Box1** is the same as before, and **CigarBox** has a volume looking suspiciously like the product of its dimensions.

The Default Constructor

Try modifying the last example by adding the declaration for **Box2** that we had previously:

```
Box Box2;        // Declare Box2 of type Box
```

Here, we have left **Box2** without initializing values. When you recompile the program you will get the error message Could not find a match for 'Box::Box()'. What this means is that the compiler is looking for a constructor **Box()** for **Box2** that doesn't need any arguments, because we haven't supplied any initializing values for the data members. Well, this statement was perfectly satisfactory in **EX7-02.CPP**, why in tarnation doesn't it work now?

The answer is that the previous example used the default constructor that was supplied by the compiler (since we didn't supply a constructor). Because in this example we supplied a constructor, the compiler assumed we were taking care of everything so didn't supply the default. So if you still want to use declarations for **Box** objects which are not initialized, you have to include the default constructor yourself. What does the default constructor look like? Well, it couldn't be simpler really as it doesn't do anything:

```
Box()    // Default constructor
{}       // Totally devoid of statements
```

Try It Out - Supplying a Default Constructor

Let's add our version of the default constructor to the last example, along with the declaration for **Box2**, plus the original assignments for the data members of **Box2**. We must enlarge the default constructor just enough to show that it is called. Here is the next version of the program:

```cpp
// EX7-04.CPP
#include <iostream.h>

class Box                       // Class definition at global scope
{
    public:
        double length;          // Length of a box in inches
        double breadth;         // Breadth of a box in inches
        double height;          // Height of a box in inches

        Box(double lv, double bv, double hv)  // Constructor definition
        {
            cout << endl << "Constructor called.";
            length = lv;                       // Set values of
            breadth = bv;
            height = hv;                       // data members
        }

        Box()
        { cout << endl << "Default constructor called."; }

        // Function to calculate the volume of a box
        double volume()
        {
            return length*breadth*height;
        }
};

int main(void)
{
    Box Box1(78.,24.0,18.0);    // Declare and initialize Box1 of type Box
    Box Box2;                   // Declare Box2 - no initial values
    Box CigarBox(8.0,5.0,1.0);  // Declare and initialize CigarBox
```

```
        double volume = 0.0;        // Store the volume of a box here

        volume = Box1.volume();   // Calculate volume of Box1
        cout << endl
            << "Volume of Box1 = " << volume;

        Box2.height = Box1.height - 10;      // Define Box2
        Box2.length = Box1.length/2.0;       // members in
        Box2.breadth = 0.25*Box1.length;     // terms of Box1

        cout << endl
            << "Volume of Box2 = "
            << Box2.volume();

        cout << endl
            << "Volume of CigarBox = "
            << CigarBox.volume();

        return 0;
}
```

How It Works

Now we have included our own version of the default constructor, there are no error messages from the compiler and everything works. The program produces this output:

```
Constructor called.
Default Constructor called.
Constructor called.
Volume of Box1 = 33696
Volume of Box2 = 6084
Volume of CigarBox = 40
```

All our default constructor does is to display a message, and evidently it was called when we declared the object **Box2**. We also get the correct value for the volumes of all three **Box** objects, so the rest of the program is working as it should.

One aspect of this example you may have noticed, is that we now know we can overload constructors. We have just run an example with two constructors that differ only in their parameter list. One has three parameters of type **double**, and the other has no parameters at all.

Assigning Default Values in a Constructor

When we discussed functions in C++, we saw how we could specify default values for the parameters to a function in the function prototype. We can also do this for class member functions including constructors. If we put the definition of the member function inside the class definition, we can put the default values for the parameters in the function header. If we only include the prototype of a function in the class definition, then the default parameter value goes in the prototype. We could decide our default size for a **Box** object was a unit box with all sides of length 1. We could alter the class definition on the last example to this:

```
class Box                          // Class definition at global scope
{
   public:
      double length;               // Length of a box in inches
      double breadth;              // Breadth of a box in inches
      double height;               // Height of a box in inches

   // Constructor definition
      Box(double lv=1.0, double bv=1.0, double hv=1.0)
      {
         cout << endl << "Constructor called.";
         length = lv;                        // Set values of
         breadth = bv;
         height = hv;                        // data members
      }

      Box()
      { cout << endl << "Default constructor called."; }

      // Function to calculate the volume of a box
      double volume()
      {
         return length*breadth*height;
      }
};
```

If we make this change to the last example, what happens? We get another error message from the compiler of course. We get this useful comment

Ambiguity between 'Box::Box(double,double,double)' and 'Box::Box()'

This means that the compiler can't work out which of the two constructors to call: the one for which we have set default values for the parameters, or the default constructor. This is because the declaration of **Box2** requires a constructor without parameters, and either constructor can now be called without parameters. The immediately obvious solution to this is to get rid of the default constructor. This is actually beneficial. Without the default constructor any **Box** object that is declared without being initialized will automatically have its members initialized to 1.

Try It Out - Supplying Default Values for a Constructor

We can demonstrate this with this example:

```
// EX7-05.CPP
#include <iostream.h>

class Box                          // Class definition at global scope
{
    public:
        double length;             // Length of a box in inches
        double breadth;            // Breadth of a box in inches
        double height;             // Height of a box in inches

// Constructor definition
        Box(double lv=1.0, double bv=1.0, double hv=1.0)
        {
            cout << endl << "Constructor called.";
            length = lv;                          // Set values of
            breadth = bv;
            height = hv;                          // data members
        }

        // Function to calculate the volume of a box
        double volume()
        {
            return length*breadth*height;
        }
};

int main(void)
{
    Box Box2;                      // Declare Box2 - no initial values

    cout << endl
         << "Volume of Box2 = "
         << Box2.volume();

    return 0;
}
```

How It Works

This program produces this output:

```
Constructor called.
Volume of Box2 = 1
```

This demonstrates that the constructor with default parameter values is doing its job of setting the values of objects that have no initializing values specified.

You shouldn't assume from this that this is the only, or even the recommended, way of implementing the default constructor. There will be many occasions where you won't want to assign default values in this way, in which case you will need to write a separate default constructor. There will even be times when you don't want to have a default constructor operating at all. This would ensure that all declared objects of a class have initializing values specified in their declaration.

Using an Initialization List in a Constructor

We can initialize the members of an object with a different technique in a class constructor, using what is called an **initialization list**. We can demonstrate this with an alternative version of the constructor for the class **Box**:

```
// Constructor definition using an initialization list
   Box(double lv=1.0, double bv=1.0, double hv=1.0): length(lv),
                                                     breadth(bv),
                                                     height(hv)

   {
      cout << endl << "Constructor called.";
   }
```

Now the values of the data members are not set in assignment statements, they are specified as initializing values using functional notation, as in a declaration. The member **length** is initialized by the value of **lv**, for example. This can be rather more efficient than using assignments as we did in the previous version. If you substitute this version of the constructor in the previous example, you will see it works just as well.

Note that the initializing list is separated from the parameter list by a colon, and each of the initializers is separated by commas. This technique is important as it is the only way of setting values for certain types of data members for an object.

Private Members of a Class

Having a constructor that sets the value of data members of a class object, yet still admitting the possibility of any part of a program being able to mess with what are really the guts of an object, is almost a contradiction in terms. To draw an analogy, once you have arranged for a brilliant surgeon such as Dr. Kildare, whose skills were honed over years of training, to do things to your insides, letting the local plumber, bricklayer or the folks from Hill Street Blues have a go at it hardly seems appropriate somehow. We need some protection for our class data members.

We can get it by using the keyword **private** when we define the class members. Class members which are **private** can only be accessed by member functions of a class in general. There is one exception but we will worry about that later. The average function has no direct means of accessing the **private** members of a class.

Try It Out - Private Data Members

We can rewrite the **Box** class to make its data members **private**.

```
// EX7-06.CPP
#include <iostream.h>

class Box                       // Class definition at global scope
{
   public:
// Constructor definition
      Box(double lv=1.0, double bv=1.0, double hv=1.0)
      {
         cout << endl << "Constructor called.";
         length = lv;                          // Set values of
         breadth = bv;
         height = hv;                          // data members
      }

      // Function to calculate the volume of a box
      double volume()
      {
         return length*breadth*height;
      }

   private:
      double length;                  // Length of a box in inches
```

```
        double breadth;          // Breadth of a box in inches
        double height;           // Height of a box in inches
};
int main(void)
{
    Box Match(2.2, 1.1, 0.5);   // Declare Match Box
    Box Box2;                    // Declare Box2 - no initial values

    cout << endl
        << "Volume of Match = "
        << Match.volume();
```

```
// Uncomment the following line to get an error
// Box2.length = 4.0;
```

```
    cout << endl
        << "Volume of Box2 = "
        << Box2.volume();

    return 0;
}
```

How It Works

The definition of the class **Box** now has two sections. The first is the **public** section containing the constructor and the member function **volume()**. The second section is **private** and contains the data members. Now, the data members can only be accessed by the member functions of the class. We don't have to modify any of the member functions. They can access all the data members of the class anyway. However, if you uncomment the statement in the function **main()** assigning a value to the member **length** of the object **Box2**, you will get a compiler error message confirming that the data member is inaccessible.

> *A point to remember is that using a constructor or a member function is now the only way to get a value into a private data member of an object. You have to make sure that all the ways in which you might want to set or modify data members is provided for.*

We could also put functions into the **private** section of a class, whereupon they can only be called by other member functions. If you put the function **volume()** in the **private** section, then you will get a compiler error from the statements that attempt to use it in the function **main()**. If you put the constructor in the private section, then you won't be able to declare any members of the class.

The example generates this output:

```
Constructor called.
Constructor called.
Volume of Box2 = 1
Volume of Match = 1.21
```

This demonstrates that the class is still working satisfactorily, with its data members defined as having the access attribute **private**. The major difference is they are now completely protected from unauthorized access and modification.

> The default access attribute which applies to members of a class if you don't specify it is *private*. You could therefore put all your *private* members at the beginning of the class definition, and let them default to *private* by omitting the keyword. However, I feel this is not good practice. It is better to take the trouble to explicitly state the access attribute in every case so there can be no doubt about what you intend.

Of course, you don't have to make all your data members **private**. If the application for your class requires it, you can have some data members defined a **private** and some as **public**. It all depends on what you are trying to do. If there is no reason to make members of a class **public**, then it is better to make them **private** as it makes the class more secure. Ordinary functions won't be able to access any of the **private** members of your class.

Accessing private Class Members

On reflection, declaring the data members of a class as **private** is a bit hard. It's all very well protecting them from unauthorized modification, but that's no reason to keep their values a secret. What we need is a Freedom of Information Act for **private** members.

You don't need to start writing to your state senator to get it. It's already available to you. All you need to do is to write a member function to return the value of a data member. Look at this member function for the class **Box**:

```
inline double Box::GetLength(void)
{ return length; }
```

This has been written as a member function definition which is external to the class just to show how it looks. It has been specified as `inline` though, since it should qualify as such. Assuming you have the declaration of the function in the public section of the class, you can use it by writing this statement:

```
len = Box2.GetLength();    // Obtain data member length
```

All you need to do is write a similar function for each data member you want to make available to the outside world, and their values can be accessed without prejudicing the security of the class.

The friend Functions of a Class

There may be circumstances when you want certain selected functions, which are not members of a class for one reason or another, to nonetheless be able to access all the members of a class - a sort of elite group with special privileges. Such functions are called **friend functions** of a class, and are defined using the keyword `friend`. You can either include the prototype of a friend function in the class definition, or you can include the function definition. Functions which are friends of a class and are defined within the class definition, are also, by default, `inline`.

Let's suppose we wanted to implement a friend function in the `Box` class to compute the surface area of a `Box` object.

Try It Out - Using a friend to Calculate the Surface Area

We could implement this in the following example.

```
// EX7-07.CPP
// Creating a friend function of a class
#include <iostream.h>

class Box                        // Class definition at global scope
{
   public:
// Constructor definition
      Box(double lv=1.0, double bv=1.0, double hv=1.0)
      {
```

```
        cout << endl << "Constructor called.";
        length = lv;                        // Set values of
        breadth = bv;
        height = hv;                        // data members
    }

    // Function to calculate the volume of a box
    double volume()
    {
        return length*breadth*height;
    }
```

```
    // friend function to calculate the surface area of a Box object
    friend double BoxSurface(Box aBox)
    {
        return 2.0*(aBox.length * aBox.breadth+
                    aBox.length * aBox.height+
                    aBox.height * aBox.breadth);
    }
```

```
  private:
    double length;              // Length of a box in inches
    double breadth;             // Breadth of a box in inches
    double height;              // Height of a box in inches
};

int main(void)
{
    Box Match(2.2, 1.1, 0.5);  // Declare Match Box
    Box Box2;                   // Declare Box2 - no initial values

    cout << endl
         << "Volume of Match = "
         << Match.volume();
```

```
    cout << endl
         << "Surface area of Match = "
         << BoxSurface( Match );
```

```
    cout << endl
         << "Volume of Box2 = "
         << Box2.volume();
```

```
    cout << endl
         << "Surface area of Box2 = "
         << BoxSurface( Box2 );
```

```
    return 0;
}
```

265

How It Works

The friend function **BoxSurface()** is defined within the class definition. The function header has the keyword **friend** at the front to indicate it is a friend function.

Note how access to the function members within the function definition is specified. They each have to be qualified by the parameter name in exactly the same way as an ordinary function, except that an ordinary function can't access the private members of a class. A **friend** function is always the same as an ordinary function except that it can access all the members of a class without restriction.

The example produces this output:

```
Constructor called.
Constructor called.
Volume of Match = 1.21
Surface area of Match  = 8.14
Volume of Box2 = 1
Surface area of Box2 = 6
```

This is exactly what you would expect. The **friend** function is computing the surface area of the **Box** objects from the values of the **private** members.

Having friend Function Definitions Outside the Class

In the last example, we could have equally placed the function definition outside of the class definition. We would then put just the prototype within the class definition, where it would have the keyword **friend** at the beginning, as in the following:

```
friend double BoxSurface(Box aBox);
```

and the function definition outside of the class definition would be written as a normal function as follows:

```
double BoxSurface(Box aBox);
{
    return 2.0*(aBox.length * aBox.breadth+
            aBox.length * aBox.height+
            aBox.height * aBox.breadth);
}
```

No **friend** keyword is necessary here. This would then operate in exactly the same way as our previous example.

The Default Copy Constructor

Suppose we declare and initialize a **Box** object **Box1** with this statement:

```
Box Box1(78.0, 24.0, 18.0);
```

We now want to create another **Box** object identical to the first. We would like to initialize the second **Box** object with **Box1**.

Try It Out - Copying Information Between Instances

We can try this out with the **main()** function which follows. We won't repeat the class definition, as it is the same as the preceding example, but the complete code is on the disk.

```
// EX7-08.CPP
// Initializing an object with an object of the same class
#include <iostream.h>
...
int main(void)
{
   Box Box1(78.0, 24.0, 18.0);
   Box Box2 = Box1;              // Initialize Box2 with Box1

   cout << endl
        << "Box1 volume = " << Box1.volume()
        << endl
        << "Box2 volume = " << Box2.volume();

   return 0;
}
```

How It Works

This example will produce this output:

```
Constructor called.
Box1 volume = 33696
Box1 volume = 33696
```

so clearly it's working as we would want. Our constructor was called only once for the creation of **Box1**, so the question is, how did **Box2** get created? The mechanism is similar to the one we experienced when we had no constructor defined, and the compiler supplied a default constructor to allow an object to be created. In this case, the compiler generates a default version of what is referred to as a **copy constructor**.

A copy constructor does exactly what we are doing here - it creates an object of a class by initializing it with an existing object of the same class. The default version of the copy constructor creates the new object by copying the existing object member by member.

This is fine for simple classes such as **Box**. But for many classes this won't work properly. Indeed, it can create serious errors in your program. In this case, you need to create your own class copy constructor. This requires a special approach, so we will look into this more fully a little later in this chapter.

The Pointer this

In our class **Box** we wrote the function **volume()** in terms of the class member names in the definition of the class. Of course, every object of type **Box** that we create contains these members, so there has to be a mechanism for the function to refer to the members for the particular object for which the function is called. When any member function executes, it automatically contains a hidden pointer with the name **this**, which points to the object used with the function call. Therefore, when the member **length** is accessed in the function **volume()** during execution, it is actually referring to **this.length**, which is the fully specified reference to the object member actually being used. The compiler takes care of adding the necessary pointer name **this** to the member names in the function.

You can use the pointer **this** explicitly within a member function if you need to.

Try It Out - Explicit Use of this

We could add a public function to our class **Box** to compare the volume of two **Box** objects.

```
// EX7-09.CPP
// Using the pointer this
#include <iostream.h>

class Box                          // Class definition at global scope
{
   public:
// Constructor definition
      Box(double lv=1.0, double bv=1.0, double hv=1.0)
      {
         cout << endl << "Constructor called.";
         length = lv;                        // Set values of
         breadth = bv;
         height = hv;                         // data members
      }

      // Function to calculate the volume of a box
      double volume()
      {
         return length*breadth*height;
      }

      // Function to compare two boxes which returns True (1)
      // if the first is greater that the second, and False (0) otherwise
      int compare(Box xBox)
      {
         return (*this).volume() > xBox.volume();
      }

   private:
      double length;              // Length of a box in inches
      double breadth;             // Breadth of a box in inches
      double height;              // Height of a box in inches

};

int main(void)
{
   Box Match(2.2, 1.1, 0.5);   // Declare Match Box
   Box Cigar(8.0, 5.0 ,1.0);   // Declare Cigar Box

   if( Cigar.compare(Match))
      cout << endl
           << "Match is smaller than Cigar";
```

```
    else
       cout << endl
            << "Match is equal to or larger than Cigar";

    return 0;
}
```

How It Works

The member function **compare()** returns 1 if the prefixed **Box** object in the function call has a greater volume than the **Box** object specified as an argument, and 0 if it doesn't. In the **return** statements, the prefix object is referred to through the pointer **this** with the expression **(*this)**. The indirection operator is necessary because we need to dereference the pointer to get at the object value. The parentheses are necessary because the direct member selection operator (the period) has a higher precedence than the indirection operator. This demonstrates that the pointer **this** exists and *does* work, but it's quite unnecessary to use it explicitly here. If you change the **return** statement in the compare function to this:

```
return volume() > xBox.volume();
```

You will find it works just as well. Any references to unadorned member names are automatically assumed to be the members of the object pointed to by **this**.

The **compare()** function is used in **main()** to check the relationship between the volumes of the objects **Match** and **Cigar**. The output from the program is as follows:

```
Constructor called.
Constructor called.
Match is smaller than Cigar.
```

which confirms that the **Cigar Box** object is larger than the **Match Box** object.

It also wasn't essential to write the **compare()** function as a class member. It could equally well have been written as an ordinary function with the objects as arguments. Note that this is not true of the function **volume()**, since it needs to access the private data members of the class. Of course, the function **compare()** implemented as an ordinary function wouldn't have the pointer **this**, but it would still be very simple:

```
// Comparing two Box objects - ordinary function version
int compare(Box B1, Box B2)
{
   return B1.volume() > B2.volume();
}
```

This has both objects as arguments and returns **True** if the volume of the first is greater than the last. You would use this function to perform the same function as in the last example with this statement:

```
if( compare(Cigar, Match) )
   cout << endl
        << "Match is smaller than Cigar";
else
   cout << endl
        << "Match is equal to or larger than Cigar";
```

If anything, this looks slightly better and easier to read than the original version. However, there is a much better way to do this which we shall see before the end of this chapter.

Arrays of Objects of a Class

We can declare an array of object of a class in exactly the same way as we have declared an ordinary array. Each element of the array causes the default constructor to be called.

Try It Out - Arrays of a Class

We can use the class definition of **Box** from the last example, but modified to include a specific default constructor:

```
// EX7-10.CPP
// Using an array of class objects
#include <iostream.h>

class Box                           // Class definition at global scope
{
   public:
// Constructor definition
      Box(double lv, double bv=1.0, double hv=1.0)
      {
         cout << endl << "Constructor called.";
```

271

```
            length = lv;                        // Set values of
            breadth = bv;
            height = hv;                         // data members
        }

        Box(void)                               // Default constructor
        {
            cout << endl
                << "Default constructor called.";
            length = breadth = height = 1.0;
        }

        // Function to calculate the volume of a box
        double volume()
        {
            return length*breadth*height;
        }

    private:
        double length;          // Length of a box in inches
        double breadth;         // Breadth of a box in inches
        double height;          // Height of a box in inches

};
int main(void)
{
    Box Boxes[5];                   // Array of Box objects declared
    Box Cigar(8.0, 5.0 ,1.0);       // Declare Cigar Box

    cout << endl
        << "Volume of Boxes[3] = " << Boxes[3].volume()
        << endl
        << "Volume of Cigar = " << Cigar.volume();
    return 0;
}
```

How It Works

We have modified the constructor so that only two default values are supplied, and we have added a default constructor, which initializes the data members to 1 after displaying a message that it was called. We will now be able to see *which* constructor was called *when*. The constructors now have quite distinct parameter lists, so there is no possibility of the compiler confusing them. The program produces this output:

```
Default constructor called.
Default constructor called.
Default constructor called.
Default constructor called.
```

```
Default constructor called.
Constructor called.
Volume of Boxes[3] = 1
Volume of Cigar = 40
```

We can see that the default constructor was called five times, once for each element of the array **Boxes**. The other constructor was called to create the object **Cigar**. It's clear from the output that the default constructor initialization is working satisfactorily, as the volume of the array element is 1.

Static Members of a Class

Both data members and function members of a class can be declared as **static**. Because the context is a class definition, there is a little more to it than the effect of the keyword **static** outside of a class, so let's look first at static data members.

Static Data Members of a Class

When we declare data members of a class as **static**, the effect is that the **static** data members are defined only once, and are shared between all objects of the class. Each object gets its own copies of each of the ordinary data members of a class, but only one instance of each static data member exists, regardless of how many class objects have been defined.

One use for a static data member is to count how many objects actually exist. We could add a static data member to the public section of the **Box** class by adding the following statement to the previous class definition:

```
static int ObjectCount;      // Count of objects in existence
```

We now have a problem. How do we initialize the static data member? We can't put it in the class definition - that is simply a blueprint for an object, and initializing values are not allowed. We don't want to initialize it in a constructor, because we want to increment it every time the constructor is called. We can't initialize it in another member function since a member function is associated with an object, and we want it initialized before any object is created. The simple answer is to write the initialization outside of the class definition, with the following statement:

```
int Box::ObjectCount = 0;    // Initialize static member of class Box
```

Note that the keyword `static` is not included here, but we do need to qualify the member name by using the class name and the scope resolution operator so that the compiler understands we are referring to a static member of the class. Otherwise we would simply create a global variable that was nothing to do with the class.

Try It Out - Counting Instances

Let's add this to the last example.

```
// EX7-11.CPP
// Using a static data member in a class
#include <iostream.h>

class Box                       // Class definition at global scope
{
   public:
      static int ObjectCount;       // Count of objects in existence

// Constructor definition
      Box(double lv, double bv=1.0, double hv=1.0)
      {
         cout << endl << "Constructor called.";
         length = lv;                      // Set values of
         breadth = bv;
         height = hv;                      // data members
         ObjectCount++;
      }

      Box(void)                            // Default constructor
      {
         cout << endl
             << "Default constructor called.";
         length = breadth = height = 1.0;
         ObjectCount++;

      }

      // Function to calculate the volume of a box
      double volume()
      {
         return length*breadth*height;
      }

   private:
```

```
     double length;              // Length of a box in inches
     double breadth;             // Breadth of a box in inches
     double height;              // Height of a box in inches

};

int Box::ObjectCount = 0;        // Initialize static member of class Box

int main(void)
{
   Box Boxes[5];                 // Array of Box objects declared
   Box Cigar(8.0, 5.0 ,1.0);     // Declare Cigar Box
   cout << endl
        << "Number of objects = " << Box::ObjectCount;

   return 0;
}
```

How It Works

This example will produce the output

```
Default constructor called.
Default constructor called.
Default constructor called.
Default constructor called.
Default constructor called.
Constructor called.
Number of objects = 6
```

The six objects are obviously the elements of the **Boxes** array, plus the object **Cigar**. It's interesting to note that **static** members of a class exist even though there may be no members of the class in existence. This is evidently the case, since we initialized the **static** member **ObjectCount** before any class objects were declared.

> *Note that you must initialize a static data member, otherwise the compiler will complain. The declaration in the class definition doesn't define a static variable, so until you define its initial value it doesn't exist.*

Static Function Members of a Class

By declaring a function member as **static** you make it independent of any particular object of the class. Referencing members of the class must be done using qualified names (as you would do with an ordinary global function). The static member function has the advantage that it exists and

275

can be called, even if no objects of the class exist. In this case, only **static** data members can be used, since they are the only ones that exist. Of course, a **static** member function can access **private** as well as **public** members of class objects, once the objects have been defined. A static function might have this prototype:

```
static void afunction ( int n );
```

A **static** function can be called in relation to a particular object by a statement such as the following:

```
aBox.afunction( 10 );
```

where **aBox** is an object of the class. The same function could also be called without reference to an object. In this case the statement would be in the following form:

```
Box::afunction( 10 );
```

where **Box** is the class name. Using the class name and the scope resolution operator serves to tell the compiler to which class the function **afunction()** belongs.

Pointers and References to Class Objects

Using pointers, and particularly references to class objects, is very important to object-oriented programming. Class objects can involve considerable amounts of data, so using a pass-by-value mechanism by specifying objects as parameters can be very time consuming and inefficient. There are also some techniques involving the use of references which are essential to some operations with classes. As we shall see, you can't write a copy constructor without using a reference parameter.

Pointers to Class Objects

You declare a pointer to a class object in the same way as you declare other pointers. For example, a pointer to objects of the class **Box** is declared in the following statement:

```
    Box* pBox = 0;              // Declare a pointer to Box
```

You can now use this to store the address of a **Box** object in an assignment in the usual way, using the address operator:

```
    pBox = &Cigar;              // Store address of object Cigar in pBox
```

As we saw when we used the pointer **this** in the definition of the member function **compare()**, you can call a function using a pointer to an object. We can call the function **volume()** for the pointer **pBox** in this statement:

```
    cout << (*pBox).volume();   // Display volume of object pointed to by pBox
```

There is a different notation we can use for this which is much clearer and makes your programs easier to follow. This means using the **indirect member selector**. We can rewrite the previous statement as follows:

```
    cout << pBox->volume();  // Display volume of object pointed to by pBox
```

This statement has exactly the same meaning as the previous version. The indirect member selection operator is formed by a minus sign followed by a 'greater than' symbol. It gets its name from the fact that it selects a class member indirectly through a pointer. It can be applied to select function members or data members equally well, and is the typical notation used by most programmers for this kind of operation, so we will use it universally from now on.

Try It Out - Pointers to Classes

Let's try this out in practice to get the feel of it. We will use the class definition as the example **EX7-09.CPP** and just show where it has changed for this example.

Try it Out!

```
// EX7-12.CPP
// Using the indirect member selection operator
#include <iostream.h>

class Box                          // Class definition at global scope
{
...
      // Function to compare two boxes which returns True (1)
      // if the first is greater that the second, and False (0) otherwise
      int compare(Box xBox)
```

```
        {
            return this->volume() > xBox.volume();
        }
    ...
};

int main(void)
{
    Box Boxes[5];                // Array of Box objects declared
    Box Match(2.2, 1.1, 0.5);    // Declare Match Box
    Box Cigar(8.0, 5.0 ,1.0);    // Declare Cigar Box
    Box* pB1 = &Cigar;           // Initialize pointer to Cigar object address
    Box* pB2 = 0;                // Pointer to Box initialized to null

    cout << endl
        << "Address of Cigar is " << pB1        // Display address
        << endl
        << "Volume of Cigar is " << pB1->volume(); // Volume of object
                                                 // pointed to

    pB2 = &Match;
    if( pB2->compare(*pB1) )                     // Compare via pointers
        cout << endl
            << "Match is greater than Cigar";
    else
        cout << endl
            << "Match is less than or equal to Cigar";

    pB1 = Boxes;                      // Set to address of array
    Boxes[2] = Match;                 // Set 3rd element to Match
    cout << endl                      // Now access thru pointer
        << "Volume of Boxes[2] is " << (pB1 + 2)->volume();
    return 0;
}
```

How It Works

The only change to the class definition is not one of substance. We have only changed the `compare()` function to use the indirect member selector with the pointer `this`. The function `main()` merely exercises pointers to `Box` type objects in various, rather arbitrary, ways.

Within the function `main()`, after declaring an array `Boxes`, and the `Box` objects `Cigar` and `Match`, we declare two pointers to `Box` objects. The first, `pB1`, is initialized with the address of the object `Cigar`, and the second, `pB2`, is initialized to null. All of this is exactly the same kind of usage that you apply with a pointer to a basic type. The fact that we are using a pointer to a type we have defined makes no difference.

278

We use **pB1** with the indirect member selection operator to generate the volume of the object pointed to, and the result is displayed. We then assign the address of **Match** to **pB2** and use both pointers in calling the compare function. Because the argument of the function **compare()** is a **Box** object passed by value, we need to dereference **pB2** when we use it as an argument to the function.

Next, we set **pB1** to the address of the first element of the array of type **Box**, **Boxes**, in order to demonstrate that we can use address arithmetic on the pointer **pB1** when using it to select the member function. In this case, we select the third element of the array and calculate its volume. This is the same as the volume of **Match**.

If you run the example, the output window from EasyWin will look something like that shown below.

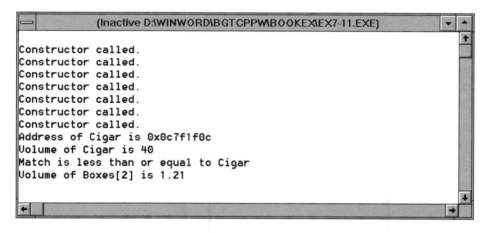

```
(Inactive D:\WINWORD\BGTCPP\BOOKEX\EX7-11.EXE)
Constructor called.
Constructor called.
Constructor called.
Constructor called.
Constructor called.
Constructor called.
Constructor called.
Address of Cigar is 0x0c7f1f0c
Volume of Cigar is 40
Match is less than or equal to Cigar
Volume of Boxes[2] is 1.21
```

*Of course, the value of the address for the object **Cigar** may well be different on your PC.*

You can see that there were seven calls of the constructor for **Box** objects, five due to the array **Boxes**, plus one each for the objects **Cigar** and **Match**.

Overall, there is virtually no difference between using a pointer to a class object, and using a pointer to a basic type such as **double**.

279

References to Class Objects

This is where references really come into their own. As with pointers, there is virtually no difference in the way you declare and use references to class objects, and the way in which we have already declared and used references to variables of basic types. To declare a reference to the object **Cigar** for instance we would write this:

```
Box& rCigar = Cigar;          // Define reference to object Cigar
```

To use a reference to calculate the volume of the object **Cigar**, you would just use the reference name where the object name would otherwise appear:

```
cout << rCigar.volume();      // Output volume of Cigar thru a reference
```

As you may remember, a reference acts as an alias for the object it refers to, so the usage is exactly the same as the original object name.

Implementing a Copy Constructor

The importance of references is really in the context of arguments and return value to functions, particularly class member functions. Let's return to the question of the copy constructor as a first toe in the water. We will sidestep the question of *when* you need to write your own copy constructor for the moment, and concentrate on the problem of *how* you can write one. We will use the class **Box** just to make the discussion more concrete.

The copy constructor is a constructor which creates an object by initializing it with an object of the same class which has previously been created. It therefore needs to accept an object of the class as an argument. We might consider writing the prototype like this:

```
Box( Box initB );
```

Let's now consider what happens when this constructor is called. If we write this declaration:

```
Box myBox = Cigar;
```

this will generate a call of the copy constructor as follows:

```
Box::Box( Cigar );
```

This seems to be no problem, until you realize that the argument is passed by value. So, before the object **Cigar** can be passed, the compiler needs to arrange to make a copy of it. Therefore, it calls the copy constructor to make a copy of the argument for the call of the copy constructor. Unfortunately, this call also needs a copy of its argument, so the copy constructor is called ... and so on and so on. We end up with an infinity of calls to the copy constructor.

The solution, as I'm sure you have guessed, is to use a **const** reference parameter. If the prototype of the copy constructor is this:

```
Box( const Box& initB );
```

the argument to the copy constructor does not now need to be copied. It will be used to initialized the reference parameter, so no copying takes place. We could implement the copy constructor as follows:

```
Box::Box( const Box& initB )
{
    length = initB.length;
    breadth = initB.breadth;
    height = initB.height;
}
```

This assumes that the copy constructor definition appears outside of the class definition. Of course, we could equally well use the initialization list to set the values of the object in this case. But this case is not an example of when we need to write a copy constructor. We will get to why and when we need to write our own copy constructor in the next chapter.

Summary

You now understand the basic ideas behind classes in C++. We are going to see more and more about using classes throughout the rest of the book.

The key points to keep in mind from this chapter are:

▶ A **class** provides a means of defining your own data types. These can reflect whatever types of **objects** your particular problem requires.

▶ A class can contain **data members** and **function members**. The function members of a class always have free access to the data members of the same class.

▶ Objects of a class are created and initialized using functions called **constructors**. These are automatically called when an object declaration is encountered. Constructors may be overloaded to provide different ways of initializing an object.

▶ Members of a class can be specified as `public`, in which case they are freely accessible by any function in a program. Alternatively, they may be specified as `private`, in which case they may only be accessed by members functions or `friend` functions of the class.

▶ Members of a class can be defined as `static`. Only one instance of each static member of a class exists which is shared amongst all instances of the class, no matter how many objects of the class are created.

▶ Every non-`static` member of a class contains the pointer `this`, which points to the current object for which the function was called.

▶ Using references to class objects as arguments to function calls can avoid substantial overhead in passing complex objects to a function.

▶ A copy constructor, which is a constructor for an object initialized with an existing object of the same class, must have its parameter specified as a `const` reference.

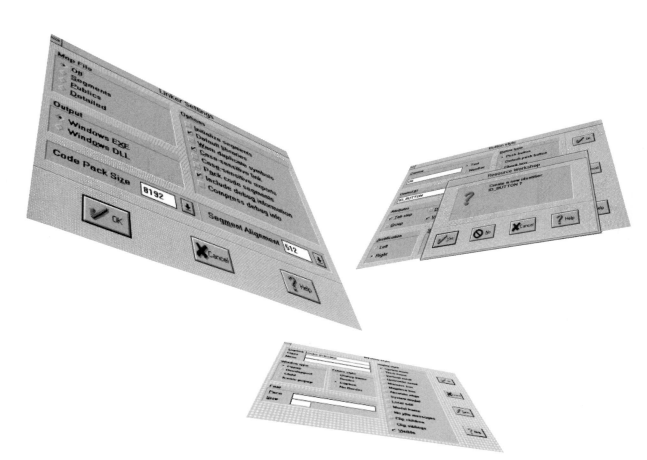

More on Classes

In this chapter you will extend your knowledge of classes by understanding how to make your class objects work more like the basic types in C++. In this chapter you will learn:

▶ What is a class destructor and when and why is it necessary.

▶ How to implement a class destructor

▶ How to allocate data members of a class in the free store, and how to delete them when they are no longer required.

▶ When you must write a copy constructor for a class.

▶ What is a union and how it can be used.

▶ How to make objects of your class work with C++ operators such as + or *.

▶ How to use classes in a practical example.

Class Destructors

Although this section heading refers to destructors, it is also about dynamic memory allocation. Allocating memory in the free store for class members can only be managed with the aid of a destructor, in addition to a constructor, of course. And it is dynamically allocated class members that will mandate the requirement for you to write your own copy constructor.

What is a Destructor?

A destructor is a function that destroys an object when it is no longer required or when it goes out of scope. It is called automatically when an object goes out of scope. Destroying an object involves freeing the memory occupied by the data members of the object (except for static members which continue to exist even when there are no class objects in existence). The destructor for a class is a member function with the same name as the class preceded by a tilde(~). The class destructor doesn't return a value and doesn't have parameters defined. For the class **Box**, the prototype of the class destructor is as follows:

```
~Box();            // Class destructor prototype
```

It's an error to specify either a return value or parameters for a destructor.

The Default Destructor

All the objects we have been using up to now have been destroyed automatically by the default destructor for the class. This is generated by the compiler in the absence of any explicit destructor being provided with a class. The default destructor doesn't delete objects or object members that have been allocated in the free store by the operator **new**. You must explicitly use the operator **delete** to destroy objects that have been created using the operator **new**, as you would with ordinary variables. If you decide to allocate memory for members of an object dynamically, you must supply a class destructor which frees any memory that was allocated by the operator **new** by using the operator **delete**.

Try It Out - A Simple Destructor

We need some practice in writing our own destructor. Firstly, we can include a destructor in the class **Box** just to show when the destructor is called. The whole code for the example is on the disk.

```
// EX8-01.CPP
// Class with an explicit destructor
#include <iostream.h>

class Box                    // Class definition at global scope
{
   public:
// Destructor definition
      ~Box()
      { cout << endl << "Destructor called.";}
   ...
};
```

```
int main(void)
{
   Box Boxes[5];                // Array of Box objects declared
   Box Cigar(8.0, 5.0 ,1.0);    // Declare Cigar Box
   Box Match(2.2, 1.1, 0.5);    // Declare Match Box
   Box* pB1 = &Cigar;       // Initialize pointer to Cigar object address
   Box* pB2 = 0;                // Pointer to Box initialized to null

   cout << endl
        << "Volume of Cigar is "
        << pB1->volume();       // Volume of obj. pointed to

   pB2 = Boxes;                 // Set to address of array
   Boxes[2] = Match;            // Set 3rd element to Match
   cout << endl                 // Now access thru pointer
        << "Volume of Boxes[2] is " << (pB2 + 2)->volume();
   return 0;
}
```

How It Works

The only thing our destructor does is to display a message showing it was called. The output is therefore as follows:

```
Constructor called.
Constructor called.
Constructor called.
Constructor called.
Constructor called.
Constructor called.
Constructor called.
```

```
Volume of Cigar is 40
Volume of Boxes[2] is 1.21
Destructor called.
Destructor called.
Destructor called.
Destructor called.
Destructor called.
Destructor called.
Destructor called.
```

We, therefore, get one call of the destructor at the end of the program for each of the objects which exist. For each constructor call that occurred, there is a matching destructor call.

Destructors and Dynamic Memory Allocation

We can use the operator **new** in a constructor to allocate space for an object member. In such a case, we must assume responsibility for deleting the space by providing a suitable destructor. Let's first define a simple class where we can do this. Suppose we want a class where each object is a message of some description, for example, a text string. We want the class to be as memory efficient as possible, so rather than defining a data member as a **char** array, we will allocate memory on the free store for a message as an object is created. Here is the class definition:

```
class Message
{
   private:
      char* pmessage;                    // Pointer to object text string

   public:

      void show_it(void)                 // Function to display a message
      {
         cout << endl << pmessage;
      }

// Constructor definition
      Message(const char* text = "Default message")
      {
         pmessage = new char[ strlen(text)+1 ]; // Allocate space for text
         strcpy( pmessage, text );              // Copy text to new memory
      }

      ~Message();                   // Destructor prototype
};
```

This class has only one data member defined, **pmessage**, which is a pointer to a text string. This is defined in the private section of the class.

In the public section, we have a function **show_it()** which will output a **Message** object to the screen. We also have the prototype for the class destructor, **~Message()**, which we will come to in a moment, and we have a definition of a constructor.

The constructor for the class accepts a string as an argument, and a default for the argument is specified. The constructor obtains the length of the string supplied as an argument, excluding the terminating null, using the function **strlen()**. To use this library function there must be an **#include** statement for the header file **STRING.H**. By adding 1 to the value the function **strlen()** returns, the constructor defines the number of bytes of memory necessary to store the string in the free store. We are assuming there is our own function to handle out of memory conditions, so we don't bother to test the pointer returned for null. Having obtained the memory for the string using the operator **new**, we copy the string supplied as an argument into the memory allocated for it using the **strcpy()** function, which is also declared in the header file **STRING.H**. This function copies the string specified by the second pointer argument to the address contained in the first pointer argument.

We now need to write a class destructor that will free up the memory allocated for a message:

```
// Destructor to free memory allocated by new
Message::~Message()
{
   cout << endl                        // Just to track what happens
        << "Destructor called.";
   delete[] pmessage;                  // Free memory assign to pointer
}
```

We need the name of the destructor qualified by the class name, **Message**, and the scope resolution operator, because we are defining it outside of the class definition. All the destructor does is display a message so we can see what is going on, and uses the operator **delete** to free the memory pointed to by the member **pmessage**. Note that we must include the square brackets with **delete** because the call to **new** was to allocate an array (of type **char**).

Try It Out - Using the Message Class

We can exercise this class with a little example.

```
// EX8-02.CPP
// Using a destructor to free memory
#include <iostream.h>          // For stream I/O
#include <string.h>            // For strlen() and strcpy()

class Message
{
...
};

// Destructor to free memory allocated by new
Message::~Message()
{
...
}
```

```
int main(void)
{
// Declare object
   Message Motto("A miss is as good as a mile.");
// Dynamic object
   Message* pM = new Message("A cat can look at a queen.");

   Motto.show_it();          // Display 1st message
   pM->show_it();            // Display 2nd message

   return 0;
}
```

How It Works

At the beginning of **main()** we declare and define an initialized **Message** object, **Motto**, in the usual manner. In the second declaration we define a pointer to a **Message** object, **pM**, and allocate memory for the object using the operator **new**. Here we are dynamically allocating space for the data member **pmessage**. The constructor will then call **new** again to allocate memory for the message text. If you run this example it will produce this output:

```
A miss is as good as a mile.
A cat can look at a queen.
Destructor called.
```

We have only one destructor call, even though we created two message objects. We said earlier that the compiler does not take responsibility for objects created in the free store. The compiler arranged to call our destructor for the object **Motto** because this is a normal automatic object, even though the memory for the data member was allocated in the free store by the constructor. The object pointed to by **pM** is different. We allocated memory for the **object** in the free store, so we have to use **delete** to remove it. You need to insert this statement:

```
delete pM;
```

just before the **return** statement in **main()**. This statement is already in the example on disk commented out. You can just remove the **//** to implement the change. If you run this version it will produce this output:

```
A miss is as good as a mile.
A cat can look at a queen.
Destructor called.
Destructor called.
```

Now we get an extra call of our destructor. This is surprising in a way. Clearly, **delete** is only dealing with the memory allocated by the call to **new** in the function **main()**. It only deleted the memory pointed to by **pM**. Since our pointer to **pM** is a pointer to a **Message** object for which a destructor has been defined, **delete** also calls our destructor to allow us to clean up the details of the members of the object. So when you use **delete** for an object created dynamically with **new**, **delete** will always call the destructor for the object allocated on the free store.

Implementing a Copy Constructor

For our class **Message**, the default copy constructor is woefully inadequate. If we have these statements:

```
Message Motto1("Radiation fades your genes.");
Message Motto2(Motto1);
```

the effect of the default copy constructor will be to copy the address in the pointer member from **Motto1** to **Motto2**, so there will be only one text string between the two objects. If **Motto1** is then destroyed, the pointer in **Motto2** will be pointing at a memory area which may now be used for something else, and chaos will surely follow. The solution is to supply a class copy constructor to replace the default. This could be implemented in the **public** section of the class as follows:

```
    Message(const Message& initM )          // Copy Constructor definition
       {
// Allocate space for text
         pmessage = new char[ strlen(initM)+1 ];
// Copy text to new memory
         strcpy( pmessage, initM.pmessage );
       }
```

This simply allocates enough memory to hold the string in the object **initM**, storing the address in the data member of the new object, and copies the text string from the initializing object. Now, our new object is identical to, but quite independent of, the old.

Sharing Memory Between Variables

As a relic of the days when 64K bytes was quite a lot of memory, we have a facility in C++ which allows more than one variable to share the same memory (but obviously not at the same time). This is called a **union**.

There are two basic ways in which you can use a union. Firstly, you can use it in a manner such that a variable **A** occupies a block of memory at one point in a program, and later the same memory is occupied by another variable **B** of a different type, because **A** is no longer required. I recommend you don't do this. It is not worth the risk of error that is implicit in such an arrangement. You can achieve the same effect by allocating memory dynamically. Secondly, you could have a situation in a program where a large array of data is required, but you don't know in advance of execution what the data type is. This will be determined by the input data. I also recommend you don't use unions for this either, since you can achieve the same result using a couple of pointers of different types and allocating the memory dynamically.

Since I can't think of a good reason to justify using a union in a particular circumstance, we won't dwell on them, but we will describe how they work so you will recognize one if you see one.

Defining Unions

A union is defined using the keyword **union**. It is best understood by taking an example of a definition:

```
union shareLD            // Sharing memory between long and double
{
   double dval;
   long lval;
};
```

This defines a union type **shareLD** which provides for the variables of type **long** and **double** to occupy the same memory. The union type name is usually referred to as a **tag name**. This statement is rather like a class definition in that we haven't defined a union instance yet, so we don't have any variables at this point. We do this in a declaration. For example:

```
shareLD MyUnion;
```

This declares an instance of the union we previously defined. If we want to refer to a member of the union, we use the direct member selection operator (the period) with the union tag name. So, we could set the long variable **lval** to 100 in the union instance **MyUnion** with this statement:

```
MyUnion.lval = 100;        // Using a member of a union
```

The basic problem with the way a union works is that you also need some means of determining which of the member values is current. This is usually achieved by maintaining another variable which acts as an indicator of the type of value stored.

A union is not limited to sharing between two variables. You can share the same memory between several variables if you wish. The memory occupied by the union will be that which is required by its largest member. For example, if we define this union:

```
union shareDLF
{
   double dval;
   long lval;
   float fval;
} uinst = 1.5;
```

it will occupy 8 bytes, as illustrated in the figure below.

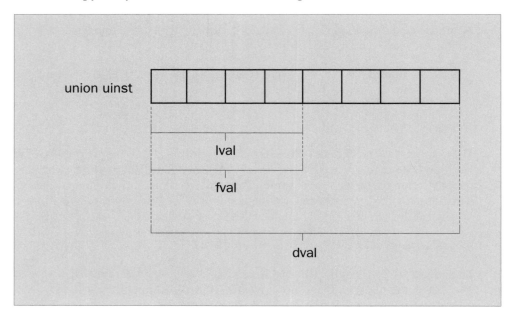

In the example, we defined an instance of the union, **uinst**, as well as the tag name for the union. We also initialized it with the value 1.5.

You can only initialize the first member of the union when you declare an instance.

Anonymous unions

You can define a union without a union type name, in which case an instance of the union is automatically declared. For example, if we define this union:

```
union
{
    char* pval;
    double dval;
    long lval;
};
```

it also defines an instance of the union with no name, so that the variables it contains may be referred to just by their names. Obviously, in any given scope, there can be only one anonymous union. As an illustration of how the anonymous union above works, to use the **double** member you could write this statement:

```
dval = 99.5;      // Using a member of an anonymous union
```

Unions in Classes

You can include an instance of a union in a class. This usually necessitates maintaining a class data member to indicate what kind of value is stored in the union. There isn't a great deal to be gained by using unions as class members.

Operator Overloading

Operator overloading enables you to make standard operators such as **+**, **-**, ***** and so on, work with objects of your own data types. It allows you to write a function which redefines a particular operator, **>** say, so that it performs a particular action when it is used with objects of a class. For example, you could redefine the operator **>**, so that when it was used with objects of the class **Box** (which we saw earlier), it would return **True** if the first **Box** argument had a greater volume than the second.

With operator overloading, you can't invent new operators. You also can't change the precedence of an operator, so your overloaded version of an operator will have the same priority in the sequence of evaluating an expression as the original base operator.

You can't overload all the operators - however, the restrictions aren't particularly oppressive. These are the operators you can't overload:

Name	Operator
The scope resolution operator	::
The conditional operator	?:
The direct member selection operator	.
The size of operator	sizeof
The dereference pointer to class member operator	.*

Anything else is fair game, which gives you quite a bit of scope. Obviously, it is a good idea to ensure that your version of the standard operators are reasonably consistent with their normal usage. It wouldn't be a very sensible approach to produce an overloaded + operator for a class that performed the equivalent of a multiply on class members. The best way to understand how operator overloading works is to work through an example, so let's implement what we just referred to, the greater than operator, >, for the class **Box**.

Implementing an Overloaded Operator

If we want to implement an overloaded operator for a class, we have to write a special function. Assuming it is a member of the class **Box**, the prototype for the function to overload the > operator will be as follows:

```
int operator > ( Box& aBox);     // Overloaded 'greater than'
```

The word **operator** here is a keyword. Combined with an operator, in this case >, it defines an operator function. The function name in this case is **operator>**. You can write an operator function with or without a space between the keyword **operator** and the operator itself, as long as there is no ambiguity. The ambiguity arises with operators using normal letters such as **new** or **delete**. If they are written without a space, **operatornew** and **operatordelete**, then they are legal names for ordinary functions, so for operator functions with these operators, you must leave a space between the keyword and the operator.

With our operator function **operator>()**, the right operand of the operator is that which is defined between parentheses. The left operand will be defined implicitly by the pointer **this**. So if we have the following **if** statement:

```
if(Box1 > Box2 )
    cout << endl << "Box1 is greater than Box2";
```

the expression between parentheses in the **if** will call our operator function. It is equivalent to this function call:

```
Box1.operator>(Box2);
```

The correspondence between the **Box** objects in the expression, and the operator function parameters, are illustrated below.

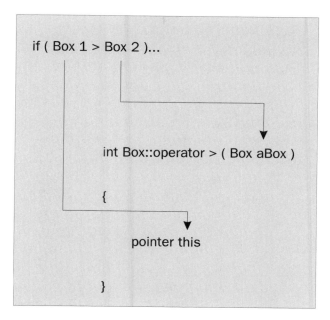

Let's write the code for the **operator>()** function:

```
// Operator function for 'greater than' which
// compares volumes of Box objects.
int Box::operator>( Box& aBox)
{
    if( (this->volume()) > (aBox.volume()) )
        return 1;
    else
        return 0;
}
```

We use a reference parameter to the function to avoid unnecessary copying when the function is called. The **if** statement expression calculates the volume of the **Box** object pointed to by **this** using the member function **volume()**, and comparing the result using the basic operator **>** with the volume of the object **aBox**.

Try It Out - Operator Overloading

We can exercise this function with an example.

```cpp
//EX8-03.CPP
// Exercising the overloaded 'greater than' operator
#include <iostream.h>                    // For stream I/O

class Box                                // Class definition at global scope
{
   public:
// Constructor definition
      Box(double lv=1.0, double bv=1.0, double hv=1.0)
      {
         cout << endl << "Constructor called.";
         length = lv;                    // Set values of
         breadth = bv;
         height = hv;                     // data members
      }

// Function to calculate the volume of a box
      double volume()
      {
         return length*breadth*height;
      }

      int operator > ( Box& aBox);     // Overloaded 'greater than'

// Destructor definition
      ~Box()
      { cout << endl << "Destructor called.";}

   private:
      double length;            // Length of a box in inches
      double breadth;           // Breadth of a box in inches
      double height;            // Height of a box in inches

};

// Operator function for 'greater than' which
// compares volumes of Box objects.
int Box::operator>( Box& aBox)
{
   if( (this->volume()) > (aBox.volume()) )
      return 1;
   else
      return 0;
}
```

```
int main(void)
{
   Box SmallBox( 4.0,2.0, 1.0 );
   Box MediumBox( 10.0, 4.0, 2.0 );
   Box BigBox( 30.0, 20.0, 40.0 );

   if(MediumBox > SmallBox )
      cout << endl
         << "MediumBox is Bigger than SmallBox";

   if(MediumBox > BigBox)
      cout << endl
         << "MediumBox is Bigger than BigBox";
   else
      cout << endl
         << "MediumBox is not Bigger than BigBox";

   return 0;
}
```

How It Works

The prototype of the operator function **operator>()** appears in the public section of the class. As the function definition is outside the class definition, it won't default to **inline**. This is quite arbitrary. We could just as well have put the definition in place of the prototype in the class definition. In this case, we wouldn't need to qualify the function name with **Box::** in front of it. As you will remember, this is needed in order to tell the compiler that this function is a member of the class **Box**.

The function **main()** has two **if** statements using the operator **>** with class members. These automatically invoke our overloaded operator. You could add an output statement to the operator function if you wanted to get confirmation of this. The output from the example as written will be as follows:

```
Constructor called.
Constructor called.
Constructor called.
MediumBox is bigger than SmallBox
MediumBox is not bigger than BigBox
Destructor called.
Destructor called.
Destructor called.
```

The output demonstrates that the **if** statements work fine with our operator function, so being able to express the solution to **Box** problems directly in terms of **Box** objects is beginning to be a realistic proposition.

Implementing Full Support for an Operator

With our operator function `operator>()`, there is still a lot of things you can't do. Specifying a problem solution in terms of `Box` objects might well involve statements such as the following:

```
if( aBox > 20.0 )
```

Our function won't deal with that. If you try to use an expression comparing a `Box` object with a numerical value you will get an error message. In order to support this we would need to write another version of the function `operator>()` as an overloaded function.

We can support the type of expression we have seen quite easily. The prototype of the function would be:

```
// Compare a Box object with a constant
int operator>( const double& value );
```

This would appear in the definition of the class. The `Box` object will be passed as the implicit pointer `this`.

The implementation is also easy. It is just one statement in the body of the function:

```
// Function to compare a Box object with a constant
int Box::operator>( const double& value )
{
    if( volume() > value )
        return 1;
    else
        return 0;
}
```

This couldn't be much simpler, could it? But we still have a problem with the operator `>` with `Box` objects. We may well want to write statements such as this:

```
if( 20.0 > aBox )
    .....                        // do something
```

You might argue that this could be done by implementing the operator function `operator<()`, which is quite true. Indeed, that is likely to be a requirement anyway for comparing `Box` objects. An implementation of support for an object type should not artificially restrict the ways in which you use the objects in an expression. The use of the objects should be as natural as possible. The problem is how to do it. A member operator function always provides the left argument as the pointer **this**. Since the left argument is of type **double** we can't implement it as a member function. That leaves us with two choices, an ordinary function or a **friend** function. Since we don't need to access the **private** members of the class we can implement it as an ordinary function. The prototype would need to be:

```
int operator>( const double& value, Box& aBox );
```

placed outside the class definition, and the implementation would be this:

```
// Function comparing a constant with a Box object
int operator>( const double& value, Box& aBox )
{
   if( value > aBox.volume() )
      return 1;
   else
      return 0;
}
```

As we have seen already, an ordinary function (and a **friend** function for that matter) accesses the data members of an object by using the direct member selection operator and the object name. The member function **volume()** is **public** so there is no problem using it here.

If the class did not have the function **volume()**, we could either use a **friend** function that could access the private data members directly, or we could provide a set of member functions to return the values of the private data members, and use those in an ordinary function to implement the comparison.

Try It Out - Complete Overloading of the > Operator

We can put all this together in an example to show how it works. We will define the member functions within the class definition since this will be the typical way of doing it more efficiently.

Try it Out!

301

```
//EX8-04.CPP
// Implementing a complete overloaded 'greater than' operator
#include <iostream.h>                  // For stream I/O

class Box                             // Class definition at global scope
{
   public:
// Constructor definition
      Box(double lv=1.0, double bv=1.0, double hv=1.0):
             length(lv), breadth(bv), height(hv)
      {
         cout << endl << "Constructor called.";
      }

      // Function to calculate the volume of a box
      double volume()
      {
         return length*breadth*height;
      }

// Operator function for 'greater than' which
// compares volumes of Box objects.
      int operator>( Box& aBox)
      {
         if( (this->volume()) > (aBox.volume()) )
            return 1;
         else
            return 0;
      }

// Function to compare a Box object with a constant
      int operator>( const double& value )
      {
         if( volume() > value )
            return 1;
         else
            return 0;
      }

// Destructor definition
      ~Box()
      { cout << endl << "Destructor called.";}

   private:
      double length;            // Length of a box in inches
      double breadth;           // Breadth of a box in inches
      double height;            // Height of a box in inches

};

int operator>( const double& value, Box& aBox ); // Function prototype
```

```
int main(void)
{
   Box SmallBox( 4.0,2.0, 1.0 );
   Box MediumBox( 10.0, 4.0, 2.0 );

   if(MediumBox > SmallBox )
      cout << endl
           << "MediumBox is Bigger than SmallBox";

   if(MediumBox > 50.0)
      cout << endl
           << "MediumBox capacity is more than 50";
   else
      cout << endl
           << "MediumBox capacity is not more than 50";

   if(10.0 > SmallBox)
      cout << endl
           << "SmallBox capacity is less than 10";
   else
      cout << endl
           << "SmallBox capacity is not less than 10";

   return 0;
}

// Function comparing a constant with a Box object
int operator>( const double& value, Box& aBox )
{
   if( value > aBox.volume() )
      return 1;
   else
      return 0;
}
```

How It Works

The constructor for the class **Box** has been updated to initialize the data members rather than use assignments, since it is a bit more efficient. Note the position of the prototype for the ordinary function version of **operator>()**. It needs to follow the class definition because it refers to a **Box** object in the parameter list. If you place it before the class definition the example will not compile. There is a way to place it at the beginning of the program file following the **#include** statement, and that is to use an **incomplete class declaration**. This would precede the prototype and would look like this:

```
class Box;                                    // Incomplete class declaration
int operator>( const double& value, Box& aBox ); // Function prototype
```

303

The incomplete class declaration identifies `Box` to the compiler as a class and is sufficient to allow the compiler to properly process the prototype for the function.

This mechanism is also essential in circumstances such as the ones where you have two classes, each of which has an object of the other class as a member. They each will then require the other to be declared first. It is possible to resolve this impasse through the use of an incomplete class declaration.

The output from the example is as follows:

```
Constructor called.
Constructor called.
MediumBox is bigger than SmallBox
MediumBox capacity is more than 50
SmallBox capacity is less than 10
Destructor called.
Destructor called.
```

After the constructor messages due to the declarations of the objects `SmallBox` and `MediumBox`, we have the output lines from the three `if` statements, each of which is working as we expected. The first of these is calling the operator function that is a class member and works with two `Box` objects. The second is calling the member function that has a parameter of type `double`. The expression in the third `if` statement calls the operator function that we implemented as an ordinary function.

As it happens, we could have made both the operator functions which are class members ordinary functions, since they only need access to the member function `volume()`, which is `public`.

> *Any comparison operator can be implemented in much the same way as we have implemented these. They would only differ in the minor details and the general approach to implementing them would be exactly the same.*

Overloading the Assignment Operator

If you don't provide an overloaded assignment operator function for your class, the compiler will provide a default. The default version will simply provide a member-by-member copying process similar to that of the default copy constructor. However, don't confuse the default copy constructor (which is called by a declaration of a class object that is initialized with an existing object of the same class), with the assignment operator (which is called when an assignment statement has a class object on both sides of the assignment operator).

For our **Box** class, the default assignment operator works without any problem, but for any class which has space for members allocated dynamically, you need to look carefully at the requirements of the class in question. There is considerable potential for chaos in your program.

Try It Out - A Bad Case of Assignment

Let's return to our message class for a moment, and see what effect the default copy operator can have. Let's suppose that we have a function member that resets a message to *****. We will call this function **reset()**.

```
// EX8-05.CPP
// Hazards of the default copy operator
#include <iostream.h>
#include <string.h>

class Message
{
   private:
     char* pmessage;                    // Pointer to object text string

   public:

     void show_it(void)                 // Function to display a message
     {
        cout << pmessage;
     }

//Function to reset a message to *
     void reset(void)
     {
        char* temp=pmessage;
        while(*temp)
           *(temp++)='*';
     }

// Constructor definition
     Message(const char* text = "Default message")
     {
        pmessage = new char[ strlen(text)+1 ]; // Allocate space for text
        strcpy( pmessage, text );               // Copy text to new memory
```

```
        }

        // Destructor to free memory allocated by new
        ~Message()
        {
            cout << endl                        // Just to track what happens
                 << "Destructor called.";
            delete[] pmessage;                  // Free memory assigned to pointer
        }
};

int main(void)
{

    Message Motto1("The devil takes care of his own");
    Message Motto2;

    Motto2 = Motto1;                        // Use default copy constructor

    cout << endl
         << "Motto2 contains - ";
    Motto2.show_it();

    Motto1.reset();                         // Setting Motto1 to * corrupts Motto2

    cout << endl
         << "Motto2 now contains ";
    Motto2.show_it();

    return 0;
}
```

How it Works

This example will produce this output:

```
Motto2 contains - The devil takes care of his own
Motto2 now contains - ******************************
Destructor called.
Destructor called.
```

It is clear that **Motto2** has been corrupted by the call to the member function **reset()** for **Motto1**. The problem is with the default assignment operator. This copies the members of the object **Motto1** to **Motto2**:

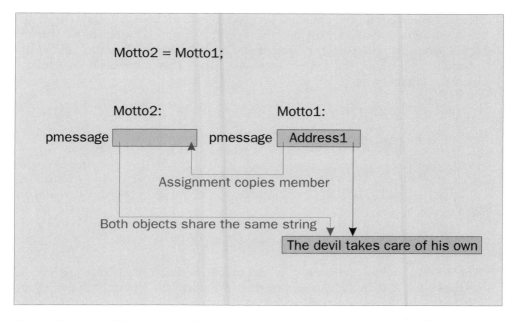

Since the two objects share the same text string, any change to the string belonging to **Motto1** modifies **Motto2**, and vice versa. What is required from the assignment operator is to copy the text to a memory area owned by the destination object, in this case **Motto2**.

Fixing the Problem

We can fix this with our own assignment operator which we will assume is defined within the class definition:

```
// Overloaded assignment operator for Message objects
   Message& operator=( const Message& aMess )
   {
// Release memory for 1st operand
      delete[] pmessage;
      pmessage = new char[ strlen( aMess.pmessage ) +1];

// Copy 2nd operand string to 1st
      strcpy( aMess.pmessage, pmessage );

// Return a reference to 1st operand
      return *this;
   }
```

There are a couple of subtleties here you need to take note of. The first is that we return a reference from the operator function because, as you may recall from our discussion of references in the last chapter, this allows the result to appear on the left of an equals sign. This is because we could have a statement such as:

```
Motto1 = Motto2 = Motto3;
```

which will translate into

```
( Motto1.operator=(Motto2) ) = Motto3;
```

with the result of the first operator function call on the left. This in turn will finally become this:

```
( Motto1.operator=(Motto2) ).operator=(Motto3);
```

The second subtlety you need to remember is that each object already has memory for a string allocated, so the first thing the operator function has to do is delete the memory allocated to the first object, and reallocate sufficient memory to accommodate the string belonging to the second object. Once this is done, the string from the second object can be copied to the new memory now owned by the first.

There is still a defect in this operator function. What if we were to write the following statement?

```
Motto1 = Motto1;
```

Obviously, you wouldn't do anything as stupid as this directly, but it could easily be hidden behind a pointer, for instance, as in the following statement:

```
Motto1 = *pMess;
```

where the pointer **pMess** points to **Motto1**. In this case, the operator function as it stands would delete the memory for **Motto1**, allocate some more memory based on the length of the string that has already been deleted, and try to copy the old memory, which by now has probably been corrupted. We can fix this with a check at the beginning of the function, so it would now become this:

```
// Overloaded assignment operator for Message objects
   Message& operator=( const Message& aMess )
   {
       if(this == &aMess )                  // Check addresses, if equal
           return *this;                    // return the 1st operand
// Release memory for 1st operand
       delete[] pmessage;
       pmessage = new char[ strlen( aMess.pmessage ) +1];

// Copy 2nd operand string to 1st
       strcpy( aMess.pmessage, pmessage );

// Return a reference to 1st operand
       return *this;
   }
```

If you put this definition of the operator function in the class definition of the previous example, you will find it will run without any problem. **Motto2** remains uncorrupted by using the **reset()** function with **Motto2**. This appears on the disk as **EX8-06.CPP**.

So let's have a golden rule out of all of this:

> *Always implement an assignment operator if you allocate space dynamically for a member of an object.*

Having implemented the assignment operator, what happens with operations such as **+=**? Well, they don't work unless you implement them. For each form of **op=** you want to use with your class objects, you need to write another operator function.

Overloading the Addition Operator

Let's look at overloading the addition operator for our **Box** class. This is interesting because it involves creating and returning a new object. The new object will be the sum (whatever we define that to mean) of the two **Box** objects that are its operands.

We can define the sum of two **Box** objects as a **Box** object with a volume which can contain the volumes of the other two, in the sense of being able to pack the two operand **Box** objects into the **Box** object that results from division. We can do this by making the new object have a **length** member which is the larger of the **length** members of the objects being added, and a **breadth** member derived in a similar way. The **height** member will be the sum of the **height** members of the two operand objects, so that the resultant **Box** object can contain the other two **Box** objects. This isn't necessarily an optimal solution, but it will be sufficient for our purposes. We can also arrange that the **length** member of a **Box** object is always greater than or equal to the **breadth** member, by altering the constructor. The addition operation is easier to explain graphically, so it is illustrated below.

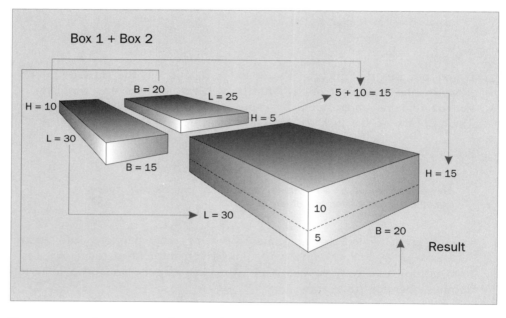

Since we need to get at the members of an object directly we will make the **operator+()** a member function. The prototype of the function will be this:

```
Box operator+( const Box& aBox );    // Function adding two Box objects
```

We define the parameter as a **const** reference to avoid unnecessary copying of the right argument when the function is called. The operation function definition would now be as follows:

```
// Function to add two Box objects
Box Box::operator+(const Box& aBox)
{
```

```
// New object has larger length and breadth, and sum of heights
   return Box( length>aBox.length? length:aBox.length,
               breadth>aBox.breadth? breadth:aBox.breadth,
               height+aBox.height);
}
```

Try It Out - Exercising Our Addition

We can see how this works in an example:

```
// EX8-07.CPP
// Adding Box objects
#include <iostream.h>                    // For stream I/O

class Box                                // Class definition at global scope
{
   public:
// Constructor definition
      Box(double lv=1.0, double bv=1.0, double hv=1.0):height(hv)
      {
          length = lv>bv ? lv : bv;          // Ensure that
          breadth = bv < lv ? bv : lv;       // length >= breadth
      }

// Function to calculate the volume of a box
      double volume()
      {
          return length*breadth*height;
      }

// Operator function for 'greater than' which
// compares volumes of Box objects.
      int Box::operator>( Box& aBox)
      {
          if( (this->volume()) > (aBox.volume()) )
             return 1;
          else
             return 0;
      }

// Function to compare a Box object with a constant
      int operator>( const double& value )
      {
          if( volume() > value )
             return 1;
          else
             return 0;
      }
```

```cpp
// Function to add two Box objects
    Box operator+(const Box& aBox)
    {
// New object has larger length and breadth, and sum of heights
        return Box( length>aBox.length? length:aBox.length,
                    breadth>aBox.breadth? breadth:aBox.breadth,
                    height+aBox.height);
    }

// Function to show the dimensions of a Box
    void ShowBox(void)
    {
        cout << length << " " << breadth << " " << height;
    }

  private:
    double length;          // Length of a box in inches
    double breadth;         // Breadth of a box in inches
    double height;          // Height of a box in inches

};

int operator>( const double& value, Box& aBox ); // Function prototype

int main(void)
{
   Box SmallBox( 4.0,2.0, 1.0 );
   Box MediumBox( 10.0, 4.0, 2.0 );
   Box aBox;
   Box bBox;

   aBox = SmallBox+MediumBox;
   cout << endl
        << "aBox dimensions are ";
   aBox.ShowBox();

   bBox = aBox+SmallBox+MediumBox;
   cout << endl
        << "bBox dimensions are ";
   bBox.ShowBox();

   return 0;
}

// Function comparing a constant with a Box object
int operator>( const double& value, Box& aBox )
{
   if( value > aBox.volume() )
      return 1;
   else
      return 0;
}
```

How It Works

In this example, we have changed the **Box** class members a little. The destructor has been deleted as it isn't necessary for this class, and the constructor has been modified to ensure that the length member is not less than the breadth member. This makes the add operation a bit easier. We have also added the function **ShowBox()** to output the dimensions of a **Box** object. This will enable us to verify that our overloaded add operation is working as we expect.

The output from this program is this:

```
aBox dimensions are 10 4 3
bBox dimensions are 10 4 6
```

This seems to be consistent with the notion of adding **Box** objects that we have defined. Note that the function also works with multiple add operations in an expression. For the computation of **bBox** the overloaded **add** operator will be called twice.

We could equally well have implemented the **add** operation for the class as a **friend** function. Its prototype would then be this:

```
friend Box operator+( const Box& aBox, const Box& bBox);
```

The method to produce the result would be much the same, except that the direct member selection operator would need to be used to obtain the members of the arguments to the function. It would work just as well as the first version of the operator function.

Using Classes

We have touched on most of the basic aspects of defining a class, so maybe we should look at how a class might be used to solve a problem. We will still need to keep the problem simple in order that this book does not entail an unreasonable number of pages! So we will consider problems in which we can use an extended version of the **Box** class.

The Idea of a Class Interface

The implementation of an extended **Box** class should incorporate the notion of a **class interface**. What we are going to provide is a tool kit for anyone wanting to work with **Box** objects, so we need to assemble a set of functions that represent the interface to the world of boxes. Since the interface will represent the only way to deal with **Box** objects, it needs to be defined to adequately cover the likely things one would want to do with a **Box** object, and be implemented as far as possible in a manner that protects against misuse or accidental errors.

The first question we need to consider is what is the nature of the problem we intend to solve, and from that derive the kind of functionality we need to provide in the class interface.

Defining the Problem

The principle function of a box is to contain objects of one kind or another, in a word our problem is *packaging*. We will attempt to provide a class that eases packaging problems in general, and then see how it might be used. We will assume that we will always be working on packing **Box** objects into other **Box** objects, since if you want to pack candy in a box, you could always represent each of the pieces of candy as an idealized **Box** object. The basic operations we might want to provide for our **Box** class include:

- Calculate the volume of a **Box**. This is a fundamental characteristic of a **Box** object and we have an implementation of this already.

- Compare the volumes of two **Box** objects to determine which is the larger. We probably should support a complete set of comparison operators for **Box** objects. We already have a version of the operator **>**.

- Compare the volume of a **Box** object with a specified value and vice versa. We also have an implementation of this for the operator **>**, but we will also need the other comparison operators.

- Add two **Box** objects to produce a **Box** object which will contain both the original objects. Thus, the result will be at least the sum of the volumes, but may be larger. We have a version of this already overloading the operator **+**.

- Multiply a **Box** object by an integer (and vice versa) to provide a **Box** object which will contain the specified number of the original object. This is effectively designing a carton.

- Determine how many **Box** objects of a given size can be packed in another **Box** object of a given size. This is effectively division, so we could overload the operator **/**.

- Determine the volume of space remaining in a **Box** object after packing it with the maximum number of **Box** objects of a given size.

We had better stop right there! There are undoubtedly other functions that would be very useful, but in the interest of saving trees we will consider the set complete, apart from ancillaries such as accessing dimensions, for example.

Implementing the Box Class

We really need to consider the degree of error protection we want to build into the **Box** class. The basic class we defined to illustrate various aspects of a class is a starting point, but we should also consider some aspects a little more deeply. The constructor is a little weak in that it doesn't ensure that we have valid dimensions for a **Box**, so perhaps the first thing we should do is ensure we always have valid objects. We could redefine the basic class as follows:

```
class Box                           // Class definition at global scope
{
   public:
// Constructor definition
      Box(double lv=1.0, double bv=1.0, double hv=1.0)
      {
         lv = lv<=0 ? 1.0 : lv;          // Ensure positive
         bv = bv<=0 ? 1.0 : bv;          // dimensions for
         hv = hv<=0 ? 1.0 : hv;          // the object

         length = lv>bv ? lv : bv;       // Ensure that
         breadth = bv < lv ? bv : lv;    // length >= breadth
      }

// Function to calculate the volume of a box
      double volume()
      {
         return length*breadth*height;
      }
```

```
// Function providing the length of a Box
    double getlen() { return length; }

// Function providing the breadth of a Box
    double getbr() { return breadth; }

// Function providing the height of a Box
    double getht() { return height; }

  private:
    double length;        // Length of a box in inches
    double breadth;       // Breadth of a box in inches
    double height;        // Height of a box in inches

};
```

Our constructor is now secure since we set any negative or zero dimension to 1. You could also consider displaying a message for a negative or zero dimension, since there is obviously an error when this occurs, and arbitrarily and silently setting a dimension to 1 might not be what is wanted.

The default copy constructor is satisfactory for our class since we have no dynamic memory allocation for data members, and the default assignment operator will also work well with the class. Perhaps now we should consider comparisons for objects of our class.

Comparing Box Objects

We should support the operators >, >=, ==, <, <= for two **Box** objects as well as for a **Box** object and a value of type **double**. We should implement these as ordinary global functions, since they don't need to be member functions. We can also write the functions to compare two **Box** objects in terms of the functions to compare a **Box** object with a **double** value, so let's start with the latter. We can repeat the **operator>()** function we had before:

```
// Function for testing if a constant is > a Box object
  int operator>( const double& value, Box& aBox )
  {
    if( value > aBox.volume() )
       return 1;
    else
       return 0;
  }
```

We can now write the `operator<()` function in a similar way:

```
// Function for testing if a constant is < Box object
   int operator<( const double& value, Box& aBox )
   {
      if( value < aBox.volume() )
         return 1;
      else
         return 0;
   }
```

The implementation of the same operators but with the arguments reversed can now be specified using these two:

```
// Function for testing if Box object is > a constant
int operator>( Box& aBox, const double& value )
{ return value<aBox; }

// Function for testing if Box object is < a constant
int operator<( Box& aBox, const double& value )
{ return value>aBox; }
```

We just use the appropriate overloaded operator function we wrote before, with the arguments from the call to this function switched.

We now need `>=` and `<=` which will be the same as the first two but with `<=` instead of `<`, and `>=` instead of `>`. The `operator==()` functions are also very similar. We won't repeat them here since they are so simple and appear on the disk along with the same operator functions with the arguments reversed.

We now have a complete set of comparison operators for `Box` objects. Also keep in mind that these will also work with expressions, as long as the expressions results in objects of the required type, so we will be able to combine these with the use of other overloaded operators.

Combining Box Objects

Now we come to the question of overloading the operators +, *, /, and %. We will take them in order. The add operation we already have from **EX8-07.CPP** has this prototype:

```
Box operator+( const Box& aBox );      // Function adding two Box objects
```

Although our original implementation of this is not an ideal solution, we will use it to avoid overcomplicating our class. A better version would need to see if the operands had any faces with the same dimension and join along those faces, but coding this can get a bit messy. Of course, if this were a practical application, a better **add** operation could be developed later and substituted for the existing version, and any programs written using the original would still run without change.

The multiply operation is very easy. It represents the process of creating a box to contain **n** boxes where **n** is the multiplier. The simplest solution would be to take the **length** and **breadth** of the object to be packed, and multiply the height by **n** to get the new **Box** object. We will make it minimally more clever by checking whether or not the multiplier is even, and if it is, stacking the boxes side by side by doubling the **breadth** and only multiplying the **height** by half of **n**. This is illustrated in the following figure:

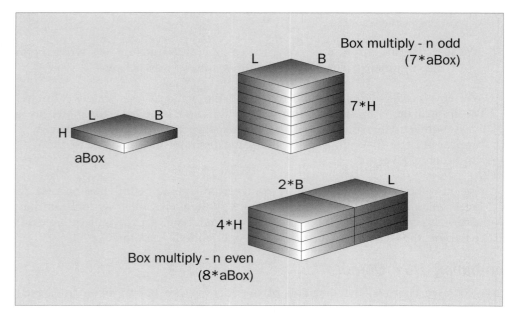

We will write the version of the operator function, **operator*()**, with the left operand as a **Box** object, as a member function:

```
// Box multiply operator aBox*n
Box operator*( int n )
{
```

```
    if( n%2 )
       return Box( length, breadth, n*height);              // n odd
    else
       return Box(length, 2.0*breadth, (n/2)*height );      // n odd
}
```

We can then use this function to write the version, with the left operand as an integer, as a non-member function:

```
// Box multiply operator n*aBox
Box operator*( int n, Box aBox )
{
   return aBox*n;
}
```

This version of the multiply operation uses the previous version directly. The only difference between the two is the operand sequence. That completes the set of combinatorial operators for **Box** objects that we defined. We can look finally at the two analytical operator functions **operator/()** and **operator%()**.

Analyzing Box Objects

We have said division will be determining how many of a **Box** object given by the right operand can be contained in the **Box** object specified by the left operand. To keep it relatively simple, we will assume that all the **Box** objects are packed the right way up, that is with the height dimensions vertical. We will also assume they are all packed the same way round, so that their length dimensions are aligned. Without these assumptions it can get rather complicated.

The problem will then amount to determining how many of the right operand objects can be placed in a single layer, and deciding how many layers we can get inside the right operand **Box**.

We will code this as a member function as follows:

```
int operator/(const Box& aBox )
{
   int tc1 = 0;      // Temporary for number in horizontal plane this way
   int tc2 = 0;      // Temporary for number in a plane that way

   tc1 = int(length/aBox.length) *
         int(breath/aBox.breadth);    // to fit this way..
   tc2 = int(length/aBox.breadth) *
```

```
        int(breadth/aBox.length;        // ...and that way

    return int(height/aBox.height)*( tc1>tc2 ? tc1:tc2); //Return best fit
}
```

This function first determines how many of the second operand **Box** can fit in a layer with the length aligned with the length dimension of the first operand **Box**. This is stored in **tc1**. We then calculate how many fit in a layer with the length of the second operand **Box** lying in the breadth direction of the first operand **Box**. We then multiply the larger of **tc1** and **tc2** by the number of layers we can pack in, and return that value. This process is illustrated below:

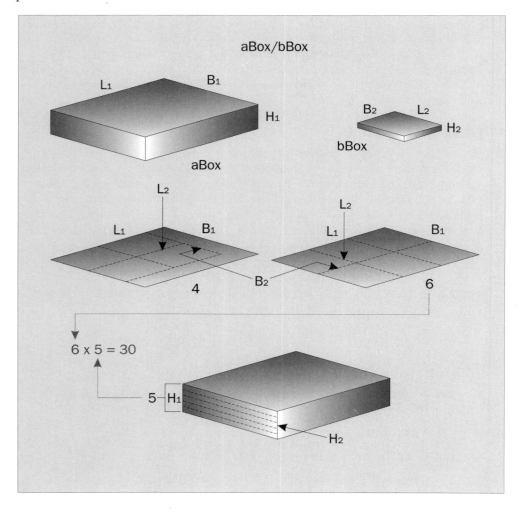

The other analytical operator function, `operator%()`, for obtaining the free volume in a packed **Box** is easier, since we can use the operator we have just written. We can write it as an ordinary global function, since we don't need access to the private members of the class.

```
// Operator to return the volume free in a packed Box
double operator%( Box& aBox, Box& bBox )
{
    return aBox.volume() - ( aBox/bBox )* bBox.volume();
}
```

This computation falls out very easily using existing class functions. The result is the volume of the big box, **aBox**, minus the volume of the **bBox** boxes in it. The number of **bBox** objects packed is given by the expression **aBox/bBox** which uses the previous overloaded operator. We multiply this by the volume of **bBox** objects to get the volume to be subtracted from the volume of the large box, **aBox**.

That completes our class interface. There are, clearly, many more functions that might be required for a production problem solver, but as an interesting working model demonstrating how we can produce a class for solving a particular kind of problem, it will suffice. We should try it out now on a problem.

Using Our Box Class

Let's suppose we need to package candies. They are on the big side, occupying an envelope 1.5 inches long by 1 inch wide by 1 inch high. We have access to a standard candy box that is 4.5 inches by 7 inches by 2 inches, and we want to know how many candies fit in the box so that we can set the price. We also have a standard carton that is 2 feet 6 inches long, by 18 inches wide, and 18 inches deep, and we want to know how many boxes of candy it can hold and how much space we are wasting.

In case the standard candy box is not a good solution, we would also like to know what custom candy box would be suitable. We know that we can get a good price on boxes with a length from 3 inches to 7 inches, a breadth from 3 inches to 5 inches, and a height from 1 inch to 2.5 inches, where each dimension can vary in steps of half an inch. We also know we need to have at least 30 candies in a box, because this is the minimum quantity consumed by our largest customers at a sitting, and the candy box should not have any empty space because the complaints from customers who think they are being cheated goes up. Further, ideally we want to pack the standard carton completely so they don't rattle around.

With our **Box** class the problem becomes almost trivial. The solution is represented by the following **main()** function:

```
// A sample packaging problem
#include <iostream.h>
#include "EX8-08F.CPP"   // This contains the Box class definition

int main(void)
{
    Box Candy(1.5,1.0,1.0);              // Candy definition
    Box CandyBox(7.0, 4.5, 2.0 );        // Candy box definition
    Box Carton(30.0, 18.0, 18.0 );       // Carton definition

// Calculate candies per candy box
    int NumCandies = CandyBox/Candy;

// Calculate candy boxes per carton
    int NumCboxes = Carton/CandyBox;

// Calculate wasted carton space
    double space = Carton%CandyBox;

    cout << endl
        << "There are " << NumCandies
        << " candies per candy box"
        << endl
        << "For the standard boxes there are " << NumCboxes
        << " candy boxes per carton " << endl << " with "
        << space << " cubic inches wasted.";

    cout << endl << endl << "CUSTOM CANDY BOX ANALYSIS (No Waste)";

// Try the whole range of custom candy boxes
    for (double length = 3.0 ; length <= 7.5 ; length += 0.5 )
       for (double breadth = 3.0 ; breadth <= 5.0 ; breadth += 0.5 )
          for (double height = 1.0 ; height <= 2.5 ; height += 0.5 )
          {
// Create new Box each cycle
              Box TryBox(length,breadth,height);

              if(Carton%TryBox < TryBox.volume() &&
                 TryBox%Candy == 0.0 && TryBox/Candy >= 30 )
                 cout << endl << endl
                     << "TryBox L = " << TryBox.getlen()
```

```
                    << " B = " << TryBox.getbr()
                    << " H = " << TryBox.getht()
                    << endl
                    << "TryBox contains " << TryBox/Candy << " candies"
                    << " and a carton contains " << Carton/TryBox
                    << " candy boxes.";
          }
      return 0;
  }
```

We should first look at how our program is structured. We have divided it into three files which is common when writing in C++. The file **EX8-08.CPP** contains our function **main()**. It includes the file **EX7-20F.CPP**, which contains the global functions and any class member functions that are defined external to the class definition. This in turn includes the file **EX8-08.H**, which contains the prototypes for the functions in **EX8-08F.CPP** which are not class members, and the definition of the class **Box**. So a C++ program can be divided into three basic files:

1   A **.H** file containing library **#include** commands, global variables, class definitions and function prototypes

2   A **.CPP** file containing further library **#include** commands and function definitions

3   Another **.CPP** file containing the function **main()**

The **#include** statement for including user defined files has the file name between double quotes. This causes TCW to search for the file in the same directory as the base **.CPP** file was found.

With complicated programs, there may well be many more than the basic three files making up the program. It is very easy to accidentally specify a file to be included in more than one place in a program. A user-defined file will therefore typically contain a sequence of what are called pre-processor commands, to ensure the contents are not accidentally include twice. The pre-processor commands are:

```
#ifndef EX8_08_H          // Tests if EX8_08_H has been defined
// If it has all the following statements down to #endif are ignored
// Otherwise all the following statements down to #endif are included
// and executed
#define EX8_08_H          // defines EX8_08_H
...
#endif                    // End of the effect of #ifndef
```

323

The pre-processor commands are those beginning with **#**. The **#ifndef** works rather like an **if** in that it tests whether the name specified has not already been defined, and if it hasn't, the following statements down to **#endif** are included. If the name exists, all the statements and commands down to **#endif** are ignored. The command **#define** defines the name.

If this file were included into a program more than once, the first **include** would include the file contents and define the name **EX8_08_H** with the **#define** command. For any subsequent inclusions of the file, the symbol **EX8_08_H** would already exist, so the **#ifndef** test would fail and the contents would be ignored.

The code in the function **main()** really doesn't need a lot of explanation. It is almost a direct expression of the definition of the problem in words, because the operators in the class interface perform problem-oriented actions on **Box** objects.

The solution to the question of the use of standard boxes is in the declaration statements, which also compute the answers we require as initializing values. We then output these values with some explanatory comment.

The second part of the problem is solved using the three nested **for** loops iterating over the possible ranges of length, breadth and height so we evaluate all possible combinations. We could output them all, but since this would involve 200 combinations of which we might only be interested in a few, we have an **if** which defines the options we are actually interested in. The **if** expression is only **True** if there is no space wasted in the Carton *and* the current trial candy box has no wasted space *and* it also contains at least 30 candies.

The output from this program is shown below.

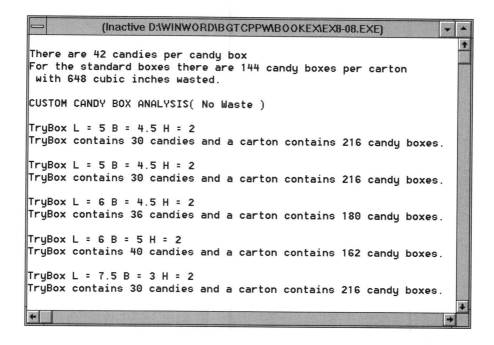

```
─                (Inactive D:\WINWORD\BGTCPPW\BOOKEX\EX8-08.EXE)        ▼ ▲
                                                                         ↑
There are 42 candies per candy box
For the standard boxes there are 144 candy boxes per carton
 with 648 cubic inches wasted.

CUSTOM CANDY BOX ANALYSIS( No Waste )

TryBox L = 5 B = 4.5 H = 2
TryBox contains 30 candies and a carton contains 216 candy boxes.

TryBox L = 5 B = 4.5 H = 2
TryBox contains 30 candies and a carton contains 216 candy boxes.

TryBox L = 6 B = 4.5 H = 2
TryBox contains 36 candies and a carton contains 180 candy boxes.

TryBox L = 6 B = 5 H = 2
TryBox contains 40 candies and a carton contains 162 candy boxes.

TryBox L = 7.5 B = 3 H = 2
TryBox contains 30 candies and a carton contains 216 candy boxes.
                                                                         ↓
←                                                                      →
```

We have a duplicate solution due to the fact that, in the nested loop, we will evaluate boxes that have a length of 5 and a breadth of 4.5, and a length of 4.5 and a breadth of 5. Because our class constructor ensures that the length is not less than the breadth, these two are identical. We could include some additional logic to avoid presenting duplicates, but it hardly seems worth the effort. You could treat it as a small exercise if you like.

Summary

In this chapter we have laid the foundations for object-oriented programming, and the basis for understanding how the Object Windows Library (OWL) in TCW works, since the OWL is based on a set of classes specially designed to make programming Windows easy. In the same way as we defined a **Box** class interface for working with **Box** objects, OWL implements a set of classes providing an easy-to-use set of tools for programming Windows. The next chapter will complete the knowledge necessary to understand how the OWL is applied.

The key points to keep in mind from this chapter are:

▶ It is essential to write a **copy constructor** for objects that have members allocated by **new**.

▶ Objects are destroyed using functions called **destructors**. It is essential to define a destructor to destroy objects which contain members that are allocated by **new**.

▶ A class may be designated as a **friend** of another class. In this case, all the function members of the **friend** class may access all the members of the other class. If class A is a **friend** of B, class B is not a **friend** of A unless it has been declared as such.

▶ Basic operators can be overloaded to provide actions specific to objects of a class. The compiler provides a default version of the assignment operator for a class, which you must replace with your own version if the objects of a class have members allocated by the operator **new**.

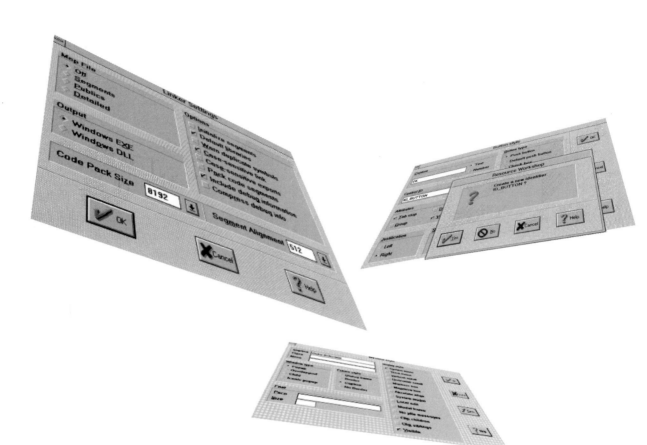

Class Inheritance

In this chapter we are going to look into what lies at the heart of object-oriented programming, and what will enable you to use the facilities of the OWL to program Windows applications. Inheritance is simply the means by which you can define a new class in terms of one you already have. You will use this in programming Windows by redefining the classes provided by OWL to suit your own particular needs, so it is important to understand inheritance.

In this chapter you will learn about

▶ How inheritance fits into the idea of object-oriented programming

▶ Defining a new class in terms of an existing one

▶ The use of the keyword **protected** to define a new access specification for class members

▶ Virtual functions and how you can use them

▶ Pure virtual functions

▶ Abstract classes

▶ Virtual destructors and when to use them

▶ Multiple inheritance

Basic Ideas of OOP

As we saw in the last chapter, a class is a data type that you define to suit your requirements. Classes in object-oriented programming also define the objects to which your program relates. You program the solution to the problem in terms of the objects of the problem, using operations that work directly with those objects. You can think of a class as representing something abstract such as a complex number - which is a mathematical concept, or a truck which is decidedly physical (especially if you run into one on the highway). So as well as being a data type, a class can also be a definition of a real world object, at least to the degree necessary to solve a given problem.

You can think of a class as defining the characteristics of a particular group of things that are specified by a common set of parameters, and share a common set of operations that may be performed on them that is essentially defined by the class interface contained in the public section of the class definition. The class **Box** that we used in the last chapter is a good example of this. This defined a box in the most elementary terms. Of course, in the real world there are also many different kinds of boxes: there are cartons, coffins, candy boxes and cereal boxes. You could differentiate them by the kind of things they hold, the materials they are made of, and in a multitude of other ways.

Even though there are many different kinds of box, they share common characteristics, so you can visualize them as actually being related to one another. You can define a particular kind of box as having the characteristics of a generic box, plus some additional parameters which serve to differentiate it. You may also find that there may be new things you can do with a particular kind of box. Equally, some objects may be the result of combining a particular kind of box with some other kind of object, a box of candy, or a crate of beer for example. An example of the kinds of relationships you could define between different sorts of objects is illustrated on the following page.

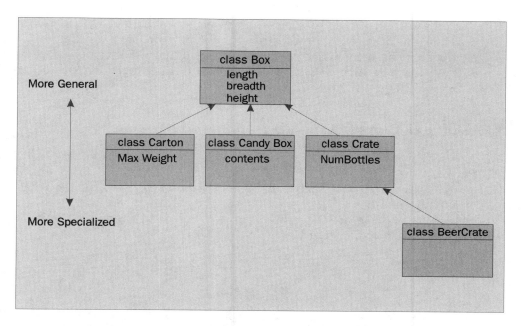

Therefore, to approximate the real world more accurately, you need to be able to define classes that are interrelated. A candy box can be considered to be a box with all the characteristics of a box, plus a few characteristics of its own. This is precisely the relationship between classes when one class is defined based on another.

Inheritance in Classes

When one class is defined in terms on another, or more generally in terms of several others, the class is referred to as a **derived class**. It automatically contains all the data members of the class or classes which are used to define it and, with some restrictions, the function members as well. In this case, the class is said to inherit the data members and function members of the classes on which it is based.

The only members of a base class which are not inherited by a derived class are the destructor, the constructors and any member functions overloading the assignment operator. All other function members, together with all the data members of a base class, will be inherited by a derived class.

What is a Base Class?

A base class is any class that is used in the definition of another class. This can be a direct base class when, for example, a class **B** is defined directly in terms of a class **A**. **A** is said to be a direct base of **B**. We shall see what this means in terms of the class definition in a moment. When a class **B** is defined in terms of a class **A**, **B** is said to be derived from **A**. This is illustrated in the following figure:

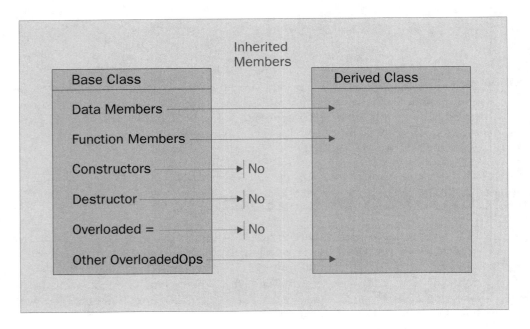

Deriving Classes from a Base Class

Let's go back to the original **Box** class we had at the beginning of the last chapter with **public** data members:

```
class Box
{
   public:
      double length;
      double breadth;
      double height;
      Box( double lv=1.0, double bv=1.0, double hv=1.0 )
      {
         length = lv;
         breadth = bv;
         height = hv;
      }
};
```

We have included a constructor in the class so that we can initialize objects when we declare them. Suppose we now need another class **CandyBox**, which is the same as a **Box** object but also has another data member, which is a pointer to a text string. We can define **CandyBox** as a derived class with the class **Box** as a base class, as follows:

```
class CandyBox : Box
{
   public:
      char* contents;

      CandyBox(char* str= "Candy" )            // Constructor
      {
         contents = new char[ strlen( str ) + 1 ];
         strcpy( contents, str );
      }

       ~CandyBox()                             // Destructor
       { delete[] contents; };
};
```

The base class, **Box**, appears after the class name for the derived class **CandyBox**, and is separated from it by a colon. In all other respects, it look like a normal class definition. We have added the new member, **contents**, and since it is a pointer to a string, we need a constructor to initialize it and a destructor to release the memory for the string. We have also put a default value for the string describing the contents of a **CandyBox** object in the constructor.

Try It Out - Using a Derived Class

We can see how our derived class works in an example:

```
// EX9-01.CPP
#include <iostream.h>                       // For stream I/O
#include <string.h>                         // For strlen() and strcpy()

class Box
{
...
};

class CandyBox : Box
{
...
};

int main(void)
{
   Box myBox(4.0,3.0,2.0);                  // Create Box object
   CandyBox myCBox;
   CandyBox myMBox("Wafer Thin Mints");     // Create CandyBox object

   cout << endl
        << "myBox occupies " << sizeof  myBox     // Show how much memory
        << " bytes" << endl
        << "myCBox occupies " << sizeof myCBox
        << " bytes" << endl
        << "myMBox occupies " << sizeof myMBox    // the objects require
        << " bytes";

   cout << endl
        << "Box length is " << myBox.length;

   myBox.length = 10.0;

// myCBox.length = 10.0;            // uncomment this for an error
   return 0;
}
```

How It Works

After declaring a **Box** object, and two **CandyBox** objects, we output the number of bytes occupied by each object, so let's look at the output:

```
myBox occupies 24 bytes
myCBox occupies 28 bytes
myMBox occupies 28 bytes
Box length is 4
```

The first is what we would expect from our discussion in the last chapter. A **Box** object has three data members of type **double**, each of which will be 8 bytes, making 24 bytes in all. Both our **CandyBox** objects are the same size - 28 bytes. The length of the string doesn't affect the size of an object, as the memory for it is allocated in the free store. The 28 bytes are made up of 24 bytes for the three **double** members inherited from the base class, **Box**, plus 4 bytes for the pointer member, **contents**. This is illustrated in the following figure:

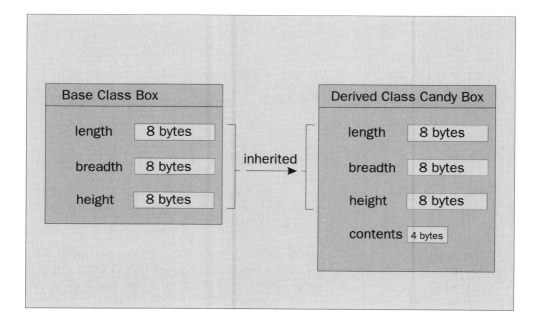

We also output the value of the **length** member of the **Box** object **myBox**. Even though we have no difficulty accessing this member of the **Box** object, if you uncomment the statement in the function **main()**:

```
// myCBox.length = 10.0;                    // uncomment this for an error
```

the program will no longer compile. The compiler will generate a message to the effect that the **length** member is not accessible. In the derived class, the member **length** has become **private**.

The reason for this is that there is a default access specifier of **private** for the base class. There always has to be an access specification for a base class, which will determine the status of the inherited members in the derived class. Omitting an access specification when specifying a base class causes the compiler to assume it is **private**. If we change the definition of the class **CandyBox** to the following:

```
class CandyBox : public Box
{
 ...
};
```

then the member **length** in the derived class will be inherited as **public** and will be accessible in the function **main()**. With the access specifier **public** for the base class, all the inherited members originally specified as public in the base class will have the same access level in the derived class.

Access Control Under Inheritance

The whole question of the access of inherited members in a derived class needs to be looked at more closely. Firstly, we should consider the **private** members of a base class in a derived class.

There was a good reason for choosing the version of the class **Box** with public data members, rather than the later, more secure, version with **private** data members. The reason was that although **private** data members of a base class are also members of a derived class, they remain **private** to the base class function members. They are only accessible in the derived class through function members of the base class that are not in the private section of the base class. You can demonstrate this very easily by changing all the **Box** class data members to **private**, and putting a function **volume()** in the derived class **CandyBox**, so that the class definitions become as follows:

```
// Version of the classes that will not compile
class Box
{
   public:

      Box( double lv=1.0, double bv=1.0, double hv=1.0 )
      {
         length = lv;
         breadth = bv;
         height = hv;
      }

   private:
      double length;
      double breadth;
      double height;

};

class CandyBox : public Box
{
   public:
      char* contents;

// Function to calculate the volume of a CandyBox object
      double volume(void)
      { return length*breadth*height; } // Error - members not accessible

      CandyBox(char* str= "Candy" )              // Constructor
      {
         contents = new char[ strlen( str ) + 1 ];
         strcpy( contents, str );
      }

      ~CandyBox()                                // Destructor
      { delete[] contents; }
};
```

A program using these classes will not compile. The function **volume()** in the class **CandyBox** attempts to access the **private** members of the base class, and this is not legal.

Try It Out - Accessing private Members of the Base Class

It is legal to use the **volume()** function in the base class however, so if you move the definition of the function **volume()** to the base class, **Box**, not only will the program compile, but you can use the function to obtain the volume of a **CandyBox** object:

```
// EX9-02.CPP
#include <iostream.h>        // For stream I/O
#include <string.h>          // For strlen() and strcpy()
class Box
{
   public:

//Function to calculate the volume of a Box object
      double volume(void)
      { return length*breadth*height; }


      Box( double lv=1.0, double bv=1.0, double hv=1.0 )
      {
         length = lv;
         breadth = bv;
         height = hv;
      }
   private:
      double length;
      double breadth;
      double height;

};

class CandyBox : public Box
{
...
};

int main(void)
{
   Box myBox(4.0,3.0,2.0);                  // Create Box object
   CandyBox myCBox;
   CandyBox myMBox("Wafer Thin Mints");    // Create CandyBox object
```

```
    cout << endl
        << "myBox occupies " << sizeof  myBox      // Show how much memory
        << " bytes" << endl
        << "myCBox occupies " << sizeof myCBox
        << " bytes" << endl
        << "myMBox occupies " << sizeof myMBox      // the objects require
        << " bytes";
    cout << endl                                    // Get volume of a
        << "myMBox volume is " << myMBox.volume();  // CandyBox object
    return 0;
}
```

How It Works

This example will produce the following output:

```
myBox occupies 24 bytes
myCBox occupies 28 bytes
myMBox occupies 28 bytes
myMBox volume is 1
```

The interesting additional output is the last line. This shows the value produced by the function **volume()**, which is now in the public section of the base class. Within the derived class, it operates on the members of the derived class that are inherited from the base. It is a full member of the derived class so it can be used freely with objects of the derived class.

The value for the volume of the derived class object is 1 because, in creating the **CandyBox** object, the default constructor **Box()** was called first to create the base class part of the object and this sets default **Box** dimensions to 1.

Constructor Operation in a Derived Class

The constructor for the base part of the derived class was called automatically in the last example. This doesn't have to be the case. We can arrange to call a particular constructor for a base class from the derived class constructor.

Try It Out - Calling Constructors

We can demonstrate this 'in action' using a modified version of the last example. We really should provide a derived class constructor which allows you to specify the dimensions of the object to make the class usable. We can produce an additional constructor to do this and call the base class constructor explicitly to set the values.

```
// EX9-03.CPP
#include <iostream.h>          // For stream I/O
#include <string.h>            // For strlen() and strcpy()

class Box
{
   public:

//Function to calculate the volume of a Box object
      double volume(void)
      { return length*breadth*height; }

// Base class constructor
      Box( double lv=1.0, double bv=1.0, double hv=1.0 )
      {
         cout << endl << "Box constructor called";
         length = lv;
         breadth = bv;
         height = hv;
      }

   private:
      double length;
      double breadth;
      double height;

};

class CandyBox : public Box
{
   public:
      char* contents;

// Constructor to set dimensions and contents
// with explicit call of Box constructor
      CandyBox(double lv, double bv, double hv, char* str= "Candy" )
         :Box(lv,bv,hv)              // Constructor
```

```
     {
         cout << endl <<"CandyBox constructor2 called";
         contents = new char[ strlen( str ) + 1 ];
         strcpy( contents, str );
     }

// Constructor to set contents
// calls default Box constructor automatically
     CandyBox( char* str= "Candy" )                          // Constructor
     {
         cout << endl << "CandyBox constructor1 called";
         contents = new char[ strlen( str ) + 1 ];
         strcpy( contents, str );
     }

     ~CandyBox()                                             // Destructor
     { delete[] contents; }
};

int main(void)
{
   Box myBox(4.0,3.0,2.0);                  // Create Box object
   CandyBox myCBox;
   CandyBox myMBox("Wafer Thin Mints");   // Create CandyBox object

   cout << endl
        << "myBox occupies " << sizeof  myBox       // Show how much memory
        << " bytes" << endl
        << "myCBox occupies " << sizeof myCBox
        << " bytes" << endl
        << "myMBox occupies " << sizeof myMBox      // the objects require
        << " bytes";
   cout << endl                                        // Get volume of a
        << "myMBox volume is " << myMBox.volume();   // CandyBox object
   return 0;
}
```

How It Works

As well as adding the additional constructor in the derived class, we have put an output statement in each constructor, so we will know when it gets called. The explicit call of the constructor for the **Box** class appears after a colon in the function header of the derived class constructor. You will have perhaps noticed that the notation is exactly the same as that used for initializing members in a constructor, which we saw in the last chapter.

```
    Box(double lv=1.0, double bv=1.0, double hv=1.0)
          :length(lv), breadth(bv), height(hv)
    {
...
    }
```

```
    CandyBox(double lv, double bv, double hv, char* str= "Candy" )
          :Box(lv,bv,hv)
      {
...
      }
```

This is quite consistent with what we are doing here, since we are initializing a **Box** sub-object of the derived class object. In the first case, we are explicitly calling the default constructors for the double types **length**, **breadth** and **height**. While in the second instance, we are calling the constructor for **Box**.

If you run this example it will produce this output:

```
Box constructor called
Box constructor called
CandyBox constructor1 called
Box constructor called
CandyBox constructor2 called
myBox occupies 24 bytes
myCBox occupies 28 bytes
myMBox occupies 28 bytes
myMBox volume is 24
```

The first line of output is due to the **Box** class constructor call originating from the declaration of the **Box** object, **myBox**. The second line of output arises from the automatic call of the base class constructor caused by the declaration of the **CandyBox** object **myCBox**.

Note how the base class constructor is always called before the derived class constructor, which outputs the next line.

The fourth line of output arises from the explicit call of the **Box** class constructor from our new constructor for **CandyBox** objects. This call passes the argument values specified for the dimensions of the object to the base class constructor. Next comes the output from the new derived class constructor itself, so constructors are again called for the base class first, followed by the derived class.

The last line shows that the initialization of the base part of the object **myMBox** is working as it should, with the private members having been initialized by the **Box** class constructor.

Having the **private** members of a base class only accessible to function members of the base isn't always convenient. There will be many instances where we want to have **private** members of a base class that can be accessed within the derived class. As you will surely have anticipated by now, C++ provides a way to do this.

Declaring protected Members of a Class

As well as the **public** and **private** access specifiers for members of a class, you can also declare members of a class as **protected**. Within the class, the keyword **protected** has exactly the same effect as the keyword **private**. Members of a class that are **protected** can only be accessed by member functions of the class, **friend** functions of the class and member functions of a class declared as a **friend** of the class. Using the keyword **protected**, we could redefine our class **Box** as follows:

```
class Box
{
   public:
       Box( double lv=1.0, double bv=1.0, double hv=1.0 )
       {
         cout << endl << "Box constructor called";
         length = lv;
         breadth = bv;
         height = hv;
       }

       // Box destructor - just to track call
       ~Box()
       { cout << endl << "Box destructor called"; }

   protected:
       double length;
       double breadth;
       double height;

};
```

Now, the data members are effectively **private**, in that they can't be accessed by ordinary global functions, but they will still be accessible to member functions of a derived class.

Try It Out - Using protected Members

We can demonstrate this by using this version of the class **Box** to derive a new version of the class **CandyBox**, which accesses the members of the base class through its own member function **volume()**.

```cpp
// EX9-04.CPP
// Using the protected access specifier
#include <iostream.h>          // For stream I/O
#include <string.h>                  // For strlen() and strcpy()

// class Box definition goes here

class CandyBox : public Box
{
    public:
        char* contents;

        // Derived class function to calculate volume
        double volume()
        { return length*breadth*height; }

        // Constructor to set dimensions and contents
        // with explicit call of Box constructor
        CandyBox(double lv, double bv, double hv, char* str= "Candy" )
            :Box(lv,bv,hv)                    // Constructor
        {
          cout << endl <<"CandyBox constructor2 called";
          contents = new char[ strlen( str ) + 1 ];
          strcpy( contents, str );
         }

        // Constructor to set contents
        // calls default Box constructor automatically
        CandyBox( char* str= "Candy" )               // Constructor
        {
          cout << endl << "CandyBox constructor1 called";
          contents = new char[ strlen( str ) + 1 ];
          strcpy( contents, str );
        }

        ~CandyBox()                                   // Destructor
        {
          cout << endl << "CandyBox destructor called";
          delete[] contents;
        }
};
```

```
int main(void)
{
   CandyBox myCBox;                                // Create CandyBox object
   CandyBox myTBox(2,3,4,"Stickjaw Toffee");   // Create CandyBox object

   cout << endl
        << "myCBox volume is " << myCBox.volume()  // Calculate volume
        << endl
        << "myTBox volume is " << myTBox.volume(); // of derived objects

// cout << endl << myTBox.length;      // Uncomment this for an error

      return 0;
}
```

How It Works

In this example, the volumes of the two **CandyBox** objects are calculated by invoking the function **volume()**, which is a member of the derived class. This function accesses the inherited members **length**, **breadth**, and **height** to produce the result. The members were declared as **protected** in the base class and remain **protected** in the derived class. The program produces the output shown below.

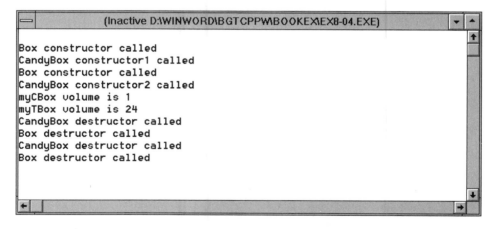

```
                (Inactive D:\WINWORD\BGTCPP\BOOKEX\EX8-04.EXE)

Box constructor called
CandyBox constructor1 called
Box constructor called
CandyBox constructor2 called
myCBox volume is 1
myTBox volume is 24
CandyBox destructor called
Box destructor called
CandyBox destructor called
Box destructor called
```

This shows that the volume is being calculated properly for both **CandyBox** objects. The first object has the default dimensions produced by calling the default **Box** constructor, so the volume is 1 and the second object has the dimension defined as initial values in its declaration.

The output also shows the sequence of constructor and destructor calls.

> *Note that destructors are called in the reverse sequence to constructors. This is a general rule that always applies. Constructors are invoked starting with the base class constructor and then the derived class constructor, whereas the destructor for the derived class is called first when an object is destroyed, followed by the base class destructor.*

You can demonstrate that the `protected` members of the base class remain `protected` in the derived class by uncommenting the statement preceding the `return` statement in the function `main()`. If you do this, you will get an error message from the compiler to the effect that the member `length` is inaccessible.

The Access Level of Inherited Class Members

We know that if we have no access specifier for the base class in the definition of a derived class, the default specification is `private`. This has the effect of causing the inherited `public` and `protected` members of the base class to become `private` in the derived class. The `private` members of the base class remain `private` to the base and therefore inaccessible to member functions of the derived class. In fact, they remain `private` to the base class regardless of how the base class is specified in the derived class definition.

We have also used `public` as the specifier for a base class. This leaves the members of the base class with the same access level in the derived class as they had in the base, so `public` members remain `public` and `protected` members remain `protected`.

The last possibility is to declare a base class as `protected`. This has the effect of making the inherited `public` members of the base, `protected` in the derived class. The `protected` (and `private`) inherited members retain their original access level in the derived class.

This is summarized in the following illustration:

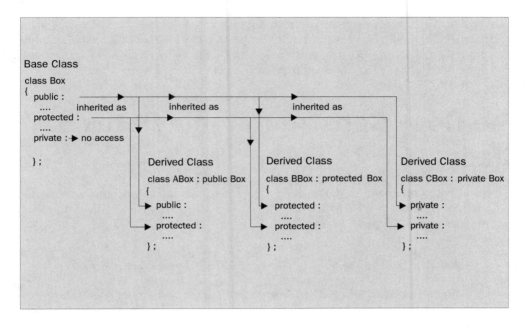

This may look a little complicated, but you can reduce it to the following three points about the inherited members of a derived class:

1   `private` members of a base class are never accessible

2   Defining a base class as `public` doesn't change the access level of its members in the derived class

3   Defining a base class as `protected` changes its `public` members to `protected` in the derived class

Being able to change the access level of inherited members in a derived class gives you a degree of flexibility, but remember that you can only make the access level more stringent. You can't in any way relax the level specified in the base class. This suggests that your base classes need to have `public` members if you want to be able to vary the access level in derived classes. This may seem to run contrary to the idea of encapsulating data in a class in order to protect it from unauthorized access, but as we shall see, it will often be the case that we construct base classes in such a manner that their only purpose is to act as a base for other classes and they are not intended to be used for instantiating objects in their own right.

The Copy Constructor in a Derived Class

You will remember that the copy constructor is called automatically when you declare an object which is initialized with an object of the same class. For example, in these statements

```
Box myBox(2.0, 3.0, 4.0);      // Calls constructor
Box CopyBox( myBox );          // Calls copy constructor
```

the first statement will call the constructor accepting three **double** arguments and the second will call the copy constructor. If you don't supply your own copy constructor the compiler will supply one that copies the initializing object member by member to the corresponding members of the new object. So that we can see what is going on during execution, let's add our own version of a copy constructor to the class **Box**. We can then use this class as a base for defining the class **CandyBox**.

```
class Box                   // Base class definition
{
   public:
      Box( double lv=1.0, double bv=1.0, double hv=1.0 )
      {
         cout << endl << "Box constructor called";
         length = lv;
         breadth = bv;
         height = hv;
      }

      // Copy constructor
      Box( const Box& initB )
      {
         cout << endl << "Box copy constructor called";
         length = initB.length;
         breadth = initB.breadth;
         height = initB.height;
      }
```

```
    // Box destructor - just to track call
    ~Box()
    { cout << endl << "Box destructor called"; }

protected:
    double length;
    double breadth;
    double height;

};
```

You will also recall that the copy constructor needs to have its parameter specified as a reference, in order to avoid an infinity of calls of itself, caused by the need to copy an argument that is transferred by value. When the copy constructor in our example is invoked, it will output a message to the screen, so we will be able to see from the output on what occasions this happens.

We can derive the **CandyBox** class exactly as before:

```
class CandyBox: public Box          // Derived class definition
{
...
};
```

This doesn't have a copy constructor added yet, so we will rely on the compiler-generated version.

Try It Out - Copy Constructor for Derived Classes

We can exercise the copy constructor we have just defined with the following example:

```
// EX9-05.CPP
// Using a derived class copy constructor
#include <iostream.h>          // For stream I/O
#include <string.h>            // For strlen() and strcpy()

class Box                     // Base class definition
{
...
};
```

```
class CandyBox: public Box              // Derived class definition
{
...
};
```

```
int main(void)
{
    CandyBox ChocBox( 2.0, 3.0, 4.0, "Chockies"); // Declare and initialize
    CandyBox ChoxBox( ChocBox );                    // Use copy constructor

    cout << endl
         << "Volume of ChocBox is " << ChocBox.volume()
         << endl
         << " Volume of ChoxBox is " << ChoxBox.volume();

    return 0;
}
```

How It Works

When you run this example, with a bit of luck it will produce this output:

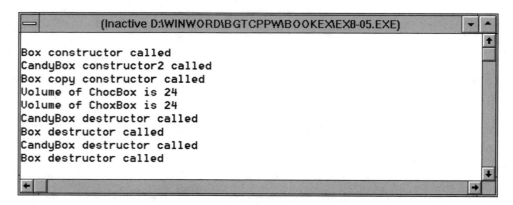

The output shows that the compiler generated copy constructor for the derived class automatically called the copy constructor for the base class.

However, all is not as it should be. In this particular case, the compiler generated copy constructor causes problems because the memory pointed to by the member **contents** of the derived class, in the second object declared, will point to the same memory as the first object. When one object is destroyed, it releases the memory occupied by the text. When the second object is destroyed, the destructor attempts to release some memory that has already been freed by the destructor call for the previous object. On my machine, this locks up the execution window for the example. It may well do the same on yours. The way to unlock it is *Ctrl-Alt-Del* in that window to terminate the task.

The way we can fix this is to supply a copy constructor for the derived class that will allocate some additional memory for the new object.

Try It Out - Fixing the Copy Constructor Bug

We can do this by adding the following code for the copy constructor to the public section of the derived class:

```
   // Derived class copy constructor
   CandyBox( const CandyBox& initCB )
   {
       cout << endl << "CandyBox copy constructor called";
// Get new memory
       contents = new char[ strlen( initCB.contents ) + 1 ];
// Copy string
       strcpy( contents, initCB.contents );
   }
```

We can now run this new version of the last example with the same function **main()** to see how our copy constructor. It appears on the disk as **EX9-06.CPP**.

How It Works

Now, when we run the example, it behaves rather better and produces the output shown in the screen below.

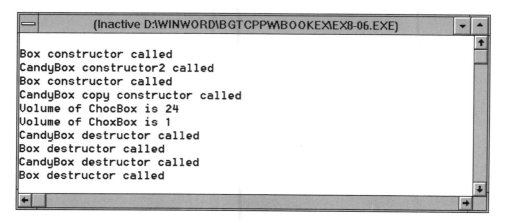

```
(Inactive D:\WINWORD\BGTCPP\BOOKEX\EX8-06.EXE)

Box constructor called
CandyBox constructor2 called
Box constructor called
CandyBox copy constructor called
Volume of ChocBox is 24
Volume of ChoxBox is 1
CandyBox destructor called
Box destructor called
CandyBox destructor called
Box destructor called
```

However, there is still something wrong. The third line of output shows that the default constructor for the **Box** part of the object **ChoxBox** is called, rather than the copy constructor. As a consequence, the object has the default dimensions, rather than the dimensions of the initializing object. The reason for this is that when you write a constructor for an object of a derived class, you are responsible for ensuring that the members of the derived class object are properly initialized. This includes the inherited members.

The fix for this is to call the copy constructor for the base part of the class in the initialization list for the copy constructor for the **CandyBox** class. The copy constructor would then become this:

```
// Derived class copy constructor
   CandyBox( const CandyBox& initCB ): Box( initCB )
   {
       cout << endl << "CandyBox copy constructor called";
// Get new memory
       contents = new char[ strlen( initCB.contents ) + 1 ];
// Copy string
       strcpy( contents, initCB.contents );
   }
```

Now, the **Box** class copy constructor is called with the **initBC** object. Only the base part of the object will be passed to it, so everything will work out. If you modify the last example by adding the base copy constructor call, the output will now be as below.

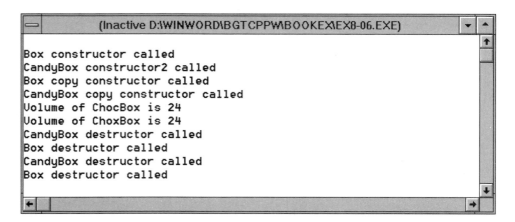

```
(Inactive D:\WINWORD\BGTCPP\BOOKEX\EX8-06.EXE)

Box constructor called
CandyBox constructor2 called
Box copy constructor called
CandyBox copy constructor called
Volume of ChocBox is 24
Volume of ChoxBox is 24
CandyBox destructor called
Box destructor called
CandyBox destructor called
Box destructor called
```

The output shows all the constructors and destructors are called in the correct sequence, and the copy constructor for the **Box** part of **ChoxBox** is called before the **CandyBox** copy constructor. The volume of the object **ChoxBox** of the derived class is now the same as that of its initializing object.

We therefore have another golden rule to remember:

> *If you write any kind of constructor for a derived class, you are responsible for the initialization of all members of the derived class object, including all its inherited members.*

Virtual Functions

We need to look more closely at the behavior of inherited member functions and their relationship to derived class member functions. Let's add a function to the class **Box** to output the volume of a **Box** object. The class would then become as follows:

```
class Box           // Base class
{
   public:

      // Function to show the volume of an object
      void ShowVolume(void)
      {
         cout << endl
             << "Box usable volume is " << volume();
      }

      // Function to calculate the volume of a Box object
      double volume(void)
      { return length*breadth*height; }

      // Constructor
      Box( double lv=1.0, double bv=1.0, double hv=1.0 )
            :length(lv), breadth(bv), height(hv){}

   protected:
       double length;
       double breadth;
       double height;

};
```

Now, we can produce the output of the usable volume of a **Box** object by just calling this function for any object for which we require the output. The constructor sets the data member values in the initialization list, so no statements are necessary in the body of the function. The data members are as before, and are specified as **protected**, so they will be accessible to the member functions of any derived class.

Let's suppose we want to derive a class for a different kind of box called a **GlassBox**, to hold glassware for instance. Because the contents are fragile, the capacity of the box is less than the capacity of a basic **Box** object because packing material is added to protect the contents. We therefore need a different **volume()** function to account for this, so we add it to the derived class:

```
class GlassBox: public Box       // Derived class
{
   public:

       // Function to calculate volume of a GlassBox
       // allowing 15% for packing
       double volume(void)
       { return 0.85*length*breadth*height; }

       // Constructor
       GlassBox( double lv, double bv, double hv ): Box(lv,bv,hv){}

};
```

There could conceivably be other additional members of the derived class, but we will concentrate on how the inherited functions work for the moment. The constructor for the derived class objects just calls the base class constructor in its initialization list to set the data member values. No statements are necessary in its body. We have included a new version of the function **volume()** to replace the version from the base class, the idea being that we can get the inherited function **ShowVolume()** to call the derived class version of the member function **volume()** when we call it for an object of the class **GlassBox**.

Try It Out - Throwing Stones in GlassBoxes

Now, we should see how our derived class works in practice. We can try this out very simply by creating an object of the base class and an object of the derived class with the same dimensions, and then verifying that the correct volumes are being calculated. The `main()` function to do this would be as follows:

```
// EX9-07.CPP
// Behavior of inherited functions in a derived class
#include <iostream.h>

...

int main(void)
{
    Box aBox(2.0, 3.0, 4.0);        // Declare a base box
    GlassBox aGBox(2.0,3.0,4.0);    // Declare a derived box of the same size

    aBox.ShowVolume();              // Display volume of base box
    aGBox.ShowVolume();             // Display volume of derived box

    return 0;
}
```

How It Works

If you run this example it will produce this output:

```
Box usable volume is 24
Box usable volume is 24
```

This is not only dull and repetitive, it is also disastrous. It isn't working the way we want at all and the only interesting thing about it is why. Evidently, the fact that the second call is for an object of the derived class **GlassBox** is not being taken account of. We can see this from the incorrect result in the output. The reason for this is that the call of the function **volume()**, in the function **ShowVolume()**, is being set once and for all by the compiler as the version defined in the base class. This is called **static resolution** of the function call, or **static linkage**. The function call is fixed before the program is executed. This is also sometimes called **early binding**, because the particular function `volume()` chosen is bound to the call from the function `ShowVolume()` during the compilation of the program.

> *Note that the function* `volume()` *here in the derived class actually hides the base class version from the view of derived class functions. If you wanted to call the base version of* `volume()` *from a derived class function, you would need to use the scope resolution operator to refer to the function as* `Box::volume()`.

What we were hoping for in this example was that the question of which `volume()` function call to use in any given instance would be resolved when the program was executed. This sort of operation is referred to as **dynamic linkage**, or **late binding**. We want the actual version of the function `volume()` called by `ShowVolume()` to be determined by the kind of object being processed, and not arbitrarily fixed by the compiler before the program is executed.

No doubt you won't be astonished that C++ does in fact provide us with a way to do this, since this whole discussion would have been otherwise futile! We need to use what is called a **virtual function**.

What's a Virtual Function?

A virtual function is a function in a base class that is declared using the keyword `virtual`. Defining a function as `virtual` in a base class that has another version in a derived class, signals to the compiler that we don't want static linkage for this function. What we *do* want is the selection of the function to be called at any given point in the program to be made based on the kind of object for which it is called.

Try It Out - Fixing the GlassBox

To make our example work as we originally hoped, we just need to add the keyword **virtual** to the definitions of the function **volume()** in the base and derived classes:

```
// EX9-08.CPP
// Using a virtual function
#include <iostream.h>

class Box            // Base class
{
   public:
...
      // Function to calculate the volume of a Box object
      virtual double volume(void)
         { return length*breadth*height; }
...
};

class GlassBox : public Box
{
   public:
...
      // Function to calculate volume of a GlassBox
      // allowing 15% for packing
      virtual double volume(void)
         { return 0.85*length*breadth*height; }
...
};

int main(void)
{
...
}
```

How It Works

If you run this version of the program with just the two little words **virtual double** added to the definition of **volume()** in the base and derived classes, it will produce this output:

```
Box usable volume is 24
Box usable volume is 20.4
```

This is now clearly doing what we wanted in the first place. The first call to the function **ShowVolume()** with the **Box** object, **aBox**, calls the inherited base version of **volume()**, and the second call with the **GlassBox** object calls the version defined in the derived class. It's not essential to put the keyword **virtual** in the derived class definition of the function **volume()**. The definition of the base version of the function as **virtual** is sufficient. However, I recommend that you *do* specify the keyword in derived classes for the virtual functions, since it makes it clear that they are virtual functions and that they will be selected dynamically.

In order for a function to behave as **virtual**, it must have the same name, parameter list and return type in any derived class, as the function has in the base class. If you use different parameters or return types the virtual function mechanism won't work. The function will operate with static linkage established and fixed at compile time.

The operation of virtual functions is an extraordinarily powerful mechanism. You may have heard the term **polymorphism** in relation to object-oriented programming. This refers to the virtual function capability. Something that is polymorphic can appear in different guises, such as a werewolf or Dr. Jekyll, for example. The same function call will produce different effects, depending on the kind of object to which it is applied.

Using Pointers to Class Objects

Using pointers with objects of a base class and of a derived class is a very important technique. A pointer to a base class object can be assigned the address of a derived class object as well as that of the base. We can thus use a pointer of the type pointer to base, to obtain different behavior with virtual functions, depending on what kind of object the pointer is pointing to. We can see how this works more clearly by looking at an example.

Try It Out - Pointers to Base and Derived Classes

Let's use the same classes as in the previous example, but make a small modification to the function **main()** so that it uses a pointer to a base class object.

```
// EX9-09.CPP
// Using a base class pointer to call a virtual function
#include <iostream.h>

    ...

int main(void)
{
   Box aBox(2.0, 3.0, 4.0);      // Declare a base box
   GlassBox aGBox(2.0,3.0,4.0);  // Declare a derived box of the same size
   Box* pBox = 0;                // Declare a pointer to base class objects

   pBox = &aBox;                 // Set pointer to address of base object
   pBox->ShowVolume();           // Display volume of base box
   pBox = &aGBox;                // Set pointer to derived class object
   pBox->ShowVolume();           // Display volume of derived box

   return 0;
}
```

How It Works

The classes are the same as in example **EX8-08.CPP**, but the function **main()** has been altered to use a pointer to call the function **ShowVolume()**. Because we are using a pointer, we have to use the indirect member selection operator, **->**. The function **ShowVolume()** is called twice, and both calls use the same pointer to base class objects, **pBox**. On the first occasion, the pointer contains the address of the base object, **aBox**, and on the occasion of the second call it contains the address of the derived class object **aGBox**.

The output produced is as follows:

```
Box usable volume is 24
Box usable volume is 20.4
```

which is exactly the same as that from the previous example using explicit objects in the function call.

We can therefore conclude from this example that the virtual function mechanism works just as well through a pointer to a base class, with the specific function being selected based on the type of object being pointed to. This is illustrated in the following figure.

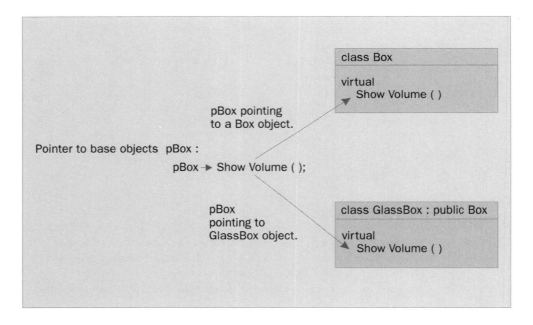

This means that, even when we don't know the precise type of the object pointed to by a base class pointer in a program (when a pointer is passed to a function as an argument for example), the virtual function mechanism will ensure that the correct function is called.

Using References With virtual Functions

A reference to a base class used as a function parameter can be passed as an argument of a derived object type, and can also select the appropriate virtual function to call. We could show this happening by modifying the function `main()` in the last example, to call a function that has a reference as a parameter.

Try It Out - Using References Instead

We can move the call to the function which outputs the volume of an object to a separate function and call that from `main()`:

```
// EX9-10.CPP
// Using a base class pointer to call a virtual function
#include <iostream.h>

class Box;                          // Required for prototype following

void Output( Box& aBox);            // Prototype of function

...

int main(void)
{
   Box aBox(2.0, 3.0, 4.0);         // Declare a base box
   GlassBox aGBox(2.0,3.0,4.0);     // Declare a derived box of the same size

   Output(aBox);                     // Output volume of base class object
   Output(aGBox);                   // Output volume of derived class object

   return 0;
}

// Function to output a volume via a virtual function call
// using a reference
void Output(Box& aBox)
{
   aBox.ShowVolume();
}
```

How It Works

At the beginning of the program we have an incomplete definition of the class **Box**. This is included so that the compiler will know of the existence of **Box** as a class when it gets to the prototype of the function **Output()**. Without this, the prototype would cause an error message to be generated.

The function **main()** now basically consists of two calls of the function **Output()**, the first with an object of the base class as an argument, and the second with an object of the derived class. Because the parameter is a reference to the base class, the function accepts objects of either class as an argument and the appropriate version of the virtual function **ShowVolume()** is called, depending on the object initializing the reference.

The program produces exactly the same output as the previous example, demonstrating that the virtual function mechanism does indeed work through a reference parameter.

Pure Virtual Functions

It is possible that you may want to include a virtual function in a base class so that it may be suitably redefined in a derived class to suit the objects of that class, but there is no meaningful definition you can put for the function in the base class.

For example, we could conceivably have a class **Container**, which could be used as a base for defining our **Box** class or a **Bottle** class, or even a **Teapot** class. The container class wouldn't have data members, but you might want to provide for a member function **volume()** as virtual for any derived classes. Since the **Container** class has no data members and therefore no dimensions, there is no sensible **volume()** definition that we can write, but we can still define the class, including the member function **volume()**, as follows:

```
class Container                        // Generic base class for specific
containers
{
   public:

      // Function for calculating a volume - no content
      // This is defined as a 'pure' virtual function, signified by '=0'
      virtual double volume(void) = 0;

      // Function to display a volume
      void ShowVolume()
      {
         cout << endl
              << "Volume is " << volume();
      }
};
```

The statement for the virtual function **volume()** defines it as having no content by placing the equals sign and zero in the function header. This is called a **pure virtual function**. Any class derived from this class must either define the **volume()** function, or redefine it as a pure virtual function.

The class also contains the function **ShowVolume()**, which will display the volume of objects of derived classes.

Abstract Classes

A class containing a pure virtual function is called an **abstract class**. It is called **abstract** because you can't define objects of a class containing a pure virtual function. It exists only for the purpose of defining classes which are derived from it. If a class derived from an abstract class still defines a pure virtual function of the base as pure, then it too is an abstract class.

Note that you should not conclude from the example of the **Container** class above that an abstract class can't have data members. An abstract class can have both data members and function members. The presence of a pure virtual function determines that a given class is abstract. Of course, an abstract class can also have more than one pure virtual function. In this case, a derived class must have definitions for every pure virtual function, if it is not to be an abstract class.

Try It Out - Abstract Container Class

We could implement a **Can** class, representing beer or cola cans perhaps, together with our original **Box** class, with both being derived from the **Container** class. The definitions of these two classes would be as follows:

```
class Box : public Container            // Derived class
{
   public:

      // Function to show the volume of an object
      void ShowVolume(void)
      {
         cout << endl
              << "Box usable volume is " << volume();
      }

      // Function to calculate the volume of a Box object
      virtual double volume(void)
      { return length*breadth*height; }

      // Constructor
      Box( double lv=1.0, double bv=1.0, double hv=1.0 ):
         length(lv), breadth(bv), height(hv){}

   protected:
      double length;
      double breadth;
      double height;

};
```

```
class Can : public Container
{
   public:
      // Function to calculate the volume of a can
      virtual double volume()
      { return 0.25*PI*diameter*diameter*height;   }

      // Constructor
      Can( double hv=4.0, double dv=2.0 ) : height(hv), diameter(dv){}

   protected:
      double height;
      double diameter;
};
```

The **Box** class is as we had it in the previous example. The **volume()** function is defined within this class (as it must be if this class is to be used to define objects). The only other option would be to specify it as a pure virtual function, since it is pure in the base class, but then we couldn't create **Box** objects.

The **Can** class also defines the volume function based on the formula $h\pi r^2$, where h is the height and r is the radius of the cross-section of a can. This is essentially the height multiplied by the area of the base to produce the volume. The expression in the function definition assumes a global constant **PI** is defined, so we will need to remember that.

We can exercise these classes with the following function **main()**:

```
// EX9-11.CPP
// Using an abstract class
#include <iostream.h>              // For stream I/O

const double PI= 3.14159265;      // Global definition for PI

   . . .
```

```
int main(void)
{
// Pointer to abstract base class initialized with address of Box object
   Container* pC1 = new Box( 2.0 ,3.0 ,4.0 );

// Pointer to abstract base class initialized with address of Can object
   Container* pC2 = new Can( 6.5, 3.0);

   pC1->ShowVolume();               // Output the volumes of the two
   pC2->ShowVolume();               // objects pointed to

   delete pC1;                      // Now clean up the free store
   delete pC2;                      // ....

   return 0;
}
```

How It Works

In this program, we declare two pointers to the base class, **Container**. Although we can't define **Container** objects because **Container** is an abstract class, we can still define a pointer to a **Container**, which we can then use to store the address of a derived class object. The pointer **pC1** is assigned the address of a **Box** object created in the free store by the operator **new**. The second pointer is assigned the address of a **Can** object in a similar manner.

The output produced by this example is as follows:

```
Volume is 24
Volume is 45.945793
```

Since **volume()** is a virtual function, the call to it is resolved when the program is executed by selecting the version belonging to the class of the object being pointed to. Thus, for the pointer **pC1**, the version from the class **Box** is called, and for the pointer **pC2**, the version in the class **Can** is called, so in each case we obtain the correct result. We could equally well have used just one pointer **pC1** and assigned the address of the **Can** object to it (after calling the **volume()** function for the **Box** object). A base class pointer can contain the address of any derived class object, even when several different classes are derived from the same base class.

Because the derived class objects were created dynamically, we need to use the operator **delete** to clean up the free store when we have finished with them.

Indirect Base Classes

At the beginning of this chapter, we said that a base class of one class could in turn be derived from another. A small extension of the last example will provide us with an illustration of this, as well as demonstrating the use of a virtual function across a second level of inheritance.

Try It Out - More Than One Level of Inheritance

All we need to do is add the class **GlassBox** to the classes we have in the last example. The relationship between the classes we now have is illustrated below.

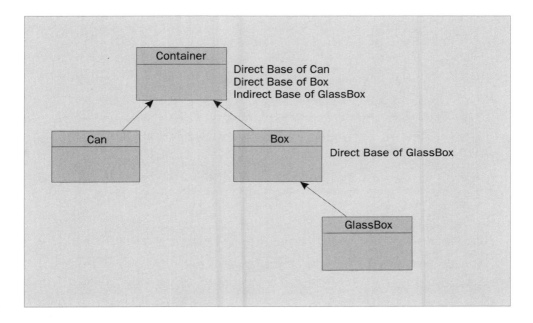

The class **GlassBox** is derived from the **Box** class exactly as before, so it doesn't need to be changed in any way. With this class hierarchy, the class **Container** is an indirect base of the class **GlassBox** and a direct base of the classes **Box** and **Can**.

Our new example, with an updated function **main()** to use the additional class in the hierarchy, will be as follows:

```
// EX8-12.CPP
// Using an abstract class
#include <iostream.h>                       // For stream I/O

const double PI= 3.14159265;        // Global definition for PI

...

class GlassBox: public Box      // Derived class
{
   public:

      // Function to calculate volume of a GlassBox
      // allowing 15% for packing
      virtual double volume(void)
      { return 0.85*length*breadth*height; }

      // Constructor
      GlassBox( double lv, double bv, double hv ): Box(lv,bv,hv){}

};

int main(void)
{
// Pointer to abstract base class initialized with address of Box object
   Container* pC1 = new Box( 2.0 ,3.0 ,4.0 );

   Can aCan( 6.5, 3.0);                    // Define Can object
   GlassBox aGBox(2.0, 3.0, 4.0);          // Define GlassBox object

// initialized with address of Can object

   pC1->ShowVolume();                      // Output the volume of Box
   delete pC1;                             // Now clean up the free store

   pC1 = &aCan;                            // Get aCan address in pointer
   pC1->ShowVolume();                      // Output the volume of Can

   pC1 = &aGBox;                           // Get aGBox address in pointer
   pC1->ShowVolume();                      // Output the volume of GlassBox

   return 0;
}
```

How It Works

We have the three-level class hierarchy shown in the previous illustration
with **Container** as an abstract base class because it contains a pure virtual
function. The function **main()** now calls the function **ShowVolume()** three
times, using the same pointer to the base class, but with the pointer

containing the address of an object of a different class each time. Of course, the function **ShowVolume()** is inherited by all derived classes we have defined. A separate branch from the base **Container** defines the derived class **Can**.

The example produces this output:

```
Volume is 24
Volume is 45.945793
Volume is 20.4
```

showing that we execute the three different versions of the function **volume()** according to the type of object involved.

> *Note that we need to delete the* Box *object from the free store before we assign another address value to it. If we don't do this, we wouldn't be able to clean up the free store because we would have no record of the original address. This is an easy mistake to make when reassigning pointers and using the free store.*

Virtual Destructors

One problem that arises with using objects of derived classes using a pointer to the base class, is that the correct destructor may not be called. We can show this effect by modifying the last example.

Try It Out - Problems Caused by Calling the Wrong Destructor

We just need to add destructors to each of the classes so that we can track which destructor is called when the objects are destroyed. Therefore, the program would be as follows:

```
// EX9-13.CPP
// Destructor calls with derived classes
// using objects via a base class pointer
#include <iostream.h>            // For stream I/O

const double PI= 3.14159265;     // Global definition for PI
```

Try it Out!

```
class Container              // Generic base class for specific containers
{
    public:
// Destructor
    ~Container()
    { cout<< endl << "Container destructor called"; }
...
};

class Box : public Container      // Derived class
{
    public:
// Destructor
    ~Box()
    { cout<< endl << "Box destructor called"; }
...
};

class Can : public Container
{
    public:
// Destructor
    ~Can()
    { cout<< endl << "Can destructor called"; }
...
};

class GlassBox: public Box      // Derived class
{
    public:
// Destructor
    ~GlassBox()
    { cout<< endl << "GlassBox destructor called"; }
...
};

int main(void)
{
// Pointer to abstract base class initialized with address of Box object
    Container* pC1 = new Box( 2.0 ,3.0 ,4.0 );

    Can aCan( 6.5, 3.0);                    // Define Can object
    GlassBox aGBox(2.0, 3.0, 4.0);          // Define GlassBox object

// initialized with address of Can object

    pC1->ShowVolume();                      // Output the volume of Box
    cout << endl << "Delete Box";
    delete pC1;                             // Now clean up the free store
```

```
pC1 = new GlassBox( 4.0, 5.0, 6.0 );    // Create GlassBox dynamically
pC1->ShowVolume();                       // ...output its volume...
cout << endl << "Delete GlassBox";
delete pC1;                              // ...and delete it

pC1 = &aCan;                             // Get aCan address in pointer
pC1->ShowVolume();                       // Output the volume of Can

pC1 = &aGBox;                            // Get aGBox address in pointer
pC1->ShowVolume();                       // Output the volume of GlassBox

return 0;
}
```

How It Works

Apart from adding a destructor to each class which outputs a message to the effect that it was called, the only other change is a couple of additions to the function **main()**. There are additional statements to create a **GlassBox** object dynamically, output its volume and then delete it, and there is a message displayed to indicate when the dynamically created **Box** object is deleted. The output generated by this example is shown below.

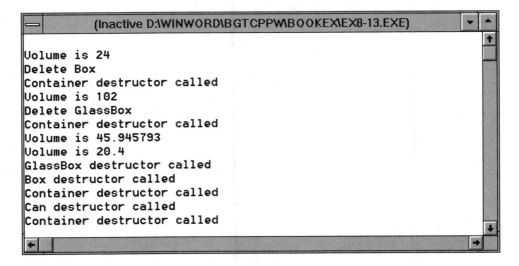

```
(Inactive D:\WINWORD\BGTCPPW\BOOKEX\EX8-13.EXE)

Volume is 24
Delete Box
Container destructor called
Volume is 102
Delete GlassBox
Container destructor called
Volume is 45.945793
Volume is 20.4
GlassBox destructor called
Box destructor called
Container destructor called
Can destructor called
Container destructor called
```

You can see from this that when we delete the **Box** object, the destructor for the base class **Container** is called. Similarly, when the **GlassBox** object that we added is deleted, again the destructor for the base class **Container** is called. For the other objects, the correct destructor calls occur, with the

371

derived class constructor being called first, followed by the base class constructor. For the first **GlassBox** object created in a declaration, three destructors are called: firstly, the destructor for the derived class, followed by the direct base destructor, and finally the indirect base destructor.

All the problems are with objects created in the free store. In both cases, the wrong destructor is called. The reason for this is that the linkage to the destructors is resolved statically, at compile time. For the automatic objects there is no problem. The compiler knows what they are and arranges for the correct destructor to be called.

With objects created dynamically, and accessed through a pointer, things are different. The only information the compiler has when the **delete** operation is executed, is that the pointer type is a pointer to the base class. The type of object the pointer is pointing to is unknown. The compiler then simply ensures that the **delete** operation is set up to call the base class destructor. In a real application, this can cause a lot of problems, with bits of objects left strewn around the free store, and possibly more serious problems depending on the nature of the objects involved.

The solution is simple. We need the calls to be resolved dynamically as the program is executed. We can organise this by using virtual destructors in our classes. As we said when we first discussed virtual functions, it is sufficient to declare the base class function as virtual, for all functions in any derived classes with the same name, parameter list and return type to be virtual as well. This applies to destructors in addition to ordinary member functions. We just need to add the keyword **virtual** to the definition of the destructor in the class **Container**, so that it becomes as follows:

```
class Container                    // Generic base class for specific
containers
{
   public:
// Destructor
     virtual ~Container()
       { cout<< endl << "Container destructor called"; }
 ...
};
```

Now, the destructors in all the derived classes are automatically **virtual**, even though you don't specify them as such explicitly. Of course, you can specify them as **virtual** if you want the code to be absolutely clear.

If you rerun the example with this modification, it will produce the following output:

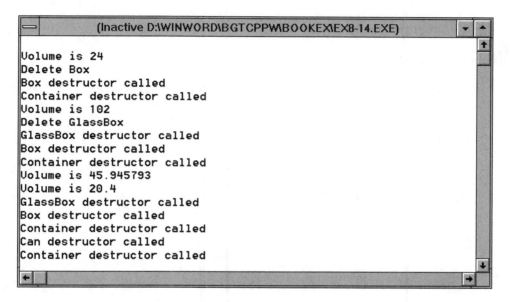

```
(Inactive D:\WINWORD\BGTCPP\WBOOKEX\EX8-14.EXE)
Volume is 24
Delete Box
Box destructor called
Container destructor called
Volume is 102
Delete GlassBox
GlassBox destructor called
Box destructor called
Container destructor called
Volume is 45.945793
Volume is 20.4
GlassBox destructor called
Box destructor called
Container destructor called
Can destructor called
Container destructor called
```

As you can see, all the objects are now destroyed with a proper sequence of destructor calls. Destroying the dynamic objects produces the same sequence of destructor calls as the automatic objects of the same type in the program. This example appears in full on the disk as the source file **EX9-14.CPP**.

It is a good idea to always declare your base class destructors as **virtual** *when using inheritance, as a matter of course. There is a small overhead in the execution of the class destructors, but you will not notice it in the majority of circumstances. Using virtual destructors ensures your objects will be properly destroyed and avoids potential program crashes that might otherwise occur.*

Multiple Inheritance

This is the last major topic before we get to writing some Windows programs, so we are nearly finished with C++ language specifics. All our derived classes so far have had a single direct base class. We're not limited to this, however. A derived class can have as many base classes as you need, which means that multiple indirect bases are also possible.

Multiple Base Classes

It is quite difficult to come up with examples of a class with multiple base classes that is based on relationships in the real world. Defining a class such as **Box** in terms of the class **Container** reflects the real world relationship between a box and a container. A box is a form of container, so we are defining a more specific object from a more general one. With most real world objects, this unidirectional specialization pattern applies. Multiple base classes are often used in practice for the convenience of implementation, rather than to reflect any particular relationships between objects. The OWL uses multiple inheritance in the definition of some of the classes you will be using in the next chapter.

However, we could consider the example of a **Package**, which might be a combination of a **Container**, or some specialized form of container such as a **Box**, together with the contents of the container defined by a class **Contents**. We could define the class **Package** as derived from both the class **Box** and the class **Contents**. This could be represented as shown in the following figure.

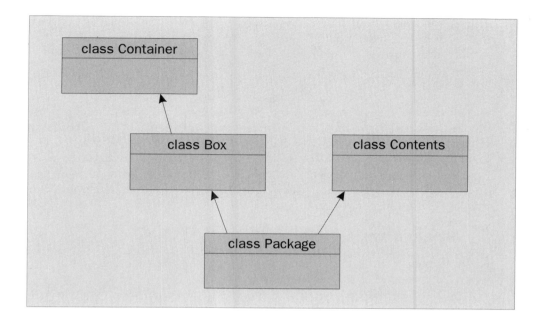

The definition of the class would look like this:

```
class Package : public Box, public Contents
{
...
};
```

The class **Package** will now inherit all the members of both classes, with the same access specifiers as appear in the definitions of the base classes, since they are defined as public base classes. The access limitations for inherited class members, as we discussed earlier in this chapter, apply equally well to classes with multiple bases.

Things can get a little more complicated now. For example, it is conceivable that both base classes could have a public member function, `show()`, to display the contents of an object. If so, a statement such as

```
aPackage.show();
```

where `aPackage` is an object of the class `Package`, will be ambiguous, since the class `Package` contains two members with the same name, `show()`, one inherited from each of the base classes. The compiler has no way of knowing which one should be called, so this will result in an error message from the compiler. If you need to call one or the other, you have to use the scope resolution operator to specify which of the two functions you want to invoke. For example, you could write this:

```
aPackage.Contents::show();
```

which makes it quite clear that you want to call the function that is inherited from the class `Contents`.

Virtual Base Classes

A further complication can arise with multiple inheritance if the direct base classes are themselves derived from another class or classes. The possibility arises that both base classes could be derived from a common class. For instance, the classes `Contents` and `Box`, which we used in the definition of the class package, could be derived from another base called `RockBottom`. Their definitions could then be something like this:

```
class Contents: public RockBottom
{
. . .
};

class Box: public RockBottom
{
. . .
};
```

Now, the class `Package` will contain two copies of the members of the class `RockBottom`, as illustrated on the following page.

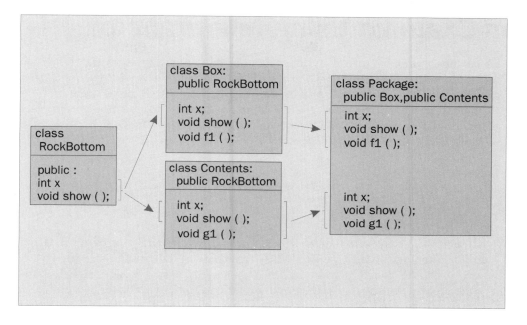

The duplication of the members of the indirect base can be at least confusing, and at worst it can cause a lot of problems. However, it is easily avoided simply by modifying the definitions of the base classes **Box** and **Contents** such that the class **RockBottom** is specified as a virtual base class. Their definitions in outline would then be as follows:

```
class Contents: public virtual RockBottom
{
    ...
};

class Box: public virtual RockBottom
{
    ...
};
```

Now, there will be only one instance of the members of the base class **RockBottom** in any class derived from these two classes and any problems with the original definition of the class **Package** disappear.

An Example Using Inheritance

You may find a more complete example of using classes would help you to understand what we have learnt in this chapter. However, it's not essential, so we won't bother to lead you through it here. We'll define the problem, then if you want to you can use it as an exercise to practice your object-oriented programming skills before we move onto Windows programming specifically in the next chapter.

> *If you prefer a more hand-holding walk-through of how to solve the problem, then the complete text is available on the disk.*

A relatively easy problem to work through is one that we have already tried when we looked at functions, that of a calculator. This time we will approach the problem from an object-oriented point of view, rather than the functional structure we developed previously. This should help you see how different the object-based approach is from the usual procedural program structure.

Defining the Problem

We will aim at a calculator with the same capabilities as the previous example. It should handle any arithmetic expression involving the operators *, /, + and -, and also allow parentheses to any depth. Numerical values can be with or without a decimal point. Here is a typical expression the calculator should be able to handle:

    3.5*(2.45*7.1 - 4.7/1.25)*(3+1.5*(8.2-7*125/88.9)/5.7)

Blanks can appear anywhere in an expression, and an expression is terminated by pressing the *Enter* key.

We will also assume the calculator will act like a real calculator in that once a result has been computed, it is retained in the display, so we could enter

    *3

to multiply it by 3.

Summary

In this chapter we have covered all of the principle ideas involved in using inheritance. The fundamentals you should keep in mind are these:

- A derived class inherits all the members of a base class except for constructors, the destructor and the overloaded assignment operator.

- Members of a base class which are declared as **private** in the base class are not accessible in any derived class. To obtain the effect of the keyword **private**, but allow access in a derived class, you should use the keyword **protected** in place of **private**.

- A base class can be specified for a derived class with the keyword **public**, **private**, or **protected**. If none is specified the default is **private**. Depending on the keyword specified for a base, the access level of the inherited members may be modified.

- If you write a derived class constructor, you must arrange for data members of the base class to be initialized properly, as well as those of the derived class.

- A function in a base class may be declared as **virtual**. This allows other definitions of the function appearing in derived classes to be selected at execution time, depending on the type of object for which the function call is made.

- You should declare the destructor in a base class containing a virtual function as **virtual**. This will ensure correct selection of a destructor for dynamically-created derived class objects.

- A virtual function in a base class can be specified as pure, by placing **=0** in the function declaration. The class will then be an abstract class for which no objects can be created. In any derived class, all the pure virtual functions must be defined; if not, it too becomes an abstract class.

- A class may be derived from multiple base classes, in which case it inherits members from all of its bases, with the exception of destructors, constructors and overloaded assignment operator functions.

▶ An indirect base class may be specified as **virtual** for derived classes in order to avoid possible multiple occurrences of its members in a class with multiple bases, two or more of which are derived from the indirect base.

You have now gone through all of the important language features of C++, and you will be applying the ideas of this last chapter particularly, when you start to use the Object Windows Library in the next chapter. It is important that you now feel comfortable with the mechanism for defining classes, deriving classes, and the process of inheritance. Windows programming with TCW will involve extensive use of these concepts. If you have any doubts, go back over the last two chapters and try playing around with the source code of the examples related to the areas that you are unsure about.

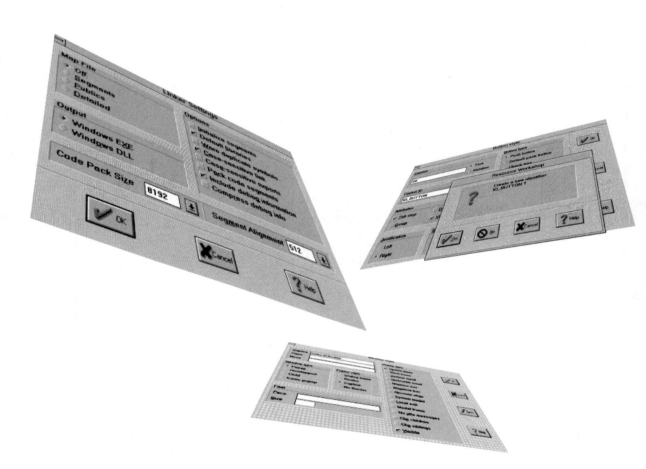

Understanding Windows Programming

This is where we write our first Windows program, making the most of the OWL and the knowledge we now have about classes and class inheritance. In this chapter you will learn:

- The basic structure and purpose of the ObjectWindows Library
- How to write a basic Windows application
- How to write text to a window
- How to program the mouse under Windows
- How to write graphics to a window
- How to write to a window so the image is not lost when the window is moved

The Structure of a Windows Program

A Windows program has a structure which is quite different to any of the programs we have seen up to now. This is a result of the nature of the Window's environment, which carries with it implicit assumptions about how a user will interact with a program. It is important that we understand why a Windows program needs to work the way it does. This will help considerably when we come to create our own Windows programs. Firstly, we should look at the basic terminology surrounding Windows, and then contrast the operation of a Windows program with what we know about procedural program organization.

Elements of a Window

As an example of a typical basic window, look at the window below.

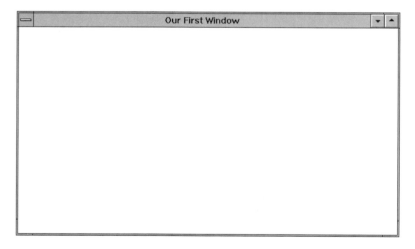

This is about as little as a program window can contain. This is the minimum Windows program. We will write the program to generate this window a little later in this chapter. Where the title appears is called the **title bar**. The text appearing here usually reflects the function of the window, Edit for an edit window for example, but it can be anything at all. Apart from a guide as to what the window is for, it also differentiates one window from another when several tasks are running.

At the top right of the window are the **Maximize** and **Minimize** buttons, which you undoubtedly recognise by now, and are used by clicking on them with the mouse. Depending on which was selected, they either enlarge the window to the maximum size which is usually, but not necessarily, full screen, or reduce the window to an icon. At the top left is the **Control Menu Box**. Clicking on this will produce a menu of all the operations you can apply to this window as a whole. This menu also appears when you click on the icon for the window when it has been minimized.

The window shown above represents quite a sophisticated program if you think about it. It may not look like much, but it has a lot of functionality. You can move the window by placing the cursor on the title bar and, holding the left button down, dragging it around the screen. You can modify the extent of the window by dragging the top or the bottom of the window, or either of its sides, and as we said you can maximize it, minimize it or show the Control Menu. Of course, you can also close it using the Control Menu Box. To implement this as a DOS program would involve a fair amount of work.

Comparing DOS and Windows Programs

There are two important differences between a typical DOS program and a Windows program:

- The relationship between the program and the computer
- How the program is organized and operates.

Let's look at both of these aspects.

When a DOS program is running it has complete control of the hardware. The actual read or write is performed by service routines of the operating system, but you have control. You can write anywhere on the screen and you can read from the keyboard in any way that you want. With a Windows program, you can do neither of these things.

Windows performs all reads from the keyboard and, if the information is destined for your application, Windows will pass it over to it. You can only ask Windows to obtain some input. Similarly, with output to the screen, your application can only write to the window it has defined, and it can't even do that directly. It has to call Windows routines to pass across what is to be written, and Windows actually does the writing. The reason for this is the multi-tasking nature of the Windows environment. There is always the basic assumption that your application is sharing the computer with a number of other active applications. With a Windows program, you are always a subsidiary task to Windows itself. It is Windows that has control of the computer. It knows which bit of the screen belongs to which application and which application can currently receive input.

Event Driven Programs

A typical DOS program, and certainly all the programs in this book so far, have a sequential nature. When data is read from the keyboard, the kind of data that is acceptable is predetermined and the program proceeds with the next activity once the data is read. Of course, there may be program logic and branches in the program, but overall execution starts at the beginning of the program and proceeds by some route through to the end. A representation of a program which is organized in this way is shown below.

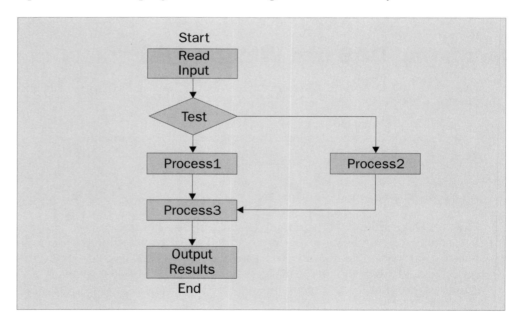

A Windows program is different. Consider the application window that was shown at the beginning of this chapter. When it is executed, the application window just sits there waiting for something to happen. The input required isn't predetermined, except that there is a finite range of possibilities. You could minimize the window or click on the Control Menu Box, or drag a window boundary, and the program will respond according to what you do. The 'event' determines what the program does next, so the sequence of actions in the program depends on you. This mode of operation is called **event-driven**, and the application is an **event-driven application**.

Event-driven programs are not limited to the Windows environment. Games programs are event-driven, so are programs which control industrial processes. The external stimuli determines which piece of the program is executed. The programs usually consist of two basic parts:

▶ Something that identifies a particular event in a set of events

▶ A set of routines to service events

With a Windows program, a lot of the work of identifying a particular event and calling the appropriate service routine is done by the OWL using the Windows API (we'll explain this in a moment). The principle task you have in writing a Windows program is writing a function that initiates the application and its main window, and creating the routines to service the events that relates to your application, although as we shall see, many of the events basic to managing a window, such as clicking the minimize or maximize buttons for example, are already taken care of by the OWL. This can give a somewhat disjointed appearance to the structure of a program, as illustrated below.

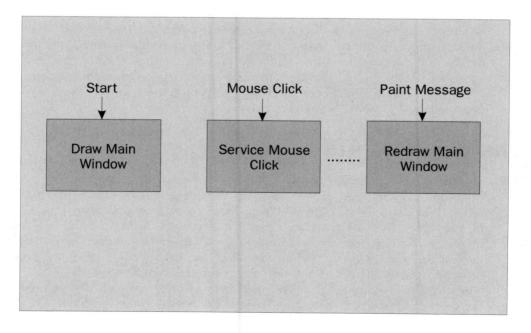

The events in a program operating under Windows, such as moving the mouse or clicking the left or right button, typically results in a Windows message that is passed to the Windows program. The process of passing a message involves calling a function in the program which has the task of analyzing the message. It then needs to be able to invoke a function to process the message in question. Operation of a Windows program usually involves hundreds of messages being passed of many different kinds. As we shall see, the facilities provided by the OWL greatly simplify the handling of Windows messages.

Essential Elements of a Windows Program

The executable module of a Windows program is a `.EXE` file which has to be in a special format that is called the New Executable file format. This is a different format from the `.EXE` file for a DOS program. It incorporates a table which allows the application to link to functions provided by Windows at execution time. These functions don't directly form part of your program. They are shared with any other programs running at the same time your program is executed and are linked to dynamically. These functions support communications with the screen, obtaining input, and so on - all the communications and functions you need through Windows to the external world.

Because your program will communicate with Windows rather than the device support routines provided by DOS, you don't get involved with the detailed characteristics of the hardware of your computer. Your program will run quite happily with a VGA screen or an SVGA screen with Windows taking care of the differences for you. The complete set of functions provided by Windows is called the **Windows API**.

The Windows API

The full name of the Windows API is the Windows Application Programming Interface. This is used by all application programs that run under Windows. One of the problems faced by a programmer in programming their first application under Windows is that the API provides more than 1000 functions. It requires a book rather larger than this one just to describe what they do. Before you close the book at this point in favor of brain surgery, note that through the magic of the OWL we don't have to worry much about this. The OWL will be providing a much easier interface for us to use, and will be taking care of calling the right Windows API in general.

Notation in Windows Programs

One aspect of the Windows API you need a little insight into is the notation used to name variables. This is referred to as **Hungarian notation**. Each variable name is prefixed by one or more lower case letters which provide information about the kind of variable it is. A variable beginning with **n** for example, **nCmdShow**, is of type **int**, whereas a variable such as **lParam** beginning with **l**, is of type **long**. The prefix **h** in **hInstance** indicates that the variable is a handle, where a handle is just a 16 bit number used to reference an object of some sort. A lot of functions will return a handle when you ask Windows for a resource of some kind for your program.

The Windows API also defines a number of new data types. These are generally named in upper case such as **HANDLE** which is the type for a handle, or **LPSTR** which is a long pointer to a string. We will introduce the meaning of the variable and type names as we go along. You will find that you soon get used to them.

ObjectWindows Basics

We are going to be using the ObjectWindows Library for the remainder of this book, so we should first have a look at what it is about in general terms. Understanding the broad principles will make it a lot easier to use.

The Ideas Behind ObjectWindows

The OWL provides a set of classes that encapsulate a great deal of the Windows API. As well as packaging many of the functions of the API, the OWL classes also contain as class members many of the data items necessary for using the API. You use the OWL classes in two ways, in some cases by defining your own classes using an OWL class as a base, so that your class inherits all of the functions and data members provided by the OWL class, and in other cases by creating and using objects of an OWL class directly.

The OWL provides default functions for handling many Windows messages. When your application needs to be able to process a message such as a mouse click in a particular way, all that you need to do normally is to include a function within your class derived from an OWL class which provides the necessary program action in response to the message.

389

The essence of creating a Windows program using OWL involves deriving classes from OWL classes, defining functions (including constructors) in your class to perform specific actions, and creating and using objects of those classes. Typically, a message from Windows that your program is to handle causes a function member of your derived class to be called.

ObjectWindows Notation

The OWL uses its own naming conventions in defining classes and class members. All the OWL classes have names that begin with **T** (such as **TWindow** or **TButton**). It also provides five data types related to those classes, for each class provided by the OWL. The name of each type is the class name, prefixed by one or two capital letters which indicate something about the type. The types are as follows:

1   **Pclass_name**: for example, **PTWindow** defines a pointer to an object of the class **TWindow**.

2   **Rclass_name**: for example, **RTWindow** defines a reference to an object of the class **TWindow**. Remember that a reference must be initialized when it is declared.

3   **RPclass_name**: for example, **RPTWindow** defines a reference to a pointer to an object of the class **TWindow**.

4   **PCclass_name**: for example, **PCTWindow** defines a pointer to a **const** object of the class **TWindow**.

5   **RCclass_name**: for example, **RCTWindow** defines a reference to a **const** object of the class **TWindow**.

ObjectWindows Class Hierarchy

The OWL provides a hierarchy of 25 interrelated classes. We are not going to go into the overall structure of the hierarchy here. You can find it in the *User's Guide* supplied with the product, if you are interested. What we *are* going to do is to look into the purpose of the important classes, gradually building our knowledge of the classes provided until we can use the whole set.

Essential Elements of an ObjectWindows Program

Windows programs which use OWL are object-oriented. You derive classes from the classes which OWL provides, and make them specific to your needs by adding function members and data members. A Windows program written using OWL must have at least two classes: an application class which you derive from an OWL class called **TApplication**, and a window class typically derived from the OWL class **TWindow**. An object of the application class defines how the application is to behave and is responsible for initializing the main window object. The main window object which can be an instance of **TWindow** defines the facilities provided with the window and its general behavior. Thus, an application will contain at least two objects:

1   An application object

2   A main window object.

Defining your Application Class

You create your application class by deriving it from the OWL class `TApplication`. The minimum you must add to your class is a member function called `InitMainWindow()` which will create a window object. We could define a minimum application class as follows:

```
// Definition of a class for our application
// with the OWL class TApplication as base.
class TBasicApp:public TApplication
{
   public:

      // Constructor for our class which calls the
      // base class constructor
      TBasicApp(LPSTR AName, HANDLE hInstance, HANDLE hPrevInstance,
            LPSTR lpCmdLine, int nCmdShow)
        :TApplication(AName, hInstance, hPrevInstance,
                  lpCmdLine, nCmdShow)
      {
```

```
         // No statements as everything required
         // is done by the base class constructor
      }

      // Declare virtual function InitMainWindow()
      // that initializes the window for the application
      virtual void InitMainWindow(void);

};
```

We have called our class **TBasicApp** using the same notation for classes as OWL. It defines the OWL class **TApplication** as a public base class, so all the inherited members of **TApplication** are accessible to member functions of our class.

Our class contains declarations for two member functions, a constructor and the **InitMainWindow()** function. The function **InitMainWindow()** is a virtual function of the base class.

The only action in our constructor is to call the base class constructor in the initialization list. This will initialize the data members of the class. The constructor for our class has five parameters which are passed on to the base class constructor. The uses of these parameters are as follows:

▶ **AName**: the name of the application, which will be stored in an inherited data member by the base class constructor.

▶ **hInstance**: a handle used to reference this particular instance of the program provided by Windows, since in general there could be other copies running. As we mentioned earlier, a handle is simply an integer value that uniquely identifies something. We will see how a program obtains the handle **hInstance** shortly.

▶ **hPrevInstance**: is the handle for a copy of a program which was initiated previous to the current one. If there isn't a previous instance of a program running, this will be zero. The handle **hPrevInstance** also originates with Windows.

▶ **lpCmdLine**: is a pointer to a string which contains any command line parameters passed to the program when it was initiated. Command line parameters are usually passed to a Windows program by entering them when the program is started from the Windows Run dialog box.

> **nCmdShow**: is a parameter that defines how the program main window is to be initially displayed. This is also passed to a program when it is started by Windows.

Creating a Window Object for Your Application

The function **InitMainWindow()** creates a main window object. By using the OWL class **TWindow**, we can do this very easily by writing the function as follows:

```
void TBasicApp::InitMainWindow(void);
{
    MainWindow = new TWindow(0, Name);
}
```

The function consists of one statement which creates a **TWindow** object in the free store using the operator **new**, and stores the pointer returned in the inherited data member **MainWindow**. The constructor for **TWindow** has two arguments here. The zero as the first argument specifies that this is the main window of the application, and the second argument is the class data member **Name**, which is a pointer to the name of the application passed to the **TBasicApp** constructor.

We now need to look at how an application object and a window object are created.

Creating Your Application Object

In a DOS program, execution starts with the function **main()**. In a Windows program, execution starts with the function **WinMain()**, so every Windows application we write will contain the function **WinMain()**. This is the function which creates an instance of our application class **TBasicApp**. Let's write this function to create and use such an object.

```
// Start of Windows program
int PASCAL WinMain(HANDLE hInstance, HANDLE hPrevInstance,
                   LPSTR lpCmdLine, int nCmdShow)
{
    // Create an object of our application class
```

393

```
    TBasicApp OurFirstApp("Our First Window", hInstance, hPrevInstance,
                                            lpCmdLine, nCmdShow );

    OurFirstApp.Run();              // Call inherited Run() for our object

    return OurFirstApp.Status;      // Return inherited data member, Status
}
```

Note the specification **PASCAL** in the function header. This provides a different calling mechanism than that used by a normal C++, and it is required for **WinMain()** (without this your programs won't run). You can see in the header that four arguments are passed to **WinMain()** by Windows. These are the entities we discussed earlier when we looked at the definition of the constructor for our application class **TBasicApp**, so this is how the values are obtained.

The first statement in **WinMain()** is a declaration of a **TBasicApp** object, initialized with a name, and the arguments passed by Windows to **WinMain()**. After the object is declared, the function **Run()** for this object is executed.

The function **Run()** is inherited from the base class **TApplication**. This function will call several other functions including **InitMainWindow()** to start up our application.

We can put all the blocks of code together to form our first Windows application. With the addition of an **#include** statement, this is all the code we need for the complete minimum Windows program.

Try It Out - Your First Windows Program

Here is the whole program.

```
// EX10-01.CPP
// The basic Windows application
#include <owl.h>        // For the Object Windows Library

// Definition of a class for our application
// with the OWL class TApplication as base.
class TBasicApp:public TApplication
{
   public:

      // Constructor for our class which calls the
```

```
        // base class constructor
        TBasicApp(LPSTR AName, HANDLE hInstance, HANDLE hPrevInstance,
                           LPSTR lpCmdLine, int nCmdShow):
          TApplication(AName, hInstance, hPrevInstance,
                           lpCmdLine, nCmdShow)
        {
          // No statements as everything required
          // is done by the base class constructor
        }

        // Define virtual function InitMainWindow
        // that initializes the window for the application
        virtual void InitMainWindow(void)
        { MainWindow = new TWindow(0, Name); }
};

// Start of Windows program
int PASCAL WinMain(HANDLE hInstance, HANDLE hPrevInstance,
                   LPSTR lpCmdLine, int nCmdShow)
{
   // Create an object of our application class
   TBasicApp OurFirstApp("Our First Window", hInstance, hPrevInstance,
                                          lpCmdLine, nCmdShow );

   OurFirstApp.Run();              // Call inherited Run() for our object

   return OurFirstApp.Status;      // Return inherited data member, Status
}
```

How It Works

The #include statements provide the definitions for the OWL classes. If you are interested, you could always browse through this file - it is regular C++. The definition of our application class is as we had it before, with the minor change that the function InitMainWindow() is defined within the class definition, just to show that you can do it. So our first Windows program turns out to be very simple - a class definition, plus a WinMain() function containing three statements.

If you run this example, it will display the window shown at the beginning of this chapter. Although there is no application function, it is a fully functional window. You can minimize it, maximize it and drag its borders to change its extent. It contains a fully operational Control Menu box which will display the menu with a single mouse click and will terminate with a double mouse click. You get all this for free - courtesy of the OWL.

You must have a project file when you run this example, as we discussed in Chapter 1. You can run DOS programs without a project file under TCW, but for a Windows program a project file is essential. If you have a project file that has the .CPP file as an entry, and the example does not execute, the most likely explanation is that TCW is not set up properly to run a Windows program, so check that the libraries have the correct directories defined, and verify that under the IDE menu option Options/ Application that Windows EXE is selected.

Reacting to Events

The next step in evolving our basic windows application is to make it respond to a windows message. We need to understand a few preliminaries before we get to doing this, but it isn't difficult.

Dealing with Windows messages is the responsibility of the class that produced the main window for the application, so we need to derive a version of **TWindow** to do what we want. We know how to derive a class using **TWindow** as a base:

```
class TNewWindow: public TWindow
{
   public:

      // Constructor just calling the base constructor
      TNewWindow(PTWindowsObject AParent, LPSTR ATitle):
                                    TWindow(AParent,ATitle)
      {}
};
```

The constructor definition simply calls the base class constructor **TWindow()**. This is necessary to enable our derived class constructor to receive the same arguments as the base class constructor and then pass them on.

However, this doesn't do any more than the base class. We need to add the mechanism for processing a windows message to this definition. This requires a member function to be added to our class, keyed to the particular message in which we are interested. This is called a **message response member function**.

Message Response Member Functions

A message response function will be called automatically when the event resulting in the message being generated by Windows occurs. A message response function is expected to accept an argument of type **RTMessage** (which you will remember from our discussion of OWL notation is a reference to an object of the class **TMessage**). The association between the message response member function is established by defining what is called a **dispatch index** for the function, within the declaration of the function in the class definition.

The dispatch index for a particular message is an integer value which is unique for that message. You can generate the dispatch index for a particular message you want to service by adding a predefined constant for the particular message, called a message constant, to a predefined base constant, **WM_FIRST**. The message constant for the message generated when you press the left mouse button is **WM_LBUTTONDOWN**, so the dispatch index for the message response function would be this:

```
WM_FIRST+WM_LBUTTONDOWN
```

When you press the right hand mouse button, a message with the message constant **WM_RBUTTONDOWN** would be generated, so the dispatch index would be this:

```
WM_FIRST+WM_RBUTTONDOWN
```

Message constants generally have names that are all capitalized and preceded by **WM_** from Windows Message, plus an underscore character. The names are also explanatory of the kind of event causing the message.

So let's define our window class derived from **TWindow**, but with a declaration of a message response function included to deal with the message generated when the right hand mouse button is pressed. This would be as follows:

```
class TNewWindow: public TWindow
{
   public:

      // Constructor just calling the base constructor
```

```
TNewWindow(PTWindowsObject AParent, LPSTR ATitle):
                                    TWindow(AParent,ATitle)
{}

// Declaration for message response function
// to be called when the right mouse button is pressed
virtual void WMRButtonDown(RTMessage Mess) =
    [WM_FIRST+WM_RBUTTONDOWN];
};
```

The first thing to note is the name of the function. It is formed from a prefix of **WM** for **W**indows **M**essage, followed by the name of the message constant, but using lower case except for the initial letters of each word. This distinguishes it from the name of the message constant and makes it easier to read. In fact, you can use any name you like, but if you follow the standard approach for naming such functions, it will make your programs more readable.

The message response function has the return value specified as void so nothing is returned from it and the parameter, **Mess**, is specified as of type **RTMessage**. This will contain all the information supplied by Windows when the right mouse button is pressed. We will come back to exactly what this is a little later.

The dispatch index within square brackets appears after the equals sign in the function declaration. This enables this particular function to be associated with the message arising from the right mouse button being pressed. Each dispatch index must only be associated with one function, otherwise the compiler would be unable to determine which function to call. For messages that don't have a response function defined, the OWL provides a default handling of the message, which in most cases is to ignore it.

The Structure of a Message

The argument passed to our message response function is a reference to an object of type **TMessage**. The data of interest is contained in the **LParam** member of the **TMessage** object passed. The **L** in **LParam** indicates it is of type **long**. For the **WM_RBUTTONDOWN** message, **LParam** actually contains two items of information in the low order two bytes and the high order two bytes of the variable. You can access these as **Mess.LP.Lo** and **Mess.LP.Hi**. (In case you are wondering how this is done, **Mess.LP.Hi** and **Mess.LP.Lo** are members of another object which shares the same memory as **LParam** in a **union**). The arrangement of these in memory is shown on the following page:

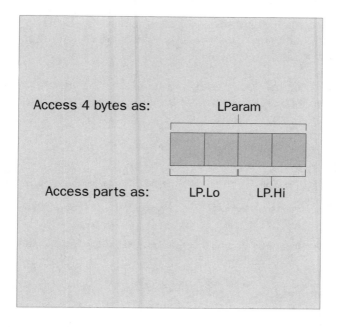

The two items of information stored in **Mess.LP.Lo** and **Mess.LP.Hi** are the x and y screen coordinates of the cursor when the mouse button was pressed. If we knew how, we could display something at the cursor position when the right mouse button is pressed, so let's look into that.

Displaying Text in a Window

We already established that the stream I/O we used in previous chapters can't be used to write to a window. We need to call a Windows function to write text to a window called **TextOut()**, but we need to get access to the windows from Windows. We do this by obtaining something called a **display context**. Windows will supply a handle to the display context for our window, which we then use with the **TextOut()** function to get our text string displayed. We get the handle to a display context using a Windows function **GetDC()** as follows:

```
OurDC = GetDC( HWindow );          // Obtain a display context handle
```

The argument **HWindow** is a data member of our class **TNewWindow** inherited from the base class. It contains a handle to our window which is used by Windows to associate the display context. The function **GetDC()** returns a handle to the display context allocated, which is stored in our variable **OurDC**, which will need to have been declared as type **HDC** (for **H**andle to a **D**isplay **C**ontext).

Let's try to drag the loose ends we have floating around together in a definition for a message response function which will respond to the right mouse button being pressed:

```
void TNewWindow::WMRButtonDown( RTMessage Mess )
{
   char* Bang = "Bang!";            // Define some text to display
   HDC OurDC;                       // Variable to hold a display context

   // Get a display context for our window and save its handle in OurDC
   OurDC = GetDC( Hwindow );

   // Write the text at the cursor position stored in the object Mess
   TextOut( OurDC, Mess.LP.Lo, Mess.LP.Hi, Bang, strlen(Bang) );

   // RELEASE the display context AT ONCE!!!
   ReleaseDC(HWindow, OurDC);
}
```

The message response function declares the pointer to a string **Bang**, which is initialized with the message we will display when the right mouse button is pressed. It also declares a variable **OurDC** which we will use to store the handle to the display context. This is obtained by means of the **GetDC()** function we previously discussed.

Once we have the display context, we are ready to write to the window using the function **TextOut()**. We pass five arguments to the function: the first is the display context, the next two are the screen coordinates where we want the message to appear, and the last two are the pointer to the text string and the length of text string returned from the function **strlen()**. The coordinates for the message are those obtained from the argument **Mess** passed to the message response function by Windows.

Once you have finished with a display context, it must be released by calling the function **ReleaseDC()**, as we do here. There are a very limited number of display contexts available for everything running under Windows, so if you forget to release it, Windows will eventually cease to operate. The function **ReleaseDC()** accepts two arguments: the handle **HWindow**, and the display context handle you obtained, which in our case is **OurDC**.

This may seem to have been a rather long and meandering road to this point, but it was all essential background, and we are now ready to assemble a program to create a window which does something.

Try It Out - Acting on a Message

If we extend the previous example to include the message response capability, the complete program will be as follows:

```
// EX10-02.CPP
// Responding to a Windows message
#include <owl.h>        // For the Object Windows Library
#include <string.h>    // For strlen()


// Definition of a class for our application
// with the OWL class TApplication as base.
class TBasicApp:public TApplication
{
   public:
      // Constructor for our class which calls the
      // base class constructor
      TBasicApp(LPSTR AName, HANDLE hInstance, HANDLE hPrevInstance,
               LPSTR lpCmdLine, int nCmdShow)
        :TApplication(AName, hInstance, hPrevInstance,
                     lpCmdLine, nCmdShow)
      {
         // No statements as everything required
         // is done by the base class constructor
      }

      // Declare virtual function InitMainWindow
      // that initializes the window for the application
      virtual void InitMainWindow(void);

};

// Definition of our window class derived from TWindow
class TNewWindow: public TWindow
{
   public:

      // Constructor just calling the base constructor
      TNewWindow(PTWindowsObject AParent, LPSTR ATitle):
                                       TWindow(AParent,ATitle)
      {}

      // Declaration for message response function
```

```
        // to be called when the right mouse button is pressed
        virtual void WMRButtonDown(RTMessage Mess) =
            [WM_FIRST+WM_RBUTTONDOWN];

};

// Definition of function to create a main window
void TBasicApp::InitMainWindow(void)
{ MainWindow = new TNewWindow(0, Name); }

// Definition of message response function for right mouse button press
void TNewWindow::WMRButtonDown( RTMessage Mess )
{
    char* Bang = "Bang!";           // Define some text to display
    HDC OurDC;                      // Variable to hold a display context

    // Get a display context for our window and save its handle in OurDC
    OurDC = GetDC( HWindow );

    // Write the text at the cursor position stored in the object Mess
    TextOut( OurDC, Mess.LP.Lo, Mess.LP.Hi, Bang, strlen(Bang) );

    // RELEASE the display context AT ONCE!!!
    ReleaseDC(HWindow, OurDC);
}
```

```
// Start of Windows program
int PASCAL WinMain(HANDLE hInstance, HANDLE hPrevInstance,
                   LPSTR lpCmdLine, int nCmdShow)
{
    // Create an object of our application class
    TBasicApp OurFirstApp("Our First Window", hInstance, hPrevInstance,
                                              lpCmdLine, nCmdShow );

    OurFirstApp.Run();              // Call inherited Run() for our object

    return OurFirstApp.Status;   // Return inherited data member Status
}
```

How It Works

An extra **#include** statement has been added for the file **STRING.H**, since
we use the function **strlen()** in our message response function
WMRButtonDown().

Our program looks as though it has grown somewhat, but much of it is
comments. Of course, as we develop more complex programs we will

accumulate quite a number of message response functions, so segmenting the code into different files, as we discussed in the previous chapter, will become essential.

Since we added our own window class **TNewWindow**, it was necessary to change the function **InitMainWindow()** in our application class **TBasicApp** to create an object of our window class instead of an object of **TWindow**.

If you run this program, a typical result you might obtain is shown below.

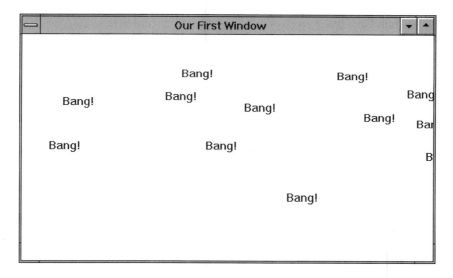

Each time you press the right mouse button, the message response function **WMRButtonDown()** is called, and the text is displayed at the cursor position. We can deduce a couple of things from the way this example works. Look at the text on the right Window boundary - it has been automatically clipped at the boundary so that anything outside the window is not displayed. Note how it will clip in the middle of a character if necessary. This is because output to the screen under Windows is always in graphics mode. The image is an array of pixels rather than a line of characters.

If you move the window in any way you will notice an unfortunate effect. Everything displayed in the window disappears like smoke in the wind with the slightest move. This is because redrawing the window itself is automatically taken care of when it is moved, but anything you displayed in the window is your responsibility. If you want the contents of the window redrawn when necessary, you have to provide the mechanism to do it. This means that you can't just display something and forget it. You must remember what you want to be displayed and where on the screen you want it to appear.

Getting the Paint Message

Whenever something happens that necessitates your program window being drawn, Windows sends a `WM_PAINT` message. This is processed by an OWL defined function, `WMPaint()` which calls a virtual function `Paint()` (`WMPaint()` is actually defined in the OWL class `TWindowsObject,` which is a base class of `TWindow`). All we have to do is to supply a version of the function `Paint()` in our window class `TNewWindow`, derived from `TWindow`, which will redraw the screen as we require.

However, the real problem is not how to draw the screen, but how to remember what should be drawn.

Remembering What to Display

The obvious answer is to create objects which represent instances of the things we want to draw. The place to do this is in our window class `TNewWindow` since the member function `Paint()`, which we need to supply to redraw the screen, is a member of `TNewWindow`.

But what kind of objects should we use to record what is to be displayed? That depends on the application. You need to devise a scheme to suit the range of entities you are dealing with and the sort of thing you might do to record text strings may well be different from what you do to record geometric elements such as lines and circles. There are a number of different approaches, but they usually involve a class for the particular sort of objects to be displayed and some mechanism for daisy-chaining them together, so that you can arrange for them all to be displayed regardless of how many there are.

Let's devise a class to represent a message to be displayed at a particular point on the screen. We could then use this with the last example to arrange to redraw the screen. The basic data members are pretty obvious. They will be the x and y coordinates of a screen position, plus a `char*` variable to point to the message. So we could start the class off as follows:

```
// Class of objects to be displayed
class TDispObject
{
   protected:
      int x;                    // Screen coordinate
      int y;                    // Screen coordinate
      char* pText;              // Pointer to string to be displayed
};
```

This is fine, but we will also need some way of tying one object to the next.

Chaining Objects Together

We could add a pointer to a **TDispObject** object which would be used to store the address of the previous object defined, then as long as we can remember the last object, we could work our way back along the chain. How should we best remember the last object? Since there is only one last object for the whole class, we don't want it to be a separate member of every object. We need just one for the whole class.

Recall how **static** data members of a class behave. Only one instance of a **static** data member exists, however many objects of the class are created, and it exists even when no objects of the class have been defined, so we can initialize it to zero. This will enable a constructor for the class to determine when the first object is created. This is precisely the mechanism we need to keep hold of the tail of a chain of objects. So we could extend the class to this:

```
// Class of objects to be displayed
class TDispObject
{
   public:

      // Constructor
      TDispObject( int xVal, int yVal, char* pStr );

   private:
      int x;                    // Screen coordinate
      int y;                    // Screen coordinate
      char* pText;              // Pointer to string to be displayed

      TDispObject* pPrev;          // Pointer to previous object
      static TDispObject*pLast;    // Pointer to last object created

      // Default constructor - we don't want it used
      TDispObject(){}

};
```

405

We have added the **static** pointer **pLast** which we need to remember to initialize at global scope. It is in the private section along with the other data members. We need to remember that this needs a declaration external to the class to initialize it. The external declaration is not the same as using it in an expression, so this doesn't violate the **private** section of the class.

We have also declared a constructor accepting a pair of screen coordinates plus a text string as arguments. In the **private** section of the class, we have defined the default constructor. Putting it in the **private** section means that if you try to use it in a program, the compiler will generate an error message and compilation will fail. This is a good way of preventing this constructor from being used accidentally. We really don't want objects of this class to be created without ensuring that they have their data members set to proper values.

What should a constructor for this class do? We can set this out in the figure shown below.

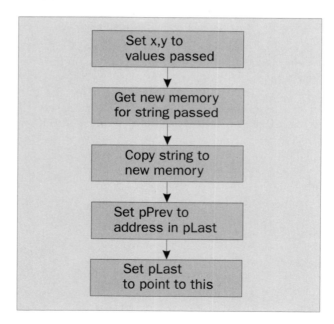

Pretty straightforward, isn't it?. We obviously need to set the screen coordinates to the arguments passed and create some space in the free store for the text we are going to display. For the first object created, the static pointer **pLast** will be zero, as we will have initialized it as such at the outset. Thus the **pPrev** member of the first object will be 0, so we will use this to recognize the end of the chain. Subsequent to the first object, **pLast** will contain the address of the previous object, so each **pPrev** member will point to its predecessor. We should be able to write the constructor quite easily now:

```
// Constructor definition
TDispObject::TDispObject( int xVal, int yVal, char* pStr )
{
    x = xVal;                             // Copy x and y
    y = yVal;                             // screen coordinates passed

    pText = new char[ strlen(pStr) + 1 ]; // Get memory for string
    strcpy( pText, pStr );                // Copy string passed

    pPrev = pLast;                        // Set pointer to previous object
    pLast = this;                         // Set to current object address
}
```

The constructor will not only initialize the data members of an object, but also add it to a chain of existing objects, as illustrated below.

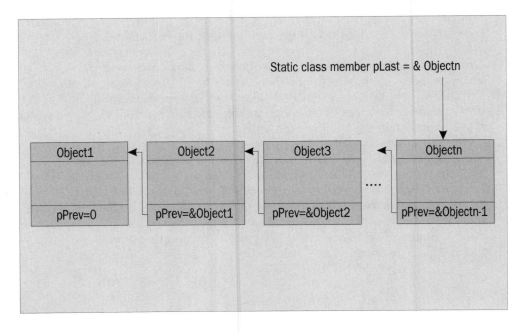

This sort of chaining of objects together is called a **linked list**. TCW also provides us with some more sophisticated built in mechanisms for doing this, which includes other methods in addition to linked lists.

Since we allocate space for the text string in the free store, we need to ensure that the destructor for the **TDispObject** class releases this memory when a **TDispObject** object is destroyed. The destructor would therefore be this:

```
// Destructor to delete memory allocated dynamically
TDispObject::~TDispObject()
{
   delete [] pText;        // Delete text string
}
```

Remember that a text string is an array of type char, *so we need to use the array form of the* delete *operator here.*

Accessing the Object Chain

We can clearly create objects of this class in our message response function by using the operator **new**, but we also need to make them accessible to the function **Paint()**, which is going to redraw the screen. This means that we must either have a data member in our window class, **TNewWindow**, which will provide access to the chain of objects to be displayed, or have some function we can call which will supply the same information.

One way of doing this is to add a data member which is a pointer to a **TDispObject** object, which can then be set by the message response function to point to the last object created. However, this is duplicating the **static** data member, which really belongs in the **TDispObject** class, and we don't want to maintain another version outside.

The alternative is to define a **static** member function of the class **TDispObject**. This has several attractions as an approach. Because it is **static**, it has global scope, and so can be called from anywhere. It also can be called even if no objects exist, so we can still get the value of **PLast** in this situation, which of course will be 0. The integrity of the **TDispObject** class is unbreached, since we don't need to maintain external records of internal data member values. We could give the function the name

`GetLast()`, and it should return the value of `pLast` which is a pointer to a `TDispObject` object. We could write this function within the class as follows:

```
// Function to get the last object address
static TDispObject* GetLast(void) { return pLast; }
```

The function `Paint()` can then use this function to grab hold of the tail of the chain of objects and, by testing for 0, determine whether or not any `TDispObject` objects have been created.

Modifying the Message Response Function

We need a new version of the message response function which doesn't directly write text to the window, but instantiates an object to be displayed instead. It then needs to be able to trigger a repaint of the window. We can do this using a Windows function `InvalidateRect()`, which essentially sends a message to Windows to the effect that some portion of the Window is invalid and should be redrawn. Windows will then send a `WM_PAINT` message to our application which will ultimately cause the `Paint()` function in `TNewWindow` to be called, which is exactly what we are looking for.

The function `InvalidateRect()` accepts three arguments. The first is a handle for the window to be updated - in our case `HWindow`. The second argument is a pointer which specifies the region that is invalid, where a zero value indicates the whole screen needs updating, so that is what we will use. The last argument is either 1 or 0, with 1 indicating that the background is to be erased within the update region, so we will use this value too.

We can now write our new version of `WMRButtonDown()`:

```
// Definition of message response function for right mouse button press
void TNewWindow::WMRButtonDown( RTMessage Mess )
{
// Create object for display
   new TDispObject(Mess.LP.Lo,Mess.LP.Hi,"Bang!");
   InvalidateRect(HWindow, 0 , 1);                   // Redraw the screen
}
```

It's actually very short - just two statements now. The first creates a new display object in the free store. We don't need to remember where it is because we can always get to the beginning of the chain of objects using the static member function of the class **TDispObject**, **GetLast()**. The second statement calls **InvalidateRect()** to cause the screen to be redrawn.

One thing we must remember though is that, since we allocate members on the free store, we should clean up afterwards. We added a destructor for the **TDispObject** class to delete the space allocated in the free store for the text string, but we still need to delete the **TDispObject** objects themselves. The best place to do this would be in the destructor for our window class **TNewWindow**, so let's write it now:

```
// Destructor definition - this needs to delete display
// objects allocated on the free store
TNewWindow::~TNewWindow()
{
// Get tail of object chain
    TDispObject* pLast = TDispObject::GetLast();
    TDispObject* pNext = pLast;              // Save last as next

    while (pNext)                            // As long as next pointer is not 0
    {
       pNext = pLast->GetPrev();             // Save pointer to previous object
       delete pLast;                         // Delete current object
       pLast = pNext;                        // Set current to previous
    }
}
```

We need two declarations for pointers to objects of the class **TDispObject**, **pLast** and **pNext**. We will use one to hold the pointer to the previous object while the current object is destroyed. We must do this so that we can remember the next object back up the chain.

Both pointers are initially set to the value of the **static** class member, **pLast**, containing the address of the last object in the chain. This is retrieved using the static member function **GetLast()**. The **delete** operation is carried out in the **while** loop as long as the pointer **pNext** is not 0, so if there happened to be no objects instantiated, **GetLast()** would return zero and the loop would not be executed at all. On each iteration, the pointer to the previous object is obtained using a member function **GetPrev()**, before deleting the current object. We need to work through a member function because the data member is **private** and can't be accessed directly. The function is very simple - its definition is:

```
TDispObject* TDispObject::GetPrev(void)
{ return pPrev; }
```

Its return type is pointer to **TDispObject**, and it returns the data member **pPrev**.

After deleting the current object the pointer **pLast** is set to the address saved in **pNext**, ready for the **delete** operation on the next iteration. All we need now is the **Paint()** function in our window class **TNewWindow**.

The Paint() Function

The **Paint()** function doesn't need to obtain a display context, because the caller function, **WMPaint()** (inherited from **TWindow**) obtains a device context and passes it as the first argument. The second argument is of type **PAINTSTRUCT&** and contains information about which part of a window is to be repainted, but we will be repainting the whole window, so we will ignore the second parameter for the time being.

The task of our **Paint()** function is then to output each **TDispObject** object to the window using the Windows function **TextOut()**. To do this it will need to obtain the values of the data members **x** and **y** for the position in the window, and access to the pointer **pText** for the string to be displayed. We can add public member functions to the class **TDispObject** to do this. These are very simple; for example, to get the pointer **pText**, the function would be written within the class definition as follows:

```
// Function to get Text value
char* GetText(void)
{ return pText; }
```

The other two function are similar, but with a return type of **int**. They all appear in full in the program **EX10-03.CPP**.

Let's have a stab at defining the **Paint()** function:

```
// Definition of Function to redraw the window contents
void TNewWindow::Paint(HDC DC, PAINTSTRUCT&)
{
// Get the tail of the chain
   TDispObject* pNext = TDispObject::GetLast();

   while (pNext)              // Output objects until the next pointer is 0
   {
```

```
    TextOut(DC, pNext->Getx(), pNext->Gety(),
            pNext->GetText(), strlen(pNext->GetText() ) );
    pNext = pNext->GetPrev();     // Get pointer to previous object
  }
}
```

The function first creates a local pointer to **TDispObject**, **pNext**, which is initialized to the address of the last object in the chain which was saved in the **static** data member of the class, **pLast**. This is returned by the **static** member function **GetLast()**.

The pointer **pNext** is used to control the **while** loop. If no objects have been created, it will be zero at the outset and the loop will not be executed. Assuming we do have some objects to display, the **TextOut()** function is called within the loop. The display context **DC** used in the call of the function **TextOut()** is received as an argument value. The remaining arguments are obtained using the member functions of the class **TDispObject** which return the values of the data members.

After each object is output to the screen, the pointer to the previous object is obtained using the function **GetPrev()** and stored back in the local pointer **pNext**. When **pNext** is zero, we have just processed the first object to be created and the loop ends.

Try It Out - Remembering the Screen

We have enough knowledge now to rebuild the last example such that we don't lose the contents of the window if it is moved. Let's review the organization of the program in three parts: the class definitions, the function definitions, and the **WinMain()** function.

The classes in our program are shown in the following figure, together with the OWL base classes for the derived classes.

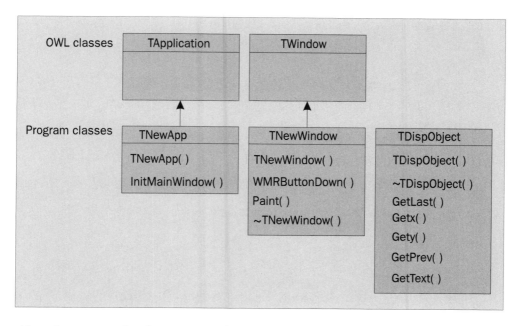

Also shown are the function in the interface to each of the classes in the program. The arrows in the figure point to base classes. The definitions of the three classes are as follows:

```
// Definition of a class for our application
// with the OWL class TApplication as base.
class TBasicApp:public TApplication
{
...
};

// Definition of our window class derived from TWindow
class TNewWindow: public TWindow
{
   public:
...

      // Function to redraw the window contents
      virtual void Paint(HDC DC, PAINTSTRUCT&);

      // Destructor declaration - this needs to delete display
      // objects allocated on the free store
      ~TNewWindow();
};
```

```cpp
// Class of objects to be displayed
class TDispObject
{
   public:

      // Function to get the last object address
      static TDispObject* GetLast(void) { return pLast; }

      // Function to get x value
      int Getx(void) { return x; }

      // Function to get y value
      int Gety(void) { return y; }

      // Function to get Text value
      char* GetText(void) { return pText; }

      // Function to get pointer to previous object
      TDispObject* GetPrev(void) { return pPrev; }

      // Constructor
      TDispObject( int xVal, int yVal, char* pStr );

      // Destructor to delete memory allocated dynamically
      ~TDispObject()
      {
         delete [] pText;        // Delete text string
      }


   private:
      int x;                   // Screen coordinate
      int y;                   // Screen coordinate
      char* pText;             // Pointer to string to be displayed

      TDispObject* pPrev;           // Pointer to previous object
      static TDispObject* pLast;    // Pointer to last object created

      // Default constructor - we don't want it used
      TDispObject(){}

};
```

Compared to the previous example, the original application class is
unchanged, and the only change to **TNewWindow** class definition is the
addition of declarations for the **Paint()** function and a destructor. There are
some changes to the internals of some of the existing functions, but we will
get to those in a moment. The substantial change here is the addition of the
class **TDispObject** where the objects represent entities to be displayed.

414

The interface to the class **TDispObject** provides functions to obtain the values of each of the data members and a constructor. The destructor is required to delete memory allocated by the constructor. All the data members are private and thus can't be referenced directly outside of the class.

The function definitions external to the classes are as follows:

```
// Definition of function to create a main window
void TBasicApp::InitMainWindow(void)
{ MainWindow = new TNewWindow(0, Name); }
```

```
// Definition of message response function for right mouse button press
void TNewWindow::WMRButtonDown( RTMessage Mess )
{
// Create object for display
   new TDispObject(Mess.LP.Lo,Mess.LP.Hi,"Bang!");
   InvalidateRect(HWindow, 0 , 1);                      // Redraw the screen
}


// Destructor definition - this needs to delete display
// objects allocated on the free store
TNewWindow::~TNewWindow()
{
// Get tail of object chain
   TDispObject* pLast = TDispObject::GetLast();
   TDispObject* pNext = pLast;                      // Save last as next

   while (pNext)                             // As long as next pointer is not 0
   {
      pNext = pLast->GetPrev();              // Save pointer to previous object
      delete pLast;                          // Delete current object
      pLast = pNext;                         // Set current to previous
   }
}


// Constructor definition
TDispObject::TDispObject( int xVal, int yVal, char* pStr )
{
   x = xVal;                                 // Copy x and y
   y = yVal;                                 // screen coordinates passed

   pText = new char[ strlen(pStr) + 1 ];     // Get memory for string
   strcpy( pText, pStr );                    // Copy string passed

   pPrev = pLast;                            // Set pointer to previous object
   pLast = this;                             // Set to current object address
}
```

```
// Definition of Function to redraw the window contents
void TNewWindow::Paint(HDC DC, PAINTSTRUCT&)
{
// Get the tail of the chain
   TDispObject* pNext = TDispObject::GetLast();

   while (pNext)              // Output objects until the next pointer is 0
   {
      TextOut(DC, pNext->Getx(), pNext->Gety(),
             pNext->GetText(), strlen(pNext->GetText() ) );
      pNext = pNext->GetPrev();        // Get pointer to previous object
   }
}
```

Only **InitMainWindow()** is still in the original version and a number of new function definitions have been added, compared to the previous example.

The function **WMRButtonDown()** in the class **TNewWindow()** is simpler than before. It just creates an object of the class **TDispObject** and calls the Windows function **InvalidateRect()** to cause the window to be redrawn. The destructor for **TNewWindow()** deletes the **TDispObject** objects created by **WMRButtonDown()**.

The constructor for **TDispObject** sets the screen coordinate members **x** and **y**, and copies the required text string to memory allocated in the free store. It also sets the value of **pPrev** to the value stored in **pLast** and the new value of the static member **pLast** to the address of the current object using the pointer **this**. Remember that the pointer **pLast** is **static** and is therefore initialized in a global declaration external to the class.

Finally, we have the **Paint()** function in the class **TNewWindow**. This is called by Windows whenever the application window is moved or otherwise interfered with and when the **InvalidateRect()** function is called from **WMRButtonDown()**. This gets the address of the last object created using the function **GetLast()** and then displays all the objects starting with the last and working back to the first.

The relationship between the principle functions of the example and their links to Windows, is shown on the following page.

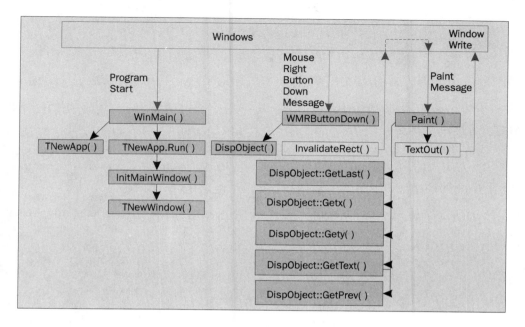

Windows acts as a unifying element in the overall program operation. The message response functions are called by Windows, as is the function **WinMain()** where application execution starts.

The last piece of our example is the function **WinMain()**:

```
// EX10-03.CPP
// Repainting a window
#include <owl.h>      // For the Object Windows Library
#include <string.h>   // For strlen()

// Class definitions
...

// Function definitions
...


TDispObject* TDispObject::pLast = 0; // initialize static data member

// Start of Windows program
int PASCAL WinMain(HANDLE hInstance, HANDLE hPrevInstance,
                                LPSTR lpCmdLine, int nCmdShow)
{
    // Create an object of our application class
```

```
      TBasicApp OurFirstApp("Our First Window", hInstance, hPrevInstance,
                         lpCmdLine, nCmdShow );

      OurFirstApp.Run();     // Call inherited Run() for our object

      return OurFirstApp.Status;    // Return inherited data member Status
   }
```

How It Works

The function **WinMain()** is exactly as before. The **static** data member of
the **TDispObject** class is initialized at global scope. The program operates
externally, exactly as before. Each mouse click will display the text string at
the cursor, but this time it always involves the function **Paint()** being
called to do the actual window write using **TextOut()**. You can now drag
the window around and the contents will automatically be maintained.

The nature of the Windows environment is such that programs have to be
organized to display the contents of the window within the **Paint()**
function, separate from their creation in a message response function or
elsewhere. In a more realistic application, management of the entities to be
displayed, and design of the scheme for their actual display in the function
Paint(), needs some care. With a complex image, it may be desirable to
track the particular portions of the screen which need to be displayed at
any given time, since redrawing the complete window may be too time
consuming. Additionally, a practical application will require some means of
deleting individual objects from the displayed image.

Managing the Mouse

We have seen that pressing a mouse button causes Windows to send a
message to the application to which the mouse action relates. Releasing a
mouse button also causes another message to be generated, and there are a
number of others which are initiated by mouse actions, too. So let's first
look at what the possibilities are.

Mouse Messages

The primary things that you can do with a mouse which result in Windows
generating a mouse message are: pressing a mouse button, releasing a
mouse button, double clicking a mouse button, and moving the mouse.
These result in the following options for mouse messages:

Code	What You Did
WM_LBUTTONDOWN	You pressed the left mouse button
WM_RBUTTONDOWN	You pressed the right mouse button
WM_LBUTTONUP	You released the left mouse button
WM_RBUTTONUP	You released the right mouse button
WM_LBUTTONDBLCLK	You double clicked the left mouse button
WM_RBUTTONDBLCLK	You double clicked the right mouse button
WM_MOUSEMOVE	You moved the mouse

What you do with these, or indeed, whether or not you do anything with them at all, will depend on the application. For each message to which you want to respond, you need to supply a suitable message response function in the window class for your application.

In order to do something a little more interesting with these, we should first look at how graphics entities can be drawn on the screen.

Drawing Graphics

There are a whole range of functions provided by Windows for drawing graphics, but we will just look at drawing lines and circles here. The Windows API is documented in the Help menu provided in TCW, so if you want to find out about others, try browsing through Windows API in the Help index.

A line is drawn from a current position in a window using a function LineTo() which has three arguments, a display context and the x and y screen coordinates of the position in the window where the line should end. A function used in association with LineTo() is the function MoveTo(), which alters the current position in the window to that specified by the arguments to the function. This is typically called to set the start position of a line, prior to calling LineTo() to actually draw the line, as illustrated on the following page.

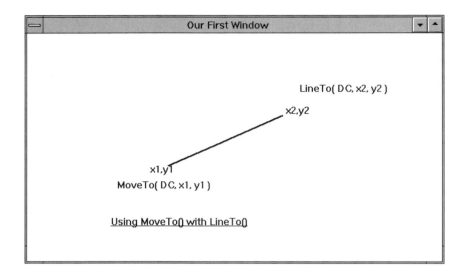

To draw a circle we have the Windows function **Ellipse()** available, which, as its name suggests, will draw ellipses as well as circles. It requires five arguments. The first is the display context handle. The next two pairs of arguments are the **x** and **y** coordinates of the top left and bottom right corners of a rectangle, which encloses the shape to be drawn, so that a circle will result if the rectangle is a square.

Many people prefer to specify a circle in terms of the center, at coordinates **Cx** and **Cy** say, and a radius **r** and we shall use this in our example. We can easily convert from a center and radius representation to the enclosing box coordinates the **Ellipse()** function expects, by using the following conversions:

Top Left of Box: **TLx** = **Cx-r**   **TLy** = **Cy+r**

Bottom Right of Box: **BRx** = **Cx+r**   **BRy** = **Cy-r**

We can show this in the following figure:

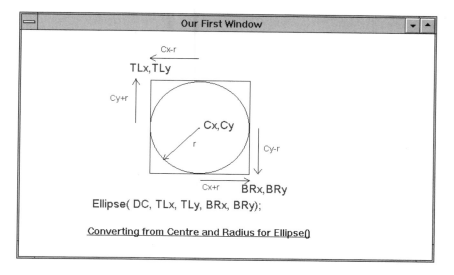

Ellipse(DC, TLx, TLy, BRx, BRy);

<u>Converting from Centre and Radius for Ellipse()</u>

A disadvantage of the function `Ellipse()` for our purposes is that it is a closed curve and it draws a shape that is filled. This means that one shape can hide another. An alternative is the Windows function `Arc()`. The first five arguments of the function `Arc()` are the same as those for the function `Ellipse()`, but it also has an additional four arguments which correspond to the x and y coordinates of the start and end points of the arc to be drawn. Since the arc is not closed, it is not filled, so we can use it to make line drawings. To draw a complete circle using the `Arc()` function, we simply need to make the start and end points for the arc the same. Any point on the circumference will do, so we could use the point with the coordinates `Cx+r,Cy` for the start point as well as the end point.

An Example Using the Mouse

Let's suppose we want to create a program which allows lines and circles to be drawn using the mouse. A line will be drawn by pressing the left mouse button for the start point and by dragging the mouse to the end point, so that when the left mouse button is released, the line is drawn. The circle will be drawn in a similar fashion, using the right mouse button. Pressing the right mouse button will identify the center of the circle and the cursor will be dragged to where the circumference should be.

421

We will need five message response functions in our window class, to deal with the messages **WM_RBUTTONDOWN**, **WM_RBUTTONUP**, **WM_LBUTTONDOWN**, **WM_LBUTTONUP** and **WM_MOUSEMOVE**, so we will need declarations in our window class, in order to define the basics of the class as follows:

```
// Window class to display graphics
class TGrfxWindow: public TWindow
{
   public:
       // Message response functions
       virtual void WMLButtonDown(RTMessage Mess) =
           [WM_FIRST+WM_LBUTTONDOWN];
       virtual void WMLButtonUp(RTMessage Mess) =
           [WM_FIRST+WM_LBUTTONUP];
       virtual void WMRButtonDown(RTMessage Mess) =
           [WM_FIRST+WM_RBUTTONDOWN];
       virtual void WMRButtonUp(RTMessage Mess) =
           [WM_FIRST+WM_RBUTTONUP];
       virtual void WMMouseMove(RTMessage Mess) =
           [WM_FIRST+WM_MOUSEMOVE];

       // Function to redraw the window contents
       virtual void Paint(HDC DC, PAINTSTRUCT&);
   ...
};
```

We will also need some classes to store our graphic objects, but we will look into this a bit later. For the moment we will call the classes **TLine** and **TCircle** when we need to refer to them.

When a graphic object is created, for either mouse button, the messages will occur in the sequence, button down, mouse move, then button up. So what should we do in each function to draw either a line or a circle? These will be the operations at the heart of our example, so it's a good place to start. Let's think about how we draw a line first, since it looks the simplest.

Drawing a Line

When the left mouse button is pressed, it sets the start point for the line, so the first thing we need to do is remember the start position which will be passed in the argument **Mess** to the message response function. We can't draw anything yet, but we do need to record the fact that the left button was pressed for the benefit of the message response function handling a mouse move. This means we will need data members in our window class,

TGrfxWindow, to remember the coordinates of the start point and a flag to record when the left button is down. Thus we will need to extend our windows class definition to this:

```
// Window class to display graphics
class TGrfxWindow: public TWindow
{
   public:
...

   private:
      int Sx;                  // Start point coordinates x,y for a line
      int Sy;                  // or the center of a circle

      BOOL LButtonDown;        // Flag = TRUE for button down
...
};
```

We will probably be able to use the data members **Sx** and **Sy** for the coordinates of the center of a circle as well for the start point of a line, since they are only used while the mouse is being moved. Once the left button is released the line will be fixed, so they then can be used for the next graphical entity (whatever it is).

Dealing with a Left Mouse Button Down Message

The flag **LButtonDown** is specified as type **BOOL**, which is a logical type not part of C++, but defined as a user type by TCW. A **BOOL** variable can have the values **TRUE** or **FALSE** and we can actually use the names **TRUE** and **FALSE** in our program, since they are also predefined.

Based on the discussion above, the message response function for the left button down event will be as follows:

```
// Definition of message response function for left mouse button press
void TGrfxWindow::WMLButtonDown( RTMessage Mess )
{
   Sx = Mess.LP.Lo;
   Sy = Mess.LP.Hi;
   if(!LButtonDown)            // If this is the first L button down
   {
      LButtonDown = TRUE;      // L button was pressed
// Make sure we track the mouse outside our window
      SetCapture(HWindow);
   }
}
```

The first thing the message response function does is to store the current cursor position coordinates passed from Windows in the data members **Sx** and **Sy** of the current **TGrfxWindow** object. The **if** which follows is just a precaution. We should get two left button down messages in a row. At least a left button up message should occur before another left button down, and we will arrange to set the flag, **LButtonDown**, to **FALSE**. Since we have a left button down message, we set the flag to **TRUE** for the benefit of the message response function handling a mouse move message.

We also call the Windows function **SetCapture()**. Calling this function ensures that we get all mouse messages sent to our window, even if the cursor is moved outside it. This will allow us to continue to draw lines where the end point lies outside the boundaries of our window, and more importantly, we will be guaranteed to get the left button up message, even if the cursor is not within our window. We will switch off capturing all the mouse messages in the message response function **WMLButtonUp()**.

Dealing with a Mouse Move Message

We are looking at drawing a line at the moment, so we will come back to how this message relates to drawing circles a little later. The next message after a button down message should be the result of moving the mouse, so the next message response function to be called will be **WMMouseMove()**. In this function, we need to check that the left button is down before we do anything, since obviously a move could occur after pressing the right button, or even without pressing a mouse button at all.

If **LButtonDown** is **TRUE**, then the button has been pressed, so we know the coordinates of the start point of a line have been stored. The action of this function should then be to create a line object from the start point to the current cursor position. If the Windows function **InvalidateRect()** is then called, the **WM_PAINT** message will be generated, and our **Paint()** function in **TGrfxWindow** will be called to redraw the window contents.

The function **WMMouseMove()** will therefore be coded as follows:

```
// Message response function to deal with a mouse move
void TGrfxWindow:: WMMouseMove(RTMessage Mess)
{
    if(LButtonDown)
    {
        // Delete last object only if this is not the first move
        if(MouseMove)
            TDispObject::DeleteLast();
```

```
        MouseMove = TRUE;                          // Record we had a mouse move
        new TLine(Sx, Sy, Mess.LP.Lo, Mess.LP.Hi ); // Create a line
        InvalidateRect(HWindow, 0, TRUE );         // Get the window redrawn
    }
}
```

The code here follows broadly the sequence of actions just described. Since
a succession of **WM_MOUSEMOVE** messages will typically occur, we need to
know whether, previous to the current execution of the message response
function, the function has already been called. We do this using a flag
MouseMove which will be a **BOOL** data member of the class **TgrfxWindow**,
and which is initialized to **FALSE** by the constructor **TGrfxWindow()**.

If the flag is **TRUE**, then we have previously created a **TLine** object, so we
first need to delete the last **TLine** object, before creating a new instance. Of
course, the first time **WMMouseMove()** is executed, the flag will be **FALSE**, so
we won't want to delete the previous object since it has been created and
finished with - it might even be a circle. We only want to delete
intermediate **TLine** objects created by the **WMMouseMove()** function, as a
whole stream of them will be created by a succession of calls to
WMMouseMove() as you drag the mouse. This will create the effect of the
end point of the line being attached to the cursor on the screen as it moves.

The line is created by calling the **TLine** class constructor. The first two
arguments are the coordinates of the start point saved in the data members
Sx and **Sy** of our window class, and the second two arguments are the
coordinates of the current cursor position passed by Windows to our
function.

Dealing with a Mouse Left Button Up Message

The **WM_LBUTTONUP** message will complete the sequence for drawing a line.
Since the line will have already been drawn by the **WMMouseMove()** message
response function, all the **WMLButtonUp()** function has to do is tidy up. This
involves resetting the flags **LButtonDown** and **MouseMove** to **FALSE**, and
calling the Windows function **ReleaseCapture()** to cancel having all the
mouse messages directed to our window - and that's it.

The code for the function will be this:

```
// Message response function for L button up
void TGrfxWindow::WMLButtonUp( RTMessage )
{
    LButtonDown = FALSE;                          // Reset button down flag
```

```
    MouseMove = FALSE;              // Reset mouse move flag
    ReleaseCapture();               // Give up mouse monopoly
}
```

Creating a line is quite simple and is accomplished by one call of **WMLButtonDown()** followed by a succession of calls to **WMMouseMove()** as the mouse is moved then finally one call to **WMLButtonUp()**.

We now need to look at how we can create a circle. There is slightly more to it, but the principle is exactly the same.

Drawing a Circle

The process of drawing a circle uses the right mouse button. We assume the start point will be the center of the circle and we will drag the cursor to form the circle with the radius we want. It starts when the right mouse button is pressed, so the first piece of code we need is the message response function called by a **WM_RBUTTONDOWN** message.

Dealing with a Right Mouse Button Down Message

The process is identical to that of a line, since all we do is save the current position, which represents the center of the circle in **Sx** and **Sy**. So let's go straight to the program code - it could look like the following:

```
// Definition of message response function for right mouse button press
void TGrfxWindow::WMRButtonDown( RTMessage Mess )
{
   Sx = Mess.LP.Lo;
   Sy = Mess.LP.Hi;
   if(!RButtonDown)               // If this is the first R button down
   {
      RButtonDown = TRUE;         // R button was pressed so set flag
      // Make sure we track the mouse outside our window
      SetCapture(HWindow);
   }
}
```

We just change the character string **LButton** to **RButton** in the **LButtonDown()** function, and we have a good **RButtonDown()** function. Or do we? We are now talking about handling two possible events which could interfere with one another. We need some protection against the possibility of some Neanderthal individual pressing the left mouse button, then pressing the right mouse button before they release the left. They could also do it the other way round. We could create a real stew out of either situation. We need to make sure that when we process a **WM_RBUTTONDOWN** message, we are not already in the middle of processing a **WM_LBUTTONDOWN** message, and vice versa. We could do this by adding a check at the beginning of each message response function to see whether the other button is still down and, if it is, to ignore the current button press message we have just received. The function for the right button would then become this:

```
// Definition of message response function for right mouse button press
void TGrfxWindow::WMRButtonDown( RTMessage Mess )
{
    // Do nothing if the other button is already pressed.
    if(LButtonDown) return;
    Sx = Mess.LP.Lo;
    Sy = Mess.LP.Hi;
    if(!RButtonDown)        // If this is the first R button down
    {
        RButtonDown = TRUE;     // R button was pressed
        // Make sure we track the mouse outside our window
        SetCapture(HWindow);
    }
}
```

WMLButtonDown() needs to be changed as well to add a check for the right button being already down. We can now be sure that only one button press is processed at one time, and only one of the flags **LButtonDown** and **RButtonDown** in our windows class is **TRUE** at one time.

We need to think about the button up processing, too.

Dealing with the Right Mouse Button Up Message

We don't want the **ReleaseCapture()** function to be called by **WMRButtonUp()**, if we are still processing a left button down message, which could be the case if the right button was pressed after the left button. We also don't want to set the **MouseMove** flag to **FALSE**. We need to remember to only call **ReleaseCapture()** and set the **MouseMove** flag **FALSE**, if **RButtonDown** is **TRUE**, which will indicate that we really are processing the right button. Otherwise, it's the same as for the line drawing message response function. The circle will have been created in the function servicing the **WM_MOUSEMOVE** message, so we just need to clean up here. So the code for the function should be as follows:

```
// Message response function for R button up
void TGrfxWindow::WMRButtonUp( RTMessage )
{
    if(!RButtonDown) return;   // If the right button isn't down, do nothing
    RButtonDown = FALSE;       // Reset button down flag
    MouseMove = FALSE;         // Reset mouse move flag

    ReleaseCapture();          // Give up mouse monopoly
}
```

The same goes for the **WMLButtonUp()** function. The version of the message response function we wrote previously to draw a line, needs this statement added at the beginning of the body of the function:

```
if(!LButtonDown) return;   // If the left button isn't down, do nothing
```

Dealing with the Mouse Move Message for a Circle

There is only one message for a mouse move, so there is only one message response function. The function **WMMouseMove()** will have to handle lines and circles. This doesn't really complicate things very much. The logic we applied to drawing a line applies equally well to drawing a circle, so we can use almost the same statements. The complete function we be as follows:

```
// Message response function to deal with a mouse move
void TGrfxWindow:: WMMouseMove(RTMessage Mess)
{
    if(LButtonDown)
    {
        // Delete last object only if this is not the first move
        if(MouseMove)
            TDispObject::DeleteLast();
        MouseMove = TRUE;                      // Record we had a mouse move
        new TLine(Sx, Sy, Mess.LP.Lo, Mess.LP.Hi ); // Create a line
        InvalidateRect(HWindow, 0, TRUE );     // Get the window redrawn
        return;                                // We are done
    }
    if(RButtonDown)
    {
        // Delete last object only if this is not the first move
        if(MouseMove)
            TDispObject::DeleteLast();
        MouseMove = TRUE;                      // Record we had a mouse move
        new TCircle(Sx, Sy, Mess.LP.Lo, Mess.LP.Hi );// Create a circle
        InvalidateRect(HWindow, 0, TRUE );     // Get the window redrawn
    }
}
```

The response function for button down message will ensure that only one or other button down flag is set, so only one of the `if` statements will be executed. If the **RButtonDown** flag is **TRUE**, we are drawing a circle and the only difference between that and the processing for a line is that we call the **TCircle** class constructor instead of the **TLine** class constructor. The arguments are the same but they represent the x and y coordinates of the center of the circle in this case, followed by a point on the circumference. We will see how these are used when we come to define the classes for our graphic objects, and now is as good a time as any to look into that.

The Graphic Object Classes

We want to be able to output objects to the window in the paint function without knowing what they are, since lines and circles can originate in any combination and in any sequence. We really need a linked list of mixed lines and circles. How can we achieve that?

We need to hark back to the last chapter and all that stuff about polymorphism. If we can arrange that the classes for both kinds of objects have a common base class, then we can use a base class pointer to hold the address of either derived class object. Our class from a previous example, **TDispObject**, looks a fairly neutral class and it has the basic elements that we might need, so let's try to hack out a version to do what we want.

```
class TDispObject
{
   public:

      // Function to get the last object address
      static TDispObject* GetLast(void) { return pLast; }

      // Function to get pointer to previous object
      TDispObject* GetPrev(void) { return pPrev; }
      virtual TDispObject () {}

   protected:                // ...so they can be accessed in a derived class

      int x;                 // Screen coordinate
      int y;                 // Screen coordinate

      TDispObject* pPrev;    // Pointer to previous object
      static TDispObject* pLast;  // Pointer to last object created

};
```

We can use the protected data members **x** and **y**, as the start point for any derived class. For a derived class for lines it will be the beginning of a line and for a class defining circles, it will be the center of a circle. All objects will require a pointer to a previous object, **pPrev**, and since this is defined as a pointer to the base class, it will happily store addresses of any derived class object.

Similarly, the **static** pointer **pLast**, used to store the address of the last object in a linked list, will store the address of any derived class object, and since it is **static**, only one copy of **pLast** will exist and will be shared between all derived classes.

We have functions which allow access to the pointers **pPrev** and **pLast** in the class interface as we had before, but we need a little extra now, since we intend to derive classes with **TDispObject** as a base.

First, we need a means of outputting an object to a window in the derived classes which will work automatically through a pointer to the base class which contains any kind of object. We therefore need to add a **virtual** function for this which we can also make pure, since we won't want to output a base class object.

We also require a function to delete the last object added to a chain for use in the **WMMouseMove()** function in the **TGrfxWindow** class, when a succession of objects are being created as the mouse is dragged with a button down. To accommodate these we need to extend the class to this:

```
// Class of objects to be displayed
class TDispObject
{
    public:

        // Function to get the last object address
        static TDispObject* GetLast(void) { return pLast; }

        // Function to delete the last object
        static void DeleteLast(void);

        // Function to get pointer to previous object
        TDispObject* GetPrev(void) { return pPrev; }

        // Pure virtual function to display an object
        virtual void Show(HDC) = 0;
```

```
        protected:              // ...so they can be accessed in a derived class

            int x;              // Screen coordinate
            int y;              // Screen coordinate
            TDispObject* pPrev;  // Pointer to previous object

            static TDispObject* pLast;  // Pointer to last object created

    };
```

The **virtual** output function is **Show()**. It is specified as pure (because of **=0** at the end) so the class is an abstract class. This means that it must be defined in a derived class to allow derived class objects to be created. It has one parameter specified of type **HDC** which is the OWL defined type for a handle to a display context. We will need this since, when the function is implemented in a derived class, it will need to pass the display context to the Windows function producing the output. Another consequence of the class **TDispObject** being abstract is that objects of the class can't be created, so we don't need any constructors for the class.

The function **DeleteLast()** is **static** so that we can access it without specifying a particular object, since we want to delete the last object in the linked list regardless of what it is. We can write the member function in the base class straight away:

```
// Function to delete last object created
void TDispObject::DeleteLast(void)
{
    if(pLast ==0 ) return;        // No objects exist - so return

    TDispObject* Temp = 0;        // Temporary pointer
    Temp = pLast->pPrev;          // Save address of object preceding the last
    delete pLast;                 // Delete the last one
    pLast = Temp;                 // Set the previous object as last
}
```

The function first checks whether the pointer **pLast** is null. If it is, we have no objects at all in the linked list, so a return is executed. When **pLast** is not null, before deleting the object pointed to by **pLast**, the address of the previous object is obtained from the **pPrev** member of the last object. The last object is then deleted and the pointer to the previous object which was saved is stored in **pLast**.

Defining the TLine Class

We are going to derive the class **TLine** from the class **TDispObject**. The only additional data members we require are for the coordinates of the end points of a line. We are also going to need a constructor, plus the function **Show()** to display a line in a window. The complete definition for **TLine** will therefore be this:

```
class TLine : public TDispObject
{
   public:
      // Constructor
      TLine(int Sx, int Sy, int Ex,int Ey)
      {
         x=Sx;                            // Initialize base members
         y=Sy;                            // storing start point

         Endx = Ex;                       // Store end point
         Endy = Ey;                       // coordinates Ex and Ey

         pPrev = pLast;                   // Set last object to previous
         pLast = this;                    // Set current object as last
      }

      // Function to display a line
      virtual void Show( HDC DC );

   protected:
      int Endx, Endy;     // End point coordinates

      TLine(){}           // Default constructor - not to be used
};
```

The parameters to the constructor are the x and y coordinates of the start and end points of a line. The constructor first initializes the members, **x** and **y**, which are inherited from the base class. These hold the coordinates of the start point of a line, so they store the first pair of parameters. The data members, **Endx** and **Endy**, are initialized with the second pair of parameters, corresponding to the end point. The **pPrev** pointer is set to the address stored in **pLast**, and **pLast** is set to the address of the current object being created, available in the pointer **this**. This adds the current object to the end of the existing chain.

The default constructor is defined in the **protected** section of the class. This will inhibit the generation of a default constructor by the compiler and any attempt to use it will result in a compiler error message. This effectively prevents uninitialized **TLine** objects being created, accidentally or otherwise.

All we need to complete the class is a definition for the member function **Show()**, to output a line to a window:

```
// Function to display a line
void TLine::Show(HDC DC)
{
   MoveTo( DC, x , y );          // Move to start point
   LineTo( DC, Endx, Endy );     // Draw Line
}
```

This is very simple. The Windows function **MoveTo()** is called first to set the current position in the window to that specified by the data members **x** and **y**, which corresponds to the start point of the line. The Windows function **LineTo()** is then called to draw a line from the current position to the point specified by the coordinates **Endx** and **Endy**. The function operates on the basis that a display context has already been obtained prior to the call, and is passed to it as an argument.

Defining the TCircle Class

The **TCircle** class will be derived from the abstract class, **TDispObject**, similarly to the class **TLine**. Its basic structure will be the same as **TLine** too, with a constructor and the function **Show()** defined in the **public** section, and the default constructor defined in the protected section to prevent it from being used:

```
class TCircle:public TDispObject
{
   public:
      // Constructor
      TCircle(int Sx, int Sy, int Ex, int Ey );

      // Function to display a circle
      virtual void Show( HDC DC );

   protected:
      // Circle radius - center coordinates are stored in
      // Sx and Sy inherited from the base class
      int Radius;

      // Default constructor
      TCircle(){}      // so it can't be used
};
```

The only data member defined here is **Radius**, in the protected section of the class definition. The coordinates for the center of a circle will be stored in the data members inherited from the base class.

We have two functions we need to define, the constructor and the function **Show()**. Let's look at the constructor first.

The defining data for a circle will be the coordinates of the center, stored by the message response function **WMRButtonDown()** in the data members of the **TGrfxWindow** object, and the coordinates of a point on the circumference, passed by Windows to the message response function **WMMouseMove()**. From these two points we need to calculate the value for **Radius**. If you remember your high school geometry, this is provided by the formula:

$$R = \sqrt{((x_e - x_s)^2 + (y_s - y_e)^2)}$$

where R is the radius and x_s, y_s and x_e, y_e are the coordinates of the center, and a point on the circumference respectively. The results from the famous theorem of Pythagorus are illustrated below.

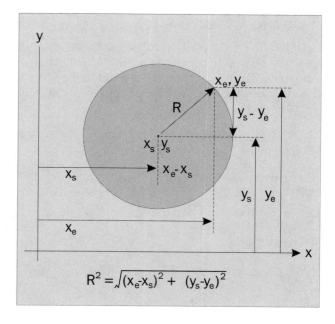

Because the differences between coordinates are squared, it doesn't matter whether you write $(y_s - y_e)^2$ or $(y_e - y_s)^2$ - the result will be the same. We can use this formula to write our constructor as follows:

```
// Constructor definition
TCircle::TCircle(int Sx, int Sy, int Ex, int Ey )
{
    double xdiff = Sx-Ex;        // x coordinate difference
    double ydiff = Sy-Ey;        // y coordinate difference

    x=Sx;                        // Initialize base members storing
    y=Sy;                        // coordinates of center

    Radius = sqrt( xdiff*xdiff+ydiff*ydiff );    // Calculate radius

    pPrev = pLast;               // Set last object to previous
    pLast = this;                // Set current object as last
}
```

We store the differences between the x and y coordinates of the points we have in temporary variables **xdiff** and **ydiff** which are of type **double**. They need to be of type **double** to use the **sqrt()** function which is declared in the header file **MATH.H**, since it takes a **double** argument and returns the square root of the argument value as a **double** result.

After storing the coordinates of the center of the circle, we calculate the radius. The result returned from the **sqrt()** will be automatically converted from **double** to **int** before being stored in the data member **Radius**. Finally, we update the pointers **pPrev** and **pLast**, as we did for a **TLine** object.

The **Show()** function for a circle will need to calculate the coordinates of the top left and bottom right of the square enclosing the circle, which are required for the Windows function **Arc()** which will actually draw the circle. We saw how to do this earlier in this chapter, so the code for the **Show()** function will be this:

```
// Function to display a circle
void TCircle::Show( HDC DC )
{
    int TLx = x-Radius;      // Calculate coordinates for
    int TLy = y+Radius;      // top left of enclosing square
    int BRx = x+Radius;      // ... and for bottom right
    int BRy = y-Radius;      // of square
    int SFx = x+Radius;      // Arc start & finish x coordinate
                             // Arc start & finish y coordinate is y
    Arc( DC, TLx, TLy, BRx, BRy,      // Now draw full circle which is
         SFx, y, SFx, y );            // arc from SFx,y to SFx,y
}
```

The function creates local int variables **TLx**, **TLy**, **BRx**, and **BRy** to contain the coordinates of the top left and bottom right of the square enclosing the circle to be drawn. A variable **SFx** is also defined which will be the x coordinate of the start and finish point of the arc. The y coordinate will be **y**, which is the y coordinate of the center. Once these coordinates have been calculated, the circle is drawn using the Windows function **Arc()**, which uses the display context, **DC**, passed as an argument.

Completing the Application Class

We can use exactly the same application class as in the previous example, so all we need to complete our example is to complete the **TGrfxApplication** class. In addition to the message response functions, the application class only needs the flags we discussed in that context, the data members **Sx** and **Sy**, a constructor and a destructor, and the **Paint()** function:

```
// Window class to display graphics
class TGrfxWindow: public TWindow
{
   public:
      // Constructor
      TGrfxWindow(PTWindowsObject AParent, LPSTR ATitle)
         :TWindow(AParent,ATitle)
      { LButtonDown = RButtonDown = MouseMove = FALSE; }

      // Destructor
      ~TGrfxWindow();

      // Message response functions
      virtual void WMLButtonDown(RTMessage Mess) =
         [WM_FIRST+WM_LBUTTONDOWN];
      virtual void WMLButtonUp(RTMessage Mess) =
         [WM_FIRST+WM_LBUTTONUP];
      virtual void WMRButtonDown(RTMessage Mess) =
         [WM_FIRST+WM_RBUTTONDOWN];
      virtual void WMRButtonUp(RTMessage Mess) =
         [WM_FIRST+WM_RBUTTONUP];
      virtual void WMMouseMove(RTMessage Mess) =
         [WM_FIRST+WM_MOUSEMOVE];

      // Function to redraw the window contents
      virtual void Paint(HDC DC, PAINTSTRUCT&);

   private:
      int Sx;                    // Start point coordinates x,y for a line
      int Sy;                    // or the center of a circle
```

```
    BOOL LButtonDown;      // Flag = TRUE for button down
    BOOL RButtonDown;      // Flag = TRUE for button down
    BOOL MouseMove;        // Flag = TRUE for previous move

};
```

All the constructor does is initialize the three flags. The destructor will need to delete the linked list of graphic objects starting with the one pointed to by the **pLast** member of the base class **DispObject**, and following the chain through via the **pPrev** pointer from each object in the list. But this is precisely what the destructor for the previous example did, so we can use the same code.

The **Paint()** function will be a little different from the previous example. There, we called the Windows functions to draw in the window directly. Here, we need to use the function **Show()** for each object, since we don't know what the objects are. It's different but it isn't very complicated. The code to do this is as follows:

```
// Definition of Function to redraw the window contents
void TGrfxWindow::Paint(HDC DC, PAINTSTRUCT&)
{
    // Get the tail of the chain
    TDispObject* pNext = TDispObject::GetLast();

    while (pNext)          // Output objects until the next pointer is 0
    {
        pNext->Show(DC);              // Display whatever it is
        pNext = pNext->GetPrev();     // Get pointer to previous object
    }
}
```

The first action is to grab the tail of the list of objects using the static member function **GetLast()**, and store it in a local pointer **pNext**. The **while** loop will continue as long as **pNext** is not null. The first action in the loop is to call the function **Show()** for the object pointed to by **pNext**. Because the function **Show()** is virtual, the version of the function will be selected dynamically according to whether **pNext** is pointing to a **TLine** object or a **TCircle** object. This mechanism could be extended to include a variety of other objects defined in classes derived from the class **DispObject**, and the **Paint()** function would take care of them without change. Isn't that neat?

437

The final action in the **while** loop is to copy the address stored in the pointer **pPrev** of the current object into **pNext**, using the member function **GetPrev()** in the **DispObject** class. This sets up **pNext** ready for the next iteration.

We are just about ready to roll with this one. All we need is a function **WinMain()** and we can start drawing.

The WinMain() Function

The function **WinMain()** is no problem. It's the same as in the previous example, but we need to add an **#include** statement for **MATH.H**:

```
// EX10-04.CPP
// Drawing lines and circles
#include <owl.h>            // For the Object Windows Library
#include <string.h>         // For strlen()
#include <math.h>           // For sqrt()

    . . .

TDispObject* TDispObject::pLast = 0;        // initialize static data member

// Start of Windows program
int PASCAL WinMain(HANDLE hInstance, HANDLE hPrevInstance,
            LPSTR lpCmdLine, int nCmdShow)
{
    // Create an object of our application class
    TBasicApp OurFirstApp("Our First Window", hInstance, hPrevInstance,
            lpCmdLine, nCmdShow );

    OurFirstApp.Run();                  // Call inherited Run() for our object

    return OurFirstApp.Status;    // Return inherited data member Status
}
```

It works quite well considering this is only our third windows program. When I ran it I obtained the following output:

More Picasso than Rembrandt I think, but definitely some talent showing. You can continue to draw lines using the left mouse button, or circles using the right mouse button to your heart's content, or at least as long as the free store holds out. Notice how you can drag the end of a line or the circle boundary as long as you keep the mouse button pressed.

If you construct a large number of objects, you may get a lot of flickering of the image as you move the mouse, depending on the horse power of your computer. Remember, we are redrawing the entire picture every time you move the mouse, so the more objects you have on the screen, the longer it is going to take. Each small movement will call our function **WMMouseMove()**, which will delete the last object, create a new one, then cause **Paint()** to be invoked to redraw the whole thing.

When you are tired of drawing, you can end the program by double clicking the control menu box.

Summary

In this chapter we have covered the essentials of Windows programming. It wasn't so difficult, was it? There were quite a few functions involved, but they are all very easy, and the OWL gives us a real head start. Let's summarize the essentials of what we have seen:

▶ The OWL provides a set of classes which encapsulate the key parts of the Windows Application Programming Interface. It enables you to derive your own classes to support your own Windows applications, which will automatically provide definitions for data members required for using the Windows API. It will also provide default behavior for many operations with your application window.

▶ The minimum Windows application requires an application class to be derived from the OWL class **TApplication**, a window class to be derived from the OWL class **TWindow**, and an application object and a window object to be instantiated.

▶ Windows communicates with your application by sending messages to your application. Sending a message means calling a message response function defined for your window object. Messages are caused by external events such as pressing a mouse button.

▶ You need to define a message response function in your window class for each message that is relevant for your application.

▶ A message response function is associated with a particular message by specifying a dispatch index in the function declaration in the window class. A dispatch index is a unique integer value associated with a given message, which is defined by adding a constant predefined by an OWL symbol to **WM_FIRST**, which is a base value also predefined by the OWL.

▶ Any event which requires a window to be redrawn will be signalled by a **WM_PAINT** message which causes the **Paint()** member function of your window class to be called. The basic window with the frame and title bar will be taken care of automatically, but you must supply a **Paint()** function which will reconstruct the image in your application Window.

Make sure you are comfortable with how the examples work in this chapter before going on to the next. There are very important basic concepts here about how a Windows program is structured. If you are not sure about what is going on, try modifying the examples to see when they don't work compared with when they do. Don't worry about crashing Windows. You can always restart with *Ctrl-Alt-Del*.

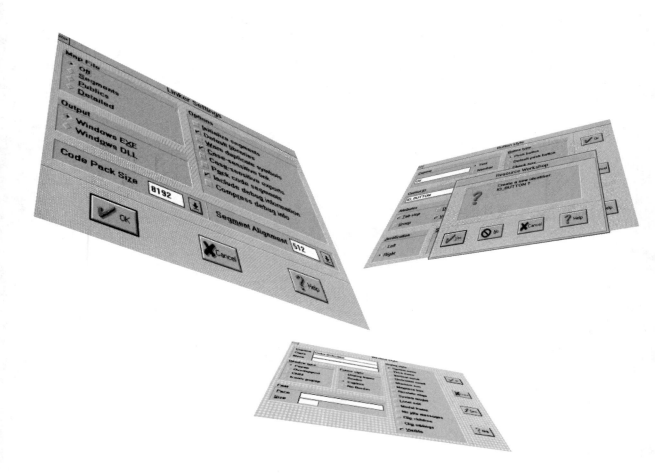

11

Understanding the Application Window

In this chapter, we will be exploring in greater depth what we can do with an application window. We will also be consolidating our programming skills in C++ by building a more substantial application example. This will use the basics we covered in the previous chapter, and will combine and develop the examples of technique introduced in the chapter, to end up with a working program for the game, NIM.

In this chapter you will learn about:

▶ The client area of your application window, and how it is addressed

▶ Drawing at specific points in the client area of a window

▶ Changing the size of a window as it is created

▶ Pen objects, and how to create and use them

▶ Deleting objects from the client area using the mouse

▶ Creating a message box

▶ Terminating your application

▶ How to manage the shut down of your application and provide a continuation option

The Application Window Client Area

The client area for an application window is the area of the window in which you can display text or graphics. In the examples in the last chapter, we placed both text and graphics in the client area using Windows API functions such as **TextOut()** and **Arc()**. However, we really didn't know where we were putting any of the items we displayed, other than that they were at the current cursor position. Suppose we want to display something at a particular position in the client area. To do this we need to understand what the screen coordinates mean and what units they are in.

Window Client Area Coordinates

A point in the window client area is specified as a pair of x,y coordinates, where the top left hand corner of the client area is 0,0. x increases towards the right, and y increases from top to bottom, as shown below.

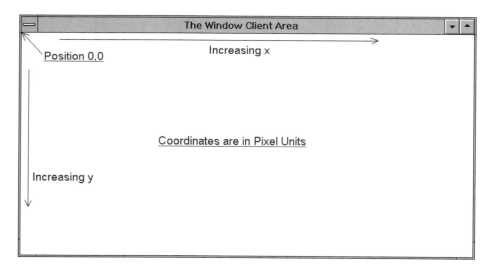

The units the coordinates are measured in are *pixels* (the word 'pixel' comes from 'picture element'). As you are likely to be aware, a pixel is a basic displayable dot on the screen, and the number of pixels on the screen depends on what sort of display adapter you have. The VGA adapter normally supports 640x480 pixels on the screen, whereas with an SVGA adapter you may have a range of possibilities from the same as that for VGA, through 800x600 to 1024x768 or even more. The upshot of this is that a particular client area coordinate position, 100,100 say, may vary in distance from the top left hand corner depending on what kind of display adapter you have on your computer.

Writing to a Specific Position

Let's produce a program to draw some lines at particular points on the screen. We will be developing this into a working game of NIM, so we will name classes accordingly. NIM is a deceptively simple game involving two or more rows of matches, with an arbitrary number of matches in each row. On your turn, you can remove any number of matches from any one row. You can remove a whole row if you wish. You must always remove at least one match. The one who removes the last match is the winner.

The Essential Application Classes

Our initial example will display a row of matches. We first need the application class and the window class defined. Here are the definitions for these:

```
// Definition of a class for our application
// with the OWL class TApplication as base.
class TGameApp:public TApplication
{
   public:
      // Constructor for our class which calls the
      // base class constructor
      TGameApp(LPSTR AName, HANDLE hInstance, HANDLE hPrevInstance,
               LPSTR lpCmdLine, int nCmdShow)
         :TApplication(AName, hInstance, hPrevInstance,
                      lpCmdLine, nCmdShow)
      {
         // No statements as everything required
         // is done by the base class constructor
      }

      // Declare virtual function InitMainWindow
      // that initializes the window for the application
      virtual void InitMainWindow(void);

};

// Definition of our application main window class
class TNimWindow:public TWindow
{
   public:
```

```
      // Constructor
      TNimWindow(PTWindowsObject AParent, LPSTR ATitle);

      // Destructor
      ~TNimWindow();

      // Function to redraw the window contents
      virtual void Paint(HDC DC, PAINTSTRUCT&);

   private:
      TGame* pTGame;                  // Pointer to a game object

};
```

Except for the addition of the pointer to a **TGame** object in the **TNimWindow** class, there is nothing new here. These are essentially the same classes as we saw in the previous chapter. The class **TGameApp** has its constructor defined within the class. It simply calls the base class constructor, which does everything we need. We need the member function **InitMainWindow()** to start things off. Here it is:

```
// Definition of function to create a main window
void TGameApp::InitMainWindow(void)
{ MainWindow = new TNimWindow(0, Name); }
```

The sole purpose of this is to instantiate a main window for the application, so it calls the constructor for our **TNimWindow** class.

The Objects to be Created

Initially, we want to be able to draw a row of matches at a particular place in the client area of our application window. The basic mechanism will be to create an object of a class we will call **TGame** in the constructor for **TNimWindow**, and the constructor for the **TGame** class will create the object to be displayed. This will involve defining two other kinds of objects: a match, which we will define in a class **TMatch**, and a row of matches, or rather a row of **TMatch** objects, which we will define in a class **TRow**. The actual displaying will be done by the **Paint()** function in the **TNimWindow** class. So let's define the class **TGame**:

```
// Class to define a game
class TGame
{
   public:
      // Constructor
      TGame()
      { aRow = new TRow( xBase, yBase ); }
```

```
      // Destructor
      ~TGame()
      { delete aRow; }


      // Display game
      void Show(HDC& DC)
      { aRow->Show(DC); }


      TRow* aRow;      // Pointer to a TRow object

};
```

It's a very simple class, with just a constructor, a destructor, and a member function **Show()**, which is intended to be called by the member function **Paint()** in the **TNimWindow** class.

The constructor creates a **TRow** object in the free store. We will come to the detail of the **TRow** class a bit later. The destructor removes the **TRow** object from the free store. The remaining function, **Show()**, will write the **TGame** object to the client area using the display context passed as a parameter. This amounts to calling the **Show()** function for the **TRow** object, **aRow**.

The TMatch Class

Let's start with the basic entity to be displayed, defined by the class **TMatch**. Since we will be creating these in rows (where a row will be a **TRow** object), it would be as well to plan for this at the outset, so we will include a pointer to a **TMatch** object as a data member, with the idea that we can create a linked list of **TMatch** objects. We can also include a function **GetNext()** to obtain the next object, as we will certainly need it eventually:

```
// Class to define a match
class TMatch
{
   public:
      // Constructor
      TMatch(int Ry, TMatch* pFirst);

      // Display a match
      void Show(HDC& DC);

      // Get next match in chain
      TMatch* GetNext(void)
      { return pNext;    }
```

```
   private:
      int x,y;                  // Screen position of a match
      TMatch* pNext;            // Pointer to next match

      // Default constructor - can't be used
      TMatch(){}

};
```

By defining the default constructor in the **private** section of the class, we prevent the compiler from generating a version and also inhibit its use.

We will assume that the row of **TMatch** objects start at the position defined by two **int** variables, **xBase** and **yBase**, which we will define at the global scope. We will also assume that **TMatch** objects are to be spaced a distance of **xDelta** pixels apart, also defined globally, so all these values will be accessible anywhere. We will draw the **TMatch** objects in a row at the relative positions shown below.

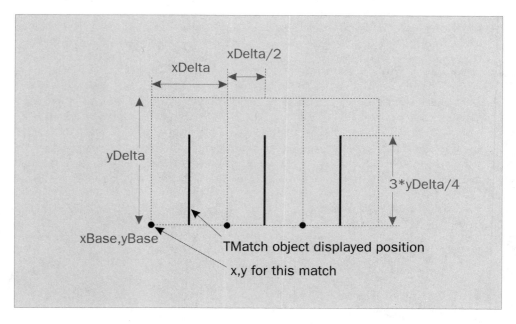

As the illustration shows, the height of a **TMatch** object will be three quarters of the length specified by another global variable, **yDelta**. A **TMatch** object is defined by the coordinates of its position in the client area, so its constructor will be the data members **x** and **y**. The **x** coordinate for the first match in a row will be **xBase**, and for successive matches it will be the **x** coordinate of the previous match plus **xDelta**.

The **y** coordinate, on the other hand, will be the same for all matches in a row, and will be the same as the **y** coordinate for the **TRow** object which created the **TMatch** object. You might think that it would be a good idea to make **y** a **static** data member, but remember that we will eventually have more than one row, and the **y** values for different rows will differ. A **static** member is shared by all members of a class, so it wouldn't help us here.

The reason for specifying **TMatch** objects in this way is that it will be more convenient later on when we want to delete some of them.

Let's write the constructor for a **TMatch** object. It has two parameters, the **y** coordinate and a pointer to the previous **TMatch** object in a row:

```
// Constructor for TMatch object has the y coordinate
// of the row, and the pointer to the last match created as arguments.
// All objects in a row will have the same y coordinate.
TMatch::TMatch(int Ry, TMatch* pFirst)
{
   pNext = pFirst;              // Next match is the last created

   y = Ry;                      // Set y coordinate as row

   if(pFirst)                   // If there is a next, then
      x = pFirst->x + xDelta;   // x coordinate is next plus xdelta
   else
      x = xBase;                // Otherwise set to base value
}
```

The next object in the row is the last one created, so we copy the address in the second parameter to the data member **pNext**. The **y** value is easy - it's simply the value of the first parameter.

For the **x** value calculation, we have two possibilities. It could be that this is the first **TMatch** object in a row, in which case the **pFirst** argument will be null, and we need to set **x** to the initial value **xBase**. If it is not the first in a row, then the **x** coordinate for this object will be the **x** coordinate for the previous object plus the increment **xDelta**.

We can now write the **Show()** function for a **TMatch** object as follows:

```
// Function to display a match
void TMatch::Show(HDC& DC)
{
    MoveTo(DC, x+xDelta/2, y);
    LineTo(DC, x+xDelta/2, y-3*yDelta/4);
}
```

This function sets the current position to a position **xDelta/2** to the right of the coordinates in the **TMatch** object. This is done using the Windows function **MoveTo()**. It then draws the **TMatch** object as a vertical line towards the top of the client area. The value for the length is subtracted from the coordinate **y**, because positive **y** is measured towards the bottom of the client area, and we want to draw the line from the current position towards the top. The function uses the display context **DC** which will be passed as a reference argument.

The TRow Class

The objects of the class **TRow** will represent a row of **TMatch** objects. The data members are going to be the coordinates of the row, and a pointer to the first **TMatch** in the row. All the links to the other objects in the row are implicit. For the interface, we need only a constructor and a destructor, plus a function to display a row in our window. The class definition will therefore be this:

```
// Class to define a row of matches
class TRow
{
    public:
        // Constructor
        TRow(int Sx, int Sy);

        // Destructor
        ~TRow();

        // Display a row
        void Show(HDC& DC);

    private:
        int x,y;                 // Screen coordinates of row object
        TMatch* pFirstMatch;     // Pointer to first match in a row
        TRow(){}                 // We don't want the default used
};
```

The constructor will accept the coordinates of the row as arguments and will create the **TMatch** objects on the free store. How will the number of objects in a row be determined? Well, we will eventually want it to be variable, but for the moment we will arbitrarily make it 15:

```
// Constructor for a TRow object
TRow::TRow(int Sx, int Sy)
{
   x = Sx;                        // Initialize position on screen
   y = Sy;
   int nMatches = 15;             // Number of matches in a row
   pFirstMatch = 0;               // Initialize pointer to first match

   for(int i = 1; i<= nMatches ; i++ )
      pFirstMatch = new TMatch(y,pFirstMatch);   // Create a row of matches
}
```

After setting the coordinates of the row as the argument values passed, a chain of **TMatch** objects is generated in the **for** loop. The current address stored in the data member **pFirstMatch** is passed to the constructor for **TMatch** objects. As space for each object is allocated, the address returned is stored back in the data member **pFirstMatch**, so this will always point to the first match in the chain.

The destructor needs to delete the chain of **TMatch** objects, starting with the first, which is pointed to by the data member **pFirstMatch**:

```
//Destructor for a TRow object
TRow::~TRow()
{
   TMatch* pNext = pFirstMatch;

   while(pNext)
   {
      pFirstMatch = pNext->GetNext();
      delete pNext;
      pNext = pFirstMatch;
   }
}
```

The destructor copies the pointer **pFirstMatch** to **pNext**, which it uses to control the loop. **pFirstMatch** is updated in the loop to the address of the next **TMatch** object from the address returned by the member function **GetNext()**. The object pointed to by **pNext** is deleted, and **pNext** is given the address stored in **pFirstMatch**. The loop continues until **pNext** is null, which will be the case when it contains the pointer to the next object stored in the data member **pNext** of the last **TMatch** object in the chain.

The **Show()** function for the class **TRow** operates with a similar sort of loop to the destructor, except in this case the **Show()** function for each **TMatch** object in the chain is called:

```
// Display a row of matches
void TRow::Show(HDC& DC)
{
   TMatch* pNext = pFirstMatch;

   while(pNext)
   {
      pNext->Show(DC);
      pNext = pNext->GetNext();
   }
}
```

In the loop, the **Show()** function for the current **TMatch** object pointed to by **pNext** is called, then the pointer **pNext** is updated to point to the next object, ready for the next iteration of the loop.

Try It Out - Outputting Our Matches

If we define the constructor and the **Paint()** function for the class **TNimWindow**, and add a **WinMain()** function, we are ready to go. The latter is virtually the same as for the previous Windows examples, so let's do it in one go:

```
// EX11-01.CPP
// Drawing at specific positions in the client area
#include <owl.h>

// Global variables
int xBase = 100;
int yBase = 100;
int xDelta = 20;
int yDelta = 80;

// Class definitions
class TRow;                    // Incomplete class declarations
class TMatch;                  // for forward references
```

```
... Class definitions
```

```
// Constructor for the main window
TNimWindow::TNimWindow(PTWindowsObject AParent, LPSTR ATitle)
    :TWindow(AParent,ATitle)
{
    pTGame = new TGame;                  // Create a TGame object
}


// Destructor for the main window
TNimWindow::~TNimWindow()
{ delete pTGame; }


// Function to output to the window
void TNimWindow::Paint(HDC DC, PAINTSTRUCT&)
{ pTGame->Show(DC); }
```

```
... plus remaining function definitions
```

```
// Start of NIM for Windows program
int PASCAL WinMain(HANDLE hInstance, HANDLE hPrevInstance,
                   LPSTR lpCmdLine, int nCmdShow)
{
    // Create an object of our application class
    TGameApp NIM("NIM", hInstance, hPrevInstance,
            lpCmdLine, nCmdShow );

    NIM.Run();               // Call inherited Run() for our object

    return NIM.Status;     // Return inherited data member Status
}
```

How It Works

The example starts up in the same way as the previous Windows examples we have seen. Other than the application class and object names, `WinMain()` is the same. When the constructor for the main window is executed, a `TGame` object, is created, which in turn creates a `TRow` object. The `TRow` constructor then creates 15 `TMatch` objects which are displayed when the member function `Paint()` in `TNimWindow` is called, when the window is created.

The window generated by the program is shown on the next page.

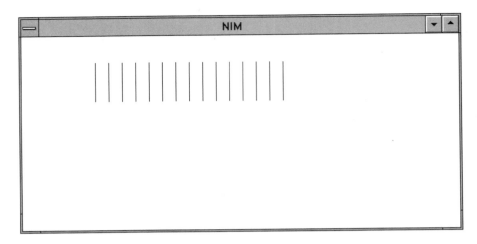

Because we draw in the client area in the function **Paint()**, you can re-size the window or drag it around, and the client area will be automatically maintained. As we have seen in the last chapter, this is the result of a **WM_PAINT** message being sent to our application when the client area needs to be redrawn. The OWL processes this by obtaining a display context and then passing it to our function **Paint()**.

The **TMatch** object spacing is the number of pixels specified in our global variable **xDelta**. You could play about with values for this and the other global variables, to see how their value affects the position of **TMatch** objects in the client area.

Changing the Size of the Main Window

The OWL automatically sets the size of the main window to default dimensions for you. However, you don't have to accept these. You can modify the initial width and height to suit your needs, or you can arrange for it to be maximized.

Altering the Width and Height of the Main Window

You can reset the size of the main window by modifying a data member **Attr** which is of type **TWindowAttr** which your window class inherits from **TWindow**. The data member **Attr** in turn includes public **int** data members **W** and **H**, which correspond to the window width and height respectively, specified in pixels. To modify the height and width of your window, you just need to set these values in the constructor for your window.

Try It Out - Modifying the Window Size

A simple demonstration of this can be arranged by modifying the constructor in the last example to change these values. We could arrange for a square window to be created, by setting them both to the value 400, say:

```
// EX11-02.CPP
// Changing the size of the main window

... globals, classes and function definitions

// Constructor for the main window
TNimWindow::TNimWindow(PTWindowsObject AParent, LPSTR ATitle):
                                        TWindow(AParent,ATitle)
{
   Attr.H = Attr.W = 400;          // Set window size as 400x400 pixels
   pTGame = new TGame;             // Create a TGame object
}

// WinMain() definition
```

How It Works

By modifying the size of the window, we don't affect the size of the objects we draw in the client area, as both are specified in terms of pixels. The size of the window as a proportion of the screen area will vary depending on your screen resolution. If you are using a standard VGA screen, the window will fill about two thirds of the screen area. If you are working with an SVGA screen at 1024x768 resolution, the window will be rather less than a quarter of the screen area. The window produced is shown below.

As you can see, the fifteen **TMatch** objects only just fit in the client area. We drew the first at a point 10 pixels to the right of the point 100,100 so it is at the point 110,100. The following 14 **TMatch** objects are at 20 pixel intervals, so the right-most one will be at the point 390,100. This is just 10 pixels inside our screen width.

Creating a Maximized Window

This is also very simple to arrange. The **Attr** object inherited in your window object has another data member **Style**. All you need to do is to add a statement to your window constructor:

```
Attr.Style |= WS_MAXIMIZE;                // Set window maximized
```

The predefined constant **WS_MAXIMIZE** is OR'd with the data member **Attr.Style**. This data member is always changed by ORing values with it. If you just use an assignment to change it, you will destroy other attributes of your window.

Using Pen Objects

The **TMatch** objects we have been creating have been a bit on the thin side. It would be nice to draw them with a thicker line so they look a bit more like matches. Lines are drawn in Windows using a **pen tool**. We can obtain different sorts of pens which will produce lines of various thicknesses, so we can have a go at updating **EX11-01.CPP** to use a pen which produces a thicker line.

Selecting a Pen

Pen objects are Windows objects, not OWL objects, so we need to use Windows API calls to manage them. It also means we are responsible for the proper creation and deletion of pens. The deletion part is very important. If you leave your pens lying around, they don't get 'borrowed' like real-world pens, they just use up memory.

When we create a pen we will need somewhere to store a handle to a pen. This will be of type **HPEN**. We can define this with this statement:

```
HPEN aPen;              // A handle to a pen
```

We will make this a member of our window class **TNimWindow**. We also need to specify the size of the pen which is an value of type **int**, so we need another data member in our window class that we can use to store the pen size. We can specify this in this statement:

```
int PenSize;            // Size of the current pen
```

We can create a pen in any member function of our window class, but if we do it in the class constructor, we then ensure it is deleted in the destructor.

To create a pen we use the Windows API function **CreatePen()**, so the constructor for our window class will be this:

```
// Constructor for the main window
TNimWindow::TNimWindow(PTWindowsObject AParent, LPSTR ATitle):
                                          TWindow(AParent,ATitle)
{
   PenSize = 5;                           // 5 pixel pen size
   aPen = CreatePen(PS_SOLID, PenSize,0); // Create a pen
   pTGame = new TGame;                    // Create a TGame object
}
```

The value set in **PenSize** will be in pixels, so here we specify it as 5 pixels wide. This will be the width of the lines drawn with a pen of this size. The call to **CreatePen()** has three arguments. The first specifies the type of line, the second is the pen size, and the third is the color of the line drawn. With **PenSize** greater than 1, the only option for the type of line is **PS_SOLID**, which specifies a solid line. If you can manage with a **PenSize** of 1, other options are available. You could use **PS_DASH** for a dashed line or **PS_DOT** for a dotted line. There are others which you can find if you look up **CreatePen()** in the TCW Help menu.

The 0 specified for the color results in a black line. If you want to jazz the output up a bit, you can use the Windows function **RGB()** to alter the color of the pen. The function **RGB()** requires three arguments corresponding to

457

the proportion of red, green and blue to be mixed to produce a color respectively. Each value can be from 0 to a maximum of 255. For example, to create a pen which will draw in a rather nice shade of yellow, we could use this statement:

```
aPen = CreatePen(PS_SOLID,PenSize,RGB(255,150,0)); // Create a yellow pen
```

The color is a mix of 255 units of red, with 150 of green and no blue.

To remove the pen in the **TNimWindow** destructor we use the windows function **DeleteObject()**. This needs one argument to be specified, the handle of the object to be deleted, in our case a pen. The destructor will therefore be this:

```
// Destructor for the main window
TNimWindow::~TNimWindow()
{
    DeleteObject(aPen);          // Delete pen object
    delete pTGame;
}
```

Try It Out - Drawing Thick Lines

By modifying the **TWindow** class, and adding the new versions of the constructor and destructor, our application has a brand new pen with a nice thick nib. The only other alteration required is to enable the **Paint()** function to use it. We use the Windows function **SelectObject()** to do that. The program is based on the ones we have already shown, so only those lines that have been changed or added are shown below.

```
// EX11-03.CPP
// Drawing using a different pen

... globals and other class definitions

// Definition of our application main window class
class TNimWindow:public TWindow
{
    public:
```

```
        // Constructor
        TNimWindow(PTWindowsObject AParent, LPSTR ATitle);

        // Destructor
        ~TNimWindow();

        // Function to redraw the window contents
        virtual void Paint(HDC DC, PAINTSTRUCT&);

    private:
        TGame* pTGame;                  // Pointer to a game object
        HPEN aPen;                      // A handle to a pen
        int PenSize;                    // Size of the current pen

};

// Constructor for the main window
TNimWindow::TNimWindow(PTWindowsObject AParent, LPSTR ATitle):
                                        TWindow(AParent,ATitle)
{
    PenSize = 5;                        // 5 pixel pen size
    aPen = CreatePen(PS_SOLID, PenSize,0);  // Create a pen
    pTGame = new TGame;                 // Create a TGame object
}

// Destructor for the main window
TNimWindow::~TNimWindow()
{
    DeleteObject(aPen);                 // Delete pen object
    delete pTGame;
}

// Function to output to the window
void TNimWindow::Paint(HDC DC, PAINTSTRUCT&)
{
    SelectObject(DC, aPen);             // Select the thicker pen
    pTGame->Show(DC); }
```

... plus the rest of the program

How It Works

The pen is created in the constructor for **TNimWindow** as we have seen. In order to use it, the function **Paint()** calls the Windows function **SelectObject()** with two arguments, the display context handle, **DC**, and the handle to the pen **aPen**. This associates the pen we have created with everything subsequently drawn, using the current display context. The output is shown below.

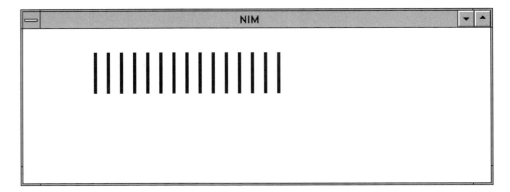

We have nice thick matches. You might want to try the effect of using the RGB() function to change the color. You could also see how different line types work if you set the pen size back to 1.

Deleting Objects from the Main Window

There are two aspects to deleting objects from the screen. One is the process of deleting the objects, once you know which ones are to be deleted, and the other is the mechanism for identifying which ones are to be deleted. The latter requires a bit more thought than the former. We can address both of these in the context of our NIM game, but first we should arrange for more than one row of matches to be displayed.

Extending the NIM Game

The game of NIM requires at least two rows, but to make our program a bit more general, we can specify the number of rows in the game by a global constant, **NROWS**. So we will add this statement:

```
const int NROWS = 3;        // Number of rows of matches in a game
```

The first point of modification is the **TGame** class and its constructor. Instead of the original pointer to a **TRow** object, we could put an array of pointers, with the dimension **NROWS**. So we could replace the original data member with this:

```
TRow* Rows[NROWS];        // Game will have NROWS rows
```

The constructor now needs to create **NROWS** objects of the class **TRow** and store their pointers in the array we have just added to the **TGame** class. We also need to consider how the rows are spaced down the client area. We could specify the row spacing using the global variable **yDelta**, which we have already used to calculate the height of a **TMatch** object. The constructor for a **TGame** object will now become this:

```
// Constructor for a game
TGame::TGame()
{
    for(int i = 0 ; i<NROWS ; i++)
        Rows[i] = new TRow(xBase,yBase+i*yDelta);    // Create row objects
}
```

This now constructs **NROWS** objects in the **for** loop. The y coordinate for the start of each row will be **yDelta** pixels below the previous one. This constructor will now work with any number of rows. The only constraint will be that we won't be able to see the rows that are drawn below the bottom of the client area for our window.

The destructor for the class **TGame** also needs to be changed to delete **NROWS** rows. This is easy, just requiring another **for** loop:

```
// Destructor for a game
TGame::~TGame()
{
    for( int i = 0; i<NROWS; i++)
        delete Rows[i];              // Delete all rows
}
```

This uses the operator **delete** to delete the object pointed to by each pointer in the array **Rows**.

Try It Out - Displaying More Than One Row of Matches

The last piece we need for a working program to display multiple rows of matches is the **Show()** function for the class **TGame**. If we put this together with the other items we are ready to go:

```
// EX11-04.CPP
// Creating multiple rows of matches
#include <owl.h>

// Global variables
const int NROWS = 3;          // Number of rows in a game
```

```
... Class definitions
```

```
// Class to define a game
class TGame
{
   public:
       // Constructor
       TGame();

       // Destructor
       ~TGame();

       // Display game
       void Show(HDC& DC);

       TRow* Rows[NROWS];       // Game will have NROWS rows

};

// Function definitions
// Constructor for a game
TGame::TGame()
{
   for(int i = 0 ; i<NROWS ; i++)
       Rows[i] = new TRow(xBase,yBase+i*yDelta);   // Create row objects
}

// Destructor for a game
TGame::~TGame()
{
   for( int i = 0; i<NROWS; i++)
       delete Rows[i];           // Delete all rows
}
```

```
// Display the current game position
void TGame::Show(HDC& DC)
{
    for(int i=0 ; i<NROWS; i++)
        Rows[i]->Show(DC);
}
```

... plus the rest

How It Works

The **Show()** function for the class **TGame** calls the **Show()** function for each **TRow** object pointed to by the elements of the array **Rows**. Everything else is taken care of automatically. The program will display the window shown below.

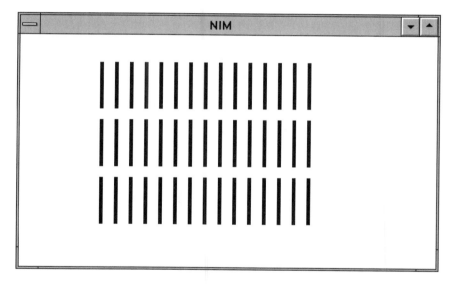

We now have three rows of solid looking matches. To prove the **NROWS** count for the number of rows works, you could rerun the example with various values set to see the effect.

The next problem is how to delete some of these matches, as this is what a move in the game will involve.

Deleting TMatch Objects

We could figure out a way to allow a player to click on the individual matches he wants to delete, but this could be tedious if a row of fifteen is to be deleted. A good alternative approach would be to enable a player to draw a line across the matches in a row that are to be deleted. We know how to draw a line with the mouse - we did that in the last chapter. We get the start point when the left button is pressed, save it and draw the line while the mouse is dragged, then when the button is released the line is fixed.

Let's add the framework to enable a line to be drawn and then worry about how we delete the **TMatch** objects afterwards. We need three message response functions corresponding to the messages **WM_LBUTTONDOWN**, **WM_MOUSEMOVE**, and **WM_LBUTTONUP**. You will remember that they go in the window class and they each need a dispatch index defined, corresponding with the type of message they will handle. The class **TNimWindow** will become this:

```
// Definition of our application main window class
class TNimWindow:public TWindow
{
   public:

      // Constructor
      TNimWindow(PTWindowsObject AParent, LPSTR ATitle);

      // Destructor
      ~TNimWindow();

      // Message response functions
      virtual void WMLButtonDown(RTMessage Mess) =
         [WM_FIRST+WM_LBUTTONDOWN];
      virtual void WMMouseMove(RTMessage Mess) =
         [WM_FIRST+WM_MOUSEMOVE];
      virtual void WMLButtonUp(RTMessage Mess) =
         [WM_FIRST+WM_LBUTTONUP];

      // Function to redraw the window contents
      virtual void Paint(HDC DC, PAINTSTRUCT&);

   private:
      TGame* pTGame;              // Pointer to a game object
      HPEN aPen;                  // A handle to a pen
      int PenSize;                // Size of the current pen
```

```
    int Sx,Sy;            // Start point of a line
    BOOL LButtonDown;     // Left button down flag - TRUE for button down
    BOOL MouseMove;       // Mouse move flag - TRUE for previous move
};
```

You can see that we have added the flags to record when the left button is down and when the first **WM_MOUSEMOVE** message has been processed. We also have added **int** members **Sx** and **Sy** in which the **WMLButtonDown()** function will save the coordinates of the start point of the line.

This is not quite enough, though. We want to create an object which represents a line, because we want the **Paint()** function to draw it. The easiest way for the **Paint()** function to work is to draw objects. This allows us to delete objects and have them automatically omitted from the display.

Let's call the class for our line **TMark**, as it will mark matches to be eventually removed. It is a very simple class definition:

```
// Class to define a mark on matches in a row
// for deletion
class TMark
{
   public:
      // Constructor
      TMark(int x1, int y1, int x2, int y2 )
      {
        Sx = x1 ; Sy = y1;           // Set start of mark coordinates
        Ex = x2 ; Ey = y2;           // and end of mark coordinates
      }

      // Display a mark
      void Show(HDC& DC)
      {
         MoveTo(DC, Sx, Sy );        // Move to start point
         LineTo(DC, Ex, Ey );        // Draw to end point
      }

   private:
      int Sx, Sy;                    // Start point coordinates
      int Ex, Ey;                    // End point coordinates
};
```

It is completely defined here, including its member functions. The only data members are the coordinates of the start and end point of a line, and the values are set by the constructor. The **Show()** function sets the start point in the client area with the **MoveTo()** function and then draws the line using the **LineTo()** function. The singular purpose of the object of this class will be to display the line as a visual cue to what is to be deleted. We will need a pointer to a **TMark** object in our window class to keep track of the current object as it is deleted, and reconstituted as the mouse is dragged. We can add the data member to the **TNimWindow** class by including this statement in the class definition:

```
TMark* pTMark;        // Pointer to Mark object
```

Defining the Message Processing Functions

The first one is very easy. It just saves the current position in the window and sets the **LButtonDown** flag:

```
// Process left button down message
void TNimWindow::WMLButtonDown(RTMessage Mess)
{
   Sx = Mess.LP.Lo;            // Save start point of Mark
   Sy = Mess.LP.Hi;
   LButtonDown = TRUE;         // Set button down flag
}
```

The next function will process the mouse move messages, so it needs to delete any previous mark object, and instantiate a new one from the start point saved by the **WMLButtonDown()** function to the current screen position. So the code for this will be much the same as we saw in the previous chapter:

```
// Process mouse move
void TNimWindow::WMMouseMove(RTMessage Mess)
{
   if(!LButtonDown)return;    // Verify mouse button is down
   if(MouseMove)
      delete pTMark;
   else
      MouseMove = TRUE;

   pTMark = new TMark(Sx,Sy, Mess.LP.Lo, Mess.LP.Hi );
   InvalidateRect(HWindow, 0, TRUE);           // Redraw window
}
```

After checking that the left mouse button really is pressed, any previously created **TMark** object is deleted. If this is the first entry into the function, no deletion occurs, but the flag **MouseMove** is set to record that this is the first time. A new **pTMark** object is created from the previously saved start point to the current position, and the Windows API function **InvalidateRect()** is called to cause the window to be redrawn.

The job of the last function will be to set the flags back to **FALSE**, and to delete the **TMark** object pointed to by **pTMark**:

```
// Process left mouse button up message
void TNimWindow::WMLButtonUp(RTMessage Mess)
{
   if( !(LButtonDown&&MouseMove) )          // Check proper sequence
   {
      LButtonDown = MouseMove = FALSE;      // If not reset and return
      return;
   }

   LButtonDown = MouseMove = FALSE;         // Reset flags
   delete pTMark;                           // Delete mark
   pTMark = 0;                              // and reset pointer
   InvalidateRect(HWindow, 0, TRUE);        // Redraw window
}
```

Try It Out - Doing More Lines

To make this a little more interesting, we will add another pen to draw the lines in red. This means we will use the members **ThickPen** and **ThinPen** to store the pen handles in the class **TNimWindow**. We just need to modify the constructor and destructor to take care of the second pen.

```
// Constructor for the main window
TNimWindow::TNimWindow(PTWindowsObject AParent, LPSTR ATitle)
   :TWindow(AParent,ATitle)
{
   LButtonDown = MouseMove = FALSE;
   pTMark = 0;
   PenSize = 3;                                     // 5 pixels pen size
   ThickPen = CreatePen(PS_SOLID, PenSize,0);       // Create a thick pen
   ThinPen = CreatePen(PS_SOLID, 1, RGB(255,0,0));  // Create a thin red pen
   pTGame = new TGame;                              // Create a TGame object
}

// Destructor for the main window
TNimWindow::~TNimWindow()
{
   DeleteObject(ThickPen);          // Delete thick pen
   DeleteObject(ThinPen);           // and thin pen
   delete pTGame;
}
```

There is also some housekeeping to be added. The constructor for our window needs to initialize the pointer **pTMark**, and the flags **LButtonDown** and **MouseMove**. We then need a new **Paint()** function:

```
// Function to output to the window
void TNimWindow::Paint(HDC DC, PAINTSTRUCT&)
{
    SelectObject(DC, ThickPen);        // Select the thicker pen
    pTGame->Show(DC);                  // Display the game

    SelectObject(DC, ThinPen);         // Select the thinner pen
    if(pTMark)pTMark->Show(DC);        // Display the mark - if any
}
```

There are only two additional lines of code: one to select the second pen and the other to display the **TMark** object after verifying that we don't have a null pointer.

How It Works

If you run this example, you will get the original three rows of 15 matches. You will be able to draw a red line in the window by pressing the left mouse button and dragging the mouse. As soon as you release the mouse button, the line will disappear, as it is deleted by the **WMLButtonUp()** function.

You may get a lot of flicker as you drag the mouse, depending on how fast your processor is. You can do two things to reduce it, change the thick pen back to 1 pixel wide and reduce the number of matches in a row.

Erasing TMatch Objects

We are now ready to implement the erase operation. It all needs to happen in the **WMLButtonUp()** function, since you only know where the end of the line is when the mouse button is released. However, we could find out which row is to be involved as soon as the left mouse button is pressed. We can find the row selected by looking for the first row from the top of the window that has a y coordinate which is greater than the y coordinate of the current position. You can see this from the illustration shown on the following page.

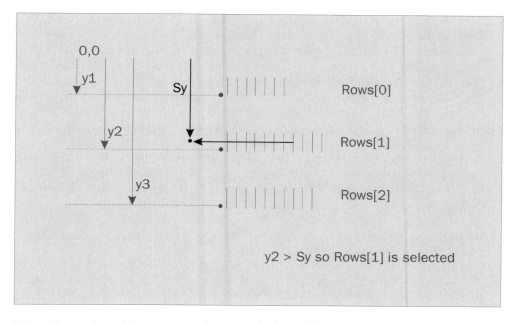

We will need a data member in the window class to record which row is selected, so the index can be picked up by the **WMLButtonUp()** function when the line is complete. Let's call it **MarkedRow** and make it type **int**. We can now modify the button down message response function:

```
// Process left button down message
void TNimWindow::WMLButtonDown(RTMessage Mess)
{
    MarkedRow = -1;              // Set MarkedRow invalid
    Sx = Mess.LP.Lo;             // Save start point of Mark
    Sy = Mess.LP.Hi;
    LButtonDown = TRUE;          // Set button down flag

    for( int i=0 ; i<NROWS ; i++ )           // Find the first row
        if (Sy < (pTGame->Rows[i]->Gety()) ) // where y is > Sy
        {
            MarkedRow = i;                    // Save the index value
            break;                            // and exit the loop
        }
}
```

The first thing this function does is to set the index to the row selected to an invalid value. This is insurance against the inevitable case of someone drawing a line which is below all the rows. We will check this in the **WMLButtonUp()** function. After storing away the coordinates of the current position in the window, we test the y value against the y value of each row in the **for** loop. The y value for a row is provided by a member function of the **TRow** class, **Gety()** (which we must remember to add). Note how this is selected. Reading from the right, for the **TGame** object defined by the pointer **pTGame**, the member **Rows[i]** is accessed, and this is used to execute the member function **Gety()** for the **TRow** object pointed to by **Rows[i]**. For the first y value greater than **Sy**, the index of the marked row is saved in the data member **MarkedRow** and the loop is immediately ended using the **break** statement.

The **WMMouseMove()** function doesn't need to be changed, so all we need to look at is the button up message function:

```
// Process left mouse button up message
void TNimWindow::WMLButtonUp(RTMessage Mess)
{
   if( !(LButtonDown&&MouseMove) )          // Check proper sequence
   {
      LButtonDown = MouseMove = FALSE;   // If not reset and return
      return;
   }

   LButtonDown = MouseMove = FALSE;          // Reset flags
   delete pTMark;                            // Delete mark
   pTMark = 0;                               // and reset pointer

   if(MarkedRow>=0)                          // Make sure row is marked
      pTGame->Rows[MarkedRow]->EraseMarked(Sx,Mess.LP.Lo);// Erase matches
   InvalidateRect(HWindow, 0, TRUE);                      // Redraw window

}
```

There are only three lines of code, but this is a slight cheat because it depends on using a member function of the class **TRow**, **ErasedMarked()**, which will sort out the **TMatch** objects to be erased, and erase them.

The first line we have added checks that we have a valid row index before we start trying to delete things. We select the **EraseMarked()** function for the object pointed to by `Rows[MarkedRow]` in the `TGame` object pointed to by `pTGame`. Since all the work is done in the function `ErasedMarked()`, we had better have a look at that next:

```
// Erase marked matches in a row
void TRow::EraseMarked( int Sx, int Ex)
{
    TMatch* pNext = pFirstMatch;
    int count = 0;                          // Count of number to be deleted
    while(pNext)
    {
        if((xDelta/2+pNext->Getx() > Sx
           && xDelta/2+pNext->Getx() < Ex)
           || (xDelta/2+pNext->Getx() > Ex
           && xDelta/2+pNext->Getx() < Sx)) // If match is between
           count++;                         // x's increment count

        pNext = pNext->GetNext();           // Set for next iteration
    }
    EraseCount(count);                      // Delete count matches from row
}
```

This function in the class **TRow** first works out how many matches are crossed by the line. This is easier than it might appear at first sight with the giant **if** condition. We need only concern ourselves with the x coordinate values for the beginning and end of the line, which are passed as arguments. If the line crosses a **TMatch** object, then the x value of the point at which the object is drawn must lie between the x values for the ends of the line. Remember though, that we draw a **TMatch** object **xDelta/2** pixels to the right of its x coordinate stored as a data member.

Because the coordinates of a **TMatch** object are **private**, we need a member function **Getx()** to retrieve the value. The expression in the **if** statement is **TRUE** if the x value of the object returned by **Getx()** plus a half of **xDelta**, is greater than **Sx**, and less than **Ex**. In this case, the variable **count** is incremented. However, this only works if the line is drawn from left to right. If the line is drawn from right to left, then the second condition will apply with **Ex** as the lower limit and **Sx** as the upper limit for the position of a crossed **TMatch** object. Thus the second condition is OR'd with the first to form a composite condition for the **if** statement.

Once all the **TMatch** objects in the row have been checked, the function **EraseCount()**, which is a member of **TRow**, is called for the current row object. Remember that the function currently being executed is a member of the **TRow** object pointed to by **Rows[MarkedRow]**, so the **EraseCount()** function will be as well. This function is as follows:

```
// Function to delete count matches from a row
void TRow::EraseCount(int count)
{

    TMatch* pNext = pFirstMatch;          // delete from the beginning
    if(!pNext)return;                     // but return if its empty
    while(count--)
    {
        pFirstMatch = pNext->GetNext();   // Set to next match

        delete pNext;                     // Delete next match
        pNext = pFirstMatch;              // Set to first for next iteration
        if(!pNext)break;                  // Check we don't fall off the end
    }
}
```

After checking that there are some matches to be deleted, the required number of **TMatch** objects are deleted, starting with the last in the chain, and working backwards. The variable **count** is decremented on each iteration and ends when it reaches zero, or we reach the end of the chain. The check for a null value in **pNext** is just to avoid using a null pointer. This would only be the case if things happened to go wrong somewhere.

With the changes we have just worked through, we should now have a program that will allow you to delete any number of matches in any given row. The rest of the program is the same as in the previous example.

To delete matches, you just need to draw a line using the mouse that straddles the number of matches you want removed. Of course, you can only delete from one row at any given time.

The deletion operation only comes into effect when the left mouse button is released after drawing a line. Using the row index saved by the **WMLButtonDown()** message response function, the function **WMLButtonUp()** calls the member function **EraseMarked()**, in the **TRow** class, for the selected row. This function counts the number of **TMatch** objects covered by the line, and calls the member function **EraseCount()** to delete that number from the row.

Completing the Game Program

To obtain a fully working game, we need to add three further capabilities to the last example. We need a variable number of matches per row, preferably different for each game; we need the computer to take a turn at removing matches; and we need to check who manages to remove the last match. We can first arrange for a variable number of matches in each row.

Generating a Random Number of Matches

TCW provides a very convenient function, **random()**, which is declared in the header **STDLIB.H**. The function accepts an integer argument **N** and returns a random integer between 0 and **N-1**. In order to start the process off, a function **randomize()** needs to be called. This is also available through **STDLIB.H**.

We can define the maximum number of matches in a row with another global variable. For reasons we will come to, it will be more convenient to specify this as the number of binary digits in the maximum value, rather than the maximum value itself. So if we call the variable defining the number of binary digits in the maximum value **NCOLS**, the maximum value will be $2^{NCOLS}-1$. For example, if **NCOLS** is 4, the maximum value is 15. We only need to change the constructor for the window **TNimWindow()** to add the initialization of the random number generator, and the constructor for **TRow** which actually generates a row, to use a random value for the number of **TMatch** objects. The constructor for our window will therefore be this:

```
// Constructor for the main window
TNimWindow::TNimWindow(PTWindowsObject AParent, LPSTR ATitle):
            TWindow(AParent,ATitle)
{
   LButtonDown = MouseMove = FALSE;
   pTMark = 0;
   PenSize = 3;                              // 5 pixels pen size
   ThickPen = CreatePen(PS_SOLID, PenSize,0);   // Create a thick pen
   ThinPen = CreatePen(PS_SOLID, 1, RGB(255,0,0));// Create a thin red pen

   randomize();                     // Initialize random number generator

   pTGame = new TGame;                       // Create a TGame object
}
```

There is just one line added to call the function **randomize()**.

The constructor for a **TRow** object only requires a little more modification than this. To generate rows of random length, it will become as follows:

```
// Constructor for a TRow object
TRow::TRow(int Sx, int Sy)
{
    x = Sx;                              // Initialize position on screen
    y = Sy;
    int nMatches = 0;                    // Number of matches in a row
    pFirstMatch = 0;                     // Initialize pointer to first match

    // Set to random value with NCOLS digits
    nMatches = 1 + random( (1<<NCOLS)-1 );

    for(int i = 1; i<= nMatches ; i++ )
        pFirstMatch = new TMatch(y,pFirstMatch);  // Create a row of matches
}
```

The first change is merely to set the initial value of the variable **nMatches**, which defines the number of matches in the row being constructed to 0, in its declaration. The only other change is the setting of **nMatches** to a random value. The argument to the function **random()** generates the number with **NCOLS** binary digits. The expression **(1<<NCOLS)** shifts 1 to the left by **NCOLS** positions. This results in the value 2^{NCOLS}, so all we then need to do is subtract 1 to get the argument value we require. The value returned by the function **random()** can be zero, so we add 1 to it to ensure that there is at least 1 **TMatch** object in a row.

Try It Out - Generating Random Matches

We can run this as it stands to make sure we are getting what we expect. The rest of the program will be the same with the exception of the changes above, and the declaration of the global variable **NCOLS**.

```
// EX11-07.CPP
// Generating random rows of matches

// Drag in functions which will drag in classes
#include "NIM1.CPP"

// Start of NIM for Windows program
int PASCAL WinMain(HANDLE hInstance, HANDLE hPrevInstance,
        LPSTR lpCmdLine, int nCmdShow)
{
```

```
    // Create an object of our application class
    TGameApp NIM("NIM", hInstance, hPrevInstance,
            lpCmdLine, nCmdShow );

    NIM.Run();                // Call inherited Run() for our object

    return NIM.Status;    // Return inherited data member Status
}
```

The program is now in three files as it is getting a bit unwieldy as a single file. The include file **NIM1.CPP** has the structure shown below:

```
// Class member function definitions for the game of NIM
#ifndef NIM1_CPP
#define NIM1_CPP
#include <stdlib.h>              // For random()
#include "NIM1.H"                // For class definitions
// Function definitions
...
#endif                           // NIM1_CPP
```

As we discussed previously, the **#ifndef** and **#endif** combination are to ensure the file does not get included more than once. This is unlikely with this example, but when you develop larger programs you may have several files involved, and then there is more potential for doing so accidentally. This file includes the file **NIM1.H**, which has this structure:

```
// Class definitions and globals for the game of NIM
#ifndef NIM1_H
#define NIM1_H
#include <owl.h>

// Global variables
const int NROWS = 3;    // Number of rows in a game
const int NCOLS = 4;    // Number of binary digits in max matches in a row

int xBase = 100;        // x coordinate of first row
int yBase = 100;        // y coordinate of first row
int xDelta = 20;        // Spacing between matches in a row
int yDelta = 80;        // Spacing between rows


// Class definitions
...
#endif                  // NIM1_H
```

This contains the definitions of the global variables and all the class definitions.

475

How It Works

If you run this you will get a variable numbers of matches in each row, and you will be able to delete as many as you like from any given row by using the mouse. A typical window is shown below.

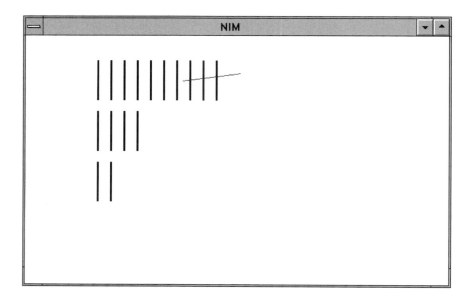

This shows the window in the middle of a delete operation with the mouse button held down. When it is released, the line disappears and the matches crossed by it are deleted. Note that we did not include the code to capture mouse messages outside of the window. Consequently if you move the mouse cursor out of the window, **WMMouseMove()** will not be executed, and if you release the mouse button, the **WMButtonUp** message will be lost. You can try it if you like, it won't do any harm. If you want the example to track the mouse off window, you simply need to add the bits to capture mouse messages from the last example in the previous chapter. The code is exactly the same.

All we need now is for the computer to take a turn, so let's implement that.

Making the Computer Play

If we make the assumption you will always take the first turn, the computer can take a turn immediately after deleting the matches that you want removed. We could add a call to function called `MyGo()` in the `WMLButtonUp()` function. We won't repeat the function call here, as its just one line of code to be added.

The interesting problem is how the computer should decide how many matches to remove. We will discuss how the decision is arrived at, but not the reason why it works, as this is not a mathematics book. For any position in the game, it's possible to determine whether or not there is a winning strategy. If we work out the sum of each of the binary digits in the number of matches in each row, and all the sums are even, there is no winning strategy, so any move will do. To take a concrete example, suppose there are 3 matches in the first row, 10 matches in the second row and 9 matches in the third row. We can write these numbers in binary form and add up corresponding digits:

3	0	0	1	1
10	1	0	1	0
9	1	0	0	1
Sum of digits	**2**	**0**	**2**	**2**

As you can see, each digit sum is even so there is no good move. In this case, the computer will remove a random number of up to half the matches from the longest row, and hope to do better next time.

If at least one of the digit sums is odd, then there is a winning strategy. This strategy is to remove a number of matches from one of the rows which will make the digit sums even.

Let's have a look at the code for the function `MyGo()` now. It is a member of the class `TNimWindow`, and is a bit longer than the function we have written so far, but it does contain quite a few comments.

```cpp
// Calculate the best go for the current position
// This is based on maintaining the total of each binary
// digit across rows, even.
void TNimWindow::MyGo(void)
{
    int RowCount[NROWS]={0};        // Numbers of matches in rows
    int TestBit[NCOLS]={0};         // Array of indicators for binary digits
    int i = 0, j = 0;               // Loop counters
    int RowGo = 0;                  // Index of row to subtract matches
    int HiCol = 0;                  // Highest order column with odd digit sum
    int OddDigit = 0;               // Odd digit flag
    int Take = 0;                   // Number of matches to subtract

    for(i=0 ; i<NROWS ; i++)        // For each row that contains matches
        if(pTGame->Rows[i])         // Get count of number of matches
            RowCount[i] = pTGame->Rows[i]->Count();

    // Set TestBit[] indicators. There is one indicator
    // for each possible binary digit in the count of matches
    // in a row. TestBit[j] will be 1 if the sum of the jth digit
    // across rows is odd, and 0 otherwise.
    for(j=0 ; j<NCOLS ; j++)    // Loop over binary digits
    {
        for(i=0 ; i<NROWS ; i++)                // For each row...
            TestBit[j] += (RowCount[i]>>j)&1; // add in current binary digit

        TestBit[j] %= 2;                        // Check for even sum of digits
        if(TestBit[j])
        {
            HiCol = j;                          // Remember highest order digit
            OddDigit = 1;                       // Set flag
        }
    }

    // For a winning strategy we must remove matches such that
    // all TestBit[] values are 0. This is done by subtracting
    // a digit corresponding to the highest order digit that is odd
    // for a row with enough matches, and adding back a digit for
    // each lower order digit that is odd.
    // If they are already 0 there is no good move,
    // so remove a random number of up to half the matches
    // from the row containing the most.

    if(!OddDigit)
    {
        // No good move so find longest row
        int Max = RowCount[0];          // Set 1st row as longest
        RowGo = 0;                      // and save index of longest row
        for(i=1 ; i<NROWS ; i++)
            if(Max<RowCount[i])
```

```
        {
            Max = RowCount[i];      // Found a longer one
            RowGo = i;              // so save value and index value
        }
        Take = random(Max/2);       // Subtract up to half the matches
        Take = Take?Take:1;         // but take at least 1
    }
    else
    {
        Take = 1<<HiCol;            // Set as that digit value
        for(i=0 ; i<NROWS ; i++)    // Find a row with enough matches
            if(RowCount[i]&Take)    // to subtract
            {
                RowGo = i;          // Found it
                break;
            }
        for( i=0 ; i<HiCol ; i++ )          // Now check lower order digits
            if(TestBit[i])                  // For an odd digit sum
                if( (RowCount[RowGo]>>i)&1 ) // If  our row has that digit,
                    Take += 1<<i;           // then increase Take by it,
                else                        // Otherwise
                    Take -= 1<<i;           // Reduce by that digit value

    }
    // Erase Take matches from row RowGo
    pTGame->Rows[RowGo]->EraseCount(Take);
}
```

The function falls into three parts. The first part simply counts how many matches are in each row, using the member function, `Count()`, of the class `TRow`, and stores the count for each row in the array `RowCount`.

The second part works out the sum of each binary digit across all the rows, and determines whether it is odd or even. This is done in a nested loop. The outer loop is over binary digits (and here we can use the global value `NCOLS`), and the inner loop is across the rows and is executed for each binary digit. The binary digit is selected by shifting the count of matches for the row to the right, by the number of positions specified by the outer loop counter. Thus the shift will be first 0 positions, then 1, position, up to `NCOLS-1` positions. By bitwise ANDing the shifted value with 1, we eliminate all the digits in the shifted value except for the right-most, which is the one we want. The sum for each digit position is checked to see if it is odd or even, and the index to the digit position corresponding of the last odd count found is saved in `HiCol` for use in the third part.

The third part either deletes a random number of matches from the longest row, if all the digit sums were even, or it works out the winning move if they were not. Finding the winning move involves finding a row containing a 1 digit in the highest odd digit sum position, removing that digit from that row, and adjusting for all the lower order odd digits by adding back or subtracting further digits from the same row. For example, if we have rows with 9, 2 and 5 matches, we can write them in binary as follows:

9	1	0	0	1
3	0	1	1	0
4	0	1	0	1
Digit sums	**1**	**2**	**1**	**2**

Counting from the right the second and fourth digits sums are odd. The first row contains a digit in the highest order odd digit position, so we are going to subtract from this row. To fix the high order odd digit we will subtract 8 matches. However, we also need to adjust the second digit position . Since the first row doesn't have a digit in this position to subtract, we effectively 'add it back' by subtracting the value of the second digit position (which is 2) from the 8 we planned to subtract, so we will actually subtract 6.

Don't worry if you don't follow all this. It is a bit involved and it is not really important to understanding the overall program. However, the small downside is that you are likely to be beaten when playing the game.

The **MyGo()** function uses the member function **Count()** which is very straightforward by comparison:

```
// Count the number of matches in a row
int TRow::Count(void)
{
   TMatch* pNext = pFirstMatch;      // Set pointer to first in the row
   int sum = 0;                       // Count of matches

   while(pNext)                       // Loop while not null
   {
      sum++;
      pNext = pNext->GetNext();       // Get address of next match
   }

   return sum;
}
```

This walks through the row of matches starting with the first, which is pointed to by the data member **pFirstMatch**. A count is accumulated until the end of the chain is found. This is indicated by a null value for the **pNext** pointer for a **TMatch** object, returned by the function **GetNext()**. We have used this technique a couple of times previously.

Deciding the Winner

With these changes, we have a working game. The computer will take its turn after you take yours. We are missing some means of determining who won however, and more importantly reporting it. Deciding when someone has won is easy. We just count up all the matches in all the rows in the message response function **WMLButtonUp()** after each turn, and if the total is zero, the last one to take a turn removed the last match and is therefore the winner. We need another bit of Windows capability to report it though. It's called a **message box**.

Creating a Message Box

We can create a message box to announce the winner using the Windows API function, **MessageBox()**. This has four parameters. The first specifies the window handle, **HWindow** in our case, the second specifies the text of the message, the third specifies the box heading and the last specifies the style of the message which determines what you must do next. We will specify **MB_OK** as the style so an OK button will appear with the message. There are a host of other possibilities, some of which we will see later, but you will find they are all documented in the TCW Help menu.

We can write a modified version of **WMLButtonUp()** now:

```
// Process left mouse button up message
void TNimWindow::WMLButtonUp(RTMessage Mess)
{
    char* YourMsg
        = "You won! You must have cheated...";    // You win message
    char* MyMsg
        ="I won! Due to outstanding skill and ability..."; // I win message
    char* BoxTitle
        = "The Winner!!!";                         // Message box title

    if( !(LButtonDown&&MouseMove) )           // Check proper sequence
    {
        LButtonDown = MouseMove = FALSE;      // If not reset and return
        return;
    }
```

```
LButtonDown = MouseMove = FALSE;      // Reset flags
delete pTMark;                        // Delete mark
pTMark = 0;                           // and reset pointer
if(MarkedRow>=0)                      // Make sure row is marked
   pTGame->Rows[MarkedRow]->EraseMarked(Sx,Mess.LP.Lo);// Erase matches

InvalidateRect(HWindow, 0, TRUE);     // Redraw window
```

```
if(pTGame->CheckWinner())           // Check unlikely possibility you won
{
    MessageBox(HWindow,YourMsg, BoxTitle, MB_OK); //You won! - you cheat
    CloseWindow();
}
MyGo();                                         // Take a go

InvalidateRect(HWindow, 0, TRUE);               // Redraw window

if(pTGame->CheckWinner())             // Check for when I win
{
    MessageBox(HWindow,MyMsg, BoxTitle, MB_OK);   //I won!
    CloseWindow();
}
```

```
}
```

We have our message box messages and title defined at the outset. The other additions are the **if** statement, which is checking for a winner with the **TGame** member function **CheckWinner()**. This will return **TRUE** if there are no matches left. When a winner is found, a message box is displayed. When you click on the OK button in the message box, the next statement is executed which calls the inherited member function **CloseWindow()**. As its name suggests, this closes the window and ends the game.

Try It Out - A Complete Game

For a complete program we only need to add the function **CheckWinner()** to the class definition and the set of functions in our **.CPP** file. This version of the program is **EX11-08.CPP** together with the files **NIM2.CPP** and **NIM2.H**. The code for the function **CheckWinner()** is this:

```
// Check for a winner
int TGame::CheckWinner(void)
{
   int sum = 0;                       // Start with zero sum
   for(int i=0 ; i<NROWS ; i++)
      sum +=Rows[i]->Count();         // Sum the matches in all rows
   return sum==0;                     // Return TRUE if sum is zero
}
```

The sum of matches in all the rows is calculated using the function `Count()` in the class `TRow`. If the value of sum is 0, `TRUE` is returned, otherwise `FALSE` is returned.

How It Works

With the changes discussed, we have a working game which should run without any problem. However, there is little error checking in the interests of limiting the amount of code, so you may well be able to crash it by doing strange things. In most cases, unless you understand the winning strategy, you will see the following message box at the end of the game:

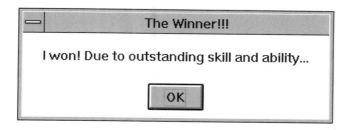

Since you have first go, you should be able to win when the starting position provides a winning opportunity, and that is down to happenstance.

Controlling When Your Application Ends

In the last version of the NIM game, we just bale out when one or the other player has won. We call the `CloseWindow()` function to end the whole thing. In fact, it doesn't end there. Calling the `CloseWindow()` function calls another function in the `TApplication` class (this is the base class for our application class) which comes back to the application for a final check.

The CanClose() Function

Our window class inherits a function `CanClose()` which gets called as a result of calling `CloseWindow()`. This provides an opportunity to see whether anything needs to be done before you definitely shut up shop. In the TCW IDE for example, you get a chance to save any files you have modified if you try to exit without saving them.

In our case, we want to provide the opportunity for another contest. We can do this by providing a `CanClose()` function in our window class:

```
// Window closing control function
BOOL TNimWindow::CanClose(void)
{
   delete pTGame;
   if(MessageBox(HWindow,"Do you want to play again?","NIM",
      MB_YESNO|MB_ICONQUESTION)==IDNO)
      return TRUE;                        // Exit on No response
   pTGame = new TGame;                    // Create a new game
   InvalidateRect(HWindow,0,TRUE);        // and redraw the window
   return FALSE;                          // Continue with a new game
}
```

Here, we delete the old game and display a message box. A new aspect is the specification of the style of the message. The two OR'd components in the style argument are **MB_YESNO** and **MB_ICONQUESTION**. The first indicates that we want a YES button and a NO button in our message box, and the second indicates we want a question mark icon in front of the message. The **MessageBox()** function will return a value depending on which button is clicked. We compare the returned value with **IDNO** (the other possibility is **IDYES**) in the **if** statement, and if this is true we exit by returning **TRUE** from `CanClose()` which will close the application.

If the YES button was clicked the expression in the **if** will be false, so we won't return a **TRUE** value. Instead, we instantiate a new **TGame** object and return **FALSE**, which allows the application to continue.

With this addition you can play as many games as you want to lose.

Summary

In this chapter you have extended your knowledge of Windows programming significantly and developed a sizeable application in the process. In case you hadn't noticed, the last version of the NIM game involved six classes and around 27 functions. You should have found the going harder than we have done before, but it is nonetheless manageable. Any aspects you feel unsure about, go back over again. Try changing the code in various ways to see what happens. Don't worry about making mistakes. The worst that can happen is likely to be that you have to reboot your PC, and the more mistakes you make - and fix - the more you will learn.

The most important thing to remember about Windows programs is that they are event-driven. Think about what the sequences of events are that drive an application. Initially, you can usually divide a problem up into relatively independent sequences of events which culminate in some specific state for your application. The button down-mouse move-button up sequence, for example. In the next chapter, we will see other sequences which are possible with Windows, but the principles will remain the same. As you will see, a lot of the more difficult bugs to discover in a program are when one or more event sequences adversely affect another.

There is nothing that you will find any more difficult in Windows than what we have covered so far. It will sometimes be a little more subtle, but mostly it will be just a little different, so if you are still with it at this point, the rest is downhill.

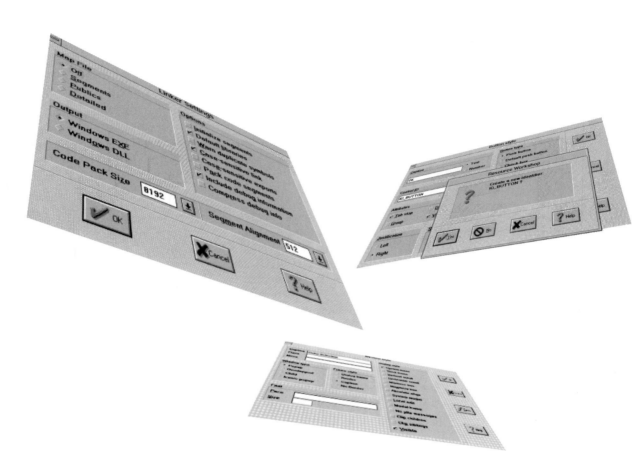

Adding Menus and Scrolling

In this chapter we will see how we can build more sophisticated application windows, and make our Windows programs more efficient. In this chapter you will learn about:

▶ Creating a main menu for your application window

▶ How to redraw only part of your application window so only the area that needs to be updated is rewritten

▶ Linking a menu into your application

▶ Menu accelerators and how to implement them

▶ Implementing scrolling in your application window

▶ Drawing in your application window when it is scrolled

▶ How to change the cursor and the background color for your application window

▶ How to create and implement your own cursor

Creating Menus

Most Windows programs have a menu, so it's about time we looked into how we can create one. We will use the example **EX9-04.CPP** as the basis. We will add a menu, and extend and improve the functionality of the program somewhat. (If you don't remember, it's the drawing program using lines and circles.)

How Menus Work

Let's first understand the general principles behind the operation of a menu, before we get into the specifics of creating one. A menu is not directly part of your program source code file. It is defined in an external file called a **resource file**, with the extension **.RC**, and the menu is referred to as a **resource**. A resource file can contain other resources besides menus, such as bitmaps, icons, and dialogs, but we shall see more about these later. In fact, virtually all of the visible bits of your Windows program that a user interacts with are defined by resources in a resource file.

You can create the resource file for a menu using a text editor, which will involve defining a menu as a text file containing a **resource script**, which consists of a set of simple commands defining various elements of the menu. A much easier way, however, is to use Resource Workshop which comes as part of the TCW package. This provides an easy-to-use mechanism for creating menus interactively, as well as anything else you are likely to want to put in a resource file, so we will use this in all our examples. We will still end up with a resource script for our menu stored in a **.RC** file, but the commands will be generated automatically as we build the menu.

When the resource file for a menu has been created, you must add the name of the file to the program project file. Then, when you compile the program, the resource script is also compiled and linked to your program. The overall process is illustrated opposite:

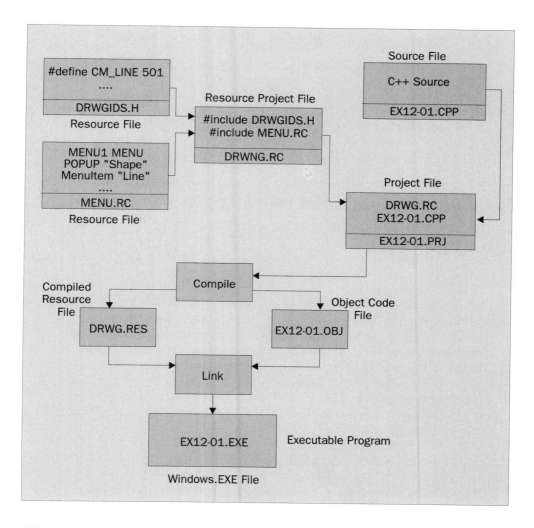

Where a program has several resources, a resource project file is usually used to manage the set for the program resources. This is simply a `.RC` file with include statements for each of the resource files. In the figure above, the resource project file points to two resource files: the file defining the menu, and a `.H` file containing definitions for symbols to be used in the program to refer to individual resources. Each resource will be have a unique identifying integer associated with it, and the `.H` file is used to define symbol equivalents for use in the program code. A mnemonic is much more readable than simply a number, particularly if you choose the symbolic name appropriately.

For example, suppose we have a menu which allows different shapes to be selected, and that one of the options is Line. We might associate, rather arbitrarily, the integer 501 with the menu option Line, but rather than use 501 in the program, we will use perhaps the symbolic constant `CM_LINE` (CM for Command Menu). So we would define it by this statement:

```
#define CM_LINE   501
```

which would appear in the `.H` file, and we would have similar definition for other menu resource items.

Windows and Command Message Response Functions

The menu items themselves are linked to your program by Windows. When you use the mouse to click on a menu option, Windows recognizes this and sends a command message to your program corresponding to the integer value associated with the particular resource, which has the effect of calling the appropriate command message response function. This works in very much the same way as with the messages Windows sends for mouse actions to be processed. A unique dispatch index associates a message processing function with a particular resource, a menu option say, so that when that menu option is selected, the message response function is called. The dispatch index is usually defined using the symbolic constants, so that for the example of the menu item Line, the dispatch index would be `[CM_FIRST+CM_LINE]`. This is analogous to what we have seen for processing mouse messages, except that the base value is `CM_FIRST`, rather than `WM_FIRST`.

Let's look into the practical side now. We will first define a menu for our drawing program. We won't do anything with it initially. We will first get to the point where the message is display, and then look at rejigging the program to work with messages afterwards.

Creating a Menu with Resource Workshop

We are not going to cover Resource Workshop in every detail, as that would require half a book, but if we do a walk-through of creating a menu step by step, you shouldn't find the rest of it too difficult.

If you have installed TCW correctly, the icon in the TCW group will be for Resource Workshop. If you double click on it, that will start the program. The initial window is very simple, with just a couple of menu options plus Help. Click on the File menu, then New project... to start a new resource project file. You will then see a pop-up window with a lot of different file type options. The one we want, .RC, will be preselected, so just select OK to accept it. If you now click on File once more, you will see the window below.

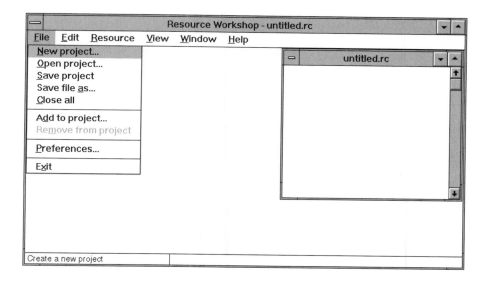

The window on the right is showing what is in your new project file - nothing at the moment.

If we want to use symbolic constants to identify resources in our program, rather than numbers, we need to create a .H file now, to hold them. Select Add to project... from the pull down menu. You will now get another pop-up window where you can enter the name of the file to add. Let's call it DRWGIDS.H, so enter that and select OK. We are now ready to start creating a menu.

Select the Resource menu option, which will display a pull down menu. We don't need to worry about identifiers, as they will be created automatically as we create the menu items, so select New... from the pull down menu, and choose menu from the options presented. You will then see the window shown on the next page.

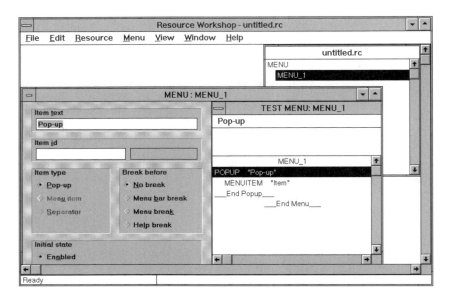

The title bar of the window contains the command MENU defining this as such, and the menu name MENU_1. We will use the menu name to associate the menu with our application window, when we get to modifying the program.

The window for the menu has three parts. The left half of the window is an interactive section, which we will use to define details of the menu. The top part of the right half is a working simulation of how the menu will appear, and the bottom part of the right half of the window shows the resource script - the commands which define the menu.

Look at the right half of the MENU window. The Item text box shows the text associated with the current highlighted line in the resource script. This relates to the pop-up menu name, which is the top level menu item - which you can see in the upper part of the right half of the window. Change the entry in the item text box to Shape and press *Enter*. Both parts of the right half of the window will be updated to reflect the change.

Next, select the next line down in the resource script, which is a MENUITEM line. The right half of the window will reflect the new line select. Select the Item text box by double clicking it, and change the text in the box to Line. This is the first menu item for the pop-up from the menu option Shape, and then select the Item id box and type CM_LINE. This will be the symbolic name we will use to identify the menu item Line in our program. You will then get a pop-up asking if a new identifier should be created, so click OK. The next pop-up shows the identifier, the integer it will represent, and the file in which it will be defined. Note that the file name is automatically the file we added to our resource project file. Let's change the number from the default 101 to 501, and press *Enter*. The right half of the window will be updated to reflect the changes.

We need to add a new menu item now for Circle, so select Menu from the main menu, and then New menu item from the pull down (note you can also use the insert key instead). A new MENUITEM will appear, and you could follow the same procedure as for Line, but use `Circle` for the item text. The number should automatically be 502. Now add another item by pressing *Insert*, use `Rectangle` for the menu text, and specify the identifier as **CM_RECTANGLE**. The number associated with the identifier should automatically be selected as 503.

Next, we want to add another main menu pop-up, Color, so select Menu from the main menu, and New pop-up from the pull down. Repeat the process we just completed for Shape, but create menu items Red, Green, Blue, Yellow, and Black, with identifiers **CM_RED**, **CM_GREEN**, and so on, in the Color pull down.

That's it. The menu is finished. You should now have a window looking like that shown below.

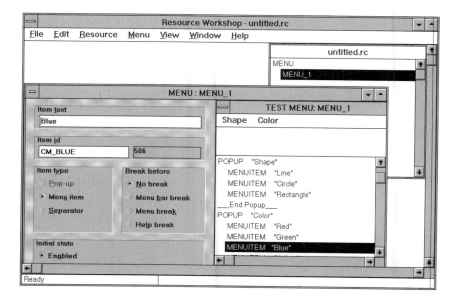

All that remains is to save the resource project, so select File and Save file as... and save the file as DRWG.RC.

Adding a Menu to a Program

To get the menu we have just created as part of **EX9-04.CPP**, we need to make the following changes:

- Add an include statements for **OWLRC.H** and **WINDOWS.H** to our program file.

- Add an include statement to our program for the **DRWGIDS.H** file we have just created along with the menu.

- Add a call to the function **AssignMenu()** to the constructor for our application window. The call will pass the menu name **MENU_1** as an argument. The function is a member of the class **TWindow**.

- Add the resource project file to our program project file.

So let's do that.

Try It Out - Adding a Menu to Our Drawing Program

Try it Out!

We will call this example **EX12-01.CPP**. The modified constructor from the base program example will be as follows:

```
// Constructor
TGrfxWindow(PTWindowsObject AParent, LPSTR ATitle):
                                  TWindow(AParent,ATitle)
{
    AssignMenu("Menu_1");                 // Associate Menu_1 with program
    LButtonDown = RButtonDown = MouseMove = FALSE;
}
```

The only addition is the line highlighted above. This identifies the name of the menu resource to be associated with this window. The function **AssignMenu()** is a member of our window class that is inherited from **TWindow**. It sets the data member **Attr.Menu** to the value supplied as an argument. If you later wanted to change to a different menu for the current window, you could call the **AssignMenu()** function again to overwrite the current value.

We need to add the required **#include** statements so the overall structure of the program will be this:

```
// EX12-01.CPP
// Drawing lines and circles plus a menu
#include <owl.h>        // For the Object Windows Library
#include <string.h>     // For strlen()
#include <math.h>       // For sqrt()
#include <owlrc.h>      // For resource file processing
#include <windows.h>
#include "drwgids.h"

// Rest of the program as before
```

After you add the file **DRWG.RC** to the program project file, the program is ready to go.

How It Works

If you run the program, it works as before, but with the menu added to the application window. A typical window now looks like that shown below:

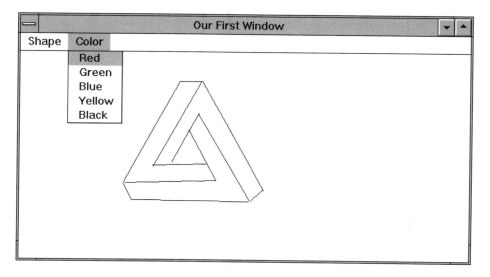

This shows a design for a useful device to set three orthogonal directions in space simultaneously. You can use it as a jig for assembling boxes for example. The menus are all working models. When you click on an option, the pull down appears, there's just no reaction when you click on an option. We need to redesign the program somewhat and add the appropriate message processing functions to make them useful within the program. Before we do that, let's take a brief detour to improve the way the program handles redrawing the window.

A Better Paint Job

You may remember with the NIM game we remarked that if you got flicker, the only thing you could do was to reduce the thickness of the `TMatch` objects drawn, or reduce their number. Well, that was a lie. You can also manage the process of drawing the window much better, and this will be much more effective in improving a program. There are two aspects to doing this.

First of all, in all the programs we have written up to now, the `Paint()` function has always redrawn the entire window client area. This is quite unnecessary. The second parameter of the `Paint()` function provides information about which area of the screen needs to be redrawn. All the `Paint()` function has to do is sort out which objects fall within the area that needs updating, and just draw those. The rest can be left.

Second of all, when we called the function `InvalidateRect()` in previous examples to get the window redrawn, by specifying the second argument as zero we indicated that the whole window was to be recreated. This is also quite unnecessary. If you can figure out which bit of the client area needs retouching, you can specify that in the second argument to the function, and the region specified will be communicated to the `Paint()` function when it is called, through its second argument.

We can update `EX12-01.CPP` to use this technique.

Implementing a Better Paint Operation

A region of the client area to be redrawn is specified as a rectangle defined by the coordinates of its top left and bottom right corners. The first thing we need to do is include in the class for each object we want to display, a data member defining a rectangle which encloses it. Then, when we delete an object from the screen for example, we simply specify its bounding rectangle as the area to be redrawn. We can use the type **RECT** which is already defined for us. This has just four data members, **top**, **left**, **bottom**, and **right**, which turns out to be amazingly convenient for our purposes.

Since every object will need a bounding rectangle to be defined, a good place to specify it would be in the base class for all our graphic objects, **TDispObject**. We could also add a function to the base to check whether an object needs to be redrawn, given that a specific area of the client window has been declared as invalid. We could call it **NeedShow()**. If the invalid region overlaps the bounding rectangle for the object, then the object will need to be redrawn. We will be able to use this function in the **Paint()** member function for the class **TGrfxWindow** to decide whether the **Show()** function for a particular object needs to be called.

We can define a new version of **TDispObject** based on this:

```
// Class of objects to be displayed
class TDispObject          // Abstract class
{
   public:

      // Function to get the last object address
      static TDispObject* GetLast(void) { return pLast; }

      // Function to delete the last object
      static void DeleteLast(void);


      // Function to get pointer to previous object
      TDispObject* GetPrev(void) { return pPrev; }

      // Pure virtual function to display an object
      virtual void Show(HDC) = 0;

      // Funtion to return value of the bounding rectangle of an object
      RECT Limit(void)
      { return Bound; }
```

```
    // Function to check whether an object needs to be displayed
    BOOL NeedShow(RECT R);


  protected:                // ...so they can be accessed in a derived class
    int x;                  // Screen coordinate
    int y;                  // Screen coordinate
    RECT Bound;             // Enclosing rectangle
    TDispObject* pPrev;     // Pointer to previous object

    static TDispObject* pLast;  // Pointer to last object created

};
```

A further function has been added to the class, **Limit()**, which returns the value of the bounding rectangle for an object. We are certain to need that, and by including it in the base, it will be automatically included in each of the classes derived from **TDispObject**.

Working Out When Rectangles Overlap

Working out whether two rectangles overlap sounds rather difficult. After all, there are all kinds of ways in which they might partially overlap. Rather than decide whether two rectangles overlap, we can approach the problem more easily by determining when they *don't* overlap.

Suppose we have a rectangle defined by a variable **R** of type **RECT**, and this represents the part of the client area that needs to be redrawn. There are four areas of the client area where an object's bounding rectangle could be, and it wouldn't overlap. Anywhere above the rectangle **R**, anywhere below the rectangle **R**, and anywhere to the right or to the left of the rectangle **R**. The first case is shown in the figure opposite.

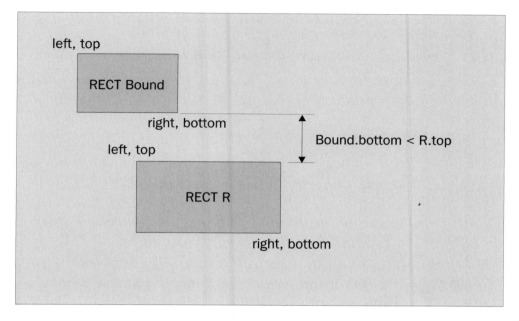

In the first case, the region is defined by any y value less than top (remember that y increases from top to bottom in the client area). So any rectangle where the y coordinate of the bottom is less than the y coordinate of the top of **R** won't overlap **R**. We can define this condition, if the second rectangle is defined by the **Bound** data member of **TDispObject**, in this expression:

```
Bound.bottom<R.top
```

Similarly, for each of the other cases, left, right, or below the rectangle **R**, the condition for non-overlap is defined by these expressions:

```
Bound.right<R.left
Bound.left>R.right
Bound.top>R.bottom
```

If none of these conditions is **TRUE**, then the rectangles *do* overlap and the object contained within **Bound** needs to be redrawn. We can now write the function **NeedShow()**, in the class **TDispObject**, which tests for overlap:

```
// Function to check if it is necessary to redraw an object
BOOL TDispObject::NeedShow(RECT R)
{
   if( (Bound.bottom<R.top)||( Bound.right<R.left)||
       (Bound.left>R.right)||( Bound.top>R.bottom) )
     return FALSE;                          // Rectangles do not overlap
   return TRUE;                             // Rectangles do overlap
}
```

The function returns a value of type **BOOL**, which is **TRUE** if the rectangles do not overlap, and **FALSE** if they do.

Implementing the Function Show()

We have to change the **Show()** function for the class **TCircle** a little, but it is actually simpler now because the bounding rectangle in the class data member **Bound** will have already been calculated by the constructor. The rectangle will need a slight adjustment to draw the circle, as we shall make each side of the bounding rectangle 1 pixel further out than the rectangle the circle occupies, as Windows does not create pixels on the boundary of an invalid rectangle. The **Show()** function will now be coded as follows:

```
// Function to display a circle
void TCircle::Show( HDC DC,RECT R )
{
   int SFx = x+Radius;             // Arc start & finish x coordinate -
                                   // Arc start & finish y coordinate is y
   Arc( DC, Bound.left+1, Bound.top+1,
          Bound.right-1, Bound.bottom-1, // Now draw full circle which is
                SFx, y, SFx, y );   // arc from SFx,y to SFx,y
}
```

We use the same check for whether we really need to draw a circle as with a line. In fact, we will be able to use the same check for any shape derived from **TDispObject**. The circle is drawn with the **Arc()** function, with the bounding rectangle defined by moving the edges of the rectangle specified by **Bound** in by one pixel.

Modifying the Shape Constructors

We now need to add the initialization of the inherited data member **Bound** to the constructors for the classes **TLine** and **TCircle**. Even though the data member is in the base class, we can only calculate the coordinates for a given shape when we know what the shape is. The **TLine** constructor is very easy:

```
TLine::TLine(int Sx, int Sy, int Ex, int Ey)
{
    x=Sx;                       // Initialize base members
    y=Sy;                       // storing start point

    Endx = Ex;                  // Store end point
    Endy = Ey;                  // coordinates Ex and Ey

    // Get bounding rectangle
    Bound.top = (Sy<Endy ? Sy : Endy)-1;
    Bound.left = (Sx<Endx ? Sx : Endx)-1;
    Bound.bottom = (Sy >=Endy ? Sy : Endy)+1;
    Bound.right = (Sx>=Endx ? Sx : Endx)+1;

    pPrev = pLast;              // Set last object to previous
    pLast = this;              // Set current object as last
}
```

We have four lines of code added to the original version. The bounding rectangle for a line is defined by the top left corner being the minimum x coordinate, the minimum y coordinate of the end points of the line, and the bottom right corner being defined by the maximum. This is illustrated in the figure below.

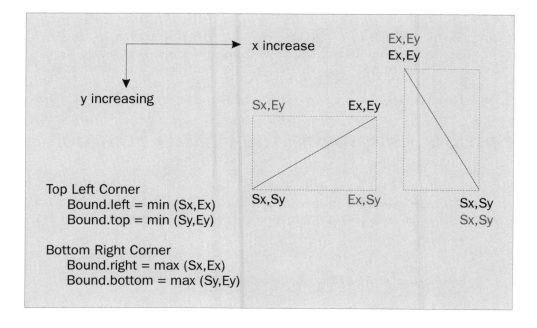

> *We actually make the rectangle one pixel larger all round, for the reason stated earlier when we discussed the* Show() *function for a circle.*

The constructor for a circle is no more difficult:

```
// Constructor definition
TCircle::TCircle(int Sx, int Sy, int Ex, int Ey )
{
    double xdiff = Sx-Ex;          // x coordinate difference
    double ydiff = Sy-Ey;          // y coordinate difference

    x=Sx;                          // Initialize base members storing
    y=Sy;                          // coordinates of center

    Radius = sqrt(  xdiff*xdiff+ydiff*ydiff ); // Calculate radius

    // Get bounding rectangle
    Bound.left = Sx-Radius-1;
    Bound.top = Sy-Radius-1;
    Bound.right = Sx+Radius+1;
    Bound.bottom = Sy+Radius+1;

    pPrev = pLast;                 // Set last object to previous
    pLast = this;                  // Set current object as last
}
```

Again the addition to the constructor is to initialize the values of the members of **Bound**. The rectangle enclosing the circle is obtained as we discussed in Chapter 9, by subtracting the **Radius** to the coordinates of the center to get the top left point, and by adding the **Radius** value to obtain the bottom right point. Here, we also make it one pixel larger all round.

Try It Out - Improving the Paint() Function

The only pieces we need to add now are a revised version of **Paint()** to take account of the rectangle passed as the second argument and to check it out with the **NeedShow()** function for each object we have to display, and to modify **WMMouseMove()** to choose the rectangle in the client area that needs to be redrawn. The **Paint()** function is easiest, so we will do that first:

```
// Definition of Function to redraw the window contents
void TGrfxWindow::Paint(HDC DC, PAINTSTRUCT& PS)
{
    RECT R;                               // Area invalidated
```

```
// Get the tail of the chain
TDispObject* pNext = TDispObject::GetLast();
R=PS.rcPaint;                           // Get rectangle invalidated

while (pNext)           // Output objects until the next pointer is 0
{
   if(pNext->NeedShow(R))               // If necessary...
      pNext->Show(DC);                  // display it, whatever it is
   pNext = pNext->GetPrev();            // Get pointer to previous object
}
}
```

The second argument to the function **Paint()** is a reference to type
PAINTSTRUCT. This contains the member **rcPaint** which is of type **RECT**, and
which defines the region to be redrawn. We retrieve this and store it in the
local variable **R** which is of type **RECT**. This is passed as the argument to
the member function **NeedShow()** for each object. If the function returns
TRUE, the **Show()** function for the object is called, otherwise the current
object is skipped, and processing continues with the next object. As a result,
only those objects which have a bounding rectangle which overlaps **R** will
be redrawn. This substantially reduces the time necessary to execute the
redraw operation in the majority of instances.

Let's consider what happens in the function **WMMouseMove()**. Typically, we
have just deleted an old object, and have created a new one. We want to
delete the object previously drawn while the left button was pressed, and
then create a new one defined by the original point when the left button
was pressed, plus the current position of the mouse. We should therefore
first get the bounding rectangle for the old object, then delete the object,
then get the area it occupied redrawn. We can then create the new object
and redraw the area that it occupies.

We can do this in a revised **WMMouseMove()** message response function
coded as follows:

```
// Message response function to deal with a mouse move
void TGrfxWindow:: WMMouseMove(RTMessage Mess)
{
   RECT R;                              // Rectangle to be redrawn

   if(LButtonDown||RButtonDown)
   {
      if(MouseMove)
      {
         // Get boundary of last object
```

```
        R = TDispObject::GetLast()->Limit();
        TDispObject::DeleteLast();              // Delete last object
        InvalidateRect(HWindow, &R, TRUE ); // Get the window redrawn

    }
    MouseMove = TRUE;                           // Record we had a mouse move

    if(LButtonDown)   // Create a line
        new TLine(Sx, Sy, Mess.LP.Lo, Mess.LP.Hi );
    else
        if(RButtonDown) // Create a circle
            new TCircle(Sx, Sy, Mess.LP.Lo, Mess.LP.Hi );

    R = TDispObject::GetLast()->Limit();    // Set to current rectangle
    InvalidateRect(HWindow, &R, TRUE );     // Get the window redrawn

    }
}
```

We first create a local variable **R** to hold invalid rectangles. We then set **R** to the enclosing rectangle of the previous object, if there was one, and the old object is deleted. We then call the Windows function **InvalidateRect()** to redraw the area previously occupied by the object we have just deleted.

We then create a new object, the choice being determined by which mouse button is down. We finally call the function **InvalidateRect()** again, using the rectangle returned by the object member function **Limit()** to get the newly created object displayed in our application window.

This example appears on the disk as **EX12-02.CPP**.

How it Works

Now when the program runs, only a local area of the screen is redrawn, where previously the whole window was redrawn each time. You should be able to see this if you use the program to strew a few circles around the screen, and then create a line using the left mouse button and drag the end around. As you move the end point of the line, you should be able to see which circles are being redrawn. Overall, it makes for a much steadier image, and a much faster response.

We should now return to the question of a menu for this example. We have the menu already there. All we need to do is make it work.

Implementing a Menu

As we discussed at the beginning of this chapter, for each menu entry we will need a message response function defined, with a dispatch index corresponding to the particular menu identifier. However, we need to think about it a bit more broadly than that. Having a menu will alter the operating philosophy of the example.

Modifying the User Interface

We need to think about how the program will be used with a menu. Since we will select the current shape from the menu, we don't need to use both mouse buttons to draw it. We could just use the left mouse button to draw the shape that is currently set, in the same way as we have drawn a line or a circle previously. We could make the shape modal. That is, whatever shape is set, it stays set for as many shapes as the user wants to draw, until he or she selects another shape using the menu. The Color menu option, which is a new capability to be added to the program, could operate similarly. Once you select Red, everything drawn subsequently will be in red unless you select another color.

Since the right mouse button is free, we could use that as a delete button. Pressing the right mouse button could erase the last object drawn. Multiple presses of the right mouse button will continue deleting the last object, until there are none left.

Implications for the Classes

Since both the shapes to be drawn and the color of the shape are modal, we will need to remember what the current shape and the current color are in our application window class, **TGrfxWindow**. The constructor for a window will also have to set an initial default shape and color (a line drawn in black would be a good choice for the initial default). Let's implement that right away. We can add the response functions for the menu options, and get rid of the right mouse button up function since we won't need it any more. The new version of the class definition will now be as follows:

505

```cpp
// Window class to display graphics
class TGrfxWindow: public TWindow
{
   public:
      // Constructor
      TGrfxWindow(PTWindowsObject AParent, LPSTR ATitle)
         :TWindow(AParent,ATitle)
      {
         AssignMenu("Menu_1");            // Associate Menu_1 with program
         LButtonDown = MouseMove = FALSE;
         Shape = line;                    // Set default shape
         Color = black;                   // Set default color
      }

      // Destructor
      ~TGrfxWindow();

      // Message response functions
      virtual void WMLButtonDown(RTMessage Mess)=
         [WM_FIRST+WM_LBUTTONDOWN];
      virtual void WMLButtonUp(RTMessage Mess)=
         [WM_FIRST+WM_LBUTTONUP];
      virtual void WMRButtonDown(RTMessage Mess)=
         [WM_FIRST+WM_RBUTTONDOWN];
      virtual void WMMouseMove(RTMessage Mess)=
         [WM_FIRST+WM_MOUSEMOVE];

      // Menu message response functions
        //...first for shape menu options
      void CMLine(RTMessage)=[CM_FIRST+CM_LINE];
      void CMCircle(RTMessage)=[CM_FIRST+CM_CIRCLE];
      void CMRectangle(RTMessage=[CM_FIRST+CM_RECTANGLE];

        // ...then for color menu options
      void CMRed(RTMessage)=[CM_FIRST+CM_RED];
      void CMGreen(RTMessage)=[CM_FIRST+CM_GREEN];
      void CMBlue(RTMessage)=[CM_FIRST+CM_BLUE];
      void CMYellow(RTMessage)=[CM_FIRST+CM_YELLOW];
      void CMBlack(RTMessage)=[CM_FIRST+CM_BLACK];

      // Function to redraw the window contents
      virtual void Paint(HDC DC, PAINTSTRUCT&);

   private:
      int Sx;                 // Start point coordinates x,y for a line
      int Sy;                 // or the center of a circle

      BOOL LButtonDown;       // Flag = TRUE for button down
      BOOL MouseMove;         // Flag = TRUE for previous move

      // Definition of current shape
      SHAPE Shape;
```

```
        // Definition of current color
        COLOR Color;

};
```

The type **SHAPE** will be defined globally as an enumeration by the following statement, ahead of the class definitions:

```
// Enumeration type
enum SHAPE{line,circle,rectangle};        // For shapes
```

We could have defined the enumeration within the class, but declaring the enumeration external to the class will enable us to use the same type name in other places in the program where we declare a variable of that type. They can only have one of the values in the list. This will make our program a bit more readable when we come to set shape values.

The color options will be defined as global constants of type **COLORREF** so that they can also be used anywhere. This requires the following statement:

```
const COLORREF red=RGB(255,0,0),
               green=RGB(0,255,0),
               blue=RGB(0,0,255),
               yellow=RGB(255,150,0),
               black=RGB(0,0,0);        // For colors
```

COLORREF is a Windows defined type for a color, which can be passed as an argument to the Windows function **CreatePen()**. Because we have these global constants defined, we can use the color names, **red**, **blue**, **green**, and so on, to set a color value anywhere in the program. We will need to create a pen of the right color for each shape as it is drawn. This will involve changing the **Show()** function for each shape class for the pen creation and selection. This is a little tricky, so we come back to it a little later.

The Menu Message Response Functions

The menu message response functions in our window class definition are named just like the Windows message response functions, except they start with **CM** for **C**ommand **M**essage instead of **WM**. The dispatch index is also defined in a similar way. The identifier for the menu we created along with the menu item is added to a base value **CM_FIRST** to define a unique dispatch index. We now have quite a number of message response functions, but the new ones are very simple. The message response function for a Circle menu selection will be this:

```
void TGrfxWindow::CMCircle(RTMessage)
{    Shape = circle;    }
```

The function for the other shape menu option will be similar. The message response function to set a color will typically be:

```
void TGrfxWindow::CMRed(RTMessage)
{   Color = red;   }
```

Hardly overwhelmingly difficult stuff, is it?

The message response function, **WMRButtonUp()**, has been deleted, along with the associated flag, **RButtonDown**, since we will not need them here. The only other change is in the constructor, with two lines added to initialize the **Shape** and **Color** data members.

Changes to the Shape Classes

For each shape class we will need to add a data member to record the color that was used to construct the shape. This is because it may be necessary to redraw the shape later, when maybe a different color value has been set, and we would want to retain the original color of the shape when it is redrawn. The easiest way to do this is to add a data member to the base class **TDispObject**. This will require one statement in the protected section of the class definition:

```
COLORREF Color;          // Color of object
```

Of course, the shape class constructor will need to be modified to accept a color value as an argument, and to initialize the value of the data member **Color**. Let's look at how the **TLine** constructor will now be written:

```
TLine::TLine(int Sx, int Sy, int Ex,int Ey, COLORREF C)
{
   x=Sx;                        // Initialize base members
   y=Sy;                        // storing start point

   Endx = Ex;                   // Store end point
   Endy = Ey;                   // coordinates Ex and Ey
   Color = C;                   // Set color

   // Get bounding rectangle
   Bound.top = (Sy<Endy ? Sy : Endy)-1;
   Bound.left = (Sx<Endx ? Sx : Endx)-1;
   Bound.bottom = (Sy >=Endy ? Sy : Endy)+1;
   Bound.right = (Sx>=Endx ? Sx : Endx)+1;

   pPrev = pLast;               // Set last object to previous
   pLast = this;                // Set current object as last
}
```

The only difference here is the additional parameter of type **COLORREF**, and the use of it to initialize the data member **Color**. The constructor for a circle will be similarly modified.

A further necessary change will be to the **Show()** functions, but only in the shape classes. The base class version can remain pure, with the same argument and return type. The derived class versions will need to select a pen of the appropriate color before drawing the shape. We can create a pen for use within the **Show()** function as we need it, and then delete it as soon as the object has been drawn.

There is, however, a complication when doing this. Once a pen has been associated with a display context using the Windows function **SelectObject()**, you need to replace it with another pen in the display context, before Windows will allow you to delete it. If you delete the display context, you can delete the pen, but we don't want to do that since we may well be drawing several shapes within the same display context which is passed by the function **Paint()**, and they all may be drawn with (potentially) successively different pens. This means that we need one basic pen that we can switch back to, after we have drawn a shape in the required color. If we don't do this, we could easily run out of memory owing to a surfeit of pens.

Let's look first at the **Show()** function for **TLine**:

```
// Function to display a line
void TLine::Show(HDC DC)
{
   HPEN aPen;                               // Pen handle

   aPen = CreatePen( PS_SOLID, 1, Color );    // Create a colored pen
   SelectObject(DC, aPen);                    // Associate the pen with current DC

   MoveTo( DC, x , y );                       // Move to start point
   LineTo( DC, Endx, Endy );                  // Draw Line

   SelectObject(DC, BasePen);                 // Select base so we can delete aPen
   DeleteObject( aPen );                      // Delete the pen
}
```

All the additions are for creating and deleting a pen. We create a pen with a pen size of 1 pixel, and a color corresponding to the object color. The **SelectObject()** function associates the pen, **aPen**, with the current display context, **DC**. After drawing the line we associate another pen, **BasePen**, with the display context, **DC**, which will replace **aPen**. This enables us to finally delete the pen, **aPen**, using the Windows API function **DeleteObject()**.

The pen **BasePen** will need to be available to all the shape classes so a good place to keep it is as a protected data member of the base class **TDispObject**. Since we only need one **BasePen** between all shape objects, we should make it **static**. If we use what is called a stock pen, we don't have to worry about deleting it. Windows provides a range of stock objects, including pens. We get one using a Windows API function **GetStockObject()** which returns a handle to the object requested as an argument. We can call it at the global scope to initialize **BasePen**.

This is now the definition of **TDispObject**:

```
// Class of objects to be displayed
class TDispObject            // Abstract class
{
   public:

      // Function to get the last object address
      static TDispObject* GetLast(void) { return pLast; }

      // Function to delete the last object
      static void DeleteLast(void);


      // Function to get pointer to previous object
      TDispObject* GetPrev(void) { return pPrev; }

      // Pure virtual function to display an object
      virtual void Show(HDC) = 0;

      // Funtion to return value of the bounding rectangle of an object
      RECT Limit(void)
      { return Bound; }

      // Function to check whether an object needs to be displayed
      BOOL NeedShow(RECT R);

   protected:               // ...so they can be accessed in a derived class
      int x;                        // Screen coordinate
      int y;                        // Screen coordinate
      RECT Bound;                   // Enclosing rectangle
      COLORREF Color;               // Color of object
      TDispObject* pPrev;           // Pointer to previous object
```

```
        static TDispObject* pLast;    // Pointer to last object created
        static HPEN BasePen;          // Basic default pen

};
```

Since **static** members need to be defined outside of the class in a defining declaration, we will need to add this statement:

```
HPEN TDispObject::BasePen = GetStockObject(BLACK_PEN );
```

just before the **WinMain()** function definition. This will initialize **BasePen** to a black pen, 1 pixel wide.

Adding a Rectangle Class

We need a new class to support rectangles, but it's very straightforward. We can define a rectangle with a pair of points representing opposite corners, so the class will be very much like the class **TLine**, which also has two defining points. Here is the definition of the class **TRectangle**:

```
// Class defining a rectangle
class TRectangle : public TDispObject
{
   public:
      // Constructor
      TRectangle(int Sx, int Sy, int Ex,int Ey, COLORREF C);

      // Function to display a rectangle
      virtual void Show( HDC DC);

   protected:
      int Endx, Endy;              // End point coordinates

      TRectangle(){}               // Default constructor - not to be used
};
```

The first defining point will be inherited from the base class, and will correspond to the position of the mouse when the left button is pressed. As the mouse is dragged, the position of the mouse will define the opposite corner of the rectangle. The constructor will need to define the bounding rectangle, which doesn't necessarily have the same pair of defining points as the **TRectangle** object. It will depend on how the rectangle is created (as illustrated in the following figure):

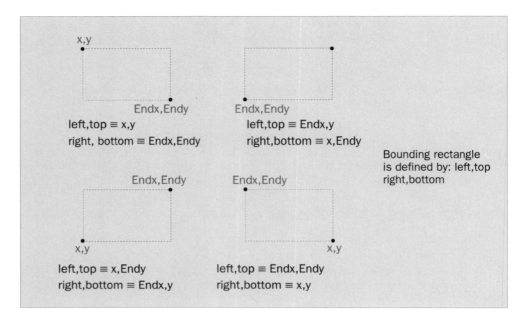

x,y

Endx,Endy

left,top ≡ x,y
right, bottom ≡ Endx,Endy

Endx,Endy

left,top ≡ Endx,y
right,bottom ≡ x,Endy

Bounding rectangle
is defined by: left,top
right,bottom

Endx,Endy

left,top ≡ x,Endy
right,bottom ≡ Endx,y

Endx,Endy

x,y

left,top ≡ Endx,Endy
right,bottom ≡ x,y

x,y

The code for the constructor will be as follows.

```
// Constructor for a rectangle
TRectangle::TRectangle(int Sx, int Sy, int Ex,int Ey, COLORREF C)
{
    x=Sx;                                    // Initialize base members
    y=Sy;                                    // storing start point

    Endx = Ex;                               // Store end point
    Endy = Ey;                               // coordinates Ex and Ey
    Color = C;                               // Set color

    // Get bounding rectangle
    Bound.top = (Sy<Endy ? Sy : Endy)-1;
    Bound.left = (Sx<Endx ? Sx : Endx)-1;
    Bound.bottom = (Sy >=Endy ? Sy : Endy)+1;
    Bound.right = (Sx>=Endx ? Sx : Endx)+1;

    pPrev = pLast;               // Set last object to previous
    pLast = this;                // Set current object as last
}
```

This is very similar to the constructor for a **TLine** object. The bounding
rectangle is defined by taking the minimum x and y coordinates of the
defining points for the rectangle as **top**, **left**, and the maximums as **right**,

bottom. As with previous shapes, the bounding rectangle is defined to be larger than the actual rectangle by 1 pixel all round.

To draw a rectangle, the easiest approach is to draw four lines. The **Show()** function for the class **TRectangle** will therefore be as follows:

```
// Function to display a rectangle
void TRectangle::Show(HDC DC)
{
   HPEN aPen;                          // Pen handle

   aPen = CreatePen(PS_SOLID, 1, Color );   // Create a colored pen
   SelectObject(DC, aPen);             // Associate the pen with current DC

   MoveTo( DC, x , y );                // Move to start point
   LineTo( DC, x, Endy );              // Draw first side
   LineTo( DC, Endx, Endy );           // Draw second side
   LineTo( DC,  Endx, y );             // Draw third side
   LineTo(DC, x, y );                  // Draw fourth side

   SelectObject(DC, BasePen);          // Select base so we can delete aPen
   DeleteObject( aPen );               // Delete the pen
}
```

We create a pen in exactly the same way as we used for the **Show()** functions for the other shapes. We draw the rectangle by moving the current position to the start point for the rectangle, and then drawing its four sides by successive calls of the **LineTo()** function. Finally, we delete the pen after selecting the pen, **BasePen**, into the current display context.

Managing the Drawing Process

The menu message response functions automatically take care of setting the type of the current object, and the current color to be used. We still need to change the message response functions for mouse events, since the operation is a little different. As we said at the outset, all shapes can now be drawn using just the left mouse button, leaving the right mouse button free to use as a delete facility. Let's do the really easy bit first, and rewrite **WMRButtonDown()** to provide a delete operation:

```
// Definition of message response function for right mouse button press
void TGrfxWindow::WMRButtonDown( RTMessage )
{
   if(LButtonDown) return; // Do nothing if the left button is pressed.
```

```
   TDispObject* pShape=0;                    // Pointer to shape
   pShape = TDispObject::GetLast();          // Get pointer to last object
   if(!pShape)return;                         // No more shapes so return

   RECT R;                                    // Place to store a rectangle
   R = pShape->Limit();                       // Get boundary for last object
   TDispObject::DeleteLast();                 // Delete last
   InvalidateRect(HWindow, &R, TRUE); // Redraw area deleted
}
```

There's not a lot to it, but it's not trivial, because we now need to get the bounding rectangle of the object to define the window area which needs to be redrawn.

We don't want to start deleting things in the middle of creating a shape, so we first check to see if the left button is down. If it is, we return immediately. If the left button isn't down, we get the pointer to the last shape using the static member function **GetLast()**. Clearly, it is possible that there are no shapes at all due to repeated deletions, so we need to check if the pointer returned is null. If it is, we simply return.

If we have a good pointer to a shape in **pShape**, we get the bounding rectangle for the last object using the member function **Limit()**, and store it in the local variable **R**. We then delete the last object, and call **InvalidateRect()** to get the area of the window defined in **R** redrawn.

The left button down response function is virtually identical to the original:

```
// Definition of message response function for left mouse button press
void TGrfxWindow::WMLButtonDown( RTMessage Mess )
{
   Sx = Mess.LP.Lo;
   Sy = Mess.LP.Hi;
   if(!LButtonDown)              // If this is the first L button down
   {
      LButtonDown = TRUE;        // L button was pressed

      // Make sure we track the mouse outside our window
      SetCapture(HWindow);
   }
}
```

The only difference is that we don't have to worry about the state of the right button. All we do here is record the current position in the members **Sx** and **Sy** of our window class, and after setting the **LButtonDown** flag, call the **SetCapture()** function to make sure we pick up all mouse events, including those outside our window.

The meat of the operation is in the function **WMMouseMove()**. We need to determine what the current object is set as, and then create the appropriate object with the current color selected. The code for the function is as follows:

```
// Message response function to deal with a mouse move
void TGrfxWindow:: WMMouseMove(RTMessage Mess)
{
   RECT R;                             // Rectangle to be redrawn

   if(LButtonDown)
   {
     if(MouseMove)
     {
        R = TDispObject::GetLast()->Limit();// Get boundary of last object
        TDispObject::DeleteLast();          // Delete last object
        InvalidateRect(HWindow, &R, TRUE ); // Get the window redrawn

     }
     else
        MouseMove = TRUE;                     // Record we had a mouse move

     switch(Shape)
     {
        case line:                          // Create a line
          new TLine(Sx, Sy, Mess.LP.Lo, Mess.LP.Hi , Color);
          break;
        case circle:                        // Create a circle
          new TCircle(Sx, Sy, Mess.LP.Lo, Mess.LP.Hi, Color );
          break;
        case rectangle:                     // Create a rectangle
          new TRectangle(Sx, Sy, Mess.LP.Lo, Mess.LP.Hi, Color);
          break;
        default:              // Error - so create a long red line
          new TLine(0, 0, 450, 450 , red );
     }

     R = TDispObject::GetLast()->Limit();     // so set to current
     InvalidateRect(HWindow, &R, TRUE );      // Get the window redrawn
   }
}
```

We define a local variable of type **RECT** to contain the definition of the window area to be redrawn. If the left button is *not* pressed, we do nothing. If it *is* pressed, we first check for a previous move. If there *is* a previous move, we need to get the bounding rectangle for whatever it was, and store it in **R**. This is because this part of the window will need to be redrawn after we delete the object. We then delete the last object and call the Windows API function to get the area it occupied redrawn. If there was no previous mouse move, we set the **MouseMove** flag to **TRUE** for next time around, when we will need to know that an interim object was created.

The next action is to decide the type of object to be drawn, which is done in the **switch** statement. The default case is defined as a safety measure - we should never reach it unless there is something wrong somewhere, and a red diagonal line will be a good signal for that. We obtain the bounding rectangle for the latest object constructed and store it in **R**. We use this as an argument to **InvalidateRect()** to get just that area of the window redrawn.

Try It Out - The Complete Drawing Program

Well, that's the program complete. The rest is the same as **EX12-02.CPP**. It appears on the disk as five files, as it's now quite a large program. The base file is **EX12-03.CPP**, which contains the **WinMain()** function. This brings in **DRAW1.CPP**, which contains all the function definitions, and in turn brings in **DRAW1.H**. This defines the globals and classes and brings in **DRWG.RC** and **DRWGIDS.H**. These are the resource file for the menu script, and the definitions for the identifiers used in the menu resource script, respectively. The latter are also used in our class definitions for the dispatch indexes.

How It Works

If you run this example you should have a drawing program with fully working menus. You can change the shape or the color at any time using the menu, and all the redrawing actions will only involve the window areas which have been changed. If you worked at it, you could produce a landscape of the quality of the one shown opposite.

Try it Out!

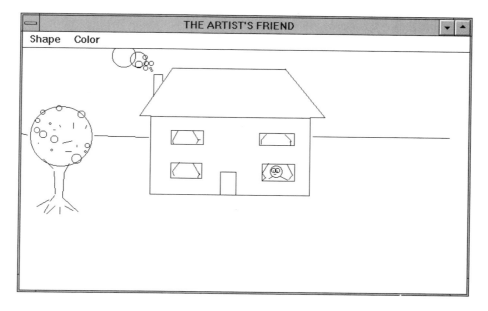

It's called *The Person Across the Street*, and it's in the style of Breughel. You should now be able to construct complex pictures without any of the flicker problems we encountered when we were redrawing the entire screen.

There is plenty of scope to extend this example. You could add more shape options, or even an additional main menu option to select line thickness. You could consider how to implement a selective erase capability.

Adding Menu Accelerators

We should first look at what a menu accelerator is. It's simply a key combination to select a menu option directly. You will have seen in other contexts that a menu item with a letter underlined can be invoked by pressing the *Alt* key and that letter. We could add that sort of capability to our menu. There are two aspects to doing it: identifying the letter to form the accelerator key combination for each menu option, and implementing the servicing of these in a program. The second of these is remarkably easy. We don't have to do anything. We don't need to modify a single line of the program. We only need to add the new version of the resource project file to the project file for the program. Using an accelerator will then call the message response function for that menu option automatically. We need only to understand how the accelerators are defined.

Defining Menu Accelerators

To define menu accelerators, it's back to our old friend, Resource Workshop. We can edit the resource file **DRWG.RC** to add accelerators. Start Resource Workshop and open the previous resource project file **DRWG.RC**. In the window showing the resource file, click on **MENU_1** - this will bring up the window for creating a menu, with the existing menu definition already loaded. If you then click on the pop-up line for Shape in the bottom right half of the window, the details will appear on the left. You then need to add an ampersand (&) preceding the letter you want to use as an accelerator - the first letter s would be a good choice. If you press *Enter*, or click on one of the menu items, the item text will have the letter s underlined. Note that all the accelerators within a menu, and within the items in each pop-up, must be different.

You will be able to click on successive menu items, adding an & in front of the letter in each menu item you want to use as an accelerator. The window after the first group of menu items have been modified is shown below.

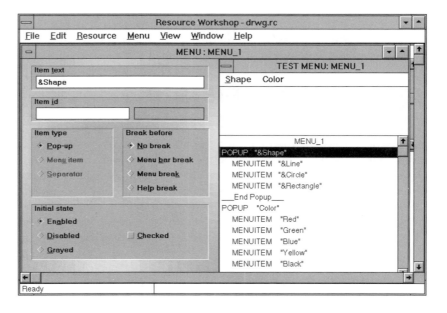

Continue to add ampersands for the rest of the menu items. When it is finished you can save it with a different name. The changes are now complete.

Try It Out - Accelerators

To run the program, we need a new project file in TCW. It contains **EX12-03.CPP** - unchanged - but with the new resource file **DRWG1.RC**. The program will run with no changes at all to the program code.

Try it Out!

How It Works

You will see that the menu items have letters underlined. Try pressing *Alt-S* for the Shape menu. The pop-up menu will appear. Each of the items will have a letter underlined. Press *Alt-C* to select the Circle option. The pop-up will close and you are now in circle drawing mode. You can access the colors in a similar manner.

You get all of this for free. The link to the message processing functions for the accelerators is made automatically. All you need to do is to specify them as you create a menu, and they will be operational in your program.

Adding Scrolling Capability to an Application

Scrolling is provided by scroll bars at the side and the bottom of a window. We can use the capabilities of the OWL to add a scrolling capability to our drawing program. We will then be able to draw on a larger area, and pan around/over it, as necessary.

Adding Scroll Bars to a Window

To add scroll bars to our application window, we need to modify the **Attr.Style** data member when the window constructor is executed. They are not separate objects, merely appendages of the window. We can add a vertical scroll bar to our window, a horizontal scroll bar, or both.

Taking the example of a horizontal scroll bar first, this is added by ORing the predefined constant **WS_HSCROLL** to the data member **Attr.Style**. We could do that with this statement:

```
Attr.Style |= WS_HSCROLL;                // Add a horizontal scroll bar
```

To add both a horizontal and a vertical scroll bar, we just have to OR an additional predefined constant **WS_VSCROLL**. The statement to add to the window constructor to do this would be as follows:

```
Attr.Style |= WS_HSCROLL|WS_VSCROLL;   // Add a horizontal scroll bar
```

It is important to use |= when updating `Attr.Style`, as this will OR the additional constants with the existing style attributes which may have been set. As has been said before, if you just use =, by accident or by design, you will overwrite all of the existing attributes which may have been set by default.

Giving Life to the Scroll Bars

To make the scroll bars operational, we can use another OWL class **TScroller**. All we need to do is to construct a **TScroller** object in our application window constructor, and save a pointer to it in the data member **Scroller**, which is already defined since it is inherited from **TWindow**.

The constructor for the class **TScroller** requires five arguments to be specified. The first is the current window handle, which we can specify in the constructor for our window as the pointer **this**. The next two specify the minimum number of pixels scrolled in the x and y directions for a scroll action. The last two specify the maximum x and y extents for the window, defined in terms of the units for the previous two arguments. For example, if we specify the minimum scroll distance for x as 5 pixels and for y as 10 pixels, then the range values will be in terms of multiples of 5 and 10 pixels respectively.

Thus if we instantiate a **TScroller** object with this statement:

```
Scroller = new TScroller( this, 20, 20, 50, 50 ); // Create scroller object
```

then the maximum range in both the x and y direction will be 1000 pixels, and the minimum increment will be 20 pixels.

Implementing Scrolling

Adding a scrolling capability need not affect the rest of the program in any way. We have already implemented the `Paint()` function so that it only redraws the part of the window specified by the `PAINTSTRUCT` parameter, so the scrolling operation is completely taken care of. The Scroller object automatically adjusts the coordinate system so that as you scroll in either x or y directions - the existing objects move accordingly. All we need to upgrade the drawing example is a new constructor for `TGrfxWindow`:

```
// Constructor for the application window
TGrfxWindow::TGrfxWindow(PTWindowsObject AParent, LPSTR ATitle):
                                                  TWindow(AParent,ATitle)
{
    AssignMenu("Menu_1");                    // Associate Menu_1 with program
    LButtonDown = MouseMove = FALSE;
    Shape = line;                                       // Set default shape
    Color = black;                                      // Set default color

    Attr.Style |= WS_HSCROLL|WS_VSCROLL;    // Add a horizontal scroll bar
    Scroller=new TScroller(this, 20, 20, 50, 50); // Create scroller object

}
```

With a drawing program, however, you would expect to be able to scroll the window to get at another part of the drawing area, and then draw some more. Unfortunately, this doesn't work out quite so easily.

For a start, our coordinates for objects are obtained from mouse positions, direct from Windows. These coordinates won't be adjusted for the scrolled position, so objects won't appear in the right place, and delete and redraw operations won't work properly. Let's look first at what we have to do for the `WMLButtonDown` function.

The coordinate values we get from Windows with the `WM_MOUSEMOVE` message are in pixels, relative to the client area origin at 0,0. When the client area is scrolled, the origin is adjusted by the `TScroller` object by the distance scrolled in x and y. The coordinates supplied by Windows will therefore need the scroll distances in x and y added, to correct for the new coordinate system at the current scrolled position.

The `TScroller` object contains data members `XPos` and `YPos` which reflect the current scrolled position. These are in multiples of the minimum scroll distance specified in the constructor call, 20 pixels in our example. The minimum scroll distance is stored in another two data members of the **TScroller** object, **XUnit** and **YUnit**. Thus we can calculate the adjustment necessary for the raw mouse position coordinates by adding **XPos*XUnit** and **YPos*YUnit** to the x and y values respectively.

We can therefore rewrite the message response function **WMLButtonDown()** as follows:

```
// Definition of message response function for left mouse button press
void TGrfxWindow::WMLButtonDown( RTMessage Mess )
{
    Sx = Mess.LP.Lo+Scroller->XPos*Scroller->XUnit; // Compensate for scroll
    Sy = Mess.LP.Hi+Scroller->YPos*Scroller->YUnit; // Compensate for scroll
    if(!LButtonDown)               // If this is the first L button down
    {
        LButtonDown = TRUE;        // L button was pressed
        SetCapture(HWindow);       // Make sure we track mouse outside window
    }
}
```

The only change is to modify the coordinates obtained from the argument supplied by Windows, before storing them in the data members of our application window.

We also need to take a look at the **WMMouseMove()** function. The coordinates supplied by Windows also need correcting for the scroll position. The revised version of this function to operate correctly in a scrolled position is as follows:

```
// Message response function to deal with a mouse move
void TGrfxWindow:: WMMouseMove(RTMessage Mess)
{
    RECT R;                                     // Rectangle to be redrawn

    if(LButtonDown)
    {
        if(MouseMove)
        {
            R = TDispObject::GetLast()->Limit();// Get boundary of last object

            // Compensate for scroll move
            OffsetRect(&R, -Scroller->XPos*Scroller->XUnit,
                           -Scroller->YPos*Scroller->YUnit);

            TDispObject::DeleteLast();          // Delete last object
            InvalidateRect(HWindow,&R,TRUE);    // Redraw rectangle R
        }
        else
            MouseMove = TRUE;                   // Record we had a mouse move
```

```
switch(Shape)
{
    case line:
        new TLine(Sx, Sy,                              // Create a line
            Mess.LP.Lo+Scroller->XPos*Scroller->XUnit,
            Mess.LP.Hi+Scroller->YPos*Scroller->YUnit , Color);
        break;

    case circle:                                       // Create a circle
        new TCircle(Sx, Sy,
            Mess.LP.Lo+Scroller->XPos*Scroller->XUnit,
            Mess.LP.Hi+Scroller->YPos*Scroller->YUnit, Color );
        break;

    case rectangle:
        new TRectangle(Sx, Sy,                         // Create a rectangle
            Mess.LP.Lo+Scroller->XPos*Scroller->XUnit,
            Mess.LP.Hi+Scroller->YPos*Scroller->YUnit, Color);
        break;

    default:                     // Error - so create a long red line
        new TLine(0, 0, 450, 450 , red );
}

// Set rectangle for current object
R = TDispObject::GetLast()->Limit();

// Compensate for scroll
OffsetRect(&R,-Scroller->XPos*Scroller->XUnit,
            -Scroller->YPos*Scroller->YUnit);

InvalidateRect(HWindow, &R, TRUE );          // Get the window redrawn
}
}
```

There are five changes to the previous version of the function, but there are only two different types of change: compensating for scrolling when defining an invalid window, and compensating for scrolling when we instantiate a shape object.

We need to alter the rectangle we invalidate so that it corresponds to compensate for the scrolled position. This involves moving the bounding rectangle for an object back by the distances scrolled in x and y. This is to get the rectangle back to Windows in the coordinate system it understands - the same one it used for the mouse position coordinates. We can do this easily using the Windows API function **OffsetRect()**. This adjusts the position of rectangle pointed to by the first argument, by the x and y distances specified in the second two arguments.

When we create a new object we need to add the scroll distances in x and y to the coordinates supplied by Windows of the current position for the mouse, just as we did for **WMLButtonDown()**. Finally, we adjust the rectangle defining the region to be redrawn for the new object, so that the area redrawn will be correct.

A further change we need to make is to the function **Paint()** for our window object. This receives a rectangle defining the area to be redrawn, but this needs to be adjusted for the current scroll position so that it is consistent with the **NeedShow()** function for the objects to be displayed. The new version of **Paint()** is as follows:

```
// Definition of Function to redraw the window contents
void TGrfxWindow::Paint(HDC DC, PAINTSTRUCT& PS)
{
    RECT R;

    R = PS.rcPaint;
    OffsetRect(&R,Scroller->XPos*Scroller->XUnit,
               Scroller->YPos*Scroller->YUnit); // Compensate for scroll

    // Get the tail of the chain
    TDispObject* pNext = TDispObject::GetLast();

    while (pNext)           // Output objects until the next pointer is 0
    {
        if(pNext->NeedShow(R))pNext->Show(DC);   // Display whatever it is
        pNext = pNext->GetPrev();              // Get pointer to previous object
    }
}
```

The alteration here is similar to the rectangle change in the previous function.

Try It Out - Drawing Over Larger Areas

We also need to change the **WMRButtonDown()** function which now deletes an object - again to adjust the rectangle specified in the call to **InvalidateRect()**. Once that is done, we are ready to go. The program is on the disk as **EX12-05.CPP** with **DRAW2.H**, and **DRAW2.CPP**, and the resource project file and **.H** file are the same as the previous example. You can now draw over a much larger area - and with working menus and accelerators.

How it Works

The changes to the operation of this program all arise because scrolling shifts the origin. The coordinate system used for the mouse messages and rectangles to be redrawn in Windows remain static, while the coordinate system in the window is moved relative to it as the window is scrolled.

It may occur to you that, in the `WMMouseMove()` function, we adjusted the rectangle as the argument to `InvalidateRect()` by subtracting the scrolled distances from x and y. Here, in the `Paint()` function, we get the same adjusted rectangle and we are adding the scroll distances back. Surely we could leave out the adjustments there, and omit them here and we would have the same position? Well, try it. Just comment out each of the `OffsetRect()` calls (these do the adjustments). You will see some strange effects when you run the program. You will find that everything works out OK, until you scroll the window and draw some more.

When we pass a rectangle back to windows as an argument to `InvalidateRect()`, is passed eventually to `Paint()`, but it is also used by Windows to define the clipping boundary for the area to be redrawn. Windows suppresses drawing outside this area, even though the draw functions such as `LineTo()` and `Arc()` may try to draw outside it. This rectangle is mapped to the client area in Windows coordinates, which are not the same as the scrolled window client area coordinates. Without the adjustment, the program doesn't work.

Window Registration

A window of your window class actually has a class. We are talking two different kinds of class here. When a window is created, it needs to have a classification so far as Windows is concerned, which determines a number of attributes associated with the window. With all the application windows we have defined up to now, we have been taking advantage of the fact that the OWL has been taking care of obtaining a class for us. Obtaining a Windows class for a window is called **window class registration**.

> *If you want to change the background color of your application window, or the cursor it uses, you must register your own class with Windows. The specific attributes such as the kind of cursor used and the background color are called registration attributes. These are specified when you register your window.*

525

Registering Your Application Window

To associate your application window with a new Windows class, you need to define two member functions in your application window class, **GetWindowClass()** and **GetClassName()**. These are already provided as defaults by the OWL, so we are substituting our versions for those inherited from **TWindow** when we derive our own window class.

Let's suppose we want to further extend our drawing example by using a cross cursor, as it is a bit more appropriate than the old arrow head for the kind of precision image we have been producing. Let's also suppose we want a background color more in keeping with our artistic temperament.

The first thing we need to do is to amend our window class definition to include the two additional functions **GetWindowClass()** and **GetClassName()** as members:

```
// Window class to display graphics
class TGrfxWindow: public TWindow
{
   public:
      // Constructor
      TGrfxWindow(PTWindowsObject AParent, LPSTR ATitle);

      // Destructor
      ~TGrfxWindow();

      // Function to define the Windows class name for our class
      LPSTR GetClassName(void)
      {  return "GrfxCrossWindow";  }

      // Function to obtain a Windows class for our window
      void GetWindowClass(WNDCLASS&);

      // Message response functions
      virtual void WMLButtonDown(RTMessage Mess)=[WM_FIRST+WM_LBUTTONDOWN];
      virtual void WMLButtonUp(RTMessage Mess)=[WM_FIRST+WM_LBUTTONUP];
      virtual void WMRButtonDown(RTMessage Mess)=[WM_FIRST+WM_RBUTTONDOWN];
      virtual void WMMouseMove(RTMessage Mess)=[WM_FIRST+WM_MOUSEMOVE];

      // Menu message response functions
        //...first for shape menu options
      void CMLine(RTMessage) = [CM_FIRST+CM_LINE];
      void CMCircle(RTMessage) = [CM_FIRST+CM_CIRCLE];
      void CMRectangle(RTMessage) = [CM_FIRST+CM_RECTANGLE];
        // ...then for color menu options
```

```
      void CMRed(RTMessage) = [CM_FIRST+CM_RED];
      void CMGreen(RTMessage) = [CM_FIRST+CM_GREEN];
      void CMBlue(RTMessage) = [CM_FIRST+CM_BLUE];
      void CMYellow(RTMessage) = [CM_FIRST+CM_YELLOW];
      void CMBlack(RTMessage) = [CM_FIRST+CM_BLACK];

      // Function to redraw the window contents
      virtual void Paint(HDC DC, PAINTSTRUCT&);

   private:
      int Sx;                 // Start point coordinates x,y for a line
      int Sy;                 // or the centre of a circle

      BOOL LButtonDown;       // Flag = TRUE for button down
      BOOL MouseMove;         // Flag = TRUE for previous move

      // Definition of current shape
      SHAPE Shape;

      // Definition of current color
      COLORREF Color;

};
```

The **GetClassName()** function is already defined here because it is trivial. All it does is return a name for the Windows class as a text string. The name is of no importance, as long as it is different from any other class names defined.

The **GetWindowClass()** member function will identify the cursor we want to use, and the background color for the client area of our window. This is done by setting the values of members of the **WNDCLASS** object which will be passed to the function as an argument.

> Note that the parameter in the specification of this member function in the class definition is a reference, so we can update the members of this object directly.

The **WndClass** members that we need to change to get a different cursor, and another background color, are **hCursor** and **hbrBackground** respectively. Let's look at the code for **GetWindowClass()** and then see what it does:

```
void TGrfxWindow::GetWindowClass(WNDCLASS& aWC)
{
   TWindow::GetWindowClass(aWC);              // Call base class function
```

```
    // Set stock cross cursor
    aWC.hCursor = LoadCursor( 0, IDC_CROSS);

    // Set our very own color!
    aWC.hbrBackground = CreateSolidBrush( RGB(255,150,75) );
}
```

We first call the corresponding function in the base class **TWindow** to do all the basics for us. We are left needing only to set the things we are interested in. In this case, we first set the cursor to the stock cursor **IDC_CROSS** which is provided by Windows. We could have used either **IDC_IBEAM** or **IDC_WAIT**. The first is the I-beam cursor which is often used with text applications, and **IDC_WAIT** is the familiar hour glass cursor that appears when your computer is busy - the slower your PC, the more you see of it. The usual default arrow head is **IDC_ARROW**.

To set the background color we create a brush using the Windows API function **CreateSolidBrush()**. This expects an argument of type **COLOREF** which is returned from the **RGB()** function we have seen previously. The color we have set here is between a Florida orange and a California orange, with a hint of betel nut.

You can use any color you like, but remember, its hard to see things that are drawn in the same color as the background!

Try It Out - Colors and Cursors

All that needs to be done is to amend the **TgrfxWindow** class definition in the previous example to include the functions **GetWindowClass()** and **GetWindowName()** as public members, and to add the function definitions in **DRAW2.CPP**. This is all done for you in **EX12-06.CPP** which combines files **DRAW3.H** and **DRAW3.CPP**, as well as the **.RC** project file from the previous example.

How it Works

The functions we have defined are called automatically, and they set the parameters which provide a new cursor and a new background color. The screen may well look like that shown opposite.

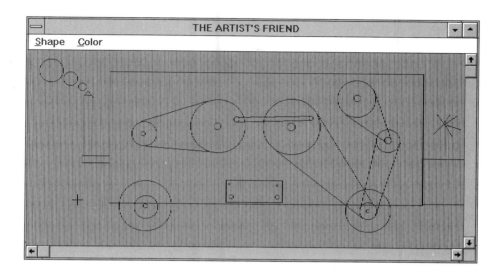

Unfortunately, the limitations imposed by a book in one color can't do justice to this picture. The window shows our new cursor, and a secret government design for a new engine to drive the economy, which runs on hot air.

There are quite a few options for creating different kinds of backgrounds with various brushes. You can run the whole gamut of solid colors using the function **CreateSolidBrush()** we have used here, or you can check out the function **CreateBrushIndirect()** which you can find details of in TCW Help. This will enable you do all kinds of wonderful things with the background - even tartan or prison stripes are possible here. If you make the background fancy enough, it could remove the necessity to draw anything at all - it may even make it impossible because you can't see what you are doing.

Creating and Using Your Own Cursor

It's very nice having the cross cursor, but it has the disadvantage of being the same as a lot of other programs. To really personalize your program, you will want to have your very own cursor. This is actually a lot easier that it sounds. Generating your own cursor with Resource Workshop is a piece of cake.

Creating a Cursor

Firstly, fire up Resource Workshop as we did before and start a new resource project file. You can copy the previous project file into it to add the menu definition which we created for the previous example. Then select Resource then New... from the menu, and then CURSOR from the options. You will then be asked what kind of file you want, so click the Microsoft compatible binary box. Finally, you will be prompted for a file name for the cursor file, and once you have entered a name, you will get a special window for creating cursors as shown below.

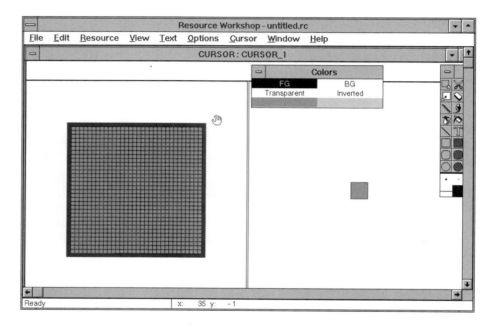

The left half of the window is an enlarged image of a blank cursor, and on the right the cursor appears normal size so you can see how it looks as you construct it. Also on the right are two small windows: one with a set of paint drawing tools, and the other showing a color palette which is limited because cursors are in only one color.

You can enlarge the working cursor image if you wish by selecting View and Zoom in from the main menu. The background of the cursor is transparent by default, which allows the window background to show through. This is the normal option for a cursor, as otherwise it will be a 32x32 pixel square, which is usually less practical for picking points in the client area.

You now need to do two things to define the cursor. Draw the shape you want to have as a cursor using the drawing tools on the right, then define the 'hotspot' for the cursor, which is the point which defines the position of the cursor (that will be reported in Windows mouse messages to your program). The drawing tools are standard paint tools so we won't dwell on them. The default pen is very easy to use, so if you haven't tried it, just poke around. You can always start over if it doesn't work out. To set the hotspot you need to know the coordinates of the point you want to set, so before selecting the Cursor menu option to set the hotspot, position the screen cursor on your design at the point you want the hotspot to be, and note the coordinates shown at the bottom of the window. You then enter these values in the window which appears when you select the Set hot spot... option. An unusual example of a cursor is shown below:

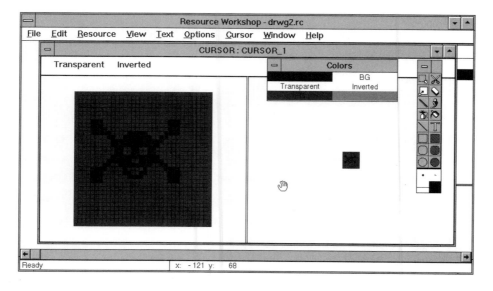

Once your cursor is finished, you can take it for a spin by selecting Cursor and Test. To reset the test, simply click the left mouse button. When you are happy with your cursor, all you need to do is save the file - this one is saved in the project file DRG2.RC. You are then ready to tie it in to your application.

Linking a Private Cursor

This is only slightly different from adding a default cursor. A slight alteration to the member function `GetWindowClass()` in our application window class will do the trick:

```
void TGrfxWindow::GetWindowClass(WNDCLASS& aWC)
{
    TWindow::GetWindowClass(aWC);             // Call base member function

    // Set up our own cursor
    aWC.hCursor = LoadCursor( GetApplication()->hInstance, "CURSOR_1");

    // Our own color!
    aWC.hbrBackground = CreateSolidBrush( RGB(255,150,75) );
}
```

The only change is to the call to the Windows API function `LoadCursor()`. This time, we have the first argument set to supply the handle to our application object. We can't reference it directly from here, but we can use the inherited member function `GetApplication()` which returns a pointer to the application object, and then use that to access `hInstance` in our application object `TBasicApp`. The second argument to `LoadCursor()` is the name assigned to the cursor resource when we created it - `CURSOR_1`. This is the default name assigned by Resource Workshop which appears in the title bar of the cursor construction window.

Try It Out - The Complete Program

Try it Out!

Aside from the alteration to `GetWindowClass()` the only other change that is necessary is to include the new resource project file `DRWG2.RC` in the program project file.

How It Works

This cursor will now be automatically available for all the client area operations. For the cursor sample shown above, you should get an application window similar to that shown opposite.

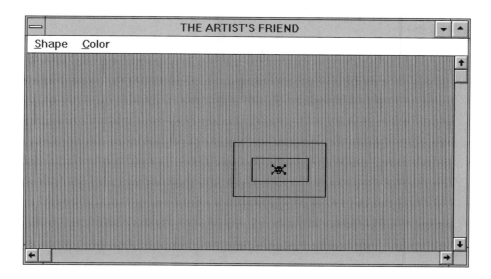

The frame was drawn in simply to give due emphasis to such an original cursor. You could use it just for Halloween, maybe. In fact, that would be an interesting exercise. Modify the example so that it produced a different cursor depending on the date. All it needs is a few more cursors, and some research on the library function to get at the date. You then just add some logic to `GetWindowClass()` to select a cursor depending on the date - a turkey for the 4th of July, holly at Christmas - the possibilities are endless. There is no problem with having several cursor resources in a program, as they take up very little space.

Try moving the cursor around. As soon as you move off the client area, it changes back into the old arrow cursor automatically. This is handled automatically by Windows. Our cursor is only applicable to the client area of our application window.

Summary

Menus are an essential part of most Windows programs, and you should now be at ease with creating and implementing them. You should spend some time experimenting wth the facilities of Resource Workshop for menu creation. You will find a lot of facilities under the covers. For example, it has built in capability to generate a standard File menu pop-up. You can create this menu item for your program with no effort at all. We will be seeing more of Resource Workshop in subsequent chapters.

The technique for redrawing part of a window is very important. It always makes the difference between whether or not a program is a bit sluggish, and for complex applications it may make the difference between whether or not the program is usable. You should make sure that you thoroughly understand how this mechanism works.

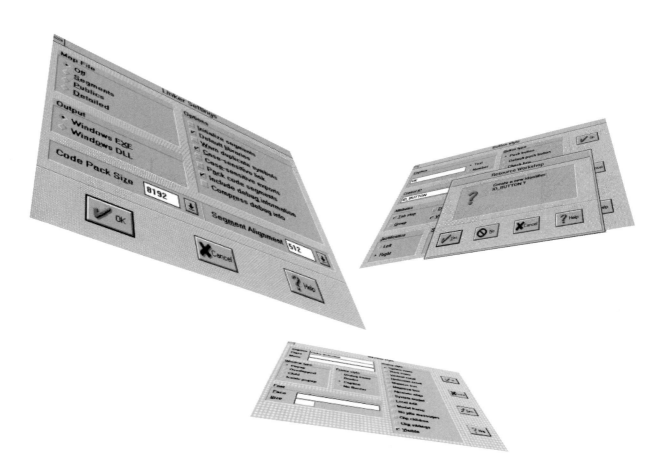

Child Windows and Dialogs

In this chapter we will look at how to add additional windows to our initial application window to provide more functionality, and to introduce more ways to interact with our program. The additional windows which are created in a program are usually **child windows** of the main window. The main window is the **parent window** of the additional windows which are created. Child windows, however, do not necessarily look like a window. In some instances, they can be very simple entities.

We will also take a look at how we can implement file input and output in a Windows program, using an interface to the user supplied by the OWL. We will do this by adding a practical extension to one of our existing examples.

In this chapter you will learn about:

- Dialogs
- Creating dialog objects using the OWL
- Creating a dialog resource using Resource Workshop
- Creating and using an input dialog
- How to get numeric data values through an input dialog
- How to create the file dialogs provided by the OWL
- How to read and write external files using the Windows API functions

Creating Child Windows

There are many ways in which child windows can be created, but perhaps the most useful mechanism is through a class provided by the OWL called **TDialog**. This provides a base class which you can use to define your own window classes for a specific sort of child window called a **dialog**. These can have a vast range of different facilities and characteristics. Dialogs are a primary means of providing communications between your windows application and the user. So far, our only means of communication has been the mouse. With dialogs, we can provide a variety of facilities for the user to interact with the program, including input from the keyboard.

For the moment, we will forgo getting any significant input into a program in order to concentrate on the mechanics of creating a dialog in an application, and we will extend our drawing package with a simple dialog. We will use the version using the cross cursor as a base, which corresponds to **EX12-06.CPP**.

Understanding Dialogs

Let's take a look at the dialog we are going to create in the drawing program we developed in the last chapter. It is shown below.

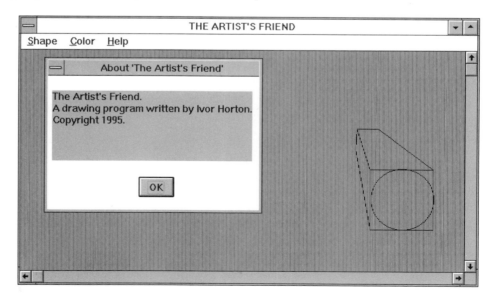

The inset window is produced by selecting Help from the main menu and the About menu item from the pop-up. Clicking on the OK button causes the child window to disappear. This could actually be done much more simply with a message box, but we want to try out the mechanism for creating a dialog.

Resource Files

The appearance of the dialog is not defined within the program, but externally within a resource file, just like the menu or the cursor we added in the last chapter. We can therefore get a lot of help in creating the necessary resource definition from Resource Workshop, as we shall see. The servicing of the About menu option is somewhat incidental, in that this is just the same as the previous menu items we actioned. It just needs a message response function. In this case, the message response function will create the dialog shown.

Modal Dialogs

A dialog can be **modal**, which means that further processing in the application depends on some action from the user, such as clicking the OK button in the window shown above. With a modal dialog, the parent window is disabled while the dialog is active. There has to be an action by the user which causes the dialog to be closed before the parent window becomes active again. A dialog can also be **modeless**, which means that processing using the main window can continue while the dialog is active. You can switch back and forth between the modeless dialog and the parent window, as you wish. Search windows for finding a particular word in a text file are often modeless. We shall create our first dialog as modal.

Creating a Dialog Resource

To create the dialog resource for the example shown, we will create a new resource project file in which we will recreate the menu we require, together with the dialog. Let's call the resource project file **DRWG3.RC**. When we open a new project in Resource Workshop, we need to add a file to hold the identifiers which we can call **DRWGIDS1.H**. We add this using the File menu option Add to project... in Resource Workshop.

Adding the extra menu is done in exactly the same way as previously, so we won't discuss it further here. The identifiers in the menu will automatically be defined in the file **DRWGIDS1.H**, so all we need to do is to place an **#include** statement for this file in the **.H** file for our program, where we define our classes. This will enable us to refer to the identifiers within our program code.

To define the dialog using Resource Workshop, we select Resource from the menu then New..., and DIALOG from the list of options that appears. We then will see the screen for creating a dialog shown below.

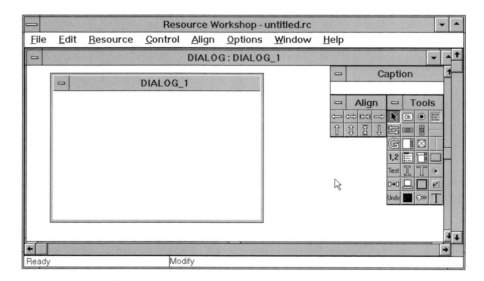

This contains a basic dialog shown on the left which we will be modifying and expanding, and a set of tools for creating and changing a dialog on the right.

The first thing we can do is to change the caption in the dialog. We can do this by double clicking on the caption in the dialog on the left. This will result in another window being displayed, enabling us to enter a new caption. The window also contains a lot of other options (ignore those for the moment). We can enter About The Artist's Friend and click on OK, and we will be back to the dialog creation window with the caption changed.

To put the message in the dialog we will use the text tool which contains a **T** and is at the bottom right hand corner of the set of tools. Drag a copy of the tool on to the dialog on the left. This will leave a small box containing the word Text in the dialog. You can enlarge this box to a suitable size by dragging its boundaries. You can also move the whole thing around within the dialog by placing the cursor inside the text box and dragging it. After moving the text box and enlarging it to a suitable size, it should then look something like the window shown below.

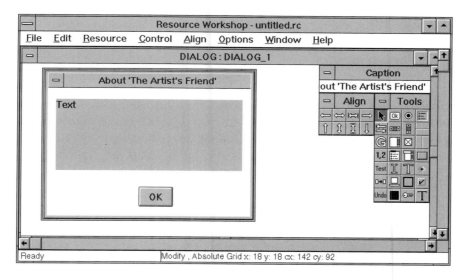

Now we need to change the text in the box. Just double click on the word Text inside the box and you will getting a pop-up allowing you to edit the text. If you want to get a newline character in the text, obviously you can't just press the *Enter* key, as that will close the box. You need to enter \n, as we did when defining text strings for output in C++.

After putting a suitable text message in the dialog, we need finally to add a button we can use to close the dialog. Drag a copy of the second tool from the first row on to the dialog and position it below the text. This will leave a button containing the word Text in the dialog. Since we want to change the text, and also create an ID for the button, you should click on the word Text in the button to edit the text. Type OK instead of Text, and type ID_BUTTON instead of the number in the Control ID edit box. You will then get an opportunity to create an identifier for the button, as shown on the following page.

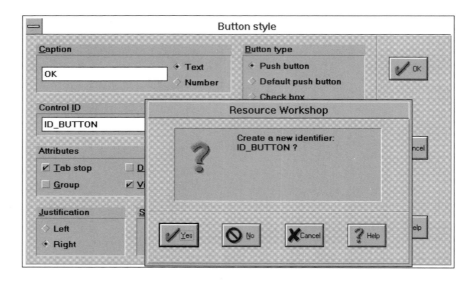

Click on Yes and assign another value for the identifier: 531 is a nice number. That's the dialog resource complete. All you need to do now is save the project file with the name DRWG3.RC, and it's finished.

Implementing a Dialog

We need a class to define our dialog object. We will derive this from the OWL class TDialog, as follows:

```
// Dialog class
class TMyDialog:public TDialog
{
   public:
      TMyDialog(PTWindowsObject aParent, LPSTR aName):
      TDialog(aParent,aName)
      {}  // All the work is done by the base constructor

      void IDButton(RTMessage) = [ID_FIRST+ID_BUTTON];
};
```

All the constructor to the class does is call the base constructor. The constructor has two parameters: the first is a pointer to the parent window and the second is a string identifying the resource for the dialog. For our dialog, it will be DIALOG_1, since this is the default name assigned to our dialog by Resource Workshop. We could have changed this if we didn't like the default by selecting Resource/Rename... from the menu. We could then enter a different name for the dialog resource.

We include the message response function **IDButton()** here in the definition of our dialog class, **TMyDialog**. This will respond to the user clicking the OK button in our dialog. This has a dispatch index defined by adding the identifier we created in the resource file, **ID_BUTTON**, to the base value **ID_FIRST**. All we want to do, in this case, is to close the dialog. We can define the function immediately, since its body could hardly be simpler, consisting of only one statement:

```
// Respond to About dialog button
void TMyDialog::IDButton(RTMessage)
{
    CloseWindow();        // Close the dialog window
}
```

This calls the function **CloseWindow()** which is a member of our class **TMyDialog**, inherited from the base class, **TDialog**. As its name suggests, this simply closes the dialog window.

To service the menu option About, we need to add a message response function **CMAbout()** to our application window class **TGrfxWindow**. We need to add the function to the class definition with this statement:

```
void CMAbout(RTMessage) = [CM_FIRST+CM_ABOUT];
```

This defines the function as a public class member with a dispatch index specified using the identifier, **CM_ABOUT**, which we created in the resource file.

The definition of the function will be this:

```
// Message response function for About menu option
void TGrfxWindow::CMAbout(RTMessage)
{
    // Create and execute a dialog
    GetModule()->ExecDialog(new TMyDialog(this, "DIALOG_1"));
}
```

This completes all the changes we need to make to **EX11-06.CPP** and its associated files. We can now take the new version for a run.

Try It Out - Adding a Dialog to Our Paint Program

This appears on the disk as **EX13-01.CPP**, with associated files **DRAWDLG.H** and **DRAWDLG.CPP**. The resource project file is **DRWG3.RC**. To see the dialog you need to click on <u>H</u>elp then select <u>A</u>bout from the pop-up. To close the dialog click on the OK button.

How It Works

Clicking on <u>A</u>bout causes the **CM_ABOUT** message to be sent to the program which calls the message response function **CMAbout()**. This creates and executes our dialog. Clicking the OK button causes the **IDButton()** function in the **TMyDialog** class to be called, which closes the dialog window.

Our dialog was modal, so it was created and executed by calling the function **ExecDialog()** in our window class, **TGrfxWindow**. For a modeless dialog, you would need to use the member function **MakeWindow()** in the window class, instead of **ExecDialog()**, to cause the dialog to appear. This is because of the different operating mechanism of a modeless dialog compared to a modal dialog. However, a modeless dialog can be closed by calling the same function we used in our example, **CloseWindow()**.

Entering Text with a Dialog

Text input is one of the easiest things to implement in a program because the OWL does most of the work for you. The OWL includes a class **TInputDialog** which provides a general dialog to input a text string. When you create an object of the class, you can customize the caption, the prompt and any default text you want to provide. This means that the class **TInputDialog** is ready to use, so you don't need to derive your own class in order to use it effectively.

The constructor for **TInputDialog** requires five arguments:

1 A pointer to the parent window

2 A pointer to the caption for the dialog

3   A pointer to the text to appear as a prompt

4   A pointer to the **char** array which will hold the input string and which is already initialized to the default string

5   Finally, the length of the input array

It could be used in a sequence of statements within a function member of the application window class, such as those shown below:

```
PTInputDialog pDlg;                     // Define a pointer to an input dialog
char Text[40] = "A text string";        // Input string initialized to default

// Create object
pDlg = new TInputDialog(this, "Text Input",
                        "Enter text:", Text, sizeof(Text));
```

This would create an instance of the **TInputDialog** class with a heading Text Input and a prompt Enter text. The input string **Text[]** is initialized with **"A text string"**, so this would appear in the dialog box when it was executed. We supply the overall length of the array **Text[]** using the **sizeof** operator.

> *Creating a dialog box using a pointer in this way is not the most usual way of using an input dialog. More commonly, it is created, used and then discarded each time an input is required. We will use this approach to implement an input dialog in our drawing program.*

To use an input dialog of the class **TInputDialog** necessitates that we add **INPUT.DLG** to our program resource file and provide an **#include** statement in the program for the file **INPUTDIA.H**. We will also need to make sure we add an **#include** before **INPUTDIA.H** for **OWLRC.H**, since this contains the definitions for the identifiers used in the dialog. If you use any OWL dialogs you need to add this **#include**, otherwise the resource file won't compile properly.

Let's now try all this out on our drawing program. It would be nice to be able to add some annotation to a drawing. We will extend the previous example to include an annotation facility, but we will omit the background color attribute from the constructor, as it's perhaps a little pretentious, not to say a bit of a nuisance when displaying objects of various colors. So in the next version we will revert to a white background.

Implementing a Text Input Dialog

We need to do a little work for this if it is going to be useful. Firstly, we need to decide how the inputting of text is going to be initiated. The obvious answer is an extra item on the main menu with the name Text. Clicking the menu option would bring up the text input dialog.

We would need another class to hold text objects, although this should be no problem if we derive it from **TDispObject**. The coordinates in the base class could contain the position of the text, so all we need to add for the derived text class is a color attribute member and a member to hold the text. However, there is something else we need. In order to define a bounding rectangle for a text string, we need to know the height and width of a typical character. A windows function **GetTextMetrics()** can provide the information we need, so we add data members to store the character width and height to **TgrfxWindow**, and can modify the constructor to set the values in an appropriate way.

Positioning the text also needs some consideration. It needs to be a little different from drawing a geometric shape since it requires a text string to be entered each time. One good approach would be to enable a positioning operation for the text using the mouse, after the text has been entered. We can store the text temporarily in a data member of the application window. We could then set a flag in the application window class to indication text mode. Since just one point defines the position for a text string, it will work more naturally if we create and display a text object as soon as the left mouse button is pressed. This will allow text to be positioned by quickly clicking the mouse, or holding the button down and dragging it around. So we can start a text positioning sequence by creating and displaying a text object in the next **WM_LBUTTONDOWN** message. The message response function for **WM_LBUTTONUP** would need to reset the text mode flag back to **FALSE**.

So, we should summarize the changes we need to make in order to use an input dialog in our drawing program. We will need to make the following alterations to the existing program:

▶ Define a **TText** class for a text object derived from **TDispObject** and add the constructor and **Show()** function for a **TText** object.

▶ Add a data item of type **char** to **TGrxWindow** to store a text string, and a flag of type **BOOL** to indicate text mode.

▶ Add data items of type **int** to **TGrfxWindow** to store the height and width of a text character.

▶ Modify the constructor for **TGrfxWindow** to initialize the new data members.

▶ Add a new main menu option <u>T</u>ext.

▶ Add a message response function in the class **TgrfxWindow** for the new text item which will create an input dialog and store the input text in a member of **TGrfxWindow**. It will also set a text mode flag in **TGrfxWindow**.

▶ Amend the message response functions for **WM_LBUTTONDOWN**, **WM_MOUSEMOVE** and **WM_LBUTTONUP** to deal with text mode.

▶ Add **INPUTDIA.DLG** to the resource project file.

▶ Add an **#include** statement for **INPUTDIA.H** to the program source file.

It looks like a lot of changes, but each step is very easy. Let's implement these in the same sequence as we have itemized them above. We will take the addition to the menu as a given, since we have added menu items in previous examples. The only point worth noting is that the additional <u>T</u>ext option to the main menu is a menu item, not a pop-up, since it doesn't have a sub-menu. We will define the identifier as **CM_TEXT** and call the resource file **DRWG4.RC**. This will also contain the necessary **#include** statements for **OWLRC.H** and **INPUTDIA.DLG**. These can be added to the files quite easily in the IDE editor.

Defining the Text Class

The new class for text items derived from **TDispObject** will be defined as follows:

```
// Class defining a text object
class TText: public TDispObject
{
   public:
      // Constructor
      TText(int X, int Y, int W, int H,  char* Str, COLORREF C);

      // Show function for text
      virtual void Show(HDC DC);
```

```
    protected:
      char String[40];
      TText(){}          // Default constructor - not to be used
};
```

The class definition adds the data member **String[]**, which stores the text, to the members inherited from **TDispObject**. It also adds a constructor and the **Show()** function to display a **TText** object. The default constructor is in the protected section of the class so as to prevent its use.

The constructor accepts six arguments. The first two are the coordinates of the text in the client area of the application window, the next two are the width and height of a character respectively and the last two are a pointer to the text string to initialize the object and the color for the text. We can write the code for the constructor as follows:

```
// Constructor for a text object
TText::TText(int X, int Y, int W, int H, char* Str, COLORREF C)
{
   x = X;                      // Set coordinates of position
   y = Y;                      // in the client area
   strcpy(String,Str);         // Get string value
   Color = C;                  // Set text color

   Bound.left = x>0 ? x-1 : x;  // Set top left of boundary
   Bound.top = y>0 ? y-1 : y;
   Bound.right = x +W*(1+strlen(String));
   Bound.bottom = y + H+1;      // ...and bottom right

   pPrev = pLast;               // Set last object to previous
   pLast = this;                // Set current object as last

}
```

The text string will be written to the client area in the member function **Show()**, using the Windows API function **TextOut()**. The coordinates supplied to **TextOut()** represent the top left corner of the string of characters. Thus we can define the top left of the bounding rectangle by subtracting one pixel from these coordinates and calculate the coordinates of the bottom right corner by adding the height to y coordinate and multiplying the number of characters in the string plus 1, by the width of a character and add that to the x coordinate. The number of characters in the string is obtained from the standard library function **strlen()**. We add the width of one character to be on the safe side when computing the coordinates of the bounding rectangle, since we are dealing with an average character width. This is illustrated on the following page:

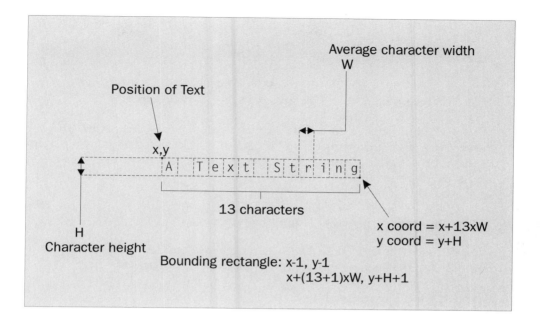

The `Show()` function works slightly differently to that of the classes defining geometric shapes:

```
// Function to display text
void TText::Show(HDC DC)
{
   SetTextColor(DC, Color);                    // Set text color
   TextOut(DC, x, y, String, strlen(String));// Output string
}
```

The color for text is not determined by the pen currently in use, but by calling a Windows API function `SetTextColor()` which sets the color for any text subsequently displayed by `TextOut()` to the color value specified. As with other color values, it is of type `COLORREF`.

Modifying TGrfxWindow

To add members to the `TGrfxWindow` class definition in order to hold the width and height of a character, we can add the following two statements to the `protected` section of the class definition:

```
   int cxChar;              // Character width
   int cyChar;              // Character height
```

Values here will be in units of pixels.

The text mode indicator can be added to the same section of the class with this statement:

```
BOOL TextMode;           // Flag = TRUE for text mode
```

This will be initialized to **FALSE** in the **TGrfxWindow** constructor, and set **TRUE** when the Text menu option is clicked. Clicking the Text menu option will be processed by a message response function, so we need to add the message response function with its dispatch index to the **public** section of the class definition:

```
void CMText(RTMessage) = [CM_FIRST+CM_TEXT];
```

The dispatch index is defined by adding the identifier, **CM_TEXT**, which we defined for the menu item, to the predefined identifier **CM_FIRST**.

Getting Text Dimensions

To get the dimensions of a text character, we can add a block of code to the constructor for **TGrfxWindow**. This will use the Windows API function **GetTextMetrics()**. We also need to initialize the flag **TextMode** to **FALSE** in the constructor. The modified version of the constructor is as follows:

```
// Constructor for the application window
TGrfxWindow::TGrfxWindow(PTWindowsObject AParent, LPSTR ATitle)
          :TWindow(AParent,ATitle)
{
    AssignMenu("Menu_1");                    // Associate Menu_1 with program
    LButtonDown = MouseMove = FALSE;
    TextMode = FALSE;                        // TextMode off
    strcpy(String, " ");                     // Set string as empty
    Shape = line;                            // Set default shape
    Color = black;                           // Set default color

    Attr.Style |= WS_HSCROLL|WS_VSCROLL;     // Add a horizontal scroll bar
    Scroller=new TScroller(this, 20, 20, 50, 50); // Create scroller object
    Scroller->AutoMode = FALSE;              // Switch off auto mode

    // Get height and width of text characters
    TEXTMETRIC TM;                      // Text information object
    HDC aDC = GetDC(HWindow);           // Get a device context
    GetTextMetrics(aDC, &TM);           // Get data on text
    cxChar = TM.tmAveCharWidth;         // Save width
    cyChar = TM.tmHeight;               // Save height
    ReleaseDC(HWindow, aDC);            // Finished with the display context
}
```

The `GetTextMetrics()` function accepts two arguments. The first is a device context containing the font we will be interested in, so we obtain a display device context by calling the Windows function `GetDC()`. The second argument is an object of type `TEXTMETRIC`. An object of this type contains a whole range of data members relating to a physical font. You can get a full description of the `TEXTMETRIC` type from the TCW Help menu. The function `GetTextMetrics()` fills out the members of the object `TM`, which we have supplied as a reference argument, with details of the font currently in effect in the display context. The two members we are interested in are `tmAveCharWidth` and `tmHeight`, which correspond to the average width and the height of characters in the current font. We store these two values in the data members we added to the `TGrfxWindow` class for that purpose. We finally release the device context since we no longer require it.

Creating the Input Dialog

We do this in the message response function for the Text menu option we have added in this example:

```
// Message response function for Text menu item
void TGrfxWindow::CMText(RTMessage)
{
    if(GetApplication()->ExecDialog(new TInputDialog(this,
        "Text Object Input", "Enter up to 39 characters:", String,
        sizeof(String)))==IDOK)
        TextMode = TRUE;
}
```

We create and execute the input dialog using the function `ExecDialog()` in much the same way as we did with the dialog for the About menu option. The expression in the `if` statement is somewhat complicated, so let's work through it step by step.

The `GetApplication()` function is an inherited member of our application window class `TGrfxWindow`, which returns a pointer to the current application object. This pointer is then used to call its member function `ExecDialog()`. The argument to `ExecDialog()` is a pointer to a `TInputDialog` object, which is created in the free store. The arguments to the `TInputDialog` constructor are a pointer to the current window, the text to appear as the caption to the dialog, the text to appear as a prompt in the dialog, a pointer to the string to hold the input, and the maximum length of the input string. The argument `String` is also assumed to contain a default string which will be displayed in the dialog.

The **ExecDialog()** function creates and executes the dialog pointed to by its argument (remember that if we execute a dialog it is modal, so processing cannot continue until the dialog is closed). The value returned by **ExecDialog()** will depend on whether the OK button or the Cancel button is selected to close the dialog. Selecting either will close the dialog automatically. A value **IDOK** returned from **ExecDialog()** indicates that the OK button was selected, the other possible return value being **IDCANCEL**. With a value returned of **IDOK**, the expression in the **if** will be **TRUE**, so we will set the flag **TextMode** to **TRUE**. This will initiate text processing mode in the message response functions handling mouse events.

Modifying Mouse Message Response Functions

The final piece required for a new version of our drawing program is to update the message response function for mouse events. We can start with the first one to be executed, **WMLButtonDown()**. Here, we need to take special action if the flag **TextMode** is **TRUE**. We need to create a text object at the current position in the client area, using the string saved in the member **String[]**. Here is the revised code:

```
// Definition of message response function for left mouse button press
void TGrfxWindow::WMLButtonDown( RTMessage Mess )
{
   // Compensate for scroll
   Sx = Mess.LP.Lo+Scroller->XPos*Scroller->XUnit;
   // Compensate for scroll
   Sy = Mess.LP.Hi+Scroller->YPos*Scroller->YUnit;
   if(!LButtonDown)              // If this is the first L button down
   {
      if(TextMode)                              // Test for text mode
      {
         // Create text object
         new TText(Sx,Sy,cxChar,cyChar,String,Color);
         RECT R = TDispObject::GetLast()->Limit();
         // Compensate for scroll
         OffsetRect(&R, -Scroller->XPos*Scroller->XUnit,
                    -Scroller->YPos*Scroller->YUnit);

         MouseMove = TRUE;                       // Pretend the mouse moved
         InvalidateRect(HWindow, &R, TRUE );   // Get the window redrawn
      }

      LButtonDown = TRUE;    // L button was pressed
      SetCapture(HWindow);   // Make sure we track the mouse outside window
   }
}
```

The new block of code is executed if **TextMode** is **TRUE**. We first create a text object at the current position specified by **Sx** and **Sy**. This will allow the text to be set in position with a single click of the left button. If we didn't create a text object here, it would be necessary to move the mouse in order for the text to appear. Once the object is created, we redraw the part of the window occupied by the text. Since we now have an object created which is potentially moveable by dragging the mouse, we need to signal the fact to the **WMMouseMove()** function. We do this by setting **MouseMove** to **TRUE**.

In the **WMMouseMove()** function, the only change necessary is to create a new **TText** object if the flag **TextMode** is **TRUE**:

```
// Message response function to deal with a mouse move
void TGrfxWindow:: WMMouseMove(RTMessage Mess)
{
    RECT R;                                          // Rectangle to be redrawn

    if(LButtonDown)
    {
        if(MouseMove)
        {
            // Get boundary of last object
            R = TDispObject::GetLast()->Limit();

            // Compensate for scroll move
            OffsetRect(&R, -Scroller->XPos*Scroller->XUnit,
                       -Scroller->YPos*Scroller->YUnit);
            TDispObject::DeleteLast();              // Delete last object

            InvalidateRect(HWindow,&R,TRUE);        // Redraw rectangle R
        }
        else
            MouseMove = TRUE;                       // Record we had a mouse move

        if(TextMode)                               // Create a text object
            new TText(Mess.LP.Lo+Scroller->XPos*Scroller->XUnit,
                      Mess.LP.Hi+Scroller->YPos*Scroller->YUnit,
                      cxChar, cyChar, String, Color);
        else
            switch(Shape)
            {
                case line:                         // Create a line
                    new TLine(Sx, Sy,
                        Mess.LP.Lo+Scroller->XPos*Scroller->XUnit,
                        Mess.LP.Hi+Scroller->YPos*Scroller->YUnit , Color);
                    break;

                case circle:                       // Create a circle
```

```
        new TCircle(Sx, Sy,
        Mess.LP.Lo+Scroller->XPos*Scroller->XUnit,
        Mess.LP.Hi+Scroller->YPos*Scroller->YUnit, Color );
        break;

    case rectangle:                          // Create a rectangle
        new TRectangle(Sx, Sy,
           Mess.LP.Lo+Scroller->XPos*Scroller->XUnit,
           Mess.LP.Hi+Scroller->YPos*Scroller->YUnit, Color);
        break;

    default:                     // Error - so create a long red line
        new TLine(0, 0, 450, 450 , red );
    }

    // Set rectangle for current object
    R = TDispObject::GetLast()->Limit();
    OffsetRect(&R, -Scroller->XPos*Scroller->XUnit,
             -Scroller->YPos*Scroller->YUnit); // Compensate for scroll

    InvalidateRect(HWindow, &R, TRUE );       // Get the window redrawn
    }
}
```

The only new bit is the introduction of the **if else** statement before the switch. This creates a **TText** object if the flag **TextMode** is set **TRUE**. This will allow a **TText** object to be dragged into position in the same way as the other objects that are displayed. All the rest of the function works as it did before.

We won't repeat the **WMLButtonUp()** function here, as the only change is the addition of one statement to reset the flag **TextMode** to **FALSE**. The right button operation remains completely unchanged.

Try It Out - Using an Edit Dialog

The complete example is on the disk as the program source files **EX13-02.CPP**, **DRAWDLG1.CPP**, **DRAWDLG1.H** and the resource project file **DRWG4.RC**. Although this is now a sizable program, all the components are relatively simple and easy to understand. It is especially important when developing Windows programs to get one part working properly before going on to the next. Finding the bugs in Windows programs can be a little more difficult than with DOS programs, because of the event-driven nature of the application and the larger number of functions that are involved, so it is as well to take small steps in implementing an application.

Try it Out!

If you run this version of the program, you will be able to obtain results such as those shown below.

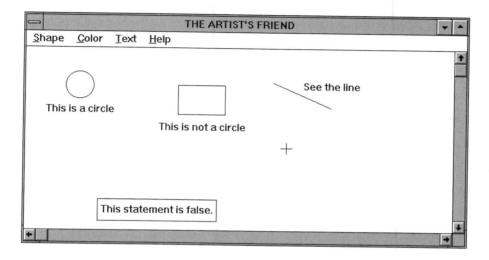

How It Works

When you click on the Text menu option, the text you enter is saved, and the message response function sets the flag **TextMode** to **TRUE**. Consequently, a **TText** object containing the text you entered is placed at the mouse position where you pressed the left button. You can then drag the text object around and the text follows the mouse position until you release the left button. You set color for text using the menu in the same way as you do for shapes. The current color that you have set, which is applicable to shapes, applies equally well to text.

The delete operation using the right mouse button works just as well with text objects as it does with shapes. Because we save the text in a data member of the application window class, clicking the Text menu option brings up the last text string you entered as the default. This is very useful for repeated text entries, and of course you can also use it as a base for new text and just modify it.

The actual use of **TInputDialog** for inputting text was very easy. As is usually the case, most of the work was around the practicalities of applying the input to some useful purpose. Since this is the primary objective in programming, this example should have given you an idea of how it can be approached.

Obtaining Numeric Values with an Input Dialog

Obviously, in many situations you will want to get a numeric value into your program, rather than a text string. Unfortunately, you have little choice but to accept a text string since that is all you can get. You have to sort out a mechanism yourself to convert the text string to whatever form of numeric data is appropriate for your application. The approach you take will depend on the nature and complexity of the input, but we can look at a couple of examples.

Converting a string to numeric form has nothing whatever to do with Windows programming, other than that it is necessary in this context. The simplest situation is when you have an integer value as a string. In this case, you can write some functions yourself to do the conversion. Assuming the string contains only numeric data, the first thing you need to do is remove blanks from the string. This can be done quite easily using a function we used in our calculator program, `eatspaces()`:

```
// Function to eliminate blanks from a string
void eatspaces(char* str)
{
   int i=0;                          // 'Copy to' index to string
   int j=0;                          // 'Copy from' index to string

   // Loop while character copied is not \0
   while( (*(str+i) = *(str+j++)) != '\0' )
      if(*(str+i) != ' ')                        // Increment i as long as
         i++;                                     // character is not a blank

   return;
}
```

Applying this to the string will leave you with a string that should only contain characters and no spaces.

To convert the string to an integer, you can use an approach which we also saw in the context of the calculator program. You need to scan the string from left to right, converting each character to its numeric value. Each numeric value is added to a running sum, which is multiplied by 10 before adding in each digit. There are many ways you can implement this, but one approach is as follows:

```
long GetInteger(char* str)
{
    long value = 0;                          // Accumulator for final value

    while(*str)                              // Loop while not /0
        value = 10*value +(*(str++)-'0');    // Add in digit value
}
```

This should be very easy to follow by now. Within the loop we subtract the character '0' from whatever the character is that is pointed to by **str**. This means that '0' will produce 0, '1' will produce 1, and so on. The contents of **value** are shifted left one decimal place by multiplying by 10 and the digit value is added in. This is repeated for as many digits as there are in the string, since the loop continues until **str** is pointing at '/0'.

You can use a similar approach for values containing a decimal point. Again, refer back to the calculator program to see how this can be done.

When you have a string containing multiple values, perhaps of different types, life gets a little more complicated and you need some help.

String Stream Processing

As well as supporting keyboard input under DOS, C++ stream I/O provides the ability to read and process data from a buffer in memory and we can use this under Windows. This requires the file **STRSTREA.H** to be included in your program. This operates in two steps. The first step defines the buffer in memory, which contains the input, to the stream operation. The second step is to read the buffer using standard stream input. We can illustrate how this works with a simple example.

Suppose we have obtained a string, **String**, through an input dialog, and suppose further that it contains three values, a value of type **int**, a floating point value of type **double** and a value of type **long**. The following code fragment shows how it could be processed:

```
#include <streastrea.h>
....
int number = 0;           // Variable to receive int value
double value = 0.0;       // Variable to receive double input
long bignum = 0L;         // Variable to receive long input
```

```
// Set String as source of input
// 'ins' is the string stream
istrstream ins(String, strlen(String) );

// Read and convert data from buffer String
ins >> number >> value >> bignum;
...
```

As you can see, step one sets the source of data as **String** and step two uses normal stream input but with the source as **ins** instead of **cin**. You can use this technique for converting data for any of the standard types.

Using File Dialogs

Most programs need to be able to read from, and write data to, external files on disk. If you think about the implications of programming this in the context of Windows, there are several things to consider.

Firstly, we need to have some dialogs available which support all the mechanisms that are normally required when using files. We need to be able to open files, save files and possibly use a 'save as' mechanism where we can provide a new file name. We also need to be able to browse through directories in order to choose the file we want to work with.

Secondly, we need to use the file support functions supported by Windows, since we have to assume there may be other programs running alongside our application, and that they may also be trying to access the same files. We need to be sure, for example, that if we are reading a file, there is no other program writing the file at the same time. Otherwise, we could get a certain amount of confusion.

Thirdly, since we are taking the object-oriented route to solving our problems, being able to perform read and write operations on a file with the standard data types will not be enough. We need to be able to read and write our own data types - the objects of our classes.

We will look into all three of these aspects and treat each of them in turn. The context we will use is the last drawing program example. The objective now is to extend it to allow a drawing to be saved in a file and subsequently retrieved.

The TFileDialog Class

As we have frequently found, in providing the basic mechanism for providing the user of our program with a dialog for file operations, the OWL comes to the rescue. The OWL provides a specialized class derived from **TDialog** called **TFileDialog** which provides a complete interface mechanism for file operations. Note this is only for the communications with the user - it has nothing to do with the read and write operations on the file. We will discuss that separately.

The constructor for **TFileDialog** accepts three arguments: a pointer to a parent window (which in our case will be the application window), a resource identifier for the dialog and a string variable. The string can contain a file name or a default setting for the file name in the dialog box, as we shall see. Since the resource dialog is also defined within the OWL, we can use one of two standard resource identifiers in the constructor call: either **SD_FILEOPEN** to open a file or **SD_FILESAVE** to save a file.

The string variable supplied as the last argument to the constructor can contain a default file designation for file open operations, such as *.*. This will cause all files to be displayed in a list in the dialog box. By specifying a partial file mask, *.txt for example, only the names of files with the extension specified will appear in the dialog. For a Save As dialog, you can also specify a default file designation, or it may contain an empty string.

A file dialog is usually modal, so the dialog is created and executed using the function **ExecDialog()** which is a member of the class **TApplication**. Thus the typical way to use a **TFileDialog** object is within an **if** statement similar to that used for the input dialog we saw earlier in this chapter. To create an open file dialog box, we could write this, for example:

```
char FileName[50];
...
strcpy(FileName, "*,drw");            // Set file mask

if(GetApplication()->ExecDialog(new TFileDialog(this,
   SD_FILEOPEN, FileName)) == IDOK)
{
   // Read the file here
}
```

This dialog provides for opening files with the extension .**DRW**. An example of the dialog box created by these statement is shown on the following page.

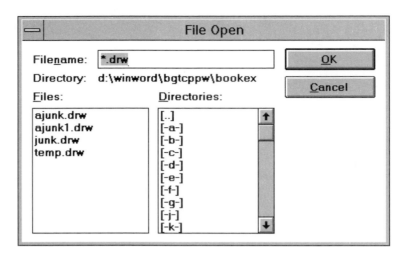

As with the input example, we use the function **GetApplication()**, which is a member of **TGrfxApplication**, to obtain a pointer to our application object, which we then use to call **ExecDialog()** member of our application object. As a result of the mask we set in the char array **FileName[]**, only files with the extension **.DRW** appear in the dialog. Of course, the user could type * . * over the default file name entry, in which case all the file names would appear. The dialog is a fully functional standard windows dialog.

To use this dialog we need to include **FILEDIAL.H** in our program source code, and the resource file **FILEDIAL.DLG** in our resource project file. Of course, we also need to update our resources to include a file menu, so let's take a look at that next.

Adding a File Menu Pop-Up

We will, of course, use Resource Workshop to help us do this. We will make a new resource project file called **DRWG5.RC** into which we can copy the resources we have already created in **DRWG4.RC**, so after starting Resource Workshop, create the new project file and copy the resources from the previous file using the Edit menu facilities. You can flip back and forth between the two files by opening them in turn.

Next, we are going to edit the menu in **DRWG5.RC**, so after opening the file, click on **MENU_1** to bring up the menu creation and editing window. Then, click on Menu in the main menu. It should look like the window shown on the following page.

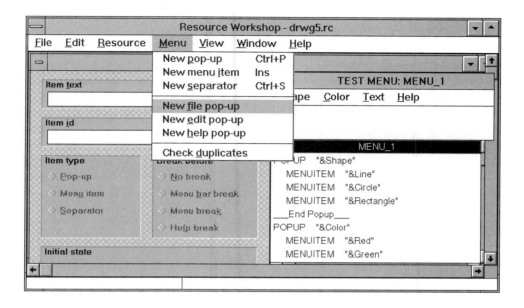

If you click on the New file pop-up option, a complete File menu will be inserted at the beginning of the file. All you now need to do is to work through each of the new menu items, assigning identifiers to the ones you want to use. We will only use Open..., New, Save, and Save as..., so you can ignore the others. Note that the Separator item just causes a line to be drawn in the pop-up to separate one group of items from another. It couldn't really have been much easier, could it? All that's now required is to save the project file.

We are ready to look at how we read and write a file under Windows now.

File Input/Output

A file is referenced using a file handle, which is an **int** value supplied by Windows when you create a file, or open a file. Opening a file is the process of telling Windows that you want to read or write an existing file. The particular file is selected by specifying the file name. We will obtain this using a **TFileDialog** object in our program.

When you have finished with a file you close it. This is the process of telling windows you no longer need the file.

Opening a File

To open an existing file, you use the Windows API function **_lopen()** - and yes, the function name does begin with the underline character. The function **_lopen()** accepts two arguments. The first is a string defining a file name which can be fully qualified - that is with a full DOS path specified - but if you supply just the file name, Windows will look in the current directory for the file. The second argument is a combination of flags which are defined in **WINDOWS.H**, and which specify what you want to do with the file and under what conditions you want to do it. You usually specify two flags OR'd together. One flag specifies that you want to read the file, write the file, or both. These correspond to the predefined identifiers **OF_READ**, **OF_WRITE**, and **OF_READWRITE** respectively. The second flag specifies the sharing option for the file, which can be **OF_SHARE_EXCLUSIVE** for exclusive use of the file, **OF_SHARE_DENY_READ** which prevents anyone else from reading the file, **OF_SHARE_DENY_WRITE** which prevents anyone else from writing the file, and lastly **OF_SHARE_DENY_NONE** which is a complete free for all - anybody can do anything they like with the file.

The **_lopen()** function returns a handle to the file if the operation was successful, and -1 otherwise. This would be a typical operation with the function:

```
int aFile = 0;                              // Declare a file handle
char FileName[50] = "MYFILE.DRW";           // Define a file name
aFile = _lopen( FileName, OF_READ|OF_DENY_WRITE);
```

This call of the function requests opening the file **MYFILE.DRW** in the current directory for reading, and allows other applications to read the file but not to write it. Clearly, someone else reading the file will not give us a problem, but allowing someone else to write to it might well do so.

> *Note that you should now test the value of* **aFile** *for a valid return value, since attempting to continue operations with an invalid file handle will certainly cause problems. Note also that in our example we will omit most error checking code to keep the number of lines of code to the minimum, but in practice you should always include it. If something can go wrong, it certainly will.*

Creating a File

To create a file you use the Windows API function `_lcreat()` - and no, there is no e on the end. It requires two arguments. The first is a string containing the file name, as with the `_lopen()` function, and the second specifies the sort of file to be created. A value of 0 specifies a normal file, a value of 1 specifies a read-only file, a value of 2 specifies a hidden file, and a value of 3 specifies a system file. You will normally use 0.

The `_lcreat()` function has the useful property that, if the file doesn't exist, it will create it, and if it does exist, it will open it. The function returns the file handle if the operation was successful, and -1 otherwise. This is a typical use of this function:

```
int aFile = 0;                              // Declare a file handle
char FileName[50] = "MYFILE.DRW";           // Define a file name
aFile = _lcreat( FileName, 0);
```

This will open or create a normal file with the name **MYFILE.DRW**.

Writing a File

To write a file you can use the Windows API function `_lwrite()`. This requires three arguments: the file handle, a pointer to a string containing the data to be written and a count of the number of bytes to be written. It returns a count of the number of bytes written and -1 if there was an error of some kind.

A typical use of this function can be illustrated by these statements:

```
char Buffer[80];                   // Output buffer
int nBytes = 0;                    // Number of bytes to be written
int aFile = 0;                     // File handle
char FileName[50] = "MYFILE.DRW";  // File name

// Prepare output data...

// Open the file for writing
aFile = _lopen( FileName, OF_WRITE|OF_SHARE_EXCLUSIVE);

if(aFile)                                    // If open was OK
    _lwrite( FileName, Buffer, nBytes );     // Write a record
```

The write operation is only undertaken if the file handle has a positive value. Since we are writing the file, we specify the **OF_SHARE_EXCLUSIVE** flag so we get the file to ourselves. It's a real recipe for trouble if anyone is writing to the file while we are doing the same, or if someone is reading the file while we are writing to it.

When a file has been created or opened, the current position in the file is maintained in a file pointer. The open operation positions the file pointer at the beginning of the file, so we will overwrite the existing contents. If you don't want to do this, you need a means of altering the file pointer.

Moving the File Pointer

Once you have opened a file, you can move the file pointer to a different position in the file using the Windows API function **_llseek()**. This function requires three arguments: the file handle, the number of bytes by which you want to move the file pointer and the reference position to which the second argument is to be applied. The reference position can be specified as 0 which means the beginning of the file, as 1 which means the current position in the file, or as 2 which means the end of the file. The second argument, specifying a number of bytes, is of type **long**.

So to add data to the end of a file you have opened, you would write this statement:

```
long FPosNow = 0L;                         // Current file position
...
FPosNow = _llseek(aFile, 0L, 2);           // Move to end of the file
```

This moves the file pointer to the end of the file. Note that the function returns the current position as a value of type **long**. If you remember the value in **FPosNow**, you can later get back to the same position with this statement:

```
_llseek(aFile, FPosNow, 0);      // Go to old position
```

The value returned is always relative to the beginning of the file.

Reading a File

The function you need to read a file is **_lread()**. This has three arguments which are the same as those for **_lwrite()**: the file handle, a buffer of type **char** to receive the data and the count of the number of bytes to be read.

The actual number of bytes read is returned from the function. So, using the same variable we have defined earlier in this section, this would be a typical read operation:

```
nBytesRead = _lread(aFile, Buffer, nBytes); // Write nBytes to the file
```

A return value of -1 signals an error.

Closing a File

The last function you need which closes a file is **_lclose()**. This requires just one argument, the file handle. Thus to close a file when you have finished with it, you need to write this statement:

```
_lclose( aFile );               // Close the file
```

This closes the file specified by the file handle **aFile**.

Implementing a File Dialog

To implement a file dialog in our drawing program, we have to add the message response functions to our application window class for the menu items in the File menu pop-up that we are interested in. These are New, Open..., Save, and Save as..., and these correspond to the identifiers we defined in our resource file: **CM_NEW**, **CM_OPEN**, **CM_SAVE**, and **CM_SAVEAS**. We also need to add data members to our window class to keep track of the current file name and the current file handle, and both of these will need to be initialized in the constructor for a **TGrfxWindow** object. Let's specify the changes to the class definition first:

```
// Window class to display graphics
class TGrfxWindow: public TWindow
{
   public:
...

        // Menu message response functions
        // for File menu options
        void CMNew(RTMessage) = [CM_FIRST+CM_NEW];
        void CMOpen(RTMessage) = [CM_FIRST+CM_OPEN];
        void CMSave(RTMessage) = [CM_FIRST+CM_SAVE];
        void CMSaveAs(RTMessage) = [CM_FIRST+CM_SAVEAS];

   private:
      // Private members as previously
      // File handle for current file
```

```
        int aFile;

        // Name of the current file
        char FileName[50];
};
```

The message response functions are named and have their dispatch indexes defined exactly as we have seen previously. Although the menu pop-up we created defined a number of other menu items, we need not worry about those. Any that we don't provide message response functions for, will simply do nothing.

The **aFile** data member will enable us to check whether a file is open or not, simply by testing the value stored. This will only work, however, as long as we initialize it to zero at the outset and take care to reset it to zero whenever we close a file. We only need one file at a time. If we needed more, we would need multiple file handles.

You may wonder why we need to record the file name in the class, as well as the file handle. We wouldn't normally leave a file open after we have saved a drawing to it, so we will close the file after each write. However, we will want the save operation to automatically save the current file with its existing name, and saving the file name will enable us to do this.

Changing the Window Class Constructor

The modification to the constructor for the **TGrfxWindow** class is extremely simple. We only need to add two statements to initialize the data members **aFile** and **FileName[]**. These are they:

```
    aFile = 0;                    // Set file handle
    strcpy(FileName,"");          // Set file name to empty
```

We set the file handle to zero, and copy an empty string into **FileName[]** using the standard library function **strcpy()**.

Saving and Restoring Objects

Before we can implement the message response functions for the additional menu items, we need to decide how we are going to save and restore our object. Firstly, let's think about what we know. When we write a file, all we can do is write a buffer, which is a given number of bytes long. There is no intelligence in the process - it's simply passing bytes to an external device. This means we need to define our objects using a standard format within a sequence of bytes, and ideally write the same number of bytes to a file, regardless of what kind of object we are dealing with.

What should the block of bytes for an object contain? The first and most obvious item is a code for an object type. Since we have no way of knowing what sort of object a block of bytes represents, we will need to include a type specifier in a standard place in the block. The rest of the block of bytes will consist of a sequence of values necessary for the creation of the object specified by the type value. All of our geometric shapes are defined by the same basic data: the coordinates of a start point, the coordinates of an end point, and a color. The text object is a little different, being defined by a start point, a color and a string containing the text. So we will represent an object as a block of bytes in one of two possible formats, depending on what it is. The two formats are illustrated here:

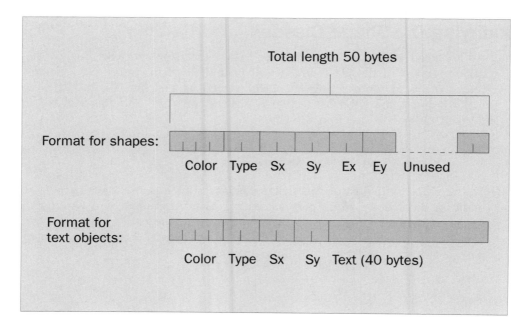

Since we allowed 40 bytes for the text in a **TText** object, we need to allow the same when we write it out, so for a **TText** object we need to allow a total of 50 bytes. We will write the same number of bytes for each object, and just ignore what we don't need.

> *In case you were wondering, the* Color *value is first because it is a 4 byte value. The other items are 2 byte values or text, so putting it first avoids any problems with boundary alignment in memory.*

> *Boundary alignment refers to the process of placing a two byte variable at an even address, a four byte variable at an address which is a multiple of four bytes, and an eight byte variable at an address which is a multiple of eight bytes. This is necessary to ensure that data is moved at an optimum speed to and from memory.*

Since we don't know what objects have been created, we will have to arrange that each class of object to be displayed contains a function which will supply the defining data for that object as a string. This function will also have to be declared as virtual in the base class, **TDispObject**, to enable us to call the appropriate function for an object automatically through a pointer.

Modifying the Shape Classes

All we need to add to **TDispObject** is a virtual member function in the public section of the class which will be redefined in the derived classes to return the data representing an object, stored as a string. We might as well make it pure, since the base class is abstract anyway, and this will force all derived classes to redefine the function:

```
// Pure virtual function to supply object data
    virtual void GetObjectData(char* pData)=0;
```

The function will fill out the string passed as an argument with the required data. If we don't pass the string as an argument, we would need to create it in the free store, which would mean the calling program would need to be responsible for deleting it. It is easier and less error prone to pass a string owned by the calling program.

Implementing Object Data Creation

How are we going to get various bits of data stored as binary values, unchanged as bytes of a string? Well, here is one example of a good use for a union. With a union we can define a **char** array 50 bytes in length, and specify it as occupying the same memory as some other variable. That takes us half way there. We want to be able to map several variables into various places in the string, so we need something else to help. That something else is a class. We can define a class with public members in the order in which we want the variables defining an object to appear. We can then put an instance of the class in a union with the string. We can then refer to the same bit of memory as individual variables, or a whole string as we wish.

We can define a class for shape data first, which will do specifying data for lines, circles and rectangles:

```
// Class for saving shape data
class ShapeData
{
   public:
      COLORREF Color;
      int Type;
      int Sx;
      int Sy;
      int Ex;
      int Ey;
};
```

This simply has each of the data entities we discussed and illustrated earlier, specified as public members, so we can access them all externally.

We need another class to organize the data for a **TText** object:

```
// Class for saving text data
class TextData
{
   public:
      COLORREF Color;
      int Type;
      int Sx;
      int Sy;
      char String[40];
};
```

This again implements the pattern we specified earlier for the sequence of defining data.

To map the shape data into a string, we can use an anonymous union such as the following to allow a string and an object of the class **ShapeData** to occupy the same memory area:

```
union
{
    char pData[OBJDATA];       // Raw input as bytes
    ShapeData Shape;           // Use this for geometric types

};
```

Now we can refer to individual members of the object **Shape** as **Shape.Sx**, **Shape.Color**, and so on. To store a value within an object into the string in its original form, we just write a statement such as this:

```
Shape.Sx = x;
```

Obtaining Object Data for the Shape Classes

Let's look at the **GetObjectData()** function for the **TLine** class first:

```
// Function to create base data for a line
void TLine::GetObjectData(char* Buffer)
{
    union
    {
        char pData[OBJDATA];       // Raw input as bytes
        ShapeData Shape;           // Use this for geometric types

    };
    Shape.Sx = x;
    Shape.Sy = y;
    Shape.Ex = Endx;
    Shape.Ey = Endy;
    Shape.Color = Color;
    Shape.Type = line;
    for(int i=0 ; i<OBJDATA ; i++)
        Buffer[i] = pData[i];
}
```

Once we have cottoned on to using a class object within a union, creating the string to be written to the file becomes simple. We have a union between a local string, **pData[]**, and a local object of the **ShapeData** class. We then copy each of the data items we need to define the object individually, set the type as **line**, and then copy the local string to the string passed as an argument, and we are done.

The **TRectangle** version is much the same:

```
// Function to create base data for a rectangle
void TRectangle::GetObjectData(char* Buffer)
{
   union
   {
      char pData[OBJDATA];          // Raw input as bytes
      ShapeData Shape;              // Use this for geometric types

   };
   Shape.Sx = x;
   Shape.Sy = y;
   Shape.Ex = Endx;
   Shape.Ey = Endy;
   Shape.Color = Color;
   Shape.Type = rectangle;
   for(int i=0 ; i<OBJDATA ; i++)
      Buffer[i] = pData[i];
}
```

In fact, the only difference here is that we set the type value to **rectangle**. The defining data elements are exactly the same. The type values **line**, **rectangle**, **circle**, and **text** which we defined in an enumeration, will be unique values for each shape, and by using the enumeration entries, the program is a bit more readable.

The function for a **TCircle** object is different, but not by very much:

```
// Function to create base data for a circle
void TCircle::GetObjectData(char* Buffer)
{
   union
   {
      char pData[OBJDATA];          // Raw input as bytes
      ShapeData Shape;              // Use this for geometric types

   };
   Shape.Sx = x;
   Shape.Sy = y;
   Shape.Ex = x+Radius;
   Shape.Ey = y;
   Shape.Color = Color;
   Shape.Type = circle;
   for(int i=0 ; i<OBJDATA ; i++)
      Buffer[i] = pData[i];
}
```

We need to deduce the coordinates for a point on the circumference of the circle, because that is what the constructor expects. The simplest way to do this is to add the **Radius** to either coordinate of the center of the circle. We have chosen the x coordinate here, but we could equally well have used the y coordinate. The rest of the function is the same as the others.

The function in the **TText** class is as follows:

```
// Function to create base data for a text object
void TText::GetObjectData(char* Buffer)
{
   union
   {
      char pData[OBJDATA];        // Raw input as bytes
      TextData Text;              // Use this for geometric types

   };
   Text.Sx = x;
   Text.Sy = y;
   strcpy(Text.String, String);
   Text.Color = Color;
   Text.Type = text;
   for(int i=0 ; i<OBJDATA ; i++)
      Buffer[i] = pData[i];
}
```

The only differences here are that an object of the class **TextData** appears in the union and we copy the **String** value from the **TText** object using the library function **strcpy()**. You might be tempted to use **strcpy()** to copy the contents of **pData[]** to **Buffer** here. This would be a serious mistake. Remember that some of our data here is not string data and will be very likely to contain a byte with '\0'. This will stop the copying process prematurely, so you will end up with garbage in much of **Buffer**. You would find out about it when you get round to reading the file back.

Recreating Shape Objects

We will need a function to recreate objects from blocks of data read from a file. This will need to deduce what the object is, and then call the constructor for the object specified using the data from the string read from the file. We won't know in advance which kind of object we are getting, so we will need to create a union containing the string and both objects specifying the possible data arrangements for an object. The code to do this is as follows:

```
// Function to create an object from base data
void TGrfxWindow::CreateObject(char* Buffer)
{
    union
    {
        char pData[OBJDATA];        // Raw input as bytes
        TextData Text;              // Use this for text type
        ShapeData Shape;            // Use this for geometric types
    };

    for(int i = 0 ; i<OBJDATA ; i++)
        pData[i] = Buffer[i];                  // Copy data passed to union

    if(Text.Type == text)                      // Test for text object
        new TText(Text.Sx, Text.Sy,
                    cxChar, cyChar, Text.String, Text.Color);
    else
    {
        switch(Shape.Type)
        {
            case line:                              // Create a line
                new TLine(Shape.Sx, Shape.Sy,
                            Shape.Ex, Shape.Ey, Shape.Color);
                break;

            case rectangle:                         // Create a rectangle
                new TRectangle(Shape.Sx, Shape.Sy,
                                Shape.Ex, Shape.Ey, Shape.Color);
                break;

            case circle:                            // Create a circle
                new TCircle(Shape.Sx, Shape.Sy,
                            Shape.Ex, Shape.Ey, Shape.Color);
                break;

            default:                        // Error if we reach here
                // Draw a long red line
                new TLine(0, 0, 400, 400,RGB(255,0,0));
        }
    }
}
```

After declaring the local union, the first action is to copy the string passed to the function into the string **pData** which is a member of the union. We can then refer to individual elements held in the string using the member of the class objects in the union.

573

The first check on the data is for a text type. If it *is* a text type, we construct a text object using the **TextData** object members, and we are finished. If it *isn't* text, it should be one of the three shape types, so the type, **Shape.Type**, is used as the switch selector. We could equally well have used **Text.Type** as they both refer to the same memory location. We have included the default entry in the switch to catch errors. Unless something goes seriously wrong, we should never reach this point.

The function has been implemented as a member of the class **TGrxWindow**. This is necessary because it needs to access the protected data members **cxChar** and **cyChar** when constructing a **TText** object.

Implementing the Message Response Functions

Let's take **CM_New()** first, since it is the easiest. We will implement it as a mechanism to reset the current drawing to blank, so it won't involve any file operations at all. It will simply delete any current objects which exist. We already do this in the destructor for **TGrfxWindow**, so if we take the code from there and put it in a new static function in the base class **TDispObject**, we can call it from anywhere. A good name for it would be **DeleteAll()**:

```
// Function to delete all objects
void TDispObject::DeleteAll(void)
{
    TDispObject* pLast = TDispObject::GetLast();// Get tail of object chain
    TDispObject* pNext = pLast;                 // Save last as next

    while (pNext)                               // As long as next pointer is not 0
    {
        pNext = pLast->GetPrev();               // Save pointer to previous object
        delete pLast;                           // Delete current object
        pLast = pNext;                          // Set current to previous
    }
    TDispObject::pLast = 0;                      // Reset pointer to last in base
}
```

This is almost identical to what was originally in the destructor for **TGrfxWindow**. The only point worth noting here is the use of **TDispObject** as a qualifier to reference the data member **pLast** in the last statement. This is because it would otherwise be hidden by the local pointer of the same name.

The destructor now only contains two statements:

```
// Destructor definition - this needs to delete display
// objects allocated on the free store
TGrfxWindow::~TGrfxWindow()
{
  TDispObject::DeleteAll();             // Delete all objects
  if(aFile)_lclose(aFile);             // If a file is open, close it
}
```

It would have been just one statement, but now that we are working with a file, we should make sure it's closed whenever we close the main window.

The code for the message response function is also very brief:

```
// Message response function for File/New
void TGrfxWindow::CMNew(RTMessage)
{
    TDispObject::DeleteAll();          // Delete everything
    InvalidateRect(HWindow,0,TRUE);    // Redraw the window
}
```

After calling the static function `DeleteAll()` in `TDispObject` to delete any displayed objects we have, we redraw the client area to make sure it is blank.

The File Open Message Response Function

The basic task of this function will be to create and execute the appropriate file dialog, and obtain the name of the file to be opened. Once a file name has been entered, the function then needs to read the data from the file and create a new set of objects. This can be done by reading the string of length `OBJDATA` from the file, and passing this to the member function `CreateObject()` to do the detailed work. The code for the `CMOpen()` function will therefore be this:

```
// Message response function for File/Open
void TGrfxWindow::CMOpen(RTMessage)
{
   char pData[OBJDATA];
   int nBytes = 0;

   strcpy(FileName, "*.drw");

   // Display dialog
```

```
if(GetApplication()->ExecDialog(
   new TFileDialog(this, SD_FILEOPEN, FileName ))
   == IDOK)
{
   aFile = _lopen(FileName, OF_READ|OF_SHARE_DENY_WRITE);// Open file

   do
   {
      nBytes = _lread(aFile, pData, OBJDATA);   // Read an object record
      if(nBytes)
         CreateObject(pData);            // Create an object if we read data
   }while(nBytes);

   _lclose(aFile);                       // We are done - so close the file
   aFile = 0;                            // Reset the file handle
   InvalidateRect(HWindow,0,TRUE);       // Redraw the window
}
}
```

We have defined a local variable **pData[]** to hold the input as we read it, and a variable **nBytes** to record the number of bytes read. We don't know how many objects have been written to the file, so we will use the number of bytes read to determine when there are no more objects to be read. We will continue to read objects until we execute a read that results in a byte count of zero.

We have assigned the file mask as ***.DRW**, assuming **.DRW** is the extension for our drawing files. However, if the user chooses something else, it won't matter. We create and execute the open dialog using the **ExecDialog()** member of our application class. The option **SD_FILEOPEN** will determine that the open dialog is created. There are two possible return values from **ExecDialog()** depending on whether the user clicks the OK button to exit, or the Cancel button. We are only interested in the **IDOK** return value, since this will indicate a file name has been specified. If the OK button was not selected, we do nothing.

Assuming the OK button was selected, we read the file in the **do while** loop. This reads a string from the file, and assuming some positive number of bytes were read, we call the function **CreateObject()** to regenerate the object specified in the string. The number of bytes read controls whether the loop continues. When the byte count is zero, no object is created and the loop ends.

The File Save Message Response Function

The save operation has two modes of execution. If a file has been opened or saved to previously, then the current drawing will be saved to that file. This can be determined by checking the contents of the data member `FileName[]`. If no file has been referenced previously, then the function needs to execute a dialog for entering a file name for a save operation. The code for the function is as follows:

```
// Message response function for File/Save
void TGrfxWindow::CMSave(RTMessage)
{
  char pData[OBJDATA];          // Object data buffer
  if(!strlen(FileName))
  {
    strcpy(FileName, "*.drw");            // No file so set mask
    // Display dialog
    if( !GetApplication()->ExecDialog(
        new TFileDialog(this, SD_FILESAVE, FileName ))
      == IDOK)
      return;
  }

  aFile =_lcreat(FileName,0);                 // Create a file

  // Get tail of object chain
  TDispObject* pNext = TDispObject::GetLast();

  while (pNext)                         // As long as next pointer is not 0
  {
    pNext->GetObjectData(pData);    // Get definition data for object
    _lwrite(aFile, pData, OBJDATA); // Write to file
    pNext = pNext->GetPrev();       // Get the next in the chain
  }
  _lclose(aFile);                   // Close the file
  aFile = 0;                        // Reset the file handle
}
```

We only need to create and execute a dialog if the data member `FileName[]` doesn't contain a file name. We check this by obtaining its length. If the length is zero, no file name has been stored, so we create and execute a file dialog using the SD_FILESAVE option. If we don't get OK back from the dialog we return, since we don't have the name of a file to save to.

Assuming we get a file name one way or another, we use the `_lcreat()` function to access it. This will open the file if it exists, and create a new one if it doesn't, so it works in any event. (But not if the disk is full - we should really check the return value.)

We then work through the objects we have in the `while` loop, starting with the last, the pointer for which is obtained using the static member of `TDispObject`, `GetLast()`. Using the pointer for each object, we call the `GetObjectData()` for the object using the pointer to the object to access the function. The string supplied is then written to the file.

When we find a null object pointer, we have written all the objects we have to the file, so the loop ends. We then close the file and reset the file handle, `aFile`, back to zero. The file name is retained in the data member `FileName[]`, so a succeeding save operation will write to the same file.

The Save As Message Response Function

Now we have written the save message response function, the Save As function is easy. It always opens a dialog before saving the object to the file, so it works essentially the same way as the save operation, when no file has been accessed previously. This will therefore be the code for this function:

```
// Message response function for File/SaveAs
void TGrfxWindow::CMSaveAs(RTMessage)
{
   char pData[50];
   if(!strlen(FileName))
      strcpy(FileName, "temp.drw");
   // Display dialog
   if( GetApplication()->ExecDialog(
         new TFileDialog(this, SD_FILESAVE, FileName ))
                                          == IDOK)
   {
     aFile = _lcreat(FileName,0);                // Create a new file
     TDispObject* pNext=TDispObject::GetLast();// Get tail of object chain

     while (pNext)                     // As long as next pointer is not 0
     {
        pNext->GetObjectData(pData);    // Get definition data for object
        _lwrite(aFile, pData, OBJDATA); // Write to file
        pNext = pNext->GetPrev();       // Get the next in the chain
     }
```

```
      _lclose(aFile);                          // Close the file
      aFile = 0;                               // Reset file handle
   }
}
```

The only significant difference with this message response function is that, if there is a file name stored in `FileName[]`, this is used as the default name in the input field in the dialog. If there is no previous file name, the name `TEMP.DRW` is used as the default. The remainder of the code for the function is the same as that for the save operation.

Try It Out - The Complete Program

The only other changes required to create a complete example is to add an `#include` statement for `FILEDIAL.H` to our program and add an `#include` statement for `FILEDIAL.DLG` to the resource project file.

This example is complete on the disk in the files `EX13-03.CPP`, `DRWDLG3.CPP`, `DRWDLG3.H` and `DRWG5.RC` as the resource project file.

If you run the example you can get a window which looks this.

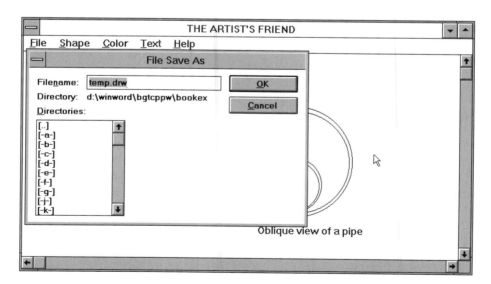

How It Works

Once you have drawn something you can save it using the File/Save or File/ Save As... menu options. You can access the menu items using the mouse, or by holding down the *Alt* key and pressing the appropriate accelerator keys. To erase the current drawing you can select New from the File pop-up.

Note that the Save function can work as a merge operation. Whatever is read from the file is added to any objects that already exist. Thus you can use the File/Open option to read any number of files successively, and end up with the current drawing containing the objects from all the files read. Of course, if you don't want to combine the contents of a file with the current drawing data, you just need to select New before you choose Open.

> *Remember that this program contains virtually no checking for error conditions. To convert it to a robust working program you would need to add error checking and recovery code wherever interaction with the user occurs, and whenever you open, create, read or write a file.*

Summary

In this chapter we have covered some of the ways in which dialogs can be used to communicate with a user, and one way in which file operations can be implemented. This is by no means an exhaustive treatment of the possibilities, either in the OWL, or in the Windows API. You should try more of the options available for dialog creation in Resource Workshop, and the creation of dialog objects using the `TDialog` class.

If you look at the last example we have created in its entirety, you will see that it is quite a sophisticated program approaching 1000 lines of source code. I hope you will also agree that the process of creating it was relatively straightforward. There are certainly a lot of different elements which make up the program, but in most instances we were able to treat them as largely independent, the major unifying factor in the application being the main application window class. Taking an object-oriented approach to the problem is also helpful in segmenting the problem into fairly self-contained and manageable chunks. You should try to exercise this approach further with a few examples of your own.

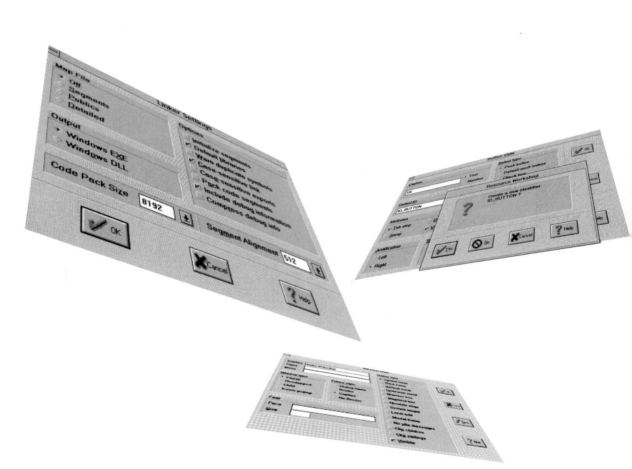

Using Controls

Controls are things which you can add to a window to provide a wide variety of ways for a user to communicate with a program. A button such as the OK button is a control; so is a scroll bar. In Windows, controls are just windows designed for a specific purpose, so you have to do all the work in managing and communicating with them. The OWL makes life very much easier by providing a set of classes for control objects. These include default behavior and automatic creation of the visible window element for the controls.

In this chapter you will learn about:

- Which controls are supported by the OWL
- Using controls in a child window
- Implementing a list box in an example
- Combo boxes and how to create them
- Using scroll bars
- Creating and using radio buttons
- Grouping radio buttons using a group box
- Using control objects in a dialog

Controls Supported by the OWL

All the control objects supported by the OWL are defined in classes derived from the OWL class `TControl`. `TControl` provides basic behavior for control objects, and since controls are windows anyway, it is derived from `TWindow`. You won't need to use `TControl` directly, since the derived classes will provide you with everything you need. The classes provided by the OWL for controls, and the specific kinds of control operations that they support, are as follows:

Controls	Operations Supported
`TButton:`	A button with text, similar to the button we used in a dialog. Typically, these are used to signal a terminating action with an input operation, such as OK or Cancel, but they can also be used as command buttons to start specific operations which can be indicated by the text on the button.
`TCheckBox:`	A box which can be checked or unchecked with a cross. This is used to select an item, and within a group of check boxes, several may be checked at one time. These are typically used to select any of number of options in a program.
`TRadioButton:`	Similar to a check box, this is also used to select an item, but selection is denoted by a filled circle. Radio buttons are usually used in groups where only one can be selected at any one time. The OWL supports this behavior automatically. We will use radio buttons to select color in our drawing program.
`TGroupBox:`	A rectangle with title text which is used to group other controls such as radio buttons and check boxes. In order to get automatic operation with radio which ensures only one selection, radio buttons need to be in a group box.
`TStatic:`	A fixed text field which can't be altered by the user.

Continued

Controls	Operations Supported
TListBox:	A box supporting a scrollable list of text items from which the user can select. We will demonstrate the use of a list box to select the type of shape in our drawing program.
TEdit:	An input field where a user can enter text. This is used for any kind of general input from the keyboard.
TComboBox:	A combination of a list box and an edit control.
TScrollBar:	A standalone scroll bar which is similar in appearance to the window scrollers we have already seen. With a scroll bar, you can use the scroll action to affect anything you like - to increase or decrease the value of a variable, for instance.

The relationships between the controls classes is shown in the following figure. The arrow heads in the figure point to base classes.

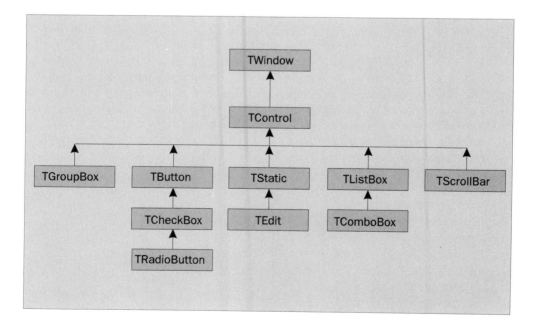

All these classes are intended to be used to create control objects inside a window. Don't confuse these with controls inside a dialog. When we created a dialog for the About menu option, the button control was defined in the resource file for the dialog. There was no object in the program corresponding to the button. With dialogs constructed with the **TDialog** class, the physical controls can be defined by the resource file, and these are managed by response functions in the class you derive from **Tdialog**. When we use control objects in this chapter, we will create objects corresponding to the controls within a child window, and the physical appearance of the control will be taken care of by the control object. No resource file is necessary for this.

Note that it is also possible to use control objects with a dialog. In this case, the physical appearance of a control is defined by a resource file, but you have the advantage of an object and its member functions corresponding to the control for managing communications with the user.

Creating Control Objects

To use control objects, you will typically create a child window which will manage a particular communication, and you create the control objects required within the constructor for the child window. This is not mandatory, of course. You are perfectly free to create control objects within your application main window, if you wish.

The control objects you construct in a window are owned by it, and they are automatically destroyed when the window is destroyed. You don't need to save pointers to any of the control objects you create unless you need to access their members during program execution. You don't even need to call **GetApplication()->MakeWindow()** for them, since they will automatically be created by their parent window once you have instantiated the control objects in their parent window constructor.

Some controls require values to be set after they have been created. List boxes, for example, usually need to have the list entries filled in. You mustn't attempt to do this within the window constructor. At this point, the control object hasn't yet been properly constructed. Where you need to perform some setup processing for a control, you can implement this in the **SetupWindow()** member function of the parent window. It is essential that you call **SetupWindow()** for the base class **TWindow** if you do this, otherwise your main window will not be constructed properly.

Implementing a List Box

Let's get straight down to a practical example of using controls. We will modify our drawing program to use a list box for the selection of the type of shape to be drawn, rather than a menu. This won't necessarily improve the program, but it will give us a chance to see how a control works in a practical context. We will use the last example in the previous chapter as the basis for the new version.

Defining a Child Window

The first thing we can do is to develop a child window class to manage the communications with the user. We will construct the list box within the child window as a **TListBox** object, and provide all the dialog with the user within this window. We will also create a **TButton** object to allow the user to close the window. The child window will also need to be able to communicate the shape selected to the main window, so we will need to work out how we can arrange for that to operate.

Since we will need to initialize the list box with text items, we will introduce our own version of the member function, **SetupWindow()**, which is inherited from **TWindow**. We will also include a pointer to our **TListBox** object in the class definition which we can use in the **SetupWindow()** function. We will also need a function to respond to choosing a shape from the list box and a function to close the window when the button is clicked.

To communicate with the application main window, we can use the pointer to the parent which is usually passed as the first argument to the constructor of a child window. Since we will want to use a function which we will add to the main window class, we will need to store the pointer as a pointer to a **TGrfxWindow** object, rather than as of type **PTWindowsObject**, because a base class pointer can only access members of the base class.

Let's write the definition for the class - we can call it **TShapeWindow**:

```
// Shape window class
class TShapeWindow:public TWindow
{
   public:
      // Constructor
      TShapeWindow(TGrfxWindow* aParent, LPSTR aName);
```

```
        // Function to initialize control objects as necessary
        void SetupWindow(void);

        // Function to handle list box event
        void HandleListBoxMsg(RTMessage)=[ID_FIRST + ID_LISTBOX];

        // Function to process button click
        void IDButton(RTMessage) = [ID_FIRST+ID_BUTTON1];

    protected:
        // List box pointer
        TListBox* pLBox;

        // Pointer to the parent window
        TGrfxWindow* TheParent;
};
```

In the constructor, the first argument for the parent window pointer is of type pointer to **TGrfxWindow** rather than **TWindowsObject** (which is used in the constructor for **TWindow**). This will enable us to save the derived class pointer in a member of our child window class, **TheParent**, and use the pointer to call a function in the parent window object to set the member **Shape** based on the input from the list box.

The **SetupWindow()** member function is called automatically when an instance of our child class is created. We will use this function to set the list of items in the list box which we will create.

Creating a List Box

We will create a list box by instantiating an object of the OWL class **TListBox**. We will need to add this statement:

```
#include <listbox.h>    // For list box controls
```

The constructor for a **TListBox** object which we will use has seven parameters, but we will ignore the last one as it has a default value set that will do for most purposes. The arguments to the constructor that we will supply are: a pointer to the parent window, a control ID which we will specify in a **#define** statement, the x and y coordinates of the position of the list box in the parent window's client area, and the width and height of the list box. We could use the following statement to construct a **TListBox** object:

```
    // Create list box object
    pLBox = new TListBox(this, ID_LISTBOX,10,10,180,70);
```

This assumes we also have the definition for the identifier **ID_LISTBOX** somewhere, so we will need to add this at a suitable point in the program:

```
#define ID_LISTBOX 801
```

As with other identifiers we have defined, the number is arbitrary, but the number assigned to each identifier in a program which is used to reference a resource or a control needs to be unique.

The list box created will be positioned at the point 10,10 in the parent window (which will be our child window **TShapeWindow**), and it will have a width and height of 180 and 70 pixels, respectively.

> *These values are chosen to provide an appropriate size and position for my display resolution, which happens to be 1024x768. If your display is different then you will need to adjust these values to suit. For standard VGA, for example, the list box will be too large. In this case, you would need to reduce the width and height by about a third. This applies to all of the child windows and controls we will be creating in this chapter.*

The default attributes of a **TListBox** object (stored in its **Attr** data member), are: **LBS_SORT** which specifies that its items are to be maintained in alphabetical order, **LBS_NOTIFY** which specifies that it will notify its parent window when events occur, **WS_BORDER** which specifies that a border should be present and **WS_VSCROLL** which specifies that the list box should have a vertical scroll bar. You can reset any of these by ANDing the complement (produced by the ~ operator) of the attribute you want to change with **Attr.Style**. For example, if you don't want the list box items sorted, you could add the following statement after the constructor call:

```
pLBox->Attr.Style &= ~LBS_SORT;        // Turn off item sorting
```

Creating a Button

We can add a button to our child window to allow it to be closed. This will require an **#include** statement for **BUTTON.H** in our program. We can create an object of the **TButton** class in the constructor for **TShapeWindow** to do this. The constructor for a **TButton** object which we need to use has all of nine parameters, of which we will specify eight, the last having a default value. The first two are the same as that of a **TListBox** constructor: a pointer to the parent window and an identifier. We will use **ID_BUTTON1** as the identifier. The next parameter is a text string specifying what is to be written on the button. We will specify it as OK. The next four parameters specify the coordinates of the position of the button in the client area of the window, followed by the width and height of the button. We finally have a parameter of type **BOOL** which specifies the push-button as of default type if it is **TRUE**. A default push button has a thick border and represents the default action of the window if the user presses the *Enter* key - pressing *Enter* becomes equivalent to clicking the button. A window must only have one default button. A normal button - that is, a non-default button - has a thin border.

We will create the **TButton** in **TShapeWindow** with the following statement:

```
new TButton(this,ID_BUTTON1,"OK",80,90,40,35,TRUE); // Create button object
```

We don't need to save the pointer to the object in the free store, as we won't need to refer to it specifically. The message to respond to a button press will be identified by a dispatch index specified using the identifier **ID_BUTTON1**. The object will be automatically destroyed when its parent window is destroyed. The button will be positioned at the point 80,90 in our child window, and will be 40 pixels wide and 35 pixels high. Again, you may need to adjust all of these values to suit your particular display resolution.

We can write the constructor for the child window next.

Constructing the Child Window

The constructor for the child window needs to call the base class constructor, as with other window classes derived from **TWindow**. It will also need to save the pointer to its parent. The code for the constructor will therefore be as follows:

```
// Constructor for child window for shape selection
TShapeWindow::TShapeWindow(TGrfxWindow* aParent, LPSTR aName)
            :TWindow(PTWindowsObject(aParent),aName)
{
   TheParent = aParent;              // Save pointer to parent
```

```
    // Create list box object
    pLBox = new TListBox(this, ID_LISTBOX,10,10,180,70);

    // Create button object
    new TButton(this,ID_BUTTON1,"OK",80,90,40,35,TRUE);
}
```

Note that in the call to the base class constructor, we need to convert the pointer to the parent class from type pointer to TGrfxWindow, to a PTWindowsObject type, since this is what the TWindow constructor requires. This conversion is no problem because the class TWindowsObject is an indirect base of the parent class, TGrfxWindow. Conversion in the opposite direction would not work.

After storing the pointer in the child window member **TheParent**, we construct the list box and the button as we have described.

We can't add text items to the list box here, as it doesn't yet exist. It will be properly created on completing execution of the constructor for the child window. The inherited member function **SetupWindow()** will be called immediately after the constructor has been executed, so to add the list items to the list box, we need to provide our own version of **SetupWindow()** in **TShapeWindow()**, which also calls the base version of the function. We can write this function as follows:

```
// Initializing list box members
void TShapeWindow::SetupWindow(void)
{
    TWindow::SetupWindow();              // Call base function

    // Put entries in list box
    pLBox->AddString("Circle");          // Add Circle to the list
    pLBox->AddString("Line");            // Add Line to the list
    pLBox->AddString("Rectangle");       // Add Rectangle to the list
}
```

After calling the base class version of the function, we use the function **AddString()** which is a member of the **TListBox** class to add the list items we want. We use the pointer to the list box, **pLBox**, to call the function. If we didn't save the pointer when we constructed the list box, we wouldn't be able to initialize the list.

Responding to Messages in the Child Window

We need to deal with two events in the child window class: a click on a list box item, and a click on the OK button. In the definition of **TShapeWindow**, we include this function as a public member of the class:

```
// Function to process button click
void IDButton(RTMessage) = [ID_FIRST+ID_BUTTON1];
```

The dispatch index is defined by adding the identifier we specified in the constructor for the **TButton** object to **ID_FIRST**, so button clicks will be serviced by this member of our child window class.

The function action is very simple - to close the child window. We can do this by calling the member function **CloseWindow()**. Thus we can code the function with just one statement:

```
// Function to process button click
void IDButton(RTMessage)
{ CloseWindow(); }            // Just close the window...
```

> *Since this is a one line function, we would do better to define the function completely within the class definition, and this is how it appears in the example on the disk.*

To service the message created when an item in the list box is clicked, we include a function in the **TShapeWindow** class definition:

```
// Function to handle list box event
void HandleListBoxMsg(RTMessage)=[ID_FIRST + ID_LISTBOX];
```

Again, we use the identifier appearing in the constructor call to specify the dispatch index for the function.

When an event occurs in the list box, the message response function will be called and the **RTMessage** argument passed will indicate what kind of event it was. The **LP.Hi** member of the argument can contain one of three values. The value **LBN_SETFOCUS** means that the list box was selected with the mouse to activate it. The value **LBN_DBLCLK** indicates that an item was selected with a double click. The value that we will look for is **LBN_SELCHANGE**, which indicates that a list item has been selected with a single mouse click. Let's take a look at how the function works:

```
// Function to process list box messages
void TShapeWindow::HandleListBoxMsg(RTMessage Msg )
{
   if(Msg.LP.Hi == LBN_SELCHANGE)
   {
     switch( pLBox->GetSelIndex())              // Choose shape based of
     {                                          // List box item selected
        case 0:
           TheParent->SetShape(circle);    // Call parent member to set
           break;                          // shape as circle
        case 1:
           TheParent->SetShape(line);      // ...or as line
           break;
        case 2:
           TheParent->SetShape(rectangle); // ...or as rectangle
           break;
     }
   }
}
```

Assuming **Msg.LP.Hi** contains the value we are looking for, we obtain an index to the list box item clicked by calling the function **GetSelIndex()** in the **TListBox** object. Each item in the list has an index value just like a regular C++ array, so the first item in the list has the index 0, the second has the index 1, and so on. Since our items will be in alphabetical order, the index values 0,1 and 2, will correspond to the Circle, Line and Rectangle items, respectively. The **switch** statement calls a **SetShape()** function in the parent window **TGrfxWindow**, to set the current shape according to the index value obtained.

With a small number of items in a fixed list such as this, we don't need any further verification of what was selected. However, where you have a list which may have items added dynamically, you may need to access the specific text string which was clicked on, particularly when the items in the list are being sorted alphabetically. **TListBox** contains a number of functions to enable you to query the list. For example, once you know the index for a list item, you could call the function **GetString()**. This function has two arguments: a pointer to a buffer to receive a string, and the index of the list item you want copied to the location specified by the first argument. A typical use of the function **GetString()** is illustrated by this statement where **Buffer** is a **char** array:

```
   pLBox->GetString(Buffer, Index );      // Get specified string
```

The function returns the length of the string, or a negative value if an error occurs.

Alternatively, you could use another member function, **GetSelString()**, in the message response function instead of **GetSelIndex()**. This function will retrieve the string selected and store it in the buffer specified by the first argument, up to the limit on the number of characters copied, as specified by the second argument. You would use this in a statement such as this:

```
pLBox->GetSelString(Buffer, sizeof(Buffer) );    // Get selected string
```

The second argument serves to ensure that you don't exceed the capacity of **Buffer**. This statement would typically be used in a message response function for a list box. The function also returns the length of the string copied to **Buffer**, or a negative value in the event of an error.

There are other functions which are very useful for accessing and modifying a list in various ways, and which you can find details on through the TCW Help facility.

Modifying the Menu Response

We no longer need all the pop-up menu items for Shape in the main menu, and we need to convert Shape to a menu item. Rather than going back to Resource Workshop, we could edit the resource file in the TCW IDE. If you retrieve **DRWG5.RC** into the IDE its contents will be as shown below.

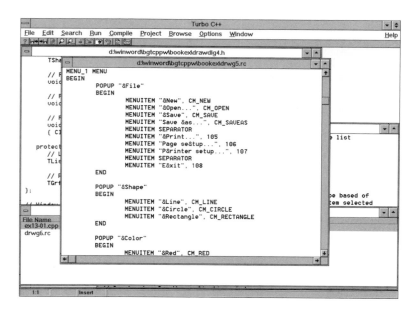

As you can see, the Shape pop-up is defined by a **POPUP** command and all the items in the pop-up are specified between **BEGIN** and **END**. The identifiers for each menu item appear after the comma in the definition of the item. We need to change this line:

```
POPUP "&Shape"
```

into a menu item for the main menu and add a suitable identifier to be associated with it, so it should be this:

```
MENUITEM "&Shape", CM_SHAPE
```

We then need to delete all the menu items that were included in the Shape pop-up. This corresponds to all the statements following the line we have just modified, between and including **BEGIN** and **END**. That's all that is necessary here. We can now save the modified file as **DRWG6.RC**. Of course, we will need to add the **#define** for the identifier **CM_SHAPE** somewhere, either at the beginning of our source code, or in a revised version of the file **DRWGIDS3.H**, (on the disk as **DRWGIDS4.H**).

The Shape Menu Message Response Function

Having deleted the menu items in the Shape pop-up, we can delete the message response functions for these from the original example, as well as their declarations as member of the **TGrfxWindow** class. The last piece of code we need to add is the message response function for the Shape menu item we have introduced. The only action necessary in this function is to create the child window with suitable attribute settings, so it will be written as follows:

```
// Message response function for Shape menu option
void TGrfxWindow::CMShape(RTMessage)
{
   PTWindow pSW;                            // Pointer to window object
   // Create window object to select a shape
   pSW = new TShapeWindow(this,"Shape Selection");

   // Set position of window
   pSW->Attr.X = 50;
   pSW->Attr.Y = 100;
```

```
    // Set size of window
    pSW->Attr.W = 220;
    pSW->Attr.H = 170;

    // Set window attributes
    pSW->Attr.Style |= WS_CAPTION|WS_POPUP|WS_THICKFRAME;

    GetApplication()->MakeWindow(pSW);          // Create window element
}
```

We need a pointer to the child window object we create by calling the constructor, since we want to be able to set its attributes. However, we can use a local variable for this as we won't need to refer to it again, and the child window will be automatically destroyed when its parent is destroyed. The two arguments to the constructor for the child window are the pointer to the current window which will own the child, and the text which is to appear in the title bar.

The position and size of the window are set by altering the members of the **Attr** data members. The window is defined to be 220 pixels wide and 170 pixels high. Change the values here to suit your display adapter, as necessary, but remember to adjust the list box and the button, both of which need to fit within this window.

The general characteristics of the window are set by ORing values with **Attr.Style**. We have specified that the window will have a caption, that it is a pop-up and that it has a thick frame. This last style specification allows the boundaries of the window to be dragged to change its size. We could also specify other options. **WS_SYSMENU**, for instance, would provide the standard system menu option containing a bar, to the right of the window title.

*Search for **WS_** under TCW Help to find out about other options.*

Try It Out - Using a Child Window

The new version of the drawing program, with all the changes for popping up a shape window when the Shape menu option is clicked, can be called up by compiling and executing the program defined by **EX14-01.PRJ** on the disk. This will produce a window such as that shown below.

Try it Out!

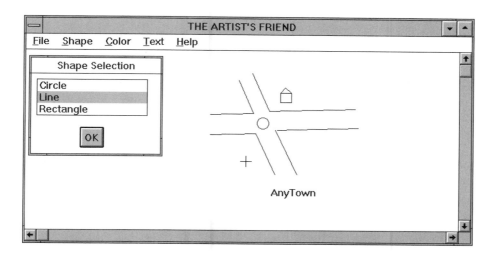

How It Works

Clicking the Shape menu option pops up the child window containing the list of shapes. You select a shape by clicking on the text item corresponding to the shape you want. You can leave the child window in the client area all the time if you wish. As soon as you use the mouse back in the main window, operation transfers to the main window and you can happily continue drawing. The active window is said to have the **focus**. When you select another shape, focus automatically changes to the Shape Selection window. Of course, you can also close the child window and re-create it again later by selecting Shape from the menu.

> *Note that you can also drag the child window around to position it where you want. You can even move it off the client area, if you wish. Try resizing it by dragging its boundaries. We get all this functionality free, gratis, and for nothing.*

Using Static Controls

Static controls provide a means of getting a text string into a window for information purposes. The user doesn't interact with a static control at all, although they can be modified in your program. Using static controls requires the following **#include** statement at the beginning of your program:

```
#include <static.h>          // For static controls
```

Because the user doesn't interact with a static control, no unique identifier needs to be created and no message response functions are involved. The constructor for the class **TStatic** which creates static controls still has the second argument providing for an ID to be passed, but you can put whatever integer value you like.

By convention, -1 is used for controls where there is no response function required.

The constructor for **TStatic** is usually called with eight arguments: the pointer to the current window, -1 for the ID value, the initial text string to be displayed, the coordinates of the controls position, the width and height of the control and the text length of the control. A typical call of the constructor, appearing in a window constructor, might be as follows:

```
pSControl = new TStatic(this, -1, "A default sample",50,50,300,30,20);
```

This creates a control with the initial text string shown and with the ability to contain up to 20 characters. A rather obvious point, but worth noting nonetheless, is that clearly the length of the control specified will need to be sufficient to accommodate the number of characters specified as a maximum.

You can alter the way the text is displayed by changing the **Attr.Style** member of the static control. The default is left-adjusted text, but you can center the text in the field by adding the attribute **SS_CENTER**, or right justify it with **SS_RIGHT**. Note that you need to switch off the default **SS_LEFT** if you want it changed, so you would need to write the following statements:

```
pSControl->Attr.Style &=  ~SS_LEFT;    // Switch off left justification
pSControl->Attr.Style |=  SS_RIGHT;    // Switch on right justification
```

The static controls corresponding to the constructor call above, and then modified to slightly different text, and right-justified using the statement we have just seen, is shown on the following page.

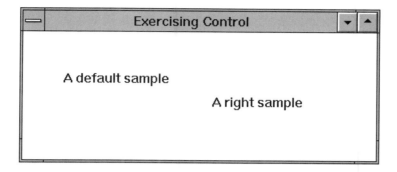

You can also underscore characters in the text you specify in the constructor for a static control, using the same technique we used for menu items in Resource Workshop - you precede each character you want to underscore with an ampersand. Of course, this means you can't include an ampersand in the string as such. If you really need to be able to include an ampersand in the text, you can specify **SS_NOPREFIX** in the **Attr.Style** member of the control.

Changing a Static Control in Your Program

To change the text in a static control, you can call the member function **SetText()** in the static control object. This has a single argument which is the new text that you want to insert, so you can use it in a statement such as this:

```
pSControl->SetText("Another message" );    // Change the static control
```

There is no return value from this function.

There are other members of a **TStatic** object which you will find useful. To find the length of the current text string, you can call the function **GetTextLen()** which returns the value as an **int**. This can be useful if you change the text in a static control in your program and you want to read back its current contents. You can find out the length of the string using **GetTextLen()** and then call the member function **GetText()** to read the text. The function `GetText()` accepts two arguments: a pointer to a buffer to store the string and an `int` value specifying the maximum number of characters to be read. You can also erase the current string by calling the member function `Clear()`.

Controls for Text Input

We saw in the previous chapter how an input dialog can provide a text input capability. A `TEdit` control provides you with the ability to add a text input field to a window. As well as accepting input from the user, an edit control also enables you to cut and paste text to the clipboard in Windows, and also implicitly provides the user with the ability to edit a text string in a control. To create `TEdit` object, you must put the following `#include` statement at the beginning of your program:

```
#include <edit.h>          // For edit controls
```

Creating an Edit Control

The constructor for a `TEdit` object provides you with the option of a control with a single line of text, or one containing multiple lines. To construct a control with a single line input field, you could use the following statement in the constructor for the window in which it is to appear:

```
pSEdit = new TEdit(this, ID_EDITS, "Initial Text",
                   50, 50, 250,30, 50, FALSE);  // Create single line edit
```

The first eight arguments are those we have seen in other controls: the pointer to the window containing the control, an ID, the initial text, the coordinates of the position of the control and its width and height, and the maximum number of characters in the control. The last argument is a `BOOL` value specifying whether or not the control is to work with multiple lines, so for a single line edit control it is `FALSE`. To specify the control as having multiple lines, this last argument would be specified as `TRUE`.

The edit control will automatically have a horizontal scroll capability for the text, and in a control accepting multiple lines of text, it will also have a vertical scrolling ability. A multiple line edit control is shown on the following page.

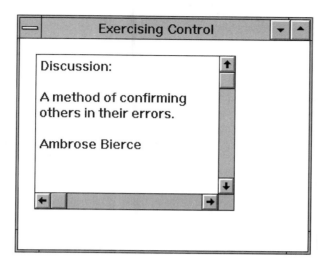

Note that the maximum number of characters that you specify in the
constructor call is not per line, it is the total for all lines, so make sure
you allow sufficient for the number of lines in the control.

Managing the Text in an Edit Control

An edit control automatically provides the user with the ability to select text
by dragging the mouse across it, just as in the IDE editor. It can then be
deleted by pressing the *Delete* key, or can be operated on by member
functions of the **TEdit** class. A **TEdit** object will contain functions **Cut()**,
Copy(), and **Paste()**, to provide the standard text editing operations with
the clipboard. None of them take an argument or return a value, they
simply operate on the selected text in the control. The **TEdit** class also has
the function **Clear()**, to erase the current text from the control.

For retrieving text from the control, **TEdit** contains the functions **GetText()**
and **GetLine()** as members. The first of these retrieves all the text up to
the number of characters specified by its second parameter, into the **char**
array specified by the first. The characters in the string retrieve will include
new line characters if their are multiple lines of text in the control.
GetText() returns the number of characters retrieved. The **GetLine()**
function uses three arguments to retrieve a line of text from a control: the
first is the **char** array to hold the text, the second is the number of
characters to be retrieved, and the third is an index value to the line

required, where lines are numbered sequentially starting with 0. **GetLine()** returns a **BOOL** value which is **TRUE**, if the operation was successful, and **FALSE** otherwise.

You can also find out how many lines of text are in an edit control with the member function **GetNumLines()**, and the number of characters in a line using the function **GetLineLength()**. Both functions return the results as an **int** and **GetLineLength()** requires an index to the particular line you are interested in, as an argument.

There are a plethora of other functions to program scrolling of the text and manipulating and modifying text in the control in myriad ways. You can find details of these in the TCW Help - searching for **TEdit** *is a good place to start.*

Using Combo Boxes

A combo box is a hybrid of a list box and an edit control, so it enables input to be entered by keying text, or selecting from a list. Combo boxes are defined by the OWL class **TComboBox**. They actually come in three flavors:

▶ Simple combo boxes, which have a list and an edit control

▶ Drop down combo boxes, which initially have their lists hidden, a list being displayed when the user clicks on a drop down arrow

▶ Dropdown list combo boxes, which are just like a drop down combo box, except that their edit controls can only display an item from a list, and the text can't be modified by the user.

Creating a Combo Box

The kind of combo box that you create is determined by an argument specified in the constructor call. You can use one of the three standard Windows identifiers - **CBS_SIMPLE**, **CBS_DROPDOWN**, or **CBS_DROPDOWNLIST** - depending on which one you want. To create a simple combo box, you could use the following statement in the constructor of the window which will own it:

```
pSCombo = new TComboBox(this, ID_SCOMBO, 30, 30, 150, 250,
                    CBS_SIMPLE, 100);      // Create a simple combo box
```

This will require an **#include** statement for the file **COMBOBOX.H** at the beginning of your program.

To add entries to the list in a **TComboBox** object, you use the **AddString()** member function as follows:

```
pSCombo->AddString("Alternatively");      // Add a line to a combo box
```

> *Remember, as with a list box, you must put the code to initialize the list in the function SetupWindow() for the parent window, not in the parent window constructor.*

By default, the list in a combo box will be sorted in alphabetical order. If you don't want it sorted, you can change the **Attr** data member with a statement such as this:

```
pSCombo->Attr.Style &= ~CBS_SORT;      // Specify an unsorted list
```

All three kinds of combo box are shown in the window below.

The headings which appear above each of the three combo boxes are static controls. The first combo box at the top is a simple version, the second combo box is a drop down type and the bottom one is a drop down list version. This last combo box has had its list already dropped down, by selecting the arrow on the top right of the box. Clicking on the arrow again would retract it. The drop down mechanism is already integrated and fully automatic. You don't have to write any code to make it work.

Because **TComboBox** is derived from **TListBox**, it inherits all the members of the base class for manipulating and querying list items.

Where you have multiple controls in a window, such as we have in the window shown above, you can arrange to shift the focus from one control to the next using the *Tab* key. To enable this, all you need to do is call the **EnableKBHandler()** member function in the constructor for the window owning the controls.

Scroll Bars

Scroll bars look just like window scrollers with a square slider you can move with the mouse and directional arrows at each end of the scroll bar, which you can also select with the mouse. The slider is also referred to as a **thumb position**.

Whereas window scrollers have a very specific function in scrolling the contents of the client area of a window, you can use a scroll bar for whatever purpose you like. For example, you could vary a color value, alter a position of an object, or simply vary a displayed value.

Scroll bars are defined by the OWL class **TScrollBar**. If you want to create objects of this class then you must add this statement:

```
#include <scrollba.h>      // For scroll bar controls
```

to your source program, prior to defining and using objects of the class.

> Note that you should not create *TScrollBar* objects in a window that has *Attr.Style* set to *WS_HSCROLL* or *WS_VSCROLL*.

Creating Scroll Bars

The constructor for a **TScrollBar** object requires seven arguments: the pointer to the owning window, an ID, the coordinates for the scroll bar, its width and height, and lastly a **BOOL** value which specifies a horizontal scroll bar if it is **TRUE**, and a vertical scroll bar if it is **FALSE**. If the width of a vertical scroll bar is zero, the scroll bar is constructed with a standard width. The same applies if the height specified is for a horizontal scroll bar. So if we write the following statement in our window constructor, we will create a horizontal scroll bar with a standard width, that is, 350 pixels long:

```
pScroll = new TScrollBar(this, ID_SCROLL,
                         30, 30, 350, 0, TRUE); // Create a scroll bar
```

Getting Feedback from a Scroll Bar

The default range of values which reflect the position of the slider is from 1 to 100. You can read the value corresponding to the current position by calling the member function **GetPosition()**. A typical statement using this function would be as follows:

```
position = pScroll->GetPosition();  // Get current scroll bar position
```

If you don't like the default range, you can change it using the member function **SetRange()**. This requires two arguments: the first specifying the lowest value, and the second the highest value. To set the scroller to have a range from 32 to 212, you could use a statement such as this:

```
pScroll->SetRange(32,212);  // Set the range - ice to steam
```

You must ensure, however, that the scroll bar has been created, so like adding items to a list in a list box, the best place to do this is in the **SetupWindow()** function of the parent window. The upper and lower limits are **int** values, so they can be negative as well as positive.

A scroll also causes a Windows message to be generated when it is scrolled, for which you can supply a message response function in the parent window. It requires a dispatch index defined by **ID_FIRST** plus the ID used in calling the constructor for the scroll bar. The type of event causing the message is identified in **Msg.WParam** rather than the usual **Msg.LP.Hi**. You can find details of these in the TCW Help, but usually you will just want to read the current position of the scroll bar, which you can do with the **GetPosition()** function we have just discussed.

Applying Group Boxes and Radio Buttons

Let's look at how we can use radio buttons in the context of our drawing example. Because radio buttons are designed to present a choice of only one out of a set of selections, they are ideal for choosing a drawing color. We will replace the Color pop-up with a Color menu item which we can link to a child window.

Firstly, let's look at how a radio button is created.

Creating Radio Buttons

Radio buttons are defined by the OWL class **TRadioButton**. To use the class, you must add an **#include** statement for **RADIOBUT.H** to your program. The class **TRadioButton** has **TCheckBox**, which defines a check box, as a base class, so check boxes and radio buttons are very closely related. You can create objects of the class **TRadioButton** within the constructor of a window. The radio buttons will then be owned by the window, and be automatically destroyed when the window is destroyed, as with the other control objects we have seen.

The constructor for a radio button in a window requires nine arguments of which the last is normally left to assume the default value. The eight arguments we will specify are a pointer to the parent window, a control ID, the text to be associated with the radio button, the coordinates of the position of the radio button, the width and height, and a pointer to an associated group box. The group box serves to define the group of radio buttons for which only one can be checked at any given time. A typical use of the constructor would be as in the following statement:

```
pTRButton = new TRadioButton(this,ID_REDBUTTON,"Red",60,50,120,20,pGBox);
```

This defines a radio button to be contained in a group box specified by the pointer **pGBox** and having the text Red associated with it. The radio button will be positioned at 60,50 within the parent window and it will be 120 pixels long and 20 pixels high.

You can also use **TRadioButton** objects to make the use of radio button with a dialog easier to manage. The **TRadioButton** class has a special constructor for this purpose, which accepts a resource ID as an argument, instead of a control ID. Since the radio button's physical appearance will be defined by a resource file, the position coordinates and the width and length of the radio button are not required.

Creating a Group Box

Group boxes are defined by the OWL class **TGroupBox**, and require that you include yet another header file in your program, **GROUPBOX.H**. The constructor for creating a group box in a window accepts the usual arguments for a control, a pointer to the parent window, a control ID, the text associated with the group box, and its position, width and height. A typical use of this constructor, which would appear in the constructor for the parent window, is as follows:

```
pGBox = new TGroupBox(this, ID_GROUPBOX,"Drawing Colors",30,15,300,200);
```

This creates a group box at coordinates 30,15 within the parent window, and with a width of 300 and a height of 200. You need to take care to adjust the height to accommodate the number of check boxes you need, allowing for some spacing between them.

You can also specify a group box to be associated with a previously defined group box associated with a **TDialog** object. Since the physical group box will be defined in the resource file for the dialog, no position coordinates, length or breadth are specified in the constructor, and a resource ID for the group box needs to be specified in place of the control ID.

Using a Group of Radio Buttons

To add a group of radio buttons to our drawing program, we will require a child window to own the group. Let's define it in a class **TColorWindow**, which we will derive from **TWindow**. We will need to include message response functions for each of the radio buttons in the class definition, and we will also need to service an OK button which the user can use to close the window. We also need to ensure one of the radio buttons is checked, and the best place to do this is in the **SetupWindow()** member of the class.

To incorporate these features, we can define the class as follows:

```
// Color window class
class TColorWindow:public TWindow
{
   public:
      // Constructor
      TColorWindow(TGrfxWindow* aParent, LPSTR aName);

      // Function to initialize controls
      void SetupWindow();

      // Function to process the OK button click
      void IDButton(RTMessage) = [ID_FIRST+ID_BUTTON1]
      { CloseWindow(); }              // Just close the window...

      // Radio button message response functions
      void HandleRedButtonMsg(RTMessage Msg) =
         [ID_FIRST + ID_REDBUTTON];
      void HandleBlueButtonMsg(RTMessage Msg) =
         [ID_FIRST + ID_BLUEBUTTON];
      void HandleGreenButtonMsg(RTMessage Msg) =
         [ID_FIRST + ID_GREENBUTTON];
      void HandleYellowButtonMsg(RTMessage Msg) =
         [ID_FIRST + ID_YELLOWBUTTON];
      void HandleBlackButtonMsg(RTMessage Msg) =
         [ID_FIRST + ID_BLACKBUTTON];

   protected:
      TGrfxWindow* TheParent;       // Pointer to the parent window
      PTRadioButton pTRButton;      // Pointer to a radio button

};
```

The class definition is very straightforward. The **public** section contains the constructor, a replacement for the **SetupWindow()** function inherited from the base class, a message response function for an OK button, and a set of message response functions for the radio buttons - one radio button for each of the color options in the program. The dispatch indexes for these are defined in the usual way by adding their ID to **ID_FIRST**.

We have defined two **protected** data members: a pointer to the parent window, **TheParent**, which will allow us to call a function to set the **Color** data member in the parent, and a pointer to a **TRadioButton** object. We only need a pointer to one of our radio buttons, since we only need to set one as checked.

Constructing the Child Window

Within the child window constructor, we must create all the controls we want to have in the window. We will first create the group box, and then use the pointer to the group box in the constructor calls for the radio buttons. Finally, we will create the OK button which will allow the window to be closed. The code for the constructor for the child window will therefore be as follows:

```
// Constructor for a color selection window
TColorWindow::TColorWindow(TGrfxWindow* aParent, LPSTR aName):
                          TWindow(PTWindowsObject(aParent),aName)
{
    PTGroupBox pGBox;              // Pointer to a group box

    TheParent = aParent;
    pGBox = new TGroupBox(this, ID_GROUPBOX,"Drawing Colors",
                          30,15,300,200);

    // Create radio button within group box
    pTRButton = new TRadioButton(this,ID_REDBUTTON,
                                 "Red",60,50,120,20,pGBox);
    pTRButton = new TRadioButton(this,ID_BLUEBUTTON,
                                 "Blue",60,80,120,20,pGBox);
    pTRButton = new TRadioButton(this,ID_GREENBUTTON,
                                 "Green",60,110,120,20,pGBox);
    pTRButton = new TRadioButton(this,ID_YELLOWBUTTON,
                                 "Yellow",60,140,120,20,pGBox);
    pTRButton = new TRadioButton(this,ID_BLACKBUTTON,
                                 "Black",60,170,120,20,pGBox);

    // Create an OK button
    new TButton(this,ID_BUTTON1,"OK",170,220,40,35,TRUE);
}
```

As we have seen previously, because we pass the pointer to the parent window to the class as a pointer to the derived class, **TGrfxWindow**, we must cast the pointer to a pointer **TWindowsObject** in order to pass it to the base class constructor, which is called in the initialization list.

The pointer to the **TGroupBox** is defined as a local variable because it is only required in the constructors calls for the radio buttons - it can then be discarded. The **TGroupBox** object we instantiate here will be automatically destroyed when the window is destroyed.

The radio buttons are constructed in the window at increments of 30 pixels vertically. The pointer to the group box, **pGBox**, is passed to all of the radio button constructor calls, in order to unify them into a single group. We will set the last radio button created, as checked, since the color associated with it corresponds to the initial default color set for the program. Thus the code for the **SetupWindow()** function will be as follows:

```
// Function to initialize controls
void TColorWindow::SetupWindow()
{
    TWindow::SetupWindow();              // Call base function
    pTRButton->Check();                  // Set last button checked
}
```

> *It is most important that you call the base class* SetupWindow() *function if you supply your own version in a class. Without it, your window will not be constructed properly.*

Each of the radio buttons corresponds to a particular color, so the task of the corresponding message response function will be to set that color in the parent to the child window. We can write a typical message response function for a radio button as follows:

```
// Respond to red radio button
void TColorWindow::HandleRedButtonMsg(RTMessage)
{
    TheParent->SetColor(red);
}
```

This uses the pointer to the parent of the child window to call the member function **SetColor()**. This will work in exactly the same way as the **SetShape()** member function we saw earlier in this chapter, so we can code it as follows:

```
// Function to set the color
void TGrfxWindow::SetColor(const COLORREF C)
{
    Color = C;
}
```

This simply sets the **Color** member of the parent window to the color value passed as an argument.

Of course, all of the control IDs for the radio buttons must be defined prior to their use. You can do this by adding statements such as this to the beginning of the program:

```
#define ID_REDBUTTON 852
```

The number assigned must be unique.

Creating the Child Window

We will create the child window in the message response function in `TGrfxWindow` for the Color menu item. This requires that the resource file be amended to delete the pop-up members and to convert Color to a menu item. You can do this by editing the resource file, just as we did to modify the Shape pop-up.

As well as constructing the child window, the message response function for the Color menu option will also need to set the size and position of the window and set its style attribute in an appropriate way. The code for the message response function is as follows:

```
// Message response function for Color menu item
void TGrfxWindow::CMColor(RTMessage)
{
   PTWindow pSW;                               // Pointer to window object
   // Create window object to select a shape
   pSW = new TColorWindow(this,"Color Selection");

   // Set position of window
   pSW->Attr.X = 400;
   pSW->Attr.Y = 100;

   // Set size of window
   pSW->Attr.W = 370;
   pSW->Attr.H = 300;

   // Set window attributes
   pSW->Attr.Style |= WS_CAPTION|WS_POPUP|WS_THICKFRAME;

   GetApplication()->MakeWindow(pSW);          // Create window element
}
```

We have declared a local pointer to the child window object which we will use to create the window after the attributes for the window have been set. We set the position of the window as 400,100 within the parent window client area. The width and height are set to 370 and 300 respectively, to accommodate the group box for the radio buttons and the OK button at the bottom of the window. As before, you should adjust these values to suit your particular display resolution, if necessary.

The **Attr.Style** member has the styles **WS_CAPTION**, **WS_POPUP** and **WS_THICKFRAME** added by ORing them with the existing value.

Try It Out - Adding RadioButtons to the Artist's Friend

Try it Out!

All the modifications necessary to implement color selection (using radio buttons as we have discussed), are incorporated into the example on the disk which has the source file **EX14-02.CPP**. If you run this example, the typical sort of window you can get is shown below.

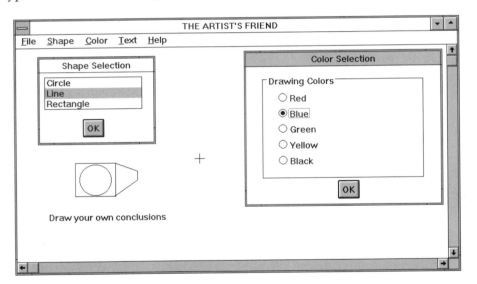

How It Works

Child windows are now created for both the Shape menu option and the Color menu option. You can leave both windows displayed while you work on a drawing, and you can move both of them around to any convenient position on your screen. You can also close them if you wish, and then select the appropriate menu item to recreate them when required.

In the Color Selection window, note how when you select a radio button, the previously selected button is automatically deselected. This is a result of the radio buttons being aggregated within a group box, and the default attribute **BS_AUTORADIOBUTTON** being set for each radio button control by the **TRadioButton** constructor. If you didn't want this behavior, you would normally use check boxes instead of radio button.

Using Control Objects in a Dialog

Throughout this chapter, we have referred to the possibility of using control objects with a dialog. This allows you to define the physical appearance of the dialog and its controls using Resource Workshop, but adds the ability to manipulate and query the controls in the dialog using the function members of associated dialog objects.

We can look at how this works by repeating the Shape menu item servicing with a **TDialog** object instead of a child window.

Defining the Dialog Class

This will take very little effort, since it will be an analog of the child window class we have already defined, but using **TDialog** as the base for our dialog class. The definition would be as follows:

```
// Color window dialog
class TColorDialog:public TDialog
{
   public:
      // Constructor
      TColorDialog(TGrfxWindow* aParent, int ResID);

      // Function to initialize controls
      void SetupWindow()
      {
         TDialog::SetupWindow();              // Call base function
         pTRButton->Check();                  // Set last button checked
      }

      // Function to process the OK button click
      void IDButton(RTMessage) = [ID_FIRST+ID_BUTTON1]
      { CloseWindow(); }          // Just close the window...
```

```
        // Radio button message response functions
        void HandleRedButtonMsg(RTMessage Msg) =
           [ID_FIRST + ID_REDBUTTON];
        void HandleBlueButtonMsg(RTMessage Msg) =
           [ID_FIRST + ID_BLUEBUTTON];
        void HandleGreenButtonMsg(RTMessage Msg) =
           [ID_FIRST + ID_GREENBUTTON];
        void HandleYellowButtonMsg(RTMessage Msg) =
           [ID_FIRST + ID_YELLOWBUTTON];
        void HandleBlackButtonMsg(RTMessage Msg) =
           [ID_FIRST + ID_BLACKBUTTON];

    protected:

        TGrfxWindow* TheParent;        // Pointer to the parent window
        PTRadioButton pTRButton;       // Pointer to a radio button

};
```

As you can see, the **TColorDialog** class is virtually identical to the **TColorWindow** class we defined in the previous example. This should be relatively unsurprising, since a dialog is a window at heart, **TDialog** being derived from **TWindowsOBject**. We will still need definitions for the IDs used to define the dispatch indexes for the message response functions, but this time they will be resource IDs which we will create in Resource Workshop and associate with the controls in the dialog. So let's look at how the dialog resource with radio buttons is created.

Creating the Dialog Resource

We can make a copy of the resource project file using the regular Windows file copy facility in File Manager. We can use the copy as the basis for a new file. Let's call the copy **DRWG8.RC**. We can also copy the file **DRWGIDS5.H** and call the copy **DRWGIDS6.H**. This will avoid messing up the file for the previous example. We can delete the old file containing the resource ID definitions from the new resource project file, and then add the copy back in. We will later be adding the additional resource IDs to this file when we create the dialog.

Having created a copy of the old resource project file, we are ready to start Resource Workshop, open the new resource project file, **DRWG8.RC**, and add the new dialog to it. We create a new dialog resource using the Resource menu item. We can change the name of the dialog to **COLOR_DIALOG** using the Resource pop-up option Rename... - we then need to verify that the creation options for the dialog are set as we require. Double click on the title of the dialog to get the window shown below.

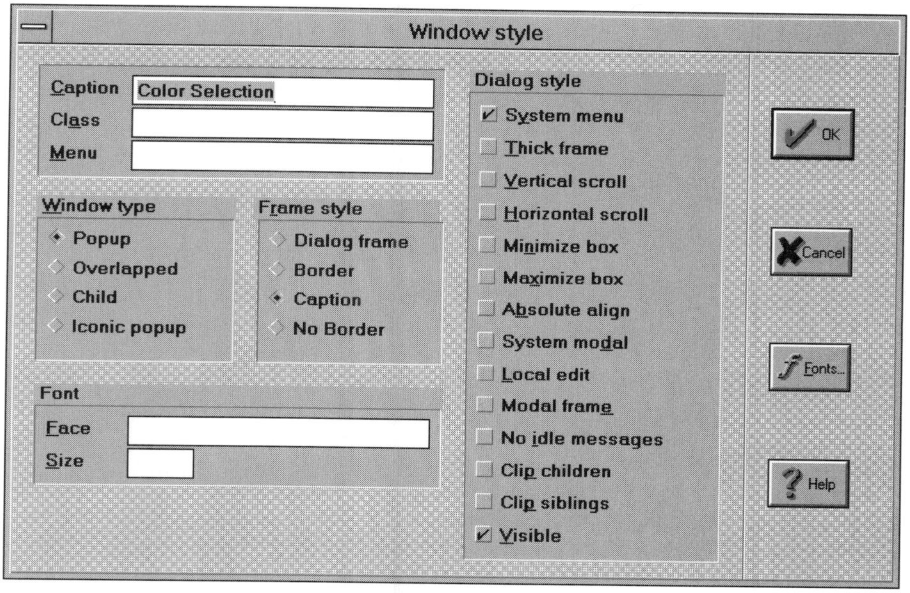

The options selected should be set as above. We want the dialog to be a pop-up, so that option is set as the window type; it should have a caption, so that is selected in the frame style; and dialog style options selected are visible, and with a system menu. This will be a modeless dialog. If we wanted the dialog to be modal, we would also select the system modal option in the dialog style. Having chosen the options, we click on OK to return to adding the controls to the dialog.

The first control we need is a group box. You can create this by choosing Group box from the Control pop-up. This will change the cursor to a tiny group box. You then click in the dialog to create it. It will certainly be too small - remember that we are going to add five radio buttons - so drag the boundaries to a suitable size, and position it to allow space for the OK button. To add the caption and the ID for the group box, double click in the caption area. You will get a pop-up window similar to that for the dialog box options, with the group box style option already selected. We can use **ID_GROUPBOX** as the ID, and select a value in the 900s to ensure it is different from the rest in the program. The definition will be automatically added to the **DRWGIDS6.H** file.

To add the radio buttons, click on Radio button in the Control menu pop-up. You can then position the radio button with the mouse, and then set its options in the button style by double clicking on the text area. Set the caption to a color, add a resource ID - **ID_REDBUTTON** for example - and make sure the Auto radio button box is checked in the button style options. You then need to add the four further buttons for the other colors. Finally, add an OK button below the group box. You should now have a window looking something like that shown below.

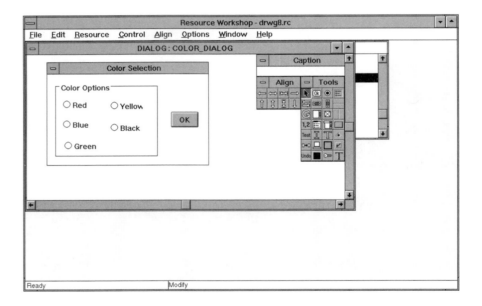

Now, you can save the project file since the dialog is complete.

Creating the Dialog

The constructor for **TColor** dialog is very similar to that of the child window in the previous example:

```
// Constructor for a color selection dialog
TColorDialog::TColorDialog(TGrfxWindow* aParent, int ResID)
            :TDialog(PTWindowsObject(aParent),ResID)
{

    PTGroupBox pGBox;            // Pointer to a group box

    TheParent = aParent;         // Create the group box

    pGBox = new TGroupBox(this, ID_GROUPBOX);

    // Create radio buttons within the group box
    pTRButton = new TRadioButton(this,ID_REDBUTTON, pGBox);
    pTRButton = new TRadioButton(this,ID_BLUEBUTTON, pGBox);
    pTRButton = new TRadioButton(this,ID_GREENBUTTON, pGBox);
    pTRButton = new TRadioButton(this,ID_YELLOWBUTTON, pGBox);
    pTRButton = new TRadioButton(this,ID_BLACKBUTTON, pGBox);

    // Create an OK button
    new TButton(this,ID_BUTTON1);
}
```

The only difference is in the version of the constructor which we call to create each control. Since the control is defined in a resource file, the physical object on screen will be created by Windows, so no information is required about the positions or dimensions of the controls. Obviously, the IDs here correspond to the resource IDs we defined in the dialog with Resource Workshop.

We will create the dialog in the message response function in **TGrfxWindow** for the <u>C</u>olor menu item:

```
// Message response function for Color menu item
void TGrfxWindow::CMColor(RTMessage)
{
    // Create a dialog object to select a shape
    GetModule()->MakeWindow(new TColorDialog(this,COLOR_DIALOG));
}
```

This has only one statement. It creates the dialog using the **MakeWindow()** member inherited from **TModule**. This creates the dialog as **modeless**, which means we can leave it on screen, and switch back and forth between the dialog and the main window. A modal dialog, on the other hand, locks out the main window until the dialog is closed. The dialog we already have in this example, for the <u>A</u>bout option, is modal.

We still need the black radio button to be checked initially, but we already provided for this in the definition of the **TColorDialog** class in exactly the same way as we did in the previous example - by redefining the **SetupWindow()** member of the class.

The message response functions for each radio button will be the same as before, except that now they will be members of **TColorDialog**.

Try It Out - Using a Dialog Rather Than a Child Window

With all the changes covered to select colors using a dialog, we are ready to run it. It is the example on the disk defined as **EX14-03.CPP**. You should be able to get a window similar to that shown below.

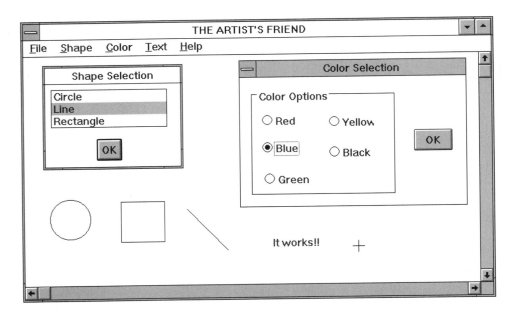

How It Works

The operation of the dialog is exactly the same as the child window in the previous example. Since it is modeless, you can leave it on screen and drag it to any convenient position on screen. The advantage of using a dialog rather than a child window is that you define it graphically, so you don't need to worry about figuring out suitable coordinates for positions or values for dimensions. You can also try out options with the dialog, using different controls. This is an easy thing to do.

If a dialog doesn't work, it's usually a result of an ID not being defined correctly, or an incompatibility between how you construct the dialog and how you define it in Resource Workshop. For example, if you want a modal dialog, the appropriate style option must be checked. If the dialog doesn't display, you probably forgot to check the Visible option.

Summary

In this last chapter, we have added basic controls to our bag of Windows programming tools. All of the OWL classes for generating these controls in a window can also be used to assist in managing the controls of a `TDialog` object, which have been defined as part of a dialog in a resource file. The capabilities of Resource Workshop to create dialogs and controls graphically is well worth experimenting with, and augmenting the `TDialog` object with objects of the classes we have discussed in this chapter will make the management of events for these controls very much easier.

Inevitably, it has been necessary to concentrate on the basics of programming Windows using the OWL. There are many more facilities to be uncovered, so you should not be afraid to try things out. Remember, the Help facility in TCW is a mine of information, including details of the Windows API functions, so if you get stuck, the TCW Help is a good place to look.

If you have stayed with it to this point you should have a good grasp of the mechanics of Windows programming. I hope you have found to be true what I said at the outset - Windows programming is not difficult, it is just messy. Enjoy your programming!

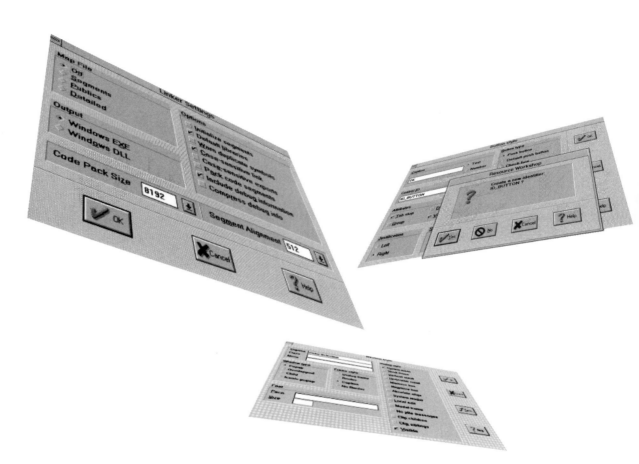

ASCII Character Code Definition

ASCII: American Standard Code for Information Interchange

The first 32 ASCII characters provide control functions. Many of these have not been referenced in this book, but are here for completeness. In the following table, only the first 128 characters have been included. The remaining 128 characters include futher special symbols and letters for national character sets.

Decimal	Hexidecimal	Character	Control
000	00	null	NUL
001	01	☺	SOH
002	02	●	STX
003	03	♥	ETX
004	04	♦	EOT
005	05	♣	ENQ
006	06	♠	ACK
007	07	•	BEL (Audible bell)

Continued

Decimal	Hexidecimal	Character	Control
008	08		Backspace
009	09		HT
010	0A		LF (Line feed)
011	0B		VT (Vertical feed)
012	0C		FF (Form feed)
013	0D		CR (Carriage return)
014	0E		SO
015	0F	¤	SI
016	10		DLE
017	11		DC1
018	12		DC2
019	13		DC3
020	14		DC4
021	15		NAK
022	16		SYN
023	17		ETB
024	18		CAN
025	19		EM
026	1A	→	SUB
027	1B	←	ESC (Escape)
028	1C	∟	FS
029	1D		GS
030	1E		RS
031	1F		US
032	20		space
033	21	!	
034	22	"	
035	23	#	
036	24	$	
037	25	%	
038	26	&	
039	27	'	
040	28	(	
041	29	)	
042	2A	*	
043	2B	+	
044	2C	,	

Continued

Decimal	Hexidecimal	Character	Control
045	2D	-	
046	2E	.	
047	2F	/	
048	30	0	
049	31	1	
050	32	2	
051	33	3	
052	34	4	
053	35	5	
054	36	6	
055	37	7	
056	38	8	
057	39	9	
058	3A	:	
059	3B	;	
060	3C	<	
061	3D	=	
062	3E	>	
063	3F	?	
064	40	@	
065	41	A	
066	42	B	
067	43	C	
068	44	D	
069	45	E	
070	46	F	
071	47	G	
072	48	H	
073	49	I	
074	4A	J	
075	4B	K	
076	4C	L	
077	4D	M	
078	4E	N	
079	4F	O	
080	50	P	
081	51	Q	

Continued

Decimal	Hexidecimal	Character	Control
082	52	R	
083	53	S	
085	55	U	
086	56	V	
087	57	W	
088	58	X	
089	59	Y	
090	5A	Z	
091	5B	[	
092	5C	\	
093	5D	]	
094	5E	^	
095	5F	_	
096	60	´	
097	61	a	
098	62	b	
099	63	c	
100	64	d	
101	65	e	
102	66	f	
103	67	g	
104	68	h	
105	69	i	
106	6A	j	
107	6B	k	
108	6C	l	
109	6D	m	
110	6E	n	
111	6F	o	
112	70	p	
113	71	q	
114	72	r	
115	73	s	
116	74	t	
117	75	u	
118	76	v	
119	77	w	

Continued

Decimal	Hexidecimal	Character	Control
120	78	x	
121	79	y	
122	7A	z	
123	7B	{	
124	7C	|	
125	7D	}	
126	7E	~	
127	7F	delete	

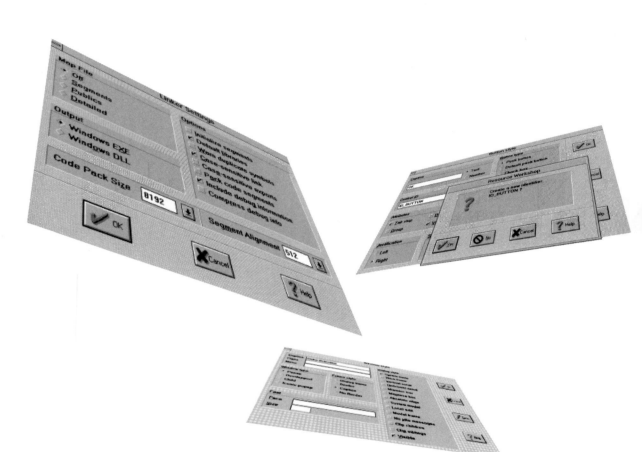

Keywords in Turbo C++ for Windows

Keywords are words used for special purposes and you must not use these words as names of objects in your program. A complete list of TCW keywords is:

_asm	else	interrupt	signed
asm	enum	_loadds	sizeof
auto	_es	long	_ss
break	_export	_near	static
case	extern	near	struct
_cdecl	_far	new	switch
cdecl	far	operator	template
char	float	_pascal	this
class	for	pascal	typedef
const	friend	private	union
continue	goto	protected	unsigned
_cs	_huge	public	virtual
default	huge	register	void
delete	if	return	volatile
do	inline	_saveregs	while
double	int	_seg	
_ds	_interrupt	short	

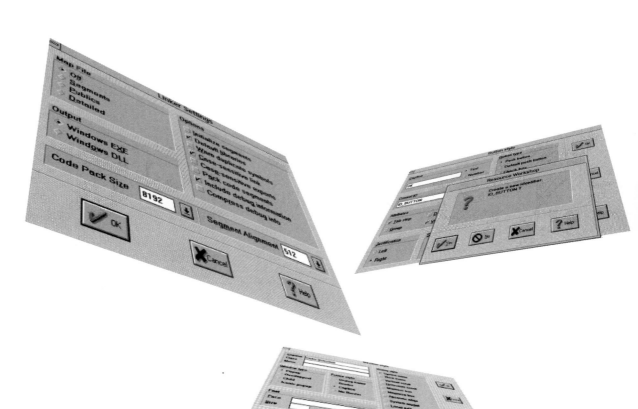

Index

Symbols

– operator 54
! operator 87, 89
!= operator 78
#include Directive 30
% operator 53
& operator 135, 138
&& operator 87
* operator 47, 133, 136
*= operator 53
+ operator 47
++ operator
  postfix form 55
+= operator 53
- operator 47
-- operator 54
.h file extension 169
.RC file extension 488
/ operator 47
< operator 78
<= operator 78
== operator 78
> operator 78
>= operator 78
>>= operator 54
?: operator 90

  as an lvalue 91
_lcreat() function 563, 578
_llseek() function 564
_lopen() function 562
_lread() function 564
_lwrite() function 563
| | operator 87, 88

A

Abstract classes 363
Adding a menu
  example 494
Address operator 135
AddString() function 603
Allocating memory dynamically 154
Anonymous unions 294
Application class
  defining 391
Application object
  creating 393
Arc() function 421
Arguments to a function 171
Arithmetic operations 47
  overloading 317
  sequence 57

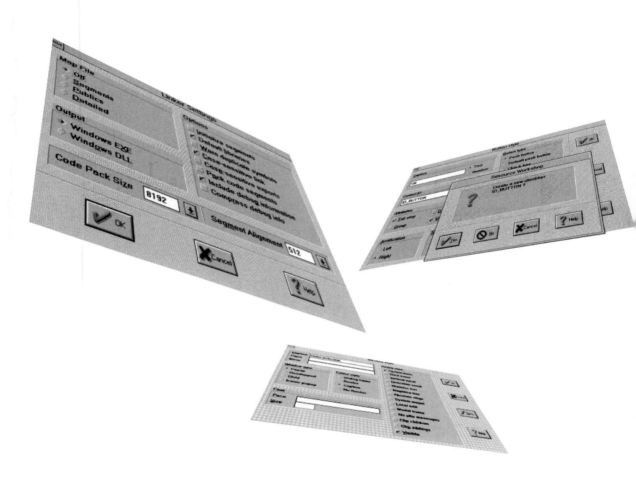

The Revolutionary Guide to Visual C++

Building on your knowledge of C, this book is a complete guide to writing C++ applications for Windows using Microsoft's Visual C++ compiler. We focus on the Microsoft Foundation Class (MFC) and show you how it can be used to produce professional looking programs. A truly comprehensive guide to all the Visual C++ tools.

Ben Ezzell   ISBN 1-874416-22-2
$39.95 / C$55.95 / £37.49

The Revolutionary Guide to OOP using C++

Benefit from the authors' years of experience using C and C++ in some of the most complex and demanding programming environments around today. This book aims to ease the difficulties in making the transition from C to C++, and will show you the power of object-oriented C++.

V. Olshevsky and A. Ponomarev   ISBN 1-874416-18-4
$39.95 / C$55.95 / £37.49

The Beginner's Guide to Visual Basic 3

If you're a beginner to programming, this book is the place to start. We'll show you how easy, fun and powerful Visual Basic can be. If you're familiar with another language, you'll learn how Visual Basic does things in terms you'll understand. Along the way, you'll get all the background information you need on Windows Programming to help you develop really professional applications.

Peter Wright   ISBN 1-874416-19-2
$29.95 / C$41.95 / £27.99

The Revolutionary Guide to Assembly Language

Take the Challenge. Learn how to design, develop and debug powerful assembly language routines. Take control of your system and increase the power of your high level programs. Why learn unnecessary information when you can accomplish the task with expert assistance. "At £35.00, it's worth every penny!" (Syd Anderson, The Association of C and C++ Users).

Vitaly Maljugin et al.   ISBN 1-874416-12-5
$39.95 / C$55.95 / £34.95

WIN FREE BOOKS

TELL US WHAT YOU THINK!

Complete and return the bounce back card and you will:

- Help us create the books you want.
- Receive an update on all Wrox titles.
- Enter the draw for 5 Wrox titles of your choice.

FILL THIS OUT to enter the draw for free Wrox titles

Name _____

Address _____

_____

_____

_____ Postcode/Zip _____

Occupation _____

How did you hear about this book ?
- ☐ Book review (name) _____
- ☐ Advertisement (name) _____
- ☐ Recommendation
- ☐ Catalog
- ☐ Other _____

Where did you buy this book ?
- ☐ Bookstore (name) _____
- ☐ Computer Store (name) _____
- ☐ Mail Order
- ☐ Other

What influenced you in the purchase of this book ?
- ☐ Cover Design
- ☐ Contents
- ☐ Use of Color
- ☐ Other (please specify)

How did you rate the overall contents of this book ?
- ☐ Excellent
- ☐ Good
- ☐ Average
- ☐ Poor

What did you find most useful about this book ?

What did you find least useful about this book ?

Please add any additional comments. _____

What other subjects will you buy a computer book on soon ?

What is the best computer book you have used this year ? _____

WROX

WROX PRESS INC.

Wrox writes books for you. Any
suggestions, or ideas about how you
want information given in your ideal
book will be studied by our team. Your
comments are always valued at WROX.

Free phone from USA 1 800 814 3461
Fax (312) 465 4063

Compuserve 100063,2152.
UK Tel. (4421) 706 6826   Fax   (4421) 706 2967

Computer Book Publishers

NB. If you post the bounce back card below in the UK, please send it to:
Wrox Press Ltd. Unit 16 Sapcote Industrial Estate, 20 James Road,
Tyseley, Birmingham B11 2BA

BUSINESS REPLY MAIL

FIRST CLASS MAIL   PERMIT#64   CHICAGO,IL

POSTAGE WILL BE PAID BY ADDRESSEE

WROX PRESS
2710 WEST TOUHY AVE
CHICAGO IL 60645-3008
USA